Readings in psychology: understanding human behavior

**Readings in psychology: understanding
human behavior/James A. Dyal, Texas
Christian University**

McGRAW-HILL BOOK COMPANY, INC.   1962

New York   San Francisco   Toronto   London

III

READINGS IN PSYCHOLOGY: Understanding Human Behavior

18530

Library of Congress Catalog Card Number: 62-14039

PREFACE

To the Professor:
Like most teachers of the introductory course in psychology you have probably occasionally felt that your course would have more impact if the students had access to original papers representative of our psychological literature. Many of you have taken time to survey portions of the literature, obtain reprints of selected articles, and place them on reserve in the library. Even at best you probably found that this procedure was time-consuming and left something to be desired in terms of actual availability of the articles to your students. An alternative approach is to make use of one of the several good anthologies of readings now available. None of these books include all of the selections which you would have chosen had you edited the book. Nevertheless, it is hoped that the scope of the present book is sufficiently broad that you will have little difficulty finding important and readable selections in each chapter.

The overall approach of the book is organismic. The biological and sociocultural factors which influence psychological processes are emphasized both in individual selections and in chapter organization. It is felt that an organismic approach is not only more understandable to the beginning student but also reflects a contemporary trend within psychology. The readings were selected to represent the major content areas of psychology. Although an attempt was made to avoid articles of a purely applied nature, a number of papers indicating how general psychological principles may be extended to everyday behavior have been included.

A further criterion for the selection of articles is implied by the title of the book. Where possible, preference was given to papers which emphasized the understanding of human behavior. This criterion by no means necessitated the exclusion of studies of lower animals. However, only those animal experiments which have either implications for human functioning or which clarify important aspects of psychological theory were selected.

The three major objectives of the book are to facilitate the teaching of the methods of experimental and clinical psychology, the communication of knowledge which has been derived by the use of these methods, and the modification of student attitudes regarding the nature of man in general and themselves in particular. The articles also seem to fall into three categories which to some degree correspond to the objectives. About one fourth of the articles consists of reports of single experiments. These selections serve to illustrate the methods of psychological experimentation and to communicate certain psychological generalizations. Another fourth of the readings represents summaries of research programs of outstanding experimental psychologists. In addition to presenting more information than the single experiments, these articles emphasize the great contributions made by long term experimental programs which extensively explore a particular problem area. Examples of this type of paper are Miller's "Recent Studies of Conflict and Drugs" and Harlow's "The Nature of Love." The remaining half of the book is devoted to psychological essays or commentaries. These are primarily designed to introduce the student to characteristic problems of psychology and to state a point of view. Some of them are theoretical papers which add to the student's knowledge or help him to reorganize knowledge that he already has, e.g., Sargent's "Reaction to Frustration—A Critique and Hypothesis" or Sperry's "On the Neural Basis of the Conditioned Response." Many of the readings of this type represent less scientifically developed areas of psychology such as personality dynamics and motivation and serve primarily to modify the student's attitudes regarding the nature of man and himself. Examples of this type of article are Horney's "Culture and Neurosis" and Rogers' "Becoming a Person."

Instead of prefacing each selection with editorial comment, I have chosen to write a brief introduction to each chapter. The purpose of these introductions is threefold: (1) to prepare the student for some of the important problems in that area of psychology; (2) to emphasize the important results and implications of the selections in the chapter which he will read; and (3) to indicate some of the relationships of that chapter to selections elsewhere in the book.

It would seem that the most effective use of this book might be attained by having students read first the relevant chapter in their basic text, then read the introduction and the appropriate selections in the readings book. Further, to be of greatest impact a book of readings must not be relegated to the category of "outside" reading but should be woven into the fabric of the course. This book may be used as a springboard for lecture topics, and in those courses in which weekly discussions are conducted it will also serve as an excellent text for use in the discussion sections.

Acknowledgments:

The bulk of the credit for this book is due to the authors of the articles themselves. The future generations of psychologists who are now in their embryonic stage of development in our courses in Introductory Psychology will do well to emulate their careful experimentations and perceptive interpretations of behavior. The authors and publishers were most generous in granting permission to reproduce their articles. Specific credits are given at the beginning of each selection. It should also be noted that although some of the articles are abridged, the specific points of abridgment are not indicated in order to avoid interference with smooth communication. Also, in order to conserve space for more text material, the references in the original papers have been omitted. Any student who wants to read additional papers in the area may look up the references in the original periodical.

The next order of credit is due my wife, Earlene, whose careful attention to the multitude of details entailed in the editing of such a book made this book an actuality. I am also indebted to my former colleagues in the psychology department at Southern Methodist University, Aaron Sartain, Alvin North, Jack Strange, Harold Chapman, and Virginia Chancey for their encouragement in undertaking this project. The assistance extended by Max Trent and Lois Bailey, directors of the S.M.U. Libraries, greatly facilitated my search for the literature. To David Coldwell of the S.M.U. Comparative Literature department goes a special appreciation for his cogent criticisms of my often cumbersome style of communication. Any shortcomings which remain in style or selection of articles are my responsibility.

James A. Dyal

CONTENTS

chapter 8 thinking, reasoning, and problem solving 245

chapter 9 intelligence 276

chapter 10 social processes: attitudes and roles 312

chapter 11 the self and behavior 337

CHAPTER 1 ◉ PSYCHOLOGY: PAST, PRESENT, AND FUTURE ◉

At the present time perhaps the most succinct and generally accepted definition of psychology is that it is the "science of behavior." However, this has not always been the case. As recently as 100 years ago psychology was neither scientific nor very much concerned about behavior. Like all sciences, psychology has emerged from the "mother of knowledge"—philosophy. Philosophers have been concerned about psychological topics for thousands of years, but their basic method of arriving at knowledge has been to "reason out" the answers, an approach known as rationalism. The generalizations thus obtained could not be called scientific, since science always involves the addition of controlled observation to the process of reasoning.

The aim of the first section of this chapter is to trace the history of the change in subject matter and method of psychology from the rational study of the mind (armchair psychology) to the study of behavior through controlled observation. The excerpt from the writings of Thomas Brown, a Scottish philosopher, reflects that during the greater portion of the last century, psychology was still the domain of philosophy. It was a "study" rather than a "science"; it was concerned with internal mental processes, or mind, rather than overt response, or behavior. However, Brown notes that "we might as well attempt to discover, by logic unaided by observation and experiment, the various coloured rays that enter into the composition of the sunbeam, as to discover, by dialectic subtleties, a priori, the various feelings that enter into the composition of a single thought or passion." This statement indicates that even at this time, in 1820, philosophers were beginning to recognize that understanding of the mind was amenable to, in fact required, controlled observation.

The next three selections represent three different approaches to the subject matter and method of psychology. These three approaches came to be formalized into three schools of psychology: Functionalism,

Structuralism, and Behaviorism. The most eminent proponents of the functionalist school were two philosopher-psychologists, William James and John Dewey. Their philosophy came to be known as Pragmatism, and it greatly influenced their views of the task and method of psychology. The term "pragmatism" itself points up the emphasis of the entire approach. It derives from the Greek word prágma, meaning action. James's psychology was a psychology of action. He criticized the older rational psychologies for concentrating on the inner faculties of man, such as reasoning and imagining, without considering how these activities are modified by the environment in which the individual exists.

The Functionalists conceived man's mind or states of consciousness as conditioned by his adaptation to his environment. To use James's words, ". . . mental life is primarily teleological"; which is to say that both mind and body were conceived as products of evolution, their primary purpose being to aid in man's survival. Thus, we can see the great influence which Charles Darwin's theory of evolution has had on psychology.

James's psychology was influenced not only by the fact that he was a philosophical pragmatist, but also by the fact that he was trained originally as a physician. He proposed that "all mental states . . . are followed by bodily activity of some sort." It was the task of psychology through introspection and experimentation to determine the physiological correlates of mental processes. Thus, in summary, the Functionalist school conceived the subject matter of psychology to be states of consciousness which were modified by man's environment and which served to facilitate his future adaptation. The method of psychology was both introspection and experimentation by an outside observer.

Selections 3 and 4 represent more extreme views regarding the subject matter and method of psychology. The Structuralist position, as represented by E. B. Titchener, was in partial agreement with the Functionalist view in that the subject matter of psychology was held to be states of consciousness. However, the Structuralists did not place as much emphasis on determining the physiological correlates of these states. Following the tradition of Wundt, Structuralism proposed that the task of psychology was to analyze complex states of consciousness into their basic, irreducible elements through the method of introspection. Thus, psychology was conceived as that science which analyzes mental contents in a manner analogous to the way in which chemistry analyzes physical properties.

Around 1912 a major revolution took place in psychology with the advent of Behaviorism. This radical position was proposed most vigorously by John B. Watson. He maintained that as long as psychology conceived that its subject matter was states of consciousness which were to be analyzed by the subjective process of introspection, it would never become an objective science. He proposed that psychology should do away with the concept of mind and concentrate on controlled observation of behavior. Internal processes, such as thinking, could not be studied directly by psychology but could only be inferred from responses of the individual, for example, verbal reports. Watsonian Behaviorism sought to establish functional relationships between the stimuli impinging on the organism and the responses which the organism made. He says, "The interest of the behaviorist in man's doings is more than the interest of the spectator—he wants to control man's reactions as physical scientists want to control and manipulate other natural phenomena. It is the business of behavioristic psychology to be able to predict and control human activity. To do this it must gather scientific data by experimental methods. Only then can the trained behaviorist predict, given the stimulus, what reaction will take place; or, given the reaction, state what the stimulation or stimulus is that has caused the reaction."[1]

In Section B we consider those characteristics which are necessary before any area of intellectual activity may be considered to be a science. In Selection 5 Chaplin and Krawiec point out the evolutionary nature of science and emphasize that the aims and methods of science differentiate it from other ways of obtaining knowledge. The next two selections examine in more detail the nature of scientific aims and methods. In Selection 6 Brown and Ghiselli suggest that the most general goal of science is understanding. The subgoals of prediction and control reflect the rational and empirical elements of science, that is, science relies on both reasoning and observation to obtain understanding. Selection 7, by Dr. T. G. Andrews, outlines the typical steps of classical scientific method. It indicates that, in comparison with other methods of observation, experimentation has the advantage of permitting more precise control of the variables which may influence the results. Through such control of variables we are better able to determine what causes a particular response.

In his article on "Psychology as a Science" (Selection 8), Professor Gregory A. Kimble applies to psychology many of the concepts which have been discussed in the previous selections. He points out that, like other sciences, the task of psychology is to establish functional relationships between variables, that is, to establish scientific laws. He notes two general types of laws which are formulated by psychologists:

[1] John B. Watson, *Behaviorism*, W. W. Norton & Company, Inc., New York, 1924, p. 11.

those which state a relationship to exist between two responses, R-R laws, and those which state a stimulus-response relationship, S-R laws. He suggests that the latter laws are preferable in that the conditions under which they are obtained offer the possibility of more precise control of extraneous variables. Although Dr. Kimble's views are definitely in the tradition of Behaviorism, they should be thought of as Neo-behavioristic. As we have seen, Watson felt that through complete control of the external stimulus he would be completely able to predict the response. Neo-behaviorists have liberalized the strict S-R formulation to include the organism as a critical source of variables which influence response. However, since we cannot observe directly the processes within the organism, they must be inferred from the relationships which obtain between stimulus and repsonse. We thus construct ideas or concepts which will help us to explain the observed relationships. These constructs vary considerably in the degree to which they include physiological terms in their definition. Some terms such as anger are inferred from physiological measures and overt responses. Other constructs which are attributed to the organism have little physiological reference, for example, the concept of attitude. But regardless which of these types of intervening variables we use, their meaning depends on the operations which we perform to demonstrate their effect on behavior. Thus, an operational definition of a construct such as anger is a statement of those observations which are necessary before we will infer that a person is in a state of being angry.

Although a large number of psychologists agree with Kimble in his Neo-behavioristic approach, others take the position that such an approach too greatly limits the types of problems with which psychology will concern itself. In Selection 9 Rollo May places psychology in its broader setting and proposes five facets of contemporary psychology which must be emphasized by the psychology of the future. Psychology will not give up its scientific orientation but will seek to apply this approach to more complex and socially relevant problems.

In conclusion, it should be noted that the approaches to understanding human behavior that we have thus far considered have tended to restrict themselves to conscious states of awareness or overt behavior. Psychoanalysis as presented by Sigmund Freud made its major departure by emphasizing the primary importance of unconscious processes. Although there was initially considerable resistance to this view, present-day psychology has integrated much of the psychoanalytic view into its attempts to explain human personality.

Contemporary psychology is an amalgam of these different emphases and methods. Viewed as a whole it is organismic in its orientation. It accepts as its subject matter the complex behavior of the human being and recognizes that many different techniques of observation must be utilized in its search for understanding. Although it has been influenced by a wide variety of "schools," in its present form psychology may be thought of as the science of the dynamics (Psychoanalysis) of the behavior of man (Behaviorism) as he adjusts to his environment (Functionalism).

selection 1 / lectures on the philosophy of the human mind / Thomas Brown, University of Edinburgh

Gentlemen,

The subject, on which we are about to enter, and which is to engage, I trust, a considerable portion of your attention for many months, is *the Philosophy of the Human Mind,*—not that *speculative* and *passive* philosophy only, which enquires into the nature of our intellectual part, and the mysterious connexion of this with the body which it animates, but that *practical* science, which relates to the duties, and the hopes, and the great destiny of man, and which, even in analyzing the powers of his understanding, and tracing all the various modifications of which it is individually susceptible, views it chiefly as a general instrument of good—an instrument by which he may have the dignity of co-operating with his beneficent Creator, by spreading to others the knowledge, and virtue, and happiness, which he is qualified at once to enjoy, and to diffuse.

The progress of intellectual philosophy may indeed, as yet, have been less considerable than was to be hoped under its present better auspices. But it is not a little, to have escaped from a labyrinth, so *very* intricate, and so *very* dark, even though we should have done nothing more than advance into sunshine and an open path, with a long journey of discovery still before us. We have at last arrived at the important truth, which now seems so very obvious a one, that the mind is to be known best by observation of the series of changes which it presents, and of all the circumstances which precede and follow these; that, in attempting to explain its phenomena, therefore, we should know *what* those phenomena are; and that we might as well attempt to discover, by logic, unaided by observation or experiment, the various coloured rays that enter into the composition of a sunbeam, as to discover, by dialectic subtilties, *a priori*, the various feelings that enter into the composition of a single thought or passion.

The mind, it is evident, may, like the body to which it is united,

Abridged from Thomas Brown, *Lectures on the Philosophy of the Human Mind*, James Ballantyne and Co., Edinburgh, 1820, vol. I, pp. 1, 6–8.

or the material objects which surround it, be considered *simply as a substance possessing certain qualities*, susceptible of various affections or modifications, which, existing successively as momentary states of the mind, constitute all the phenomena of thought and feeling. The general circumstances in which these changes of state succeed each other, or, in other words, the *laws* of their succession, may be pointed out, and the phenomena arranged in various classes, according as they may resemble each other, in the circumstances that precede or follow them, or in other circumstances of obvious analogy. There is, in short, a science that may be terméd *mental physiology*, as there is another science relating to the structure and offices of our corporeal frame, to which the term physiology is more commonly applied; and as, by observation and experiment, we endeavour to trace those series of changes which are constantly taking place in our *material* part, from the first moment of animation to the moment of death; so, by *observation*, and in some measure also by *experiment*, we endeavour to trace the series of changes that take place in the *mind*, fugitive as these successions are, and rendered doubly perplexing by the reciprocal combinations into which they flow. The innumerable changes, corporeal and mental, we reduce, by generalizing, to a few classes; and we speak, in reference to the mind, of its faculties or functions of *perception, memory, reason*, as we speak, in reference to the body, of its functions of *respiration, circulation, nutrition*. This *mental physiology*, in which the mind is considered simply as a *substance endowed with certain susceptibilities, and variously affected or modified in consequence*, will demand of course our first inquiry; and I trust that the intellectual analyses, into which we shall be led by it, will afford results that will repay the labour of persevering attention, which they may often require from you.

selection 2 / the definition of psychology / William James, Harvard University

The definition of Psychology may be best given in the words of Professor Ladd, as the *description and explanation of states of consciousness as such*. By states of consciousness are meant such things as sensations, desires, emotions, cognitions, reasonings, decisions, volitions, and the like. Their 'explanation' must of course include the study of their causes, conditions, and immediate consequences, so far as these can be ascertained.

Abridged from William James, *Psychology*, Henry Holt and Company, Inc., New York, 1892, pp. 1–8. Reprinted by permission of the publisher.

Psychology is to be treated as a natural science in this book. This requires a word of commentary. Most thinkers have a faith that at bottom there is but one Science of all things, and that until all is known, no one thing can be completely known. Such a science if realized, would be Philosophy. Meanwhile it is far from being realized; and instead of it, we have a lot of beginnings of knowledge made in different places, and kept separate from each other merely for practical convenience' sake, until with later growth they may run into one body of Truth. These provisional beginnings of learning we call 'the Sciences' in the plural. In order not to be unwieldy, every such science has to stick to its own arbitrarily-selected problems, and to ignore all others. Every science thus accepts certain data unquestioningly, leaving it to the other parts of Philosophy to scrutinize their significance and truth. All the natural sciences, for example, in spite of the fact that farther reflection leads to Idealism, assume that a world of matter exists altogether independently of the perceiving mind. Mechanical Science assumes this matter to have 'mass' and to exert 'force,' defining these terms merely phenomenally, and not troubling itself about certain unintelligibilities which they present on nearer reflection. Motion similarly is assumed by mechanical science to exist independently of the mind, in spite of the difficulties involved in the assumption. So Physics assumes atoms, action at a distance, etc., uncritically; Chemistry uncritically adopts all the data of Physics; and Physiology adopts those of Chemistry. Psychology as a natural science deals with things in the same partial and provisional way. In addition to the 'material world' with all its determinations, which the other sciences of nature assume, she assumes additional data peculiarly her own, and leaves it to more developed parts of Philosophy to test their ulterior significance and truth. These data are—

1. *Thoughts and feelings*, or whatever other names transitory *states of consciousness* may be known by.

2. *Knowledge*, by these states of consciousness, of other things. These things may be material objects and events, or other states of mind. The material objects may be either near or distant in time and space, and the states of mind may be those of other people, or of the thinker himself at some other time.

All mental states (no matter what their character as regards utility may be) are followed by bodily activity of some sort. They lead to inconspicuous changes in breathing, circulation, general muscular tension, and glandular or other visceral activity, even if they do not lead to conspicuous movements of the muscles of voluntary life. Not only certain particular states of mind, then (such as those called volitions, for example), but states of mind as such, *all* states of mind, even mere thoughts and feelings, are *motor* in their consequences. This will be made manifest in detail as our study advances. Meanwhile let it be set down as one of the fundamental facts of the science with which we are engaged.

It was said above that the 'conditions' of states of consciousness must be studied. The immediate condition of a state of consciousness is an activity of some sort in the cerebral hemispheres. This proposition is supported by so many pathological facts, and laid by physiologists at the base of so many of their reasonings, that to the medically educated mind it seems almost axiomatic. It would be hard, however, to give any short and peremptory proof of the unconditional dependence of mental action upon neural change. That a general and usual amount of dependence exists cannot possibly be ignored.

This conception is the 'working hypothesis' which underlies all the 'physiological psychology' of recent years, and it will be the working hypothesis of this book. Taken thus absolutely, it may possibly be too sweeping a statement of what in reality is only a partial truth. But the only way to make sure of its unsatisfactoriness is to apply it seriously to every possible case that can turn up. To work an hypothesis 'for all it is worth' is the real, and often the only, way to prove its insufficiency. I shall therefore assume without scruple at the outset that the uniform correlation of brain-states with mind-states is a law of nature.

selection 3 / mind, consciousness and the method of psychology / Edward B. Titchener, Cornell University

We have defined mind as the sum-total of human experience considered as dependent upon the experiencing person. We have said, further, that the phrase 'experiencing person' means the living body, the organised individual; and we have hinted that, for psychological purposes, the living body may be reduced to the nervous system and its attachments. Mind thus becomes the sum-total of human experience considered as dependent upon a nervous system. And since human experience is always process, occurrence, and the dependent aspect of human experience is its mental aspect, we may say, more shortly, that mind is the sum-total of mental processes. All these words are significant. 'Sum-total' implies that we are concerned with the whole world of experience, not with a limited portion of it;

Abridged from Edward Bradford Titchener, A *Textbook of Psychology*, The Macmillan Company, New York, 1911, pp. 15–20. Reprinted with permission of the Estate of Edward Bradford Titchener.

'mental' implies that we are concerned with experience under its dependent aspect, as conditioned by a nervous system; and 'processes' implies that our subject-matter is a stream, a perpetual flux, and not a collection of unchanging objects.

Consciousness, as reference to any dictionary will show, is a term that has many meanings. Here it is, perhaps, enough to distinguish two principal uses of the word.

In its first sense, consciousness means the mind's awareness of its own processes. Just as, from the common-sense point of view, mind is that inner self which thinks, remembers, chooses, reasons, directs the movements of the body, so is consciousness the inner knowledge of this thought and government. You are conscious of the correctness of your answer to an examination question, of the awkwardness of your movements, of the purity of your motives. Consciousness is thus something more than mind; it is "the perception of what passes in a man's own mind"; it is "the immediate knowledge which the mind has of its sensations and thoughts."

In its second sense, consciousness is identified with mind, and 'conscious' with 'mental.' So long as mental processes are going on, consciousness is present; as soon as mental processes are in abeyance, unconsciousness sets in.

The first of these definitions we must reject. It is not only unnecessary, but it is also misleading, to speak of consciousness as the mind's awareness of itself. The usage is unnecessary, because, as we shall see later, this awareness is a matter of observation of the same general kind as observation of the external world; it is misleading, because it suggests that mind is a personal being, instead of a stream of processes. We shall therefore take mind and consciousness to mean the same thing. But as we have the two different words, and it is convenient to make some distinction between them, we shall speak of mind when we mean the sum-total of mental processes occurring in the life-time of an individual, and we shall speak of consciousness when we mean the sum-total of mental processes occurring *now*, at any given 'present' time. Consciousness will thus be a section, a division, of the mind-stream.

The method of psychology

Scientific method may be summed up in the single word 'observation'; the only way to work in science is to observe those phenomena which form the subject-matter of science. And observation implies two things: attention to the phenomena, and record of the phenomena; that is, clear and vivid experience, and an account of the experience in words or formulas.

In order to secure clear experience and accurate report, science has recourse to experiment. An experiment is an observation that can be repeated, isolated and varied. The more frequently you can *repeat* an observation, the more likely are you to see clearly what is there and to describe accurately what you have seen. The more strictly you can *isolate* an observation, the easier does your task of observation become, and the less danger is there of your being led astray by irrelevant circumstances, or of placing emphasis on the wrong point. The more widely you can *vary* an observation, the more clearly will the uniformity of experience stand out, and the better is your chance of discovering laws. All experimental appliances, all laboratories and instruments, are provided and devised with this one end in view: that the student shall be able to repeat, isolate and vary his observations.—

The method of psychology, then, is observation. To distinguish it from the observation of physical science, which is inspection, a looking-at, psychological observation has been termed introspection, a looking-within. But this difference of name must not blind us to the essential likeness of the methods.

selection 4 / what is behaviorism? / John B. Watson, Johns Hopkins University

THE OLD AND NEW PSYCHOLOGY CONTRASTED

Before beginning our study of "behaviorism" or "behavioristic" psychology, it will be worth our while to take a few minutes to look at the conventional school of psychology that flourished before the advent of behaviorism in 1912—and that still flourishes. Indeed we should point out at once that behaviorism has not as yet by any means replaced the older psychology—called *introspective psychology*—of James, Wundt, Külpe, Titchener, Angell, Judd, and McDougall. Possibly the easiest way to bring out the contrast between the old psychology and the new is to say that all schools of psychology except that of behaviorism claim that *"consciousness" is the subject matter of psychology*. Behaviorism, on the contrary, holds that the subject matter of human psychology is the *behavior or activities of the human being*. Behaviorism claims that "consciousness" is neither a definable nor a usable concept; that it is merely another word for the "soul" of more ancient times. The old psychology is thus dominated by a kind of subtle religious philosophy.

From John B. Watson, *Behaviorism*, 1st ed., W. W. Norton & Company, Inc., New York, 1924, pp. 3–7. Copyright 1924, 1925 by The People's Institute Publishing Company, Inc.; 1930, rev. ed., W. W. Norton & Company, Inc.; 1952, 1953, by John B. Watson. Reprinted by permission of W. W. Norton & Company, Inc., New York.

An examination of consciousness

From the time of Wundt on, consciousness becomes the keynote of psychology. It is the keynote of all psychologies today except behaviorism. It is a plain assumption just as unprovable, just as unapproachable, as the old concept of the soul. And to the behaviorist the two terms are essentially identical, so far as concerns their metaphysical implications.

To show how unscientific is the concept, look for a moment at William James' definition of psychology. "Psychology is the description and explanation of states of consciousness as such." Starting with a definition which *assumes* what he starts out to prove, he escapes his difficulty by an *argumentum ad hominem*. Consciousness—Oh, yes, everybody must know what this "consciousness" is. When we have a sensation of red, a perception, a thought, when we *will* to do something, or when we *purpose* to do something, or when we desire to do something, we are being *conscious*. All other introspectionists are equally illogical. In other words, they do not tell us what consciousness is, but merely begin to put things into it by assumption; and then when they come to analyze consciousness, naturally they find in it just what they put into it. Consequently, in the analyses of consciousness made by certain of the psychologists you find such elements as *sensations* and their ghosts, the *images*. With others you find not only sensations, but so-called *affective elements*; in still others you find such elements as *will*—the so-called conative element in consciousness. With some psychologists you find many hundreds of sensations of a certain type; others maintain that only a few of that type exist. And so it goes. Literally hundreds of thousands of printed pages have been published on the minute analysis of this intangible something called "consciousness." And how do we begin work upon it? Not by analyzing it as we would a chemical compound, or the way a plant grows. No, those things are material things. This thing we call consciousness can be analyzed only by *introspection*—a looking in on what goes on inside of us.

As a result of this major assumption that there is such a thing as consciousness and that we can analyze it by introspection, we find as many analyses as there are individual psychologists. There is no way of experimentally attacking and solving psychological problems and standardizing methods.

The advent of the behaviorists

In 1912 the behaviorists reached the conclusion that they could no longer be content to work with intangibles and unapproachables. They decided either to give up psychology or else to make it a natural science. They saw their brother-scientists making progress in medicine, in chemistry, in physics. Every new discovery in those fields was of prime importance; every new element isolated in one laboratory could be isolated in some other laboratory; each new element was immediately taken up in the warp and woof of science as a whole. May I call your attention to the wireless, to radium, to insulin, to thyroxin, and hundreds of others? Elements so isolated and methods so formulated immediately began to function in human achievement.

In his first efforts to get uniformity in subject matter and in methods the behaviorist began his own formulation of the problem of psychology by sweeping aside all mediaeval conceptions. He dropped from his scientific vocabulary all subjective terms such as sensation, perception, image, desire, purpose, and even thinking and emotion as they were subjectively defined.

The behaviorist's platform

The behaviorist asks: Why don't we make what we can *observe* the real field of psychology? Let us limit ourselves to things that can be observed, and formulate laws concerning only those things. Now what can we observe? Well, we can observe *behavior—what the organism does or says*. And let me make this fundamental point at once: that *saying* is doing—that is, *behaving*. Speaking overtly or to ourselves (thinking) is just as objective a type of behavior as baseball.

The rule, or measuring rod, which the behaviorist puts in front of him always is: Can I describe this bit of behavior I see in terms of "stimulus and response"? By stimulus we mean any object in the general environment or any change in the tissues themselves due to the physiological condition of the animal, such as the change we get when we keep an animal from sex activity, when we keep it from feeding, when we keep it from building a nest. By response we mean anything the animal does—such as turning towards or away from a light, jumping at a sound, and more highly organized activities such as building a skyscraper, drawing plans, having babies, writing books, and the like.

At this point let me diverge to emphasize the fact that almost from infancy society begins to prescribe behavior. A Chinese baby must use chop sticks, eat rice, wear certain kinds of clothes, grow a queue, learn to speak Chinese, sit in a certain kind of way, worship his ancestors, and the like. The American baby must use a fork, learn quickly to form habits of personal cleanliness, wear certain kinds of clothes, learn reading, writing and arithmetic, become monogamous, worship the Christian God, go to church and, yes, even to speak upon a public platform. It is presumably not the function of the behaviorist to discuss whether these things which society prescribes serve as a help or a hindrance to the growth or adjustment of an individual. The behaviorist is working under the mandates of society and consequently it does come within his province to say to society: "If you decide that the human organism should behave in this way, you must arrange situations of such and such kinds." I would like to point out here that some time we will have a behavioristic ethics, experimental in type, which will tell us whether it is advisable from the standpoint of present and future adjustments of the individual to have one wife or many wives; to have capital punishment or punishment of any kind; whether prohibition or no prohibition; easy divorces or no divorces; whether many of our other prescribed courses of conduct make for adjustment of the individual or the contrary, such for example as having a family life or even knowing our own fathers and mothers.

selection 5 / the evolution of scientific method in psychology / J. P. Chaplin, University of Vermont, and T. S. Krawiec, Skidmore College

The story of science as it unfolds down the ages is a record of man's greatest intellectual achievement. It is a history of the continuous struggle against ignorance, fear, and superstition—a struggle which has not always been successful in any given age, but which over the span of recorded history is a proud and Promethean accomplishment indeed. During his brief tenancy of this planet man has reached out far beyond the solar system to chart the fringes of outer space and unravel the mysteries of the creation of the galaxies. And, here on earth, he has kindled those stellar fires which only yesterday seemed forever beyond his reach. Even the darkest mystery of all, the nature of life itself, seems well within his grasp; for, within the short span of a few generations, the geneticist has learned the secret of the transmission of living matter and can modify it at will in lower forms. So rapid has been the march of science in our time, it has been estimated we have learned more about our universe in one generation than the sum total of all past scientific knowledge up to the twentieth century.

Meanwhile, what have we learned of man with his unrivaled mind and complex behavior patterns? Part of the recent mushrooming of scientific endeavor and accomplishment has been the coming of age of psychology, the science of human behavior. It was less than a century ago that man first turned the powerful weapons of science against his

From J. P. Chaplin and T. S. Krawiec, *Systems and Theories of Psychology*, Holt, Rinehart and Winston, Inc., New York, 1960, pp. 1–6. Copyright © 1960. Reprinted by permission of the publisher.

own ignorance of himself. Of course, men of thought have always been interested in human nature. Philosophers, artists, writers, and theologians have sought to interpret human conduct from their particular points of view, and many of our valued insights into human nature have come from these avenues of approach. But the notion that those methods of investigation which won so much knowledge for the natural scientist could be applied to the study of man himself is a relatively recent one. In a sense, the task of psychology has been to take over the problems and questions about human nature that were its heritage from the prescientific past and seek the answers in the light of modern science. In view of recent political and military developments, thoughtful people would agree that there is no more pressing, urgent task to which science could address itself. We have too much knowledge, it seems, of the world around us and too little knowledge of the world within.

Science and methodology

Today, it is almost a truism to say that science not only begins with a method but that its very essence *is* its methodology. To put it another way, the heart of science is the set of rules which must be followed by anyone who aspires to be a scientist. This statement implies, contrary to a widespread popular view, that any such science as chemistry, biology, geology, or psychology is not so much a compilation of facts or collection of impressive apparatus as it is an attitude or willingness on the part of the scientist to follow the rules of the scientific game. Facts have an annoying way of changing, and what is truth today may be error tomorrow. Therefore, facts alone are only the transient characteristics and not the enduring stuff of true science. Apparatus, too, however imposing it may appear, is not science but only the tool of science whose application may or may not be scientific. Anyone can purchase a white robe and a laboratory full of "scientific" paraphernalia, but the possession of such equipment does not qualify him as a scientist. Rather, both his scientific status and the value of the information he is collecting are evaluated according to the manner in which he *plans* his investigations, the *procedures* he employs in collecting data, and the way in which he *interprets* his findings. It is his standing on these three fundamental steps in scientific methodology that tells us whether he is a scientist, an amateur riding a hobbyhorse, or possibly a crackpot. So crucial is the methodology followed in any scientific investigation that no reputable scientist will accept a fellow scientist's results as valid until he knows precisely what procedures were employed in arriving at those results. This cautious, conservative attitude has been dignified by the special name, *operationism*, and has been elevated into a basic working principle of the natural sciences. In formal terms we may define operationism as follows: *The validity of any scientific finding or concept depends on the validity of the procedures employed in arriving at that finding or concept.* In effect, this means that both the results of an experiment and the conclusions the investigator derives from it can never transcend the methodology employed.

Bearing in mind this brief analysis of the importance of methodology, it becomes clear that in order to understand systems, schools, or theoretical points of view in psychology we must first have some appreciation of the methodology which lies at their very foundation. In the last analysis, the exposition of a systematic point of view is a statement of its *aims, methods,* and *findings.* From what has already been said, the value of the findings is contingent upon the validity of the methods used in the investigation. However, aims, too, tend to be interwoven with methods. Obviously if the scientist's goal is to investigate the nature of the solar system, his methodology will be quite different from that which he would employ if he were embarking on a study of Australian mammals. As a consequence of this relationship between aims and methods, it becomes apparent that while it is correct to speak of *the* scientific method, each science has its own specialized methodology. It is largely this specialization in aims and procedures which distinguishes each science from every other.

To summarize, it seems logical to begin our survey of systematic psychology with a study of the aims and methods which were instrumental in establishing the various systems, for this approach alone makes possible an operationistic frame of reference.

selection 6 / the aims of science / Clarence W. Brown and Edwin E. Ghiselli, University of California

UNDERSTANDING AS THE GENERAL AIM OF SCIENCE

Understanding and the search for truth One of the most general statements of the aim of science is: to discover truth about natural events. To do this requires knowledge about the events, and this knowledge comes from the experiencing of the events. Experiencing natural phenomena gives the scientist his facts, and his aim is to discover, accumulate, and interpret facts and relationships among facts.

Facts about the natural universe are not isolated events but are pat-

From Clarence W. Brown and Edwin E. Ghiselli, *Scientific Method in Psychology,* McGraw-Hill Book Company, Inc., New York, 1955, pp. 36–42. Reprinted by permission of the publisher.

terned and related in diverse ways that in most instances are unknown to the scientist. Sometimes facts are initially experienced in ways that are meaningful, but most of the time the scientist's effort is expended in arranging the known facts in new patterns in an effort to discover unknown meanings and relationships. Through rational analysis he organizes the facts into more and more abstract and general systems. The end result is the formulation of general principles or laws under which all of the facts and relationships within some restricted domain of experience can be subsumed. The word understanding best expresses the end result of this "search for truth," and it expresses more accurately than any other word the general aim of all scientific work.

A continuum of understanding Experience, knowledge, and understanding are closely related. They should be placed on a common continuum with experience at the beginning and understanding at the end. From experience we pass through knowledge on our way to attaining understanding. There are no sharp lines of demarcation between them. They are really three different points or levels on a common axis.

It is obvious that understanding is more than experiencing. Sometimes, having experienced a phenomenon on several occasions, an individual will declare that he understands it. He may be in error, and this type of error frequently occurs in everyday life. Mere repetition of the experience of an event does not necessarily result in an understanding of the event. We all can recall having experienced some phenomenon many times, and of knowing little more about it after the last experience than we knew after the first one. Most housewives do not understand electricity although they have used it in many ways over many years. Experience is a first step, and an important step, toward understanding—but it is not understanding.

Understanding is more than knowledge. Knowledge is a second step toward understanding. By manipulation of experience through the thought processes old meanings are reinterpreted and new meanings are discovered. The end result is knowledge. This knowledge is then further enlarged, organized, and systematized, and the end result is understanding. Knowledge, then, must be integrated and ordered before we have understanding.

The continuous expansion of understanding Understanding is characterized as continuously growing and expanding. At the beginning it waits upon experience and knowledge, but after it comes into being in its own right it does not remain static. Additional experiences and further knowledge increase understanding, so it is continuously evolving. Gaining understanding is a never-ending process, because with each increment of understanding further doubt arises, and this doubt, in turn, creates a need for more experience and knowledge. In some individuals, understanding begets complacency; in others, uncertainty. If we were forced to classify the scientist, we would, of course, place him among those whose understanding causes them continually to question the *status quo* and thus to seek further experience and knowledge.

PREDICTION AS AN AIM OF SCIENCE

The meaning of prediction No scientist is content to stop after he has made a discovery, confirmed a hypothesis, or explained a complex phenomenon. He wants to make some use of his results. He therefore projects his generalizations to situations in which he believes they will hold; he makes predictions concerning the way the principles he develops will operate in new situations.

Suppose that in studying the intelligence of a class of eighth-grade children we learn that the brightest child obtains a score twice the amount of the lowest score achieved. Such a large discrepancy might lead us to conclude that the progress in school attainable by the children getting the highest and lowest scores would differ considerably if differences in intelligence were reflected in school achievement. We might predict that the brightest child could progress faster if given more work, or that the social adjustment of the dullest child would improve if he were not forced to compete with the brightest child. Thus on the basis of this present knowledge we are forecasting what would take place if we used this knowledge in a given specific way.

Prediction and understanding Prediction is based on understanding. Understanding forms the springboard from which prediction into the unknown is made. In turn, prediction contributes toward the further testing and verification of understanding. One check we can apply to our understanding of a phenomenon is the success with which we can use that understanding in new situations. If our prediction is unsuccessful, then our understanding of the phenomenon is to be questioned and challenged in reference to the particular predicted situation.

In the aforementioned example, our predictions concerning the improvement in the rate of progress of the brightest child or the improvement in social adjustment of the dullest child might turn out to be successful, thus verifying the application of our findings. We might then recommend the segregation of students in school in terms of their intelligence-test scores. We could make a broad prediction that the school progress and social adjustment of all children would be improved if they were allowed to work with children of their own intelligence level. Our prediction might then be found in error. The social adjustment of children might be more closely associated with their ages than with their intelligence-test scores. Equalizing the children in terms of intelligence would exaggerate differences in the ages of the children occupying the same classroom. If there were a very close relation between age and social adjustment, we would have to revise our notion about segregating all of the children in terms of their intelligence. Regardless of whether our prediction turned out to be correct or incorrect, the result of our prediction would have a direct effect upon our understanding of the problem involved.

Tentative nature of a prediction The predicted situation always differs from the predictor situation. Sometimes the difference is small, as when a given situation is being duplicated with a minimum of change. For example, having determined the learning scores of rats in an alley maze, we might predict a similar distribution of scores for these rats on an elevated maze. Sometimes the difference is large, as when several factors are allowed to vary between the predictor and predicted situations. Having determined the distribution of scores of some rats on a brightness-discrimination problem, we might then destroy different parts of the visual areas of the brain and predict that the brightness-discrimination function would be lost. In this instance the brain damage may produce differences in health and differences in motivation as well as differences in learning ability, and consequently our prediction has more likelihood of failure than if only differences in learning ability were present.

Regardless of whether the difference between the predictor and predicted situations is large or small, in a prediction we set up a relationship which cannot be completely verified by a utilization of knowledge from the past. The unknown factors that are present force us to accept the prediction as only tentatively correct. Our confidence in the prediction will, of course, vary with the degree to which the predicted situation corresponds to the predictor situation. The wider the discrepancies between the two situations, the less confidence we shall have that the prediction will turn out successfully.

The testing of predictions We must include a testing situation as part of prediction. A prediction that cannot be tested is of no value. It forever remains an unknown.

The test may be either rational or empirical in nature. In a rational test we may show, through reasoning, that the outcome of our particular explanation or theory ought to be of a certain kind or have particular characteristics. If our prediction concerns relationships that are only partially understood, we may be able, through reasoning, to increase this understanding by introducing into the relationships additional meanings that at first were thought to be irrelevant.

Suppose we are interested in explaining how we see color. We recall that there are two kinds of retinal structures, the rods and the cones, and that the latter are color-sensitive. We also know from our color-mixing experiments that the spectral colors can be obtained from variations in the mixture of three colors, viz., a certain red, a certain yellow, and a certain blue. Associating these facts together might lead us to the notion that there are three color-sensitive structures in the retina, one for each of these colors. We now can explain how we see color by stating that the light rays differentially activate one or more of these three color-sensitive structures in the retina. With this explanation we can now proceed to predict what might happen if there were radical changes in these structures. We might, for instance, predict that if a person were born without any one of them he would be color-blind to certain hues. Or again, if the color-sensitive structures were not evenly and uniformly distributed in the retina, a person might see certain hues and fail to see certain other hues in some given part of the visual field. We are pleased with our explanation because it enables us to give plausible predictions about other events in which we are interested.

Tests of the rational kind are one of the most valuable tools of the theoretical scientist. Although he may not be interested in knowing if his ideas have practical value in everyday-life situations, he nevertheless is concerned with any forward reference that his data, explanations, or theories may have. Consequently, he finds prediction a valuable aid in forecasting in "conceptual space" what can be expected from his ideas.

In an empirical test, the prediction is applied to conditions in the natural world. The relationships stipulated in the findings are projected to natural phenomena and these phenomena are then carefully observed to determine if these relationships occur according to the demands of the prediction.

Let us consider again the example of the predictive value of our explanation of how we see color. After having predicted that if people were born without one of these sensitive color processes in their retina they would be blind to certain particular colors, we could then explore the possibility that there are color-blind persons who fit our predicted descriptions. We would first describe (predict) the types of color blindness that would occur, depending on which color process or combinations of color processes were absent in the retina. For example, if the retina contained no red-sensitive process the person should not see red hues, or if all three sensitive processes were absent the person should be totally color-blind. Having calculated the various types of blindness, we would then study color-blind people and learn if their actual blindness corresponded to the blindness predicted by our color-vision explanation. If we found a relatively high correspondence, we would have empirical evidence supporting our explanation.

Eventually, all predictions should be brought to some kind of empirical test. Empirical conditions offer the most easily understood types of situation. They usually allow for the coincident observation of the phenomena by many individuals, and therefore increase the probability of reaching agreement among different investigators.

CONTROL AS AN AIM OF SCIENCE

The meaning of control As an aim of science, control refers to the manipulation of the conditions determining a phenomenon in order to achieve some desired end. In utilizing present understanding to control the functioning of any factor, we are thus testing and verifying this understanding.

Ready examples of the use of control are to be found in the area of vocational guidance. Aptitude-test scores have been found to correlate rather highly with success in college. From this finding we can now exercise a more intelligent control over the admission of students to college training. We can advise an individual who has very low aptitude scores that he should not attempt college work. In such an instance we might save the person from many serious frustrations and direct his activities to areas where he would achieve marked success. We would be exercising control over his behavior, and the resulting achievement would serve to verify the understanding gained concerning the relation between aptitude-test scores and college success.

Control and prediction Control is a corollary aim to prediction. Actually, the two are inseparable when interpreted as general aims of science. To achieve any prediction, regardless of how simple it might be, some control of the determinants of the behavior is required. In the problem of predicting college success from aptitude-test scores, we have exercised control by permitting only certain kinds of behavior to be expressed, i.e., those behaviors that are elicited by the particular tests used. Likewise, regardless of the behavior we desire to control, there is always an uncertainty about the end result, so whether we consciously make a prediction or not the conditions characteristic of prediction are present. When we speak of the relationship between aptitude and college success in connection with the advice we give a high school graduate who is considering going to college, there is implied a predictive relation between the two types of variables.

Control and application Sometimes the term control is restricted to situations of a practical nature, such as the example of segregating school children in terms of their intelligence-test scores. This is a narrow interpretation of the term. Control serves equally well at the abstract and theoretical levels on which the "pure" scientist works. His task is to form inferences from his theory and to devise new conceptual situations to which the theory can be applied. He must logically show how an end result of a given kind can be produced by controlling the conceptual situations according to the implications of his theory. For example, the concept of control can be found throughout Einstein's theory of relativity, although what Einstein did can in no sense be construed to be control of practical situations.

THE EMPIRICAL AND RATIONAL PHASES OF SCIENCE

The scientist capitalizes on any type of approach that he thinks will enhance his chances of gaining knowledge. Some of these involve the direct manipulation of the natural phenomena he is studying, whereas some of them involve the use of the higher mental processes by which he thinks about these phenomena. There are then both empirical and rational phases, and the scientific method is an intelligent combination of these two types of procedures.

The empirical phases of science The meaning of empirical should not be restricted to the meaning of "that which is sensed." Experiences of natural phenomena are the first facts the scientist collects. The original experiences he gains in collecting the facts are of great significance because they are the "stock" with which he "sets up housekeeping."

In addition to the sensory experiences themselves, empirical refers to the techniques and procedures in which sensory experience plays an important role. Beyond the original observations, empirical features are to be found in all of the subsequent steps in which sensory experience is present. For example, the experimentalist, in the designing, constructing, and operating of apparatus, depends heavily upon empirical procedures. This is also true for various types of analysis of the data. Frequently the scientist reduces his data to graphic form and through the examination of diagrams, figures, and drawings he discovers many new meanings. These are empirical procedures.

Empirical facts are the point of origin of evidence. The scientist tests his ideas under natural conditions. These tests thus provide the means for confirming and justifying all of his work. They are the court of final appeal where he must be content to rest his case.

In the realm of the production of hunches, ideas, and hypotheses, empirical procedures by themselves are strictly limited in scope. Alone, raw sensory experience provides us with only a rather elemental type of meaning. Mere awareness of an object is very limited. We add little to knowledge if we terminate our activity at this point. The full import and significance of an experience results from various intellectual manipulations of the sensed data gained in the experience. Rational phases, then, are essential to higher-order meanings.

The rational phases of science Whether or not the facts of experience eventually add significantly to our knowledge depends upon the kind of rational manipulations we perform and the accuracy with which we perform these manipulations. We can study the data statistically or logically; we can analyze them into more elemental structures or combine them into complex patterns; we can note their similarities or their differences. These rational manipulations of sensory and inferential meanings are the "heart" processes of our descriptions, explanations, generalizations, and theories. Through these manipulations we learn about the relationships between other variables and the phenomena under study and the significance that these relationships have for future understanding.

The rational phases of the scientific method include all procedures in which higher-order meanings are involved and include such individual processes as memory, abstraction, inference, reasoning, generalization, judgment, and the like.

Certainly, as scientists, we must use rational procedures from the beginning of an investigation right through to the end. Science particularly requires rational processes in the setting up of the problem, in the analysis of the results, and in the interpretation of the findings.

The rational procedures of formal logic are a valuable part of the scientific method. As indicated earlier, scientists must practice "straight" or "sound" reasoning. Logic sets up patterns of reasoning for us to follow, patterns which, if followed, will lead us to what are considered logically correct conclusions. Logic aids in the accurate formulation of propositions so they can be evaluated against other possible alternatives. It enables us to state our postulates so their full implications can be developed through further reasoning. "Straight" thinking is required in every stage of a scientific inquiry, and therefore we should not depreciate or ignore a procedure that has as its fundamental purpose the description of the conditions for accurate thinking.

selection 7 / the methods of psychology / T. G. Andrews, University of Chicago

The general plan of scientific method

The scientist selects a tentative explanation as the beginning step in his inquiry, and this tentative suggestion is taken as an *hypothesis*, which directs the search for corroborative or negating facts. The hypothesis is merely a question and is usually quite narrow in scope. These hypotheses are piecemeal but not haphazardly so; each is a question recognized as belonging to a larger family of questions.

An investigation is designed in such a way that it involves a direct analysis of all the major conditions of the hypothesis. Preferably the investigation takes the form of an *experiment*, which is carried out

From T. G. Andrews, ed., *Methods of Psychology*, John Wiley & Sons, Inc., New York, 1948, pp. 3–5, 6–8. Reprinted by permission of the publisher.

under rigidly controlled conditions during the systematic variation of one of these conditions in particular. These characteristics allow the *reproducibility* of the conditions under which a given experiment is performed. When experimentation is impossible, however, the investigator may employ other methods. Psychological science is founded upon but not limited by the experimental method.

If the results of the investigation are not controversial, the hypothesis may be confirmed (although not proved), and the next step involves tying together the results of a large number of scientifically tested propositions which have some system of relationship. The results of this last step may involve the formulation of a *scientific law*, which is only a type of mental shorthand by which a number of facts or relations are subsumed under one simplified statement. A natural law, then, is merely a résumé of a longer and more detailed description.

Another stage, although not an absolutely necessary one, is the organization of a *theory* to account for the laws. The laws, as well as the theories, represent generalizations from which formal deductions can be made. These deductions are then set up as hypotheses for further scientific investigation. A particular law or theory is thus tested objectively according to whether or not the things which it predicts (which may be deduced from it) are supported or discredited empirically. As more and more correct predictions are added for a particular theory or law, we say that *truth is approached* (not *attained*) by the theory or law.

The process of induction from empirical evidence always involves a treacherous step because the evidence is never complete. In testing a certain hypothesis about human behavior, we can never study *all* humans but must obtain what is believed to be a "representative" sample from the hypothetical population of all humans. Generalizations are thus of necessity made on the basis of partial evidence, and so they are made only as *probable inferences*. The degree of probability—or confidence—that can be attached to scientific inferences differs from one to another, and to this extent the business of science is directed toward diminishing error in the general process of scientific problem solving.

The scientific method becomes more than a mere circular game played by scientists when prediction directs investigation to seek something that has not been previously suspected. Furthermore, some of the most spectacular achievements of science have been produced by the rather straightforward system of inducing a generalization and then deducing from the generalization. Good experimentation, then, is not a hit-or-miss affair or purely random trial and error, and this fact led Darwin to the pregnant statement, "How odd it is that anyone should not see that all observation must be for or against some view, if it is to be of any service."

Theory and experiment are the helpmates of scientific pursuit, theory suggesting the pattern of the maze, and experiment determining the blind alleys and the short cuts. Whenever such a maze is found to be composed only of blind alleys, it is modified or discarded, or at least it should be. To this extent the term *science* should be reserved to describe a body of *verified knowledge*, and the most satisfactory criterion of science is in terms of the method of verification. Knowledge of facts without knowledge of the procedures to discover the facts does not constitute science, and this is especially true in psychology. Knowing about the behavior of people does not qualify one as a psychologist.

Experimental methods

Experimentation holds the central position in psychological science, as it does in all other sciences, for the reason that it best exemplifies the principles of scientific method. The experiment consists of objective observations of actions performed under rigidly controlled conditions. The hypothesis for investigation is chosen and is stated in such a manner that it can be tested rather completely. One factor, the "causal" one, is usually varied through a predetermined range of values. In the more classical scheme, changes are produced in one variable at a time, and the effects of these changes are observed and measured or recorded while all other important variables of influence are held constant in their effects.

The independent and the dependent variable

One manner of illustrating a typical design for a psychological experiment is shown in Fig. 1. This diagram indicates that a certain type of specified action, the *dependent variable*, is observed while it is influenced by arbitrarily produced changes in some specified stimulating condition, the *independent variable*. Other stimulating conditions that might influence the dependent variable are not allowed to vary during the course of the experiment; i.e., their influences are held constant. On the other hand, actions other than those of one particular dependent variable are quite naturally being carried on by the organism, and these are indicated by the lines R_1 and R_3. In some experiments measures of these other responses are recorded during the whole process, and under such conditions more than one dependent variable exists in the experiment. Such is the case in an experiment which is designed to determine the effects on both mood and efficiency, (two dependent variables) of changes in oxygen content of the air breathed by the subjects in the experiment.

Thus there is only one independent variable in an experiment of

Fig. 1. This diagram represents the scheme of a psychological experiment.

the classical design, and so we often hear of the *law of the independent variable*. This law states that we are to keep all causal factors constant except one, which is to be systematically varied while observations of concomitant or successive changes in the dependent variables are made. Such a procedure rules out all other possibilities of producing in the results effects not attributable to the one independent variable. Certain systematic experimental designs are now available that enable the experimenter to employ more than one independent variable in a single experiment.

The foregoing description is not to be taken as indicating that all the factors involved in any experiment are under the investigator's control. If the observations could be completely controlled, the experimenter would need to make only as many observations as there are degrees of change in the independent variable. This may be the situation in certain physical sciences, but certainly not in the behavioral sciences, where the behavior of the organism is quite variable and is influenced by a multitude of factors, both internal and external. Because of the relatively great variability of behavior, it is necessary for the experimenter to obtain several observations under each condition of the experiment. An average tendency among the observations for each level of the independent variable is then computed, and that average tendency is accepted as a more dependable and representative value for the dependent variable.

Importance of controls

Many of the factors that would influence and modify the behavior specified by a particular dependent variable must have their influence removed from the experimental situation. Insuring adequate controls is one of the most important problems for the experimentalist to face.

The influences of uncontrolled factors may obscure the results of experiments that would otherwise be critical, and yet psychology cannot exert control over all the possible sources of influence that are extraneous to the independent variable. The result of this seeming impasse is that all experiments must be repeated (replicated) and must produce consistency of results under a variety of conditions before they become accepted as demonstrating "facts." The scientist must always be prepared to scrap his results whenever they are demonstrated to be untenable in the light of replication under more precise control.

selection 8 / psychology as a science / Gregory A. Kimble, Duke University

The approach I would like to take to this discussion of psychology as a science is simply that, whether or not such is generally the case now, it is possible to approach the problems of psychology scientifically. Furthermore, it seems to me that about our only hope in this task lies in making use of the things that the philosophers of science are able to tell us. I have, therefore, tried to decide just what lessons these philosophers can teach us and how they can be applied to psychology. My sincere hope is that the summary of my thinking on the topic which I am about to present does not do the philosophers too great an injustice, or, if it does, that they can at least be philosophical about it.

Let us begin by stating the subject matter with which psychology deals. The standard definition of psychology is that it is *the science of behavior*. This definition probably needs clarification. On the one hand it covers less than you may have expected. On the other, it covers too much. Note first that the definition says nothing about mind, or experience, or consciousness. This is not merely an attempt to finesse the problems raised by these three terms. If they are to be used at all in a science of psychology, they will have to be introduced in a way to be described later. A second point is that the behavior with which the psychologist deals tends to be limited to its grosser aspects. Where internal physiological processes are a part of psychology, they are conceived as aids to conceptualization rather than as a part of its basic subject matter. I shall return more than once to the question of the relationship between psychology and physiology; let us turn now to a discussion of the use of the term, "science" in the expression, "science of behavior."

The word, science, refers to the attempt that people called scientists

From Gregory A. Kimble, "Psychology as a Science," *Scientific Monthly*, 77: 156–160, 1953. Reprinted by permission of the publisher.

make to bring order into the world of observable events. Scientists are, of course, not the only ones trying to bring order into the world. Others are the theologians, some literary people, and the philosophers. The scientific way of approaching the task differs from these latter ways, chiefly in terms of its initial data. All science begins with the sensory experience of a perceiving scientist. These sensory experiences, which are private and not a part of science, give rise to its initial data, that is, to a publicly observable *report* of such experiences. In this sense, psychology is exactly like any other science. The report with which psychologists are provided may be about rats running a maze, physiological processes, test results, or even the scientist's own introspection. But the element of all of this that is useful is the report that is open to public inspection.

The particular task which the psychologist has taken for himself is that of trying to make some sense of behavior. But we have just seen that, as scientists, psychologists must concern themselves with events that are publicly observable and, therefore, verifiable. This restriction on the activities of psychologists raises a question: Just what kinds of observations can they make on behavior that are of this sort? The answer to this question comes in two parts. First, psychologists have found (just as other scientists in other fields have found) that human behavior is so complicated that it is impossible even to talk about all of the activity of an individual at any one time. So, in practice, they restrict their observation to limited portions of behavior called responses. Second, even responses cannot, without the aid of photographic assistance, be recorded in detail. So, their reports of behavior typically deal with some abstracted characteristic like the speed or the magnitude of the response.

Having stated the general manner in which the psychologist views behavior, a word must now be said about a primary assumption, which is that these various aspects of behavior are related to events in the person's past and present environment. Although the collection of variables in this category might better be called antecedent and attendant circumstances, the psychological convention is to call them stimuli. When the psychologist speaks of stimuli he usually is referring more or less broadly to events or changes in events in the environment. So far as these stimulus variables are concerned, they are so numerous that no attempt to enumerate them here is possible. A few examples will have to do. In the field of learning, for one example, the efficiency of a learned reaction is known to depend in a regular fashion upon the number and spacing of practice trials, upon the amount of reward the subject is given for making the response, and upon many other variables. In vision, what a person sees (really what he *says* he sees) is known to depend upon the area of the visual stimulus, upon its brightness, upon the duration of its presentation in the visual field, and so on. One thing that should be noticed about these particular examples of environmental events is that they are quantifiable in terms of some standard physical measuring scale. Not all variables with which psychologists have to deal are yet subject to measurement in any very respectable sense of the word. For the kind of information that is needed to build a science of psychology, however, quantification of these independent variables is a necessity of which psychology is acutely aware.

The final task in the development of a behavior science is simply that of stating the relationships that exist among the variables that have been isolated. What psychologists are after is a set of laws of the general type: $R = f(S)$, where R is some aspect of a response, S is a stimulus event and f represents the functional relationship. These are what I will call S-R laws. It should, of course, be realized that the formula, $R = f(S)$, is highly schematized. Behavior is seldom predictable from knowledge of a single S-variable. The S in this equation stands for an indefinite number of antecedent conditions which in actual practice will have to be discovered along with their relevance to behavior.

Because of this complexity in the determination of behavior, the S-R laws have turned out to be very difficult to discover. Where this has happened, psychologists have sometimes had more success using a different approach, in an attempt to discover the relationships that exist among *response* variables. As a convenient example of this, one may take the very important work of the clinical psychologists and the psychological testers. They almost never deal with the S-R type of relationship at all. Instead they use what are sometimes called R-R laws. The distinction between these two types of relationship is shown in the following example. There is some rather good evidence to suggest that an individual who is frustrated in his various strivings develops a tendency toward aggressive behavior. For purposes of exposition, it can be assumed that this is a well-established relationship. On this basis, if one knew that an individual had been frustrated many times in his efforts to achieve important goals, it could be predicted that he would show aggressive behavior. In this case, an S-R law would be used to make the prediction. The determining S-variable is the frequent blocking of goal-directed behavior, and the dependent response variable is the aggressive behavior. If it were known that aggressive behavior in some form always occurs as a consequence of frustration and that it never occurs in the absence of frustration, there would be some point in saying that aggression occurs *because* of frustration. Furthermore, given a control over the person's environment and a knowledge of the S-R law, the amount of his aggressive behavior could be controlled.

A clinical psychologist, on the other hand, might give this same person a psychological test and come out with the statement that he has strong aggressive tendencies and may be expected to show a great deal of hostile behavior on many occasions. This prediction (which would be as correct as the other one) would be made in terms of a different kind of law. What the clinician has done is to observe a small segment of the individual's behavior in a controlled situation called a test, and, from his behavior in this situation, to make a prediction about other behavior. His prediction is made in terms of an $R_2 = f(R_1)$ kind of relationship, in which R_2 is the predicted aggressive behavior, R_1 is the predicted-from-test behavior, and the function is a correlation coefficient. These R-R laws are diagnostic laws, and carry no implications of causality. (The statement that the person tested is aggressive because the clinician has given him a test is obviously absurd, at least until such a time as the clinician's services are more expensive and, therefore, more frustrating than they are now.) Furthermore, the R-R laws provide no control over behavior in the absence of further information of the S-R type.

The commodities in which the psychologist deals are, then, two types of relationship which I have called S-R and R-R laws. The precise statement of a large number of such laws would be extremely valuable, but it would not make psychology a high-order science. What would still be needed would be the collection of the S-R and R-R relationships into some more orderly or integrated kind of formulation. In actual practice, it has been found useful to attempt the formulation without the comprehensive set of empirical laws it is hoped eventually to integrate. Such attempts at formalization are called systematic psychology or psychological theory.

The form that psychological theorizing has taken has been toward the development of intervening state variables which are considered as standing between S and R or between R_1 and R_2, depending upon the kind of relationship. The intervening states that have been postulated have been of two general sorts, physiological states and hypothetical constructs. If we consider first the type of intervening variable used by the more physiologically minded psychologists, the paradigm in terms of which they attempt to explain behavior may be expressed in the following way: S-O-R. Stimulation according to this scheme is thought of as producing some physiological or organic change in the individual. And this physiological change, in turn, is thought of as being responsible for whatever behavior is being observed. Such psychologists investigate the relationships between neural, glandular, circulatory, and muscular events, on the one hand, and behavioral events on the other.

Another large group of psychologists make use of the hypothetical construct type of intervening variable in their explanation of behavior. The paradigm, in terms of which such psychologists work, is the following: S-H-R. Antecedent stimulus conditions are thought of as defining a hypothetical intervening state in terms of which responses are predicted. Examples of such hypothetical constructs in fairly general use are: habit, motivation, fatigue, attitude, symbolic processes, and the like. About these hypothetical constructs, there are a number of things that need to be said. The first of these is that there is no reason in the world to assume that they *must* have any actual existence inside the organism or anywhere else. Some of them, at least, are analogous to the physicists' concept of velocity which derives its meaning from its definition: $V = S/T$. The physicists do not spend much time worrying about what or where velocity really is. Psychologists, on the other hand, spend a good bit of time looking for the neurophysiological events which they think *have* to exist and to correspond to their concepts, however imperfect. What is worse, they spend even more time speculating about them. There are just two comments that I wish to make about this. One is that, although all behavior probably has its neurophysiological aspects, mere speculation about them is a fruitless procedure. The other is that, although physiological *information* may someday turn out to be useful for psychology, there is nothing in the program of psychology which makes such information indispensable. For all practical purposes, it is possible to construct a science of psychology in which the organism is considered as empty. For my own part, I can conceive of a psychology based on stimulus and response events entirely, one in which the existence of the organism is a completely unimportant fact. The scientific account will, after all, deal with behavior in the abstract. Such a science no more needs to refer to the organism than the science of gravitation needs to refer to stones or to the Leaning Tower of Pisa.

Whether the constructs that are introduced between stimuli and responses are physiological or purely hypothetical, they have to meet certain criteria to be acceptable. The most important of these criteria can be summed up in one word: *meaningfulness*. Intervening variables must be meaningful in two ways. The first is what has been called *operational meaning*. The meaningfulness of a concept in this sense depends upon the adequacy of its definition. A concept may be said to be adequately defined providing there exists a set of defining statements for it which lead eventually to phenomena in the sensory experience of the scientist, and providing further that these statements are such that any properly qualified and equipped person can put them to a test. This requirement is no more than a particular application of the more general criterion of public observability.

Concepts for which no such definition is *possible* are of no use to science. This is not, however, to say that concepts which have never been adequately defined never will be. They may or may not be. Concepts such as mind, consciousness, and experience are in the class of intervening variables for which no satisfactory operational definition exists. This is in part because of the complexity of the phenomena involved, and in part because of their inherent privacy. But this state of affairs does not demand the conclusion that respectable definition is impossible.

On the other hand, an operational definition of these terms (assuming it is achieved) does not guarantee their utility. The second kind of meaningfulness remains to be demonstrated. This point can be made clear with the aid of an illustration. I can define a construct as follows: Kappa (for Kimble) = the square root of the number of hairs on my head divided by my diastolic blood pressure minus the length of my great toe. This concept, Kappa, although its operational definition is impeccable, has not been used much in psychology because, so far as we know, it has no meaningful relationship to any of the events with which psychologists are supposed to be dealing. In this second sense, a concept is meaningful if it is related to behavior, or aids in its prediction.

Just as there are two major kinds of laws with which the psychologist deals, there are two kinds of operations in terms of which a concept may acquire operational meaning. The first of these is by definition in terms of antecedent stimulus conditions. The second is by an inference from behavior. To illustrate, let us consider a case in which both types of definition have been used and return to the example of aggression. It has already been pointed out that predictions of aggressive behavior might be made either from a knowledge of an individual's history of frustration or from his behavior on a test. Using exactly the same evidence, there can be developed two different definitions of the concept aggression. In terms of antecedent conditions, aggression can be defined as a positive function of the number of frustrations a person has experienced. In terms of behavior, it can be said that a person is aggressive if his pattern of test responses is so and so. The one thing we cannot say is that we now have two different definitions of the "same thing." Different definitions define different concepts. In psychology, especially, there is the need to be cautioned against the tendency to treat things as identical just because they have the same name. Whether the frustration-produced aggression has anything to do with the test-defined aggression is an empirical question which can be decided by research.

As I see it, just one final point needs to be made with respect to the science of psychology as it is developing. It must be presented as a sort of confession. Not all psychologists agree with the analytical, behavioristic (what James would have called "tough-minded") sort of analysis I have been presenting of the field. In psychology, we hear a great deal about "the total situation," "the whole child," "the whole personality," and "global intelligence." Psychologists who use these expressions object to the type of account I have given, chiefly because of the analytical approach which it implies. This cold analysis, they say, is wrong because it fails to capture the warmth and vitality of human behavior as we know it in our common-sense, firsthand experience. Unfortunately for common sense, that is how it is with science. Common sense tells us that the world is flat; science says that it is round. Our firsthand experience tells us that the sun moves slowly around us; science says that we are moving around the sun, and at a breakneck speed. Direct observation tells us that the chairs in which we are sitting are solid; science says that they are mostly empty space. The mere fact that some line of scientific argument produces a description of the world that fails to correspond to our naive experience of it is no obstacle to that argument. And if there are aspects of behavior that cannot be handled in the way I have been describing, I know of no way of finding this out without giving it a try.

At a somewhat different level, the opponents of behavioristic psychology sometimes object that the analysis of behavior destroys its essentially continuous or integrated character, and robs it of its wholeness. They now propose what they call a field theoretical approach to human behavior and very bitterly deplore what they call the *mechanism* of the sort of argument I have been expounding. They say that their new field theories stand to the more orthodox psychology as does the theory of relativity to Newtonian mechanics. The adequacy of this analogy, of course, depends upon some understanding of what the term, "field," means in physics. It seems to have been used in two rather different ways. Basically, by a "field," the physicist means a system of interrelated variables that differs from other systems of physics partly in the kind of calculus which expresses the interdependencies. Unfortunately, the mathematics are difficult, even for a physicist. So, for their nonmathematical brethren, the theoretical physicists have constructed models (as, for example, the Rutherford-Bohr atom) in an attempt to convey what is involved in their equations. Since the so-called field theories in psychology consist of anthropomorphic models in this second sense, it seems to me that they cannot be called field theories in the sense that the theoretical physicist uses the expression. On the other hand, if one wished to consider as field theories approaches to psychology that come closer to the actual mathematical statement of the interdependencies involved, then the very people who bear the stigma, "mechanistic," would have to qualify as the greatest field theorists of them all.

Finally, it must be pointed out that science is concerned with the regularities in the world; that is, with events that repeat themselves. Whole situations do not repeat themselves, at least not very often. Analysis of the elements common to somewhat different situations will be absolutely essential in order to achieve a science of psychology.

This, then, is what the science of psychology, as it begins to be rather definitely defined, is like. It is concerned with the prediction of behavior either in terms of other behavior or else in terms of antecedent stimulus conditions. Its proponents are trying to develop a consistent body of scientific knowledge expressed in terms of whatever lawful relationships may be found to exist among these variables. Because of the tremendous complexity of this task, it has been necessary to use concepts that are considered formally as intervening between stimuli and responses in one case and between predicted responses and predicted-from responses in another. Furthermore, different psychologists develop different kinds of concepts. Some use mechanistic ones, some use field theoretical ones, others think physiologically. Which of these approaches is the best cannot be decided on the basis of *type* of concept. What really counts is the extent to which these concepts aid in the primary task of psychology—the understanding of behavior.

selection 9 / the historical meaning of psychology as a science and profession / Rollo May, The William Alanson White Institute of Psychiatry, Psychoanalysis and Psychology

Psychology, until about 100 years ago, was part of philosophy and ethics. The great psychological insights before the time of Freud are to be found in the writings of philosophers and religious teachers such as Socrates, Plato, Augustine, Pascal, Spinoza, Kierkegaard, and Nietzsche. The first emergence of psychology in the experimental scientific sense was relatively late; Wundt established his psychological laboratory in Leipzig in 1879 for the exploration of physiological psychology.

To understand the meaning and development of contemporary psychology, we need to see briefly what has happened in man's relation to nature and to himself in the modern period. Since the Renaissance,

From Rollo May, "The Historical Meaning of Psychology as a Science and Profession," *Transactions of the New York Academy of Sciences*, Ser. II, 17: 312–314, 1955. Reprinted by permission of the author and the publisher.

as is well known, a new view of the objectivity of man arose. For complex reasons that we shall not discuss here, natural science in its modern mathematical form was founded on a career to be marked by tremendous progress. When Descartes made his famous dichotomy in the 17th century between extension—matter which can be measured— and thought, which cannot be measured, modern man was given a methodology by means of which he thereupon devoted himself, with great emphasis, to the measuring and control of physical nature. The sciences which best fit this method made the greatest strides: physics, for example; later, chemistry; and so on. Thus, medicine made greater strides than psychology and, in the psychological field itself, psychophysics was the most advanced until the last few years. The Newtonian classical physical view that went along with this development is well known. I wish only to emphasize that the philosophical concomitants during this period were, understandably, a great emphasis on rationalism and, later, a devotion of philosophy to an elucidation of scientific method.

During the last part of the 19th century, radical changes occurred in the social systems of Western man. These changes are portrayed in the work of Freud, Marx, Nietzsche, and others, who pointed out that the inherited ways of understanding experience no longer had the same validity. The disunity that became evident during that period in the various sciences is graphically presented by Ernst Cassirer in his lectures at Yale, published under the title An Essay on Man. These basic changes and evidences of disunity in modern society had a great deal to do with the emergence of psychology as a centrally important science in its own right.

As is well known, psychology in this country, when it broke off from theology and philosophy in the last half of the 19th century, devoted itself largely to laboratory and experimental work. Though it was kept broad by such leaders as William James, nonetheless, psychology, predominantly in America, has followed until recently the emphasis upon experimental laboratory methods.

The importance of Freud and the later development of clinical and therapeutic psychology can be seen when we realize that Freud sought to find some bases for psychological unity amid the progressively disunified tendencies characterizing persons of the Victorian culture. In essence, Freud pointed out that the rationalistic view of man—that is, man trying to live his life solely by reason and repressing the irrational, unpredictable, and unmeasureable tendencies —was not only unsatisfactory but led to the breakdown of personality.

There is no doubt that clinical psychology and the more intensive forms of psychotherapy are here to stay in our civilization chiefly because of the great and pressing social need for these psychological services.

The bringing together of clinical and traditional scientific psychology presents a number of problems, some of which remain unsolved. I believe that the development of new theory is necessary. This theory in psychology may well be parallel to the new theory in physics as elaborated by Heisenberg, Einstein, Bohr, and others. The essence of the new physical theory is that objective nature can no longer be understood as detached from man. The human being is actor as well as spectator. The parallel to this in psychology would be that we must view man as subject as well as object. I see the new development in physics as symptomatic of far-reaching and necessary changes in our attitude toward man and nature in the Western World. The changes in psychology will occur not because physics now gives us "permission," but rather because of changes running through the basic concepts of Western society.

Psychology needs to work out the theory and method which will be most fruitful for its particular subject matter and aims. The new theory for psychology, which will also serve as a basis for psychotherapy, will include at least the following five aspects:

First, it will preserve the careful methods of experimental psychology. But it will put these methods in a broader understanding of the nature of man. The experimentalist will be aware that, whenever we experiment on a person, we are necessarily leaving out some elements of the whole autonomous human being.

Second, the new theory will include human self-awareness. For we can never see man whole except as we see him, including ourselves, as the mammal who has a distinctive capacity for awareness of himself and his world. Herein lie the roots of man's capacity to reason and deal in symbols and abstract meanings, and herein lies also the basis for a sound view of human freedom.

Third, the new theory will include some concept of the dynamism of the self. It is not satisfactory to assume the person "grows" like a plant or that the self merely is characterized by a "thrust towards health" like the body. We need some understanding of the aspect of the human being which Allport sought to describe in his term "functional autonomy" and which Goldstein characterizes as "self-actualization."

Fourth, it will include the aspect of culture. For man always lives, moves, and has his being in a social, interpersonal world.

Fifth, the new theory will include the historical dimension of the human being. For man is the mammal who, unlike other animals, can have self-awareness of his past, can transcend the present moment of time, can project himself into the future, thus can learn from the past and, to some extent, can mold his future. It is not generally realized that scientific psychology has treated man almost entirely as an ahistorical unit and, to my mind, this has meant a considerable truncation of understanding.

The sixth aspect of the new theory should be the relation of psychology to ethics. For it is clear from the implications above that man's behavior always influences his own future and impinges upon the rest of the community.

CHAPTER 2 ❋ THE DEVELOPMENT OF BEHAVIOR ❋

In a very real sense a complete understanding of the development of behavior would necessarily entail consideration of all the facets of behavior which are discussed throughout the remainder of this book. However, because we cannot conveniently consider everything at once, we leave the elaboration of more specific aspects of functioning to the relevant chapters. In this chapter we examine some of the kinds of evidence which support the general psychological principle that the structure and behavior of the organism depend on a continual interaction of hereditary mechanisms with environmental factors.

With regard to the biological development of the organism, this principle implies that no anatomical structure can be said to be exclusively determined by gene structure per se. On the contrary, biological structure is determined by the biochemical composition of the genes in interaction with *the surrounding intracellular and extracellular biochemical environment. Thus, as Montagu points out in Selection 10, "What the organism inherits is a genotype and an environment." He goes on to illustrate how this biochemical environment may be modified by a great number of factors outside the intrauterine environment of the developing organism. He emphasizes that later behavior of the child may be greatly influenced by such extrauterine factors.*

The influence of genetic mechanisms does not end with birth. Their continued influence manifests itself in uniform patterns of development of structure and behavior which we call maturation. In Selection 11 Dr. Gesell, an internationally known expert on the development of behavior, summarizes some of these dominant maturational patterns. He emphasizes the innate tendency of the child toward growth, but at the same time he notes the importance of culture in providing the necessary support for this unfolding development.[1]

In Selection 12 Hebb adds new meaning to the importance of adequate environmental stimulation for effective growth. He provides both clinical and experimental evidence to support the generalization that "early environment has a lasting effect on the form of adjustment at maturity." He cites studies of sensory deprivation to indicate that the functioning of the mature organism is similarly dependent on adequate environmental support. Hebb develops the further generalization that with regard to the phylogenetic scale, "the greater the development of intelligence the greater the vulnerability to emotional breakdown," but points out how man's culture serves to protect him from strong emotional disturbances. It should be noted that this principle seems to apply only to increases in intelligence as we move up the phylogenetic scale. The bulk of the scientific evidence does not support the common sense generalization that, at the human level, the more intelligent one is the more likely he is to be emotionally unstable.

Gesell refers to culture as a "gigantic conditioning apparatus." Dr. Ruth Benedict, a cultural anthropologist, elaborates this view in her article "Continuities and Discontinuities in Cultural Conditioning." She examines several types of role conflicts which are dictated by the child's biology but which may be ameliorated to a greater or less degree by his culture. Her paper, thus, emphasizes the interaction of biological, psychological, and cultural determinants of behavior by illustrating the wide range of "adjustments which are possible within a universally given, but not so drastic, set of physiological facts."

[1] Note that Maslow's theory of motivation (Selections 15 and 16), which emphasizes the concept of self-actualization, implies a similar tendency toward growth; and Rogers (Selection 47) makes a "growth hypothesis" basic to his theory of personality and practice of psychotherapy.

selection 10 / constitution and prenatal factors in infant and child health / M. F. Ashley Montagu, The New School for Social Research

Introduction

This review of the materials relating to constitutional and prenatal factors in infant and child health should be regarded as of suggestive

Abridged from M. F. Ashley Montagu, "Constitutional and Prenatal Factors in Infant and Child Health," *Symposium on the Healthy Personality,* Milton rather than of determinative value. That is to say, it should be read as suggesting areas for research to research workers, and to parents it should suggest something of the nature of the care and caution they need to exercise even before the baby is born. In short, most statements made in this review should be read with the phrase, "The evidence suggests . . ." mentally affixed.

It is important to bear in mind that much of our knowledge of what conditions affect the unborn fetus is drawn from the field of disease, from pathology. This fact should not cause the reader to develop an exaggerated view of the dangers to which the fetus is exposed nor to marvel at what might seem the surprising fact that so many human beings have survived unmarred. The pathological cases are fortunately in the minority. Their value, and their use here, lies in the fact that they show, as it were, in high relief the kind of conditions which can influence the development of the fetus, as well as something of the probable mode of action of the more normal conditions. They also show us how the development of the fetus can be influenced for better or for worse. Indeed, if there is one important lesson to be learned from the findings which are discussed in this paper, it is that we can do much to make the prenatal development of the infant a satisfactory one.

Constitution, heredity, and environment

Constitution is the sum total of the structural, functional, and psychological characters of the organism. It is in large measure an integral of genetic potentialities influenced in varying degrees by internal and external environmental factors. What, in fact, we are concerned with here is the answer to the following questions: (1) What are the inherited genetic potentialities (the genotype) of the organisms?, (2) How are these influenced by the internal and external environmental factors during prenatal life?, and (3) What role does each of these factors play in influencing the subsequent physical and mental health of infant and child?

What we mean by these questions is what we mean by "constitution," for constitution is at first a series of operative questions that even by the time of birth have not yet become final declarative answers. Indeed, there is little that is final about constitution, for constitution is a *process* rather than an unchanging entity. In brief, it is important to understand at the outset that constitution is not a biologically *given* structure predestined by its genotype to function in a predetermined manner. The manner in which all genotypes

J. Senn, ed., Josiah Macy, Jr. Foundation, New York, 1950, pp. 148–175. Reprinted by permission of the publisher.

function is determined by the interaction of the genotype with the environment in which it undergoes development. What, so to speak, the genotype—the complex of genetic potentialities with which the organism is endowed—asks is: What kind of responses are going to be made to my autocatalytic enzymatic (chemically accelerating) overtures, my tentative advances? How will I impress? How will I be impressed? For the outcome of all this will be my constitution.

The point that must be emphasized here is that every genotype is a unique physiochemical system comprising particular kinds of potentialities having definite limits. These limits vary from individual to individual, so that were the genotype to be exposed to identical environmental conditions its interactive expression would nevertheless continue to vary from individual to individual. But in point of fact the environmental conditions never are the same for two individuals, not including single-egg or so-called "identical" twins. This fact renders it necessary for us to recognize that heredity is not merely constituted by the genotype, but by the genotype as modified by the environment in which it has developed. It is necessary to grasp clearly the fact that what the organism inherits is a genotype *and* an environment. That heredity is the dynamic integral of the genotype and the environment—the resultant of the dynamic interaction between the two.

If it is true that the organism inherits a genotype and an environment, and that the resultant of the interaction between the two is heredity, then it follows that it would be possible to influence the heredity of the developing organism by controlling its environment. This we know to be true by virtue of numerous experiments involving plants and non-human animals, and we have good evidence that it is also true for man. The question of an earlier day which asked whether heredity was more important than environment or vice versa has been dismissed by some experts as a spurious question. It has been said that heredity and environment are equally important, since both are necessary if the genes are to develop, or rather if the genes are to produce development. Genes always act within the conditioning effects of an environment. Some have gone further and stated that the genotype is more important than the environment, and others have asserted the opposite.

Clearly, the genotype is fundamental in that it is biologically determined as a complex of potentialities with inherent limitations for development. But since those potentialities are always considerably influenced by the environment, the question of importance becomes a relative one, depending upon whether one takes the view that the genotype can be favorably influenced by controlled environmental factors or that it cannot. Since it is through its environment alone that the developing "human" organism can be influenced, it seems clear that it is the most important means through which we can work to secure the optimum development of the genotype in its final expression in what we see, which we call the phenotype. The importance of the genotype is affirmed as potentiality or potentialities, a statement which implies the necessity of emphasizing its complementary, the importance of the developer of those potentialities—the environment.

Genes determine, not characters nor traits, but responses of the developing organism to the environment. Since the expression of the genotype is a function of the environment, it is to a certain extent amenable to human control. The practical significance of this statement cannot be overemphasized for those of us who are interested in understanding, and to some extent controlling, the character and influence of prenatal factors upon the developing fetus and their effects upon the health of infant and child.

Inherited potentialities and environmental influences

We may now turn to our three questions and the answers to them. The first two questions are best answered together.

What are the inherited genetic potentialities of the organism, and how are these influenced by internal and external environmental factors during prenatal life?

The inherited genetic potentialities are contained in the genes in the 24 chromosomes transmitted from the mother and in the 24 chromosomes transmitted from the father. Three different observers, by three different methods, have independently estimated the number of genes in man to be somewhere in the vicinity of 30,000. Genes are autocatalytic, enzymatic, self-duplicating giant protein molecules of great complexity. That is to say, genes are the organic catalysts which accelerate essential chemical reactions, the original builders of the body which they serve to differentiate according to the type of medium and other conditions which surround them in their interactive chemical relations. These chemical relations are inherent in the chemical properties of the genes and will be *more or less* broadly realized according to a determinate pattern under all environments. The *more* or the *less* will depend upon the nature of the environment in which the genes find themselves. The important point to understand, however, is that the same genes may be influenced to express themselves differently and to have different end effects as a consequence of the different environments in which they function. It is in this way, we believe, that the different parts of the body come to be developed by essentially the same genes. Furthermore, from fertilization onward small random or accidental changes in the environment of the egg or embryo may be operative and can have a decisive effect upon development. A gene on the verge of expressing itself may be affected by random variations in the constitution of the cell substance. Variations in the prenatal environment during the limited period of the action of certain genes may substantially affect their manifestation.

A great many constitutional defects in children are believed to be owing to disturbances during the prenatal development of the organism. The evidence for this is in part derived from experimental studies on nonhuman animals and in part from the factual data for man himself.

Is there a connection between the nervous systems of mother and child?

Until recently there has been a widespread belief that the fetus is so well insulated in the womb and so well protected by the placental barrier that it lives a nirvana-like existence completely sufficient unto itself. Some have described this condition as a state of uterine bliss. According to them this uterine state of bliss leaves its mark upon the mind of the organism and, unconsciously recollected in later life, usually in anything but tranquillity, determines the person's search for such a state of bliss. This "Maginot Line" view of uterine existence is no longer in agreement with the facts. Indeed, we begin to perceive that there is more than a modicum of truth in the remark, uttered by Samuel Taylor Coleridge more than a hundred years ago, "Yes, the history of man for the nine months preceding his birth, would, probably, be far more interesting, and contain events of greater moment, than all the threescore and ten years that follows it."

A still widely prevalent belief has it that there is no connection between the nervous systems of mother and fetus. This notion is based on a very narrow conception of the nervous system. It is through the neurohumoral system, the system comprising the interrelated nervous and endocrine systems acting through the fluid medium of the blood (and its oxygen and carbon-dioxide contents), that nervous changes in the mother may affect the fetus. The common endocrine pool of the mother and fetus forms a neurohumoral bond between them. The endocrine systems of mother and fetus complement each other.

All this is not to say that there is anything at all in the old wives' tale of "maternal impressions." The mother's "impressions," her "psychological states" as such, cannot possibly be transmitted to the fetus. What are transmitted are the gross chemical changes which occur in the mother and, so far as we know at the present time, nothing more.

While it is believed that some hormonal molecules are not small enough to pass through the placenta, there is no doubt that many maternal hormones are composed of molecules of small enough size to be able to pass very readily through the placenta.

Are the mother's emotional states communicated to the fetus? If so, how? Possible effects.

The answer to this compound question is: Yes, there is good evidence that the mother's emotional states are, at least in chemical form, transmitted to the fetus. The Fels Institute workers at Antioch College, Yellow Springs, Ohio, have found that emotional disturbances in the pregnant mother produce a marked increase in the activity of the fetus. Mothers undergoing periods of severe emotional distress have fetuses which show considerably increased activity. Moreover, the Fels workers have found that mothers having the highest rates for the functioning of that part of the nervous system which is mostly under unconscious control, and is concerned with the regulation of visceral activities, the autonomic nervous system in such measures as skin conductance, resting heart rate, respiration rate, variability of respiration and variability of heart rate under basic conditions, have the most active fetuses. In view of these facts, it has been postulated that "the psychophysiological state of the mother exerts an influence upon the behavior pattern of the normal fetus."

The Fels Institute workers have observed that fatigue in the pregnant mother will also produce hyperactivity in the fetus. Supporting these observations, other observers have found that the activity of the fetus is greatest in the evening.

How are the mother's emotional states capable of affecting the fetus?

Through the neurohumoral system, which has already been defined as being composed of the interrelated nervous and endocrine systems acting through the fluid medium of the blood. For example, stimuli originating in the cerebral cortex (the external gray matter of the brain) may set up reflexes which pass directly into the autonomic nervous system (through the autonomic representation in the cerebral cortex) or are mediated through the feeling-tone center or relay station known as the thalamus to the lower autonomic centers of the hypothalamus, the great coordinating center of the autonomic nervous system situated at the base of the brain. By whatever route such reflexes travel, the autonomic nervous system acts upon the endocrine glands and these pour their secretions into the blood. In the pregnant mother such secretions are known to be capable of passing through the placenta to the fetus, with the possible exception of some of the hormones of the pituitary gland. Stimuli originating in the central nervous system of the mother can therefore indirectly produce changes in the fetus by leading to chemical changes in the mother which affect the fetus. Acetylcholine, which is a substance given off along the course of a nerve fiber during the passage of a nerve impulse, and adrenaline, the secretion of the glands situated on top of the kidneys, the adrenal glands, are almost certainly two among the many substances involved. But we may well consider this under the heading of the third part of our question: What are the possible effects of the mother's emotional states upon the fetus?

The infants of mothers who were emotionally disturbed during pregnancy frequently exhibit evidences of an irritable and hyperactive autonomic nervous system. The cases observed by Sontag presented disturbances in gastrointestinal motility, tone, and function manifested by excessive regurgitation, dyspepsia, and perhaps diarrhea. In some cases there is increase in heart rate, increased vasomotor irritability (irritability of the blood vessels in terms of constriction and dilation), and changes in respiratory pattern. Sontag says:

Irritable or poorly balanced adrenergic-cholinergic systems probably constitute an important part of the rather poorly defined syndrome commonly labeled constitutional inadequacy or nutritional diaphysis. Early feeding difficulties based on motor and sensory abnormalities of the gastrointestinal system are in many instances of autonomic origin. The presence of feeding difficulties of a motor or secretory nature from birth must presume their etiology and basic disturbances during intrauterine life. In prenatal development of such a condition, prolonged nervous and emotional disturbances of the mother during the later months of pregnancy seem to be important.

The suggestion is that the autonomic nervous system of the fetus becomes sensitized through the hyperactivity of the mother's neurohumoral system.

The Fels Institute workers have found that if the mother undergoes severe emotional stresses during pregnancy, especially during the latter part of pregnancy, her child will be born as, and develop as, a hyperactive, irritable, squirming infant who cries for his feeding every two or three hours instead of sleeping through the four-hour interval between feedings. The irritability of such infants involves the control of the gastrointestinal tract, causing emptying of the bowel at frequent intervals, as well as regurgitation of food. As Sontag puts it:

He is to all intents and purposes a neurotic infant when he is born—the result of an unsatisfactory fetal environment. In this instance he has not had to wait until childhood for a bad home situation or other cause to make him neurotic. It has been done for him before he has even seen the light of day.

Greenacre has suggested that the evidence indicates the possible existence of preanxiety reactions in fetal life without, necessarily, any psychic content. She suggests that traumatic stimuli, such as sudden sounds, vibrations, umbilical-cord entanglements, and the like, may produce a predisposition to anxiety which, whether combined or not with constitutional and traumatizing birth experiences, might be an important determinant in producing the severity of any neurosis.

That the fetus is capable of being conditioned . . . has long been thought to be a possibility. The possibility has now been turned into a certainty. Spelt has shown that the fetus *in utero* during the last two months of pregnancy can be taught to respond to the secondary association of a primary original stimulus. . . .

These are important findings, for they indicate that the potentialities for conditioning and probably learning (the ability to increase the strength of any act through training) are already present in the unborn fetus, as well as the possibility of its acquiring certain habits of response while still in the womb.

Other environmental factors which may affect the prenatal development of the organism may be considered under the following eight headings: (I) physical agents, (II) nutritional effects, (III) drugs, (IV) infections, (V) maternal dysfunction, (VI) maternal sensitization, (VII) maternal age, (VIII) maternal parity.

I Physical agents The fetus will respond to sounds originating outside the mother's body at the thirtieth week, when, for example, a doorbell buzzer is held opposite its head. Under such conditions the fetal responses are of a convulsive nature. The startle reflex is easily elicited. It has been found that very slight tapping upon the amnion at the time of hysterectomy under local anesthesia will result in quick fetal movements at a much earlier period in prenatal life. Tapping indirectly, as upon the side of a bathtub in which a pregnant woman was lying, induced a sudden jump on the part of the fetus thirty-one days before it was born. Orchestral or piano music or the vibration of a washing machine, during the last two months of pregnancy, resulted in marked increase in fetal activity. It is now known that the human fetus *in utero* is capable of being stimulated by, and responding to, a wide range of tones.

It is believed that the ability to receive stimuli originating within the organism, the proprioceptive sense, is developed very early in the fetus, and that muscle-joint responses are capable of being produced not only by proprioceptive but also by stimuli originating outside the organism (exteroceptive stimulation). Differences in pressure *in utero*, whether induced through internal or external forces; differences in position, umbilical-cord entanglements, and similar factors may more or less adversely affect the development of the organism. Deformity may be caused by faulty position, mechanical shaking, temperature changes; asymmetry of the head may be produced by pressure of the head downward upon the thorax; wryneck (torticollis) has been observed, and pressure atrophy of the skin indicates the kind of continuous stimulation to which the fetus may be exposed.

Exposure to massive doses of x-rays within the first two months of pregnancy will, in many cases, produce abortion of the embryo. Where abortion does not follow, serious injury has been found to result in a large percentage of cases. Thus, Murphy found that in a series of 74 recorded cases of therapeutic maternal irradiation, there were only 36 normal children born; there were 23 imbeciles with heads of abnormal size and 15 offspring otherwise malformed or diseased. In other words, 51.3% of the children were abnormal.

II Nutritional effects From the standpoint of the physical growth and development of the organism, it is known that such environmental factors as are produced by the mother's nutrition and occupation during all stages of pregnancy, her health, general hygiene, and sanitation can affect the development of the fetus. These conditions generally reflect the socioeconomic status or the nutritional status of the mother. Fetuses and infants of mothers of low socioeconomic status are smaller and have a higher mortality rate than those of mothers of higher socioeconomic status. In itself small size is not necessarily a handicap, but in many cases it is a symptom of basic organic deficiencies which will play an important role in the later developmental history of the organism. Children who may otherwise appear to be normal will usually exhibit evidences of deficient intrauterine environment in the form of radio-opaque white striae which may be seen in the tarsal bones by the end of the first postnatal month. These striae, corresponding to the lines of retarded growth seen in the long bones of older children and adults and caused by periods of prolonged illness, indicate that disturbances in nutrition, from whatever cause, during prenatal life are capable of inscribing their effects very substantially upon the structure of the developing organism.

III Drugs Drugs taken by the pregnant mother may seriously affect the fetus. Many cases of congenital deafness have been traced to the mother's use of quinine for malaria during pregnancy. Morphinism has been reported in the infants of mothers who were morphine addicts. Inhalation of amyl nitrite by the mother for a few seconds induced an increase in fetal heart rate, beginning during the third minute following the mother's inhalation. Subsequent inhalations produced a diphasic (excitor-depressor) response.

The obstetrical practice of dosing the pregnant mother with barbiturates and similar drugs prior to delivery may so overload the fetal blood stream as to produce asphyxiation in the fetus at birth, with either permanent brain damage or subtle damage of such a kind as to lead to mental impairment. Fortunately, the trend today is away from heavy sedation.

It is known that a barbiturate derivative such as "sodium seconal," usually prescribed as a sedative, when given to the pregnant mother will pass into the blood stream of the fetus and cause a cortical electrical depression in its brain waves which can be measured at, and persists for some time after, birth.

Is there any evidence that the pregnant mother's smoking affects the fetus? There is. It has been found that the smoking of one cigarette generally produced an increase in the heart rate, sometimes a decrease in the heart rate. The maximum individual increase in fetal heart beats per minute was 39.6, the greatest drop 16.8. The maximum effect is observed between the eighth and twelfth minutes after the cigarette, and the cardiovascular response is more marked after the eighth month. It is quite possible that the products of tobacco may adversely affect not only the heart of the fetus but its whole cardiovascular system, not to mention the possibility of many other organs. This is a subject upon which we need more research. At the present time we have no definite evidence that the mother's intake of tobacco smoke actually harms the fetus. This is a question which further research alone can settle.

IV Infections Some virus and bacterial diseases can be transmitted from pregnant mother to fetus, with considerable damage to the latter. Rubella (German measles) is an example of a virus disease which, contracted by the mother in early pregnancy, may produce cataract and deafness with mental defect.

Swan has shown that if the monther contracts rubella during the first four months of pregnancy she has a three to one chance of giving birth to a congenitally defective child. Equine encephalomyelitis, fortunately very rare, is another virus disease which can cause changes in the fetus which produce idiocy. Smallpox, chickenpox, measles, mumps, scarlet fever, erysipelas, and recurrent fever have long been known to be transmissible from mother to fetus. There is also good experimental evidence indicating that the virus of *influenza* A can produce serious deformities in the developing embryo. The bacterium of congenital syphilis, *Treponema pallidum*, can actually enter the embryo. If this happens, miscarriage occurs. If the bacterium enters at a later fetal age, the child is born with signs of congenital syphilis, or the disease may not show itself till later, as congenital paresis. Tuberculosis is also transmissible to the fetus from the mother by means of the *Bacillum tuberculosis*. The fetal death rate from tuberculosis is high, while those infants who are born with the disease usually die within the first year.

V Maternal dysfunction By maternal dysfunction is meant noninfectious functional disease in the pregnant mother. Such disorders in the mother may seriously affect the development of the fetus. Pregnant women suffering from hypertensive disease (high blood pressure) show a very high rate both of fetal loss and of maternal mortality, as well as of other serious conditions. Chesley and Annetto have reported that in 301 pregnancies in 218 women with essential hypertension (disease due to no known cause), the gross fetal loss in the first hypertensive pregnancy reached the staggeringly high figure of 38% and increased with the increase in blood pressure. There were thirteen maternal deaths, or a total of 4.3%, some 200 times higher than occurs in general obstetrical practice. Gasper found that out of 49 deliveries in 45 pregnant diabetics there were 19 still births and 6 neonatal deaths, in other words a fetal mortality rate of 51%!

VI Maternal sensitization In instances in which the genotype of mother and fetus differ in the substances borne on the surfaces of the red blood corpuscles, the mother may become sensitized and produce antibodies inimical to fetal development. This usually results in causing anemia at a relatively late fetal age. The Rh incompatibilities constitute a well-known example of this. When the blood of the rhesus monkey is injected into rabbits or guinea pigs, a special serum is obtained. The serum will "clump" the blood of about 85% of all white persons. The factor in the blood which makes it clump in response to the serum is the Rh factor. Persons who have this type of blood are said to be Rh positive. Persons who do not are Rh negative. The exact way in which the Rh factor is inherited is extremely complicated. Three distinct Rh factors are known, and at least six major genes are involved. These result in twenty-one combinations of genotypes which produce eight Rh blood types.

Understanding how the Rh factor operates and how it is inherited is extremely important in biology and medicine. And the practical implications for human health are great.

When a woman who is Rh negative marries a man who is Rh positive, the first-born child of such a marriage is usually normal. However, during following pregnancies the fetus may be lost by miscarriage. Or it may be born in such an anemic and jaundiced state that it lives only a few hours after birth. The infant usually dies from a disease called erythroblastosis. The name means that the red blood corpuscles —the erythrocytes—have been subject to wholesale destruction.

The disease is caused by the fact that the fetus has inherited an Rh positive gene from its father. The fetus produces Rh positive substances called antigens in its blood. These substances pass through the placenta into the mother's blood, where the antigens stimulate the production of large numbers of antibodies. These antibodies in turn pass through the placenta into the blood system of the fetus. There they start destroying the red blood corpuscles of the fetus.

Fortunately this disease does not occur as often as the facts of heredity might lead us to expect. Erythroblastosis takes place in about one out of every two hundred pregnancies. Actually, about one in twelve pregnancies involves an Rh negative mother carrying an Rh positive fetus. Therefore, in theory we should have children suffering from erythroblastosis born in one out of twelve instead of one out of two hundred pregnancies. If we omit firstborn children—who are seldom affected—this figure would work out to one in seventeen or eighteen pregnancies.

Understanding the importance of the Rh factor is of great practical importance. Every woman planning marriage should consult her physician to find out the Rh types both of herself and of her prospective husband. There are various ways in which the evil effects of clashing Rh factors may be partially averted if doctors know about them beforehand.

VII Maternal age There is a high correlation between age of mother and maldevelopment of the fetus. The cause of this is obscure. Half the known cases of Mongolism were born to mothers of thirty-eight years of age or more. Congenital hydrocephalus is also significantly correlated with late maternal age. Indeed, statistically speaking, abnormal conditions appear with significantly higher frequency in the infant of the older mother than in any other group. The incidence of two-egg twinning also increases with maternal age. The evidence is now fairly complete that infant and maternal mortality rates, prematurity, stillbirths, and miscarriage rates are highly correlated with age of mother. The optimum period for childbearing seems to lie between the years of twenty-three and twenty-nine. Before twenty-three years of age, on the average, the younger the mother—and after twenty-nine years of age, the older the mother—the higher are the maternal and infant mortality rates. In the younger mothers the responsible factor appears to be inadequate development of the reproductive system. In the older mothers the progressive decline in the functions of that system is almost certainly responsible. Since these functions are largely endocrine in nature, it is likely that in some cases the fetus is adversely affected developmentally.

VIII Parity or number of previous pregnancies of mother There is evidence that first-born children, as well as those born at the end of a long series of pregnancies, are less viable than those born in between, irrespective of maternal age. Fetal malformations are slightly more common in the children of mothers having their first pregnancies (primiparae) than in those of the second and third. It is known that disturbances due to sensitization become more marked with increasing age of the mother, but the reason for this is at present unknown.

It should be remembered that these are statistical findings, and that there are plenty of first-born and last-born children, as well as children who were born well after their mother's thirty-eighth birthday, who are in every way perfectly healthy. . . .

The question has been asked whether some children from birth are more likely than others to find the achievement of healthy personality development difficult. Some of the facts already mentioned in the preceding pages should make it quite clear that the answer to this question is in the affirmative.

Excluding physical malformations from our discussion in the present connection, the indications are that a child which as a fetus was traumatized by such factors as have already been discussed is likely to find the achievement of healthy personality development more difficult, other things being equal, than a child who as a fetus was not so traumatized. Some children, as Sontag has pointed out, are born "neurotic" as a result of their intrauterine experiences.[1]

[1] A more exhaustive discussion of this subject may be found in Ashley Montagu, *Prenatal Influences*, C. C. Thomas, Springfield, Ill., 1962.

selection 11 / growth potentials of the human infant / Arnold Gesell, Yale University

All educability is dependent upon innate capacities of growth. This intrinsic growth is a gift of nature. It can be guided, but it cannot be created; nor can it be transcended by any educational agency.

The problem of human educability therefore must reckon with two closely related concepts, namely *learning* and *growth*. Darwin understood this when he suggested toward the end of his life that more accurate knowledge of the development of infants would probably give a foundation for some improvement in their education.

From the vantage point of post-Darwinian science, we begin to see each child as the focal end product of age-old processes of evolution. Biologically considered, infancy is a period of formative immaturity, which is most prolonged and most intensified in the very species which stands highest in the life scale—presumably in our own! Bernard Shaw rather deplores this circumstance. Accordingly, in his *Metabiological Pentateuch*, he arranges matters otherwise; and on a summer afternoon in the year A.D. 31,920, the Newly Born emerges from a fabulous eggshell (some "filaments of spare albumen clinging to her here and there")—an exquisite creature endowed with speech and the full-fledged intelligence of a seventeen-year-old youth. With such a precocious start and a Back-to-Methuselah life cycle, the race may indeed be in a better position to cope with its cultural problems.

The infant of today, nevertheless, is born with prodigious powers of psychological growth. Note how swiftly and progressively he gains

From Arnold Gesell, "Growth Potentials of the Human Infant," *Scientific Monthly*, 68:252–256, 1949. Reprinted by permission of the publisher.

command of his eyes and hands. Very soon after birth he is able to fixate an eye upon an object of interest; first he fixates with one eye, then with the other, later with each in rapid rhythmic alternation, and later conjointly and convergently. At four weeks he gives sustained binocular regard to an object brought into his line of vision; at eight weeks he follows it with head rotation; at twelve weeks he looks regardfully at his own hand; at sixteen weeks, when seated in a supportive chair in front of a test table, he can focus eyes upon a tiny pellet 7 mm in diameter. He takes hold of the world with his eyes before he does so with his hands. But at twenty-four weeks he can pick up a one-inch block on sight. His early manual grasp is pawlike, palmar and ulnar. Soon it becomes digital and radial. At forty weeks he picks up the pellet with fingertips by precise pincer prehension. At fifteen months he releases this same pellet into a bottle; he adaptively superimposes one block upon another. At eighteen months he builds a tower of three blocks; at two years, a wall; at three years, a bridge.

I rehearse this brief tale because it illustrates what the infant himself rehearses by way of his own ontogenetic development. The significant fact about these patterns of eye-hand behavior is that they are not products of formal instruction, training, nor of education in a narrow sense. They are self-taught, self-initiated. In sequence and form they represent a generic ground plan of child development. The ground plan is primarily determined by genes. Environmental factors support, inflect, and modify, but they do not generate, the basic progressions of development. When the infant enters the world, he is already in possession of fundamental growth potentials which are distinctively his own, though phyletic in their origin. With the aid of motion-picture cameras at the Yale Clinic, we have documented thousands of behavior patterns and pattern phases at thirty-four progressive age levels, from the period of fetal infancy through the first ten years of life. Growth gradations were charted in four major fields of behavior: motor, language, adaptive, personal-social. These objective records show that, although no two individuals are exactly alike, all normal children tend to follow a general sequence of growth characteristic of the species and of a cultural group. Every child has a unique pattern of growth, but that pattern is a variant of a basic ground plan. The species sequences are part of an established order of nature. Accordingly, the eyes take the lead, the hands follow; palmar grasp comes before digital; creeping before walking; crying before laughing; towers before walls; vertical crayon strokes before horizontal, and horizontal before oblique. First the blade, then the ear.

Growth is a step-by-step process. Each step is made possible by the step that preceded. The mind thus grows by natural stages. Maximum educability is realized only when educational measures are attuned to the maturity status of the organism. We have demonstrated the significance of maturity factors by extensive use of the method of co-twin control. One of a pair of extremely similar, single-egg twins was intensively trained for periods of six to eight weeks in a specific activity; the other twin was reserved as a comparative control. Objective data supported by cinemanalysis were gathered for stair climbing, constructive play with blocks, vocabulary training, digit and object memory, and motor skills in ring tossing and paper cutting. In none of these activities was it possible to confer a permanent advantage of skill upon either twin. After a lapse of a few weeks or months, the performances of the twins on the various tests were as similar to each other as at the beginning of the given experiment. I hasten to say that this does not prove that twins (or singletons) should not be educated. We simply have demonstrated in quantitative terms that the efficacy of training varies enormously with the developmental readiness of the infant and child.

Maturation is the net sum of gene effects operating in a self-limited life cycle. If you are reluctant to acknowledge the educational importance of genes, you may say, "This is all very well for such physical reactions as walking, stair climbing, block building, writing, drawing, and motor skills. But does it apply to emotions, to morals, to personality, and to the spiritual aspects of childhood?"

Our studies show that the higher psychical manifestations of child life also are profoundly subject to laws of development. From the standpoint of development, body and mind are indivisible. The child comes by his mind as he comes by his body, through the organizing processes of growth. Psychically, he inherits nothing fully formed. Each and every part of his nature has to grow—and his sense of self, his fears, his affections and his curiosities, his feelings toward mother, father, playmates, and sex, his judgments of good and bad, of ugly and beautiful, his respect for truth and property, his sense of humor, his ideas about life and death, crime, war, nature, and deity. All his sentiments, concepts, and attitudes are products of growth and experience. For all these diverse areas of behavior it is possible to formulate gradations and gradients of growth which represent the natural maturational stages by which the child assimilates the complex culture into which he is born.

The culture also assimilates him through its "gigantic conditioning apparatus." But the process of acculturation is fundamentally delimited and pervasively patterned by the mechanisms of maturation inherent in the individual.

Educability is delimited and configured by the selfsame mechanisms; for educability does not depend upon a formless kind of plasticity. It depends upon the structured nascencies of the mind as a growing organism. The human mind is a minutely architectured action system which has an embryogenesis and a developmental morphology, manifested in patterns of behavior. The forms and lawful sequences of these patterns can be defined by scientific methods. This is the task of a genetic and clinical science of child development.

More knowledge needs to be applied at the beginnings of the life cycle to reduce the mounting tide of adolescent instability and of adult abnormalities of behavior. Through broadened methods of developmental diagnosis and supervision in infancy, through individualized growth guidance in nursery and elementary schools, we can strengthen the stamina of the child and of the family unit. We can foster basic virtues and discover distinctive gifts and talents—academic and nonacademic—in the early years of life. We cannot make democracy a genuine folkway, unless we bring into the homes of the people a *developmental philosophy* of child care that is rooted in scientific research.

No one has to teach a baby the elements of growing. He knows all that by heart, for nature drilled it into him through countless ages of evolution. What is more, nature compounded him so ingeniously that no one just like him will ever be born again. He is an individual. Under given environmental conditions, his inborn growth potentials will govern the extent and the modes of his maturing. His growth characteristics constitute the very core of his individuality, and by the same token his educability. To rear him aright, whether at home or at school, we must understand his individuality.

He manifests this individuality from the very beginning in his natural rhythms of feeding, sleep, and self-activity. Given wisely managed opportunity he seems to know when to sleep, when to be hungry, and how much to sleep and eat. His educability is not so bland and undifferentiated that he responds neatly to an iron-clad feeding schedule. Things work out better, if his own self-regulation mechanisms, which are really growth mechanisms, are given a reasonable scope. The discerning physician makes no arbitrary distinctions between physical and mental factors; he gives conjoint consideration to the infant's nutritional status, to his immunities, allergies, and behavior traits. The child grows as a unit.

The task of the culture, likewise, is to watch for signs and symptoms of the child's total well-being with a special concern for psychological health. We must go along with the baby far enough to build up in him a sense of security. Step by step it is possible to build up his self-confidence through strengthening his confidence in his caretakers. Gradually he gains in morale and social insights, not through sheer indulgence, but through perceptive guidance on the part of his elders. And the more these elders know about the processes of growth, the more they will enjoy the truly remarkable progress which normal children make even in the first five years of life.

The intrinsic badness of children has, in my opinion, been vastly exaggerated by distorting interpretations. Well-constituted children with healthy inheritance have an intrinsic charm—a charm which betokens intrinsic goodness. The growth potentials for good far outweigh those for evil, unless the cultural odds are too heavily weighted against the child.

It is too freely said that science is indifferent to human values. I would say in this connection that science by implication is always concerned with values, and the life sciences which deal with the physiology and the pathologies of growth are coming profoundly to grips with the deepmost determiners of human values. The race evolved, the child grows. And we shall not have the requisite self-knowledge to manage our culture until we make a more sedulous effort to understand the ways of all growth and the potentials of child growth, which are the culminating evidences and products of organic evolution.

This evolution has not ceased; and to that degree man still remains educable. He seems to have reached the very acme of mass cruelty, confusion, conflict, and destructiveness. Therein lies a tithe of hope. It would seem that on sheer evolutionary grounds of survival, man must and can shift to a higher cerebral plane of attitude and action. Among other things, he surely needs a science of behavior, a systematically prosecuted science, which will not only probe the lingering wickedness of old Adam, but which will explore with unrelenting penetration the rich repository of potentials for good, which are revealed with awesome mystery in the sequences of child development.

selection 12 / the mammal and his environment / D. O. Hebb, McGill University

The original intention in this paper was to discuss the significance of neurophysiological theory for psychiatry and psychology, and to show, by citing the work done by some of my colleagues, that the attempt to get at the neural mechanisms of behavior can stimulate and clarify purely behavioral—that is, psychiatric and psychological—thinking. The research to be described has, I think, a clear relevance to clinical problems; but its origin lay in efforts to learn how the

From D. O. Hebb, "The Mammal and His Environment," *American Journal of Psychiatry*, 111:826–831, 1955. Reprinted by permission of the publisher.

functioning of individual neurons and synapses relates to the functions of the whole brain, and to understand the physiological nature of learning, emotion, thinking, or intelligence.

In the end, however, my paper has simply become a review of the research referred to, dealing with the relation of the mammal to his environment. The question concerns the normal variability of the sensory environment and this has been studied from two points of view. First, one may ask what the significance of perceptual activity is during growth; for this purpose one can rear an animal with a considerable degree of restriction, and see what effects there are upon mental development. Secondly, in normal animals whose development is complete, one can remove a good deal of the supporting action of the normal environment, to discover how far the animal continues to be dependent on it even after maturity.

The role of the environment during growth

The immediate background of our present research on the intelligence and personality of the dog is the work of Hymovitch on the intelligence of rats. He reared laboratory rats in 2 ways: (1) in a psychologically restricted environment, a small cage, with food and water always at hand and plenty of opportunity for exercise (in an activity wheel), but with no problems to solve, no need of getting on with others, no pain; and (2) in a "free" environment, a large box with obstacles to pass, blind alleys to avoid, other rats to get on with, and thus ample opportunity for problem-solving and great need for learning during growth. Result: the rats brought up in a psychologically restricted (but biologically adequate) environment have a lasting inferiority in problem-solving. This does not mean, of course, that environment is everything, heredity nothing: here heredity was held constant, which prevents it from affecting the results. When the reverse experiment is done we find problem-solving varying with heredity instead. The *same* capacity for problem-solving is fully dependent on both variables for its development.

To take this further, Thompson and others have been applying similar methods to dogs. The same intellectual effect of an impoverished environment is found again, perhaps more marked in the higher species. But another kind of effect can be seen in dogs, which have clearly marked personalities. Personality—by which I mean complex individual differences of emotion and motivation—is again strongly affected by the infant environment. These effects, however, are hard to analyze, and I cannot at present give any rounded picture of them.

First, observations during the rearing itself are significant. A Scottish terrier is reared in a small cage, in isolation from other Scotties and from the human staff. Our animal man, William Ponman, is a dog lover and undertook the experiment with misgivings, which quickly disappeared. In a cage 30 by 30 inches, the dogs are "happy as larks," eat more than normally reared dogs, grow well, are physically vigorous: as Ponman says, "I never saw such healthy dogs—they're like bulls." If you put a normally-reared dog into such a cage, shut off from everything, his misery is unmistakable, and we have not been able to bring ourselves to continue such experiments. Not so the dog that has known nothing else. Ponman showed some of these at a dog show of national standing, winning first-prize ribbons with them.

Observations by Dr. Ronald Melzack on pain are extremely interesting. He reared 2 dogs, after early weaning, in complete isolation, taking care that there was little opportunity for experience of pain (unless the dog bit himself). At maturity, when the dogs were first taken out for study, they were extraordinarily excited, with random, rapid movement. As a result they got their tails or paws stepped on repeatedly—but paid no attention to an event that would elicit howls from a normally reared dog. After a few days, when their movements were calmer, they were tested with an object that gave electric shock, and paid little attention to it. Through 5 testing periods, the dog repeatedly thrust his nose into a lighted match; and months later, did the same thing several times with a lighted cigar.

A year and a half after coming out of restriction they are still hyperactive. Clipping and trimming one of them is a 2-man job; if the normal dog does not stand still, a cuff on the ear will remind him of his duty; but cuffing the experimental dog "has as much effect as if you patted him—except he pays no attention to it." It seems certain, especially in view of the related results reported by Nissen, Chow, and Semmes for a chimpanzee, that the adult's perception of pain is essentially a function of pain experience during growth—and that what we call pain is not a single sensory quale but a complex mixture of a particular kind of synthesis with past learning and emotional disturbance.

Nothing bores the dogs reared in restriction. At an "open house," we put 2 restricted dogs in one enclosure, 2 normal ones in another, and asked the public to tell us which were the normal. Without exception, they picked out the 2 alert, lively, interested animals—not the lackadaisical pair lying in the corner, paying no attention to the visitors. The alert pair, actually, were the restricted; the normal dogs had seen all they wanted to see of the crowd in the first 2 minutes, and then went to sleep, thoroughly bored. The restricted dogs, so to speak, haven't the brains to be bored.

Emotionally, the dogs are "immature," but not in the human or clinical sense. They are little bothered by imaginative fears. Dogs suffer from irrational fears, like horses, porpoises, elephants, chimpanzees, and man; but it appears that this is a product of intellectual development, characteristic of the brighter, not the duller animal. Our dogs in restriction are not smart enough to fear strange objects. Things that cause fear in normal dogs produce only a generalized, undirected excitement in the restricted. If both normal and restricted dogs are exposed to the same noninjurious but exciting stimulus repeatedly, fear gradually develops in the restricted; but the normals, at first afraid, have by this time gone on to show a playful aggression instead. On the street, the restricted dogs "lead well," not bothered by what goes on around them, while those reared normally vary greatly in this respect. Analysis has a long way to go in these cases, but we can say now that dogs reared in isolation are not like ordinary dogs. They are both stupid and peculiar.

Such results clearly support the clinical evidence, and the animal experiments of others, showing that early environment has a lasting effect on the form of adjustment at maturity. We do not have a great body of evidence yet, and before we generalize too much it will be particularly important to repeat these observations with animals of different heredity. But I have been very surprised, personally, by the lack of evidence of emotional instability, neurotic tendency, or the like, when the dogs are suddenly plunged into a normal world. There is, in fact, just the opposite effect. This suggests caution in interpreting data with human children, such as those of Spitz or Bowlby. Perceptual restriction in infancy certainly produces a low level of intelligence, but it may not, by itself, produce emotional disorder. The observed results seem to mean, not that the stimulus of another attentive organism (the mother) is necessary from the first but that it may become necessary only as psychological *dependence* on the mother develops. However, our limited data certainly cannot prove anything for man, though they may suggest other interpretations besides those that have been made.

The environment at maturity

Another approach to the relation between the mammal and his environment is possible: that is, one can take the normally reared mammal and cut him off at maturity from his usual contact with the world. It seems clear that thought and personality characteristics develop as a function of the environment. Once developed, are they independent of it? This experiment is too cruel to do with animals, but not with college students. The first stage of the work was done by Bexton, Heron, and Scott. It follows up some work by Mackworth on the effects of monotony, in which he found extraordinary lapses of attention. Heron and his co-workers set out to make the monotony more prolonged and more complete.

The subject is paid to do nothing 24 hours a day. He lies on a comfortable bed in a small closed cubicle, is fed on request, goes to the toilet on request. Otherwise he does nothing. He wears frosted glass goggles that admit light but do not allow pattern vision. His ears are covered by a sponge-rubber pillow in which are embedded small speakers by which he can be communicated with, and a microphone hangs near to enable him to answer. His hands are covered with gloves, and cardboard cuffs extend from the upper forearm beyond his fingertips, permitting free joint movement but with little tactual perception.

The results are dramatic. During the stay in the cubicle, the experimental subject shows extensive loss, statistically significant, in solving simple problems. He complains subjectively that he cannot concentrate; his boredom is such that he looks forward eagerly to the next problem, but when it is presented he finds himself unwilling to make the effort to solve it.

On emergence from the cubicle the subject is given the same kind of intelligence tests as before entering, and shows significant loss. There is disturbance of motor control. Visual perception is changed in a way difficult to describe; it is as if the object looked at was exceptionally vivid, but impaired in its relation to other objects and the background—a disturbance perhaps of the larger organization of perception. This condition may last up to 12 or 24 hours.

Subjects reported some remarkable hallucinatory activity, some which resembled the effects of mescal, or the results produced by Grey Walter with flickering light. These hallucinations were primarily visual, perhaps only because the experimenters were able to control visual perception most effectively; however, some auditory and somesthetic hallucinations have been observed as well.

The nature of these phenomena is best conveyed by quoting one subject who reported over the microphone that he had just been asleep and had a very vivid dream and although he was awake, the dream was continuing. The study of dreams has a long history, and is clearly important theoretically, but is hampered by the impossibility of knowing how much the subject's report is distorted by memory. In many ways the hallucinatory activity of the present experiments is indistinguishable from what we know about dreams; if it is in essence the same process, but going on while the subject can describe it, not merely hot but still on the griddle), we have a new source of information, a means of direct attack, on the nature of the dream.

In its early stages the activity as it occurs in the experiment is probably not dream-like. The course of development is fairly consistent. First, when the eyes are closed the visual field is light rather than dark. Next there are reports of dots of light, lines, or simple geometrical patterns, so vivid that they are described as being a new experience. Nearly all experimental subjects reported such activity. (Many of course could not tolerate the experimental conditions very long, and left before the full course of development was seen.) The next stage is the occurrence of repetitive patterns, like a wallpaper design, reported by three-quarters of the subjects; next, the appearance of isolated objects, without background, seen by half the subjects; and finally, integrated scenes, involving action, usually containing dreamlike distortions, and apparently with all the vividness of an animated cartoon, seen by about a quarter of the subjects. In general, these amused the subject, relieving his boredom, as he watched to see what the movie program would produce next. The subjects reported that the scenes seemed to be out in front of them. A few could, apparently, "look at" different parts of the scene in central vision, as one could with a movie; and up to a point could change its content by "trying." It was not, however, well under control. Usually, it would disappear if the subject were given an interesting task, but not when the subject described it, nor if he did physical exercises. Its persistence and vividness interfered with sleep for some subjects, and at this stage was irritating.

In their later stages the hallucinations were elaborated into everything from a peaceful rural scene to naked women diving and swimming in a woodland pool to prehistoric animals plunging through tropical forests. One man saw a pair of spectacles, which were then joined by a dozen more, without wearers, fixed intently on him; faces sometimes appeared behind the glasses, but with no eyes visible. The glasses sometimes moved in unison, as if marching in procession. Another man saw a field onto which a bathtub rolled: it moved slowly on rubber-tired wheels, with chrome hub caps. In it was seated an old man wearing a battle helmet. Another subject was highly entertained at seeing a row of squirrels marching single file across a snowy field, wearing snowshoes and carrying little bags over their shoulders.

Some of the scenes were in 3 dimensions, most in 2 (that is, as if projected on a screen). A most interesting feature was that some of the images were persistently tilted from the vertical, and a few reports were given of inverted scenes, completely upside down.

There were a few reports of auditory phenomena—one subject heard the people in his hallucination talking. There was also some somesthetic imagery, as when one saw a doorknob before him, and as he touched it felt an electric shock; or when another saw a miniature rocket ship maneuvering around him, and discharging pellets that he felt hitting his arm. But the most interesting of these phenomena the subject, apparently, lacked words to describe adequately. There were references to a feeling of "otherness," or bodily "strangeness." One said that his mind was like a ball of cottonwool floating in the air above him. Two independently reported that they perceived a second body, or second person, in the cubicle. One subject reported that he could not tell which of the 2 bodies was his own, and described the 2 bodies as overlapping in space—not like Siamese twins, but 2 complete bodies with an arm, shoulder, and side of each occupying the same space.

Theoretical significance

The theoretical interest of these results for us extends in 2 directions. On the one hand, they interlock with work using more physiological methods, of brain stimulation and recording, and especially much of the recent work on the relation of the brain stem to cortical "arousal." Points of correspondence between behavioral theory and knowledge of neural function are increasing, and each new point of correspondence provides both a corrective for theory and a stimulation for further research. A theory of thought and of consciousness in physiologically intelligible terms need no longer be completely fantastic.

On the other hand, the psychological data cast new light on the relation of man to his environment, including his social environment, and it is this that I should like to discuss a little further. To do so I must go back for a moment to some earlier experiments on chimpanzee emotion. They indicate that the higher mammal may be psychologically at the mercy of his environment to a much greater degree than we have been accustomed to think.

Studies in our laboratory of the role of the environment during infancy and a large body of work reviewed recently by Beach and Jaynes make it clear that psychological development is fully dependent on stimulation from the environment. Without it, intelligence does not develop normally, and the personality is grossly atypical. The experiment with college students shows that a short period—even a day or so—of deprivation of a normal sensory input produces personality changes and a clear loss of capacity to solve problems. Even at maturity, then, the organism is still essentially dependent on a normal sensory environment for the maintenance of its psychological integrity.

The following data show yet another way in which the organism appears psychologically vulnerable. It has long been known that the chimpanzee may be frightened by representations of animals, such as a small toy donkey. An accidental observation of my own extended this to include representations of the chimpanzee himself, of man, and of parts of the chimpanzee or human body. A model of a chimpanzee head, in clay, produced terror in the colony of the Yerkes Laboratories, as did a lifelike representation of a human head, and a number of related objects such as an actual chimpanzee head, preserved in formalin, or a colored representation of a human eye and eyebrow. A deeply anesthetized chimpanzee, "dead" as far as the others were concerned, aroused fear in some animals and vicious attacks by others.

I shall not deal with this theoretically. What matters for our present purposes is the conclusion, rather well supported by the animal evidence, that the greater the development of intelligence the greater the vulnerability to emotional breakdown. The price of high intelligence is susceptibility to imaginative fears and unreasoning suspicion and other emotional weaknesses. The conclusion is not only supported by the animal data, but also agrees with the course of development in children, growing intelligence being accompanied by increased frequency and strength of emotional problems—up to the age of 5 years.

Then, apparently, the trend is reversed. Adult man, more intelligent than chimpanzee or 5-year-old child, seems not more subject to emotional disturbances but less. Does this then disprove the conclusion? It seemed a pity to abandon a principle that made sense of so many data that had not made sense before, and the kind of theory I was working with—neurophysiologically oriented—also pointed in the same direction. The question then was, is it possible that something is concealing the adult human being's emotional weaknesses?

From this point of view it became evident that the concealing agency is man's culture, which acts as a protective cocoon. There are many indications that our emotional stability depends more on our successful avoidance of emotional provocation than on our essential characteristics: that urbanity depends on an urbane social and physical environment. Dr. Thompson and I reviewed the evidence, and came to the conclusion that the development of what is called "civilization" is the progressive elimination of sources of acute fear, disgust, and anger; and that civilized man may not be less, but more, susceptible to such disturbance because of his success in protecting himself from disturbing situations so much of the time.

We may fool ourselves thoroughly in this matter. We are surprised that children are afraid of the dark, or afraid of being left alone, and congratulate ourselves on having got over such weakness. Ask anyone you know whether he is afraid of the dark, and he will either laugh at you or be insulted. This attitude is easy to maintain in a well-lighted, well-behaved suburb. But try being alone in complete darkness in the streets of a strange city, or alone at night in the deep woods, and see if you still feel the same way.

We read incredulously of the taboo rules of primitive societies; we laugh at the superstitious fear of the dead in primitive people. What is there about a dead body to produce disturbance? Sensible, educated people are not so affected. One can easily show that they are, however, and that we have developed an extraordinarily complete taboo system—not just moral prohibition, but full-fledged ambivalent taboo —to deal with the dead body. I took a poll of an undergraduate class of 198 persons, including some nurses and veterans, to see how many had encountered a dead body. Thirty-seven had never seen a dead body in any circumstances, and 91 had seen one only after an undertaker had prepared it for burial; making a total of 65% who had never seen a dead body in, so to speak, its natural state. It is quite clear that for some reason we protect society against sight of, contact with, the dead body. Why?

Again, the effect of moral education, and training in the rules of courtesy, and the compulsion to dress, talk and act as others do, adds up to ensuring that the individual member of society will not act in a way that is a provocation to others—will not, that is, be a source of strong emotional disturbance, except in highly ritualized circumstances approved by society. The social behavior of a group of civilized persons, then, makes up that protective cocoon which allows us to think of ourselves as being less emotional than the explosive 4-year-old or the equally explosive chimpanzee.

The well-adjusted adult therefore is not intrinsically less subject to emotional disturbance: he is well-adjusted, relatively unemotional, as long as he is in his cocoon. The problem of moral education, from this point of view, is not simply to produce a stable individual, but to produce an individual that will (1) be stable in the existing social environment, and (2) contribute to its protective uniformity. We think of some persons as being emotionally dependent, others not; but it looks as though we are all completely dependent on the environment in a way and to a degree that we have not suspected.

selection 13 / continuities and discontinuities in cultural conditioning / Ruth Benedict, Columbia University

All cultures must deal in one way or another with the cycle of growth from infancy to adulthood. Nature has posed the situation dramatically: on the one hand, the new born baby, physiologically vulnerable, unable to fend for itself, or to participate of its own initiative in the life of the group, and, on the other, the adult man or woman. Every

From Ruth Benedict, "Continuities and Discontinuities in Cultural Conditioning," Psychiatry, 1:161–167, 1938. Copyright held by The William Alanson White Psychiatric Foundation, Inc. Reprinted by special permission of The William Alanson White Psychiatric Foundation, Inc.

man who rounds out his human potentialities must have been a son first and a father later, and the two roles are physiologically in great contrast; he must first have been dependent upon others for his very existence, and later he must provide such security for others. This discontinuity in the life cycle is a fact of nature and is inescapable. Facts of nature, however, in any discussion of human problems, are ordinarily read off not at their bare minimal but surrounded by all the local accretions of behavior to which the student of human affairs has become accustomed in his own culture. For that reason, it is illuminating to examine comparative material from other societies in order to get a wider perspective on our own special accretions. The anthropologist's role is not to question the facts of nature, but to insist upon the interposition of a middle term between "nature" and "human behavior"; his role is to analyze that term, to document local man-made doctorings of nature, and to insist that these doctorings should not be read off in any one culture as nature itself. Although it is a fact of nature that the child becomes a man, the way in which this transition is effected varies from one society to another, and no one of these particular cultural bridges should be regarded as the "natural" path to maturity.

From a comparative point of view, our culture goes to great extremes in emphasizing contrasts between the child and the adult. The child is sexless, the adult estimates his virility by his sexual activities; the child must be protected from the ugly facts of life, the adult must meet them without psychic catastrophe; the child must obey, the adult must command this obedience. These are all dogmas of our culture, dogmas which, in spite of the facts of nature, other cultures commonly do not share. In spite of the physiological contrasts between child and adult, these are cultural accretions.

It will make the point clearer if we consider one habit in our own culture in regard to which there is not this discontinuity of conditioning. With the greatest clarity of purpose and economy of training, we achieve our goal of conditioning everyone to eat three meals a day. The baby's training in regular food periods begins at birth, and no crying of the child and no inconvenience to the mother is allowed to interfere. We gauge the child's physiological make-up and at first allow it food oftener than adults, but, because our goal is firmly set and our training consistent, before the child is two years old it has achieved the adult schedule. From the point of view of other cultures, this is as startling as the fact of three-year-old babies perfectly at home in deep water is to us. Modesty is another sphere in which our child training is consistent and economical; we waste no time in clothing the baby, and, in contrast to many societies where the child runs naked till it is ceremonially given its skirt or its pubic sheath at adolescence, the child's training fits it precisely for adult conventions.

In neither of these aspects of behavior is there need for an individual in our culture to embark before puberty, at puberty, or at some later date upon a course of action which all his previous training has tabooed. He is spared the unsureness inevitable in such a transition.

The illustration I have chosen may appear trivial, but, in larger and more important aspects of behavior, our methods are obviously different. Because of the great variety of child training in different families in our society, I might illustrate continuity of conditioning from individual life histories in our culture, but even these, from a comparative point of view, stop far short of consistency; and I shall, therefore, confine myself to describing arrangements in other cultures in which training which with us is idiosyncratic is accepted and traditional and does not, therefore, involve the same possibility of conflict. I shall choose childhood rather than infant and nursing situations, not because the latter do not vary strikingly in different cultures, but because they are nevertheless more circumscribed by the baby's physiological needs than is its later training. Childhood situations provide an excellent field in which to illustrate the range of cultural adjustments which are possible within a universally given, but not so drastic, set of physiological facts.

The major discontinuity in the life cycle is of course that the child who is at one point a son must later be a father. These roles in our society are strongly differentiated; a good son is tractable, and does not assume adult responsibilities; a good father provides for his children and should not allow his authority to be flouted. In addition, the child must be sexless so far as his family is concerned, whereas the father's sexual role is primary in the family. The individual in one role must revise his behavior from almost all points of view when he assumes the second role.

I shall select for discussion three such contrasts that occur in our culture between the individual's role as child and as father: (1) responsible-non-responsible status role; (2) dominance-submission; (3) contrasted sexual role. It is largely upon our cultural commitments to these three contrasts that the discontinuity in the life cycle of an individual in our culture depends.

Responsible-non-responsible status role

The techniques adopted by societies which achieve continuity during the life cycle in this sphere in no way differ from those we employ in our uniform conditioning to three meals a day. They are merely applied to other areas of life. We think of the child as wanting to play and the adult as having to work, but in many societies the mother takes the baby daily in her shawl or carrying net to the garden or to gather roots, and adult labor is seen even in infancy from the pleasant security of its position in close contact with its mother. When the child can run about, it accompanies its parents still, doing tasks which are essential and yet suited to its powers, and its dichotomy between work and play is not different from that its parents recognize, namely the distinction between the busy day and the free evening. The tasks it is asked to perform are graded to its powers, and its elders wait quietly by, not offering to do the task in the child's place. Everyone who is familiar with such societies has been struck by the contrast with our child training. Dr. Ruth Underhill tells me of sitting with a group of Papago elders in Arizona when the man of the house turned to his little three-year-old grand-daughter and asked her to close the door. The door was heavy and hard to shut. The child tried, but it did not move. Several times the grandfather repeated: "Yes, close the door." No one jumped to the child's assistance. No one took the responsibility away from her. On the other hand there was no impatience, for after all the child was small. They sat gravely waiting till the child succeeded and her grandfather gravely thanked her. It was assumed that the task would not be asked of her unless she could perform it, and, having been asked, the responsibility was hers alone just as if she were a grown woman.

The essential point of such child training is that the child is from infancy continuously conditioned to responsible social participation, while at the same time the tasks that are expected of it are adapted to its capacity. The contrast with our society is very great. A child does not make any labor contribution to our industrial society except as it competes with an adult; its work is not measured against its own strength and skill but against high-geared industrial requirements. Even when we praise a child's achievement in the home, we are outraged if such praise is interpreted as being of the same order as praise of adults. The child is praised because the parent feels well disposed, regardless of whether the task is well done by adult standards, and the child acquires no sensible standard by which to measure its achievement. The gravity of a Cheyenne Indian family ceremoniously making a feast out of the little boy's first snowbird is at the furthest remove from our behavior. At birth the little boy was presented with a toy bow, and from the time he could run about serviceable bows suited to his stature were specially made for him by the man of the family. Animals and birds were taught him in a graded series beginning with those most easily taken, and as he brought in his first of each species his family duly made a feast of it, accepting his contribution as gravely as the buffalo his father brought. When he finally killed a buffalo, it was only the final step of his childhood conditioning, not a new adult role with which his childhood experience had been at variance.

The Canadian Ojibwa show clearly what results can be achieved. This tribe gains its livelihood by winter trapping, and the small family of father, mother, and children live during the long winter alone on their great frozen hunting grounds. The boy accompanies his father and brings in his catch to his sister as his father does to his mother; the girl prepares the meat and skins for him just as his mother does for her husband. By the time the boy is twelve, he may have set his own line of traps on a hunting territory of his own and return to his parent's house only once in several months—still bringing the meat and skins to his sister. The young child is taught consistently that it has only itself to rely upon in life, and this is as true in the dealings it will have with the supernatural as in the business of getting a livelihood. This attitude he will accept as a successful adult just as he accepted it as a child.

Dominance-submission

Dominance-submission is the most striking of those categories of behavior where like does not respond to like, but where one type of behavior stimulates the opposite response. It is one of the most prominent ways in which behavior is patterned in our culture. When it obtains between classes, it may be nourished by continuous experience; the difficulty in its use between children and adults lies in the fact that an individual conditioned to one set of behavior in childhood must adopt the opposite as an adult. Its opposite is a pattern of approximately identical reciprocal behavior; the societies which rely upon continuous conditioning characteristically invoke this pattern. In some primitive cultures, the very terminology of address between father and son, and, more commonly, between grandchild and grandson or uncle and nephew, reflects this attitude. In such kinship terminologies, one reciprocal expresses each of these relationships so that son and father, for instance, exchange the same term with one another, just as we exchange the same term with a cousin. The child later will exchange it with his son. "Father-son," therefore, is a continuous relationship he enjoys throughout life. The same continuity, backed up by verbal reciprocity, occurs far oftener in the grandchild-grandson relationship or that of mother's brother–sister's son. When these are "joking" relationships, as they often are, travellers report wonderingly upon the liberties and pretensions of tiny toddlers in their dealing with these family elders. In place of our dogma of respect to elders, such societies employ in these cases a reciprocity as nearly identical as may be. The teasing and practical joking the grandfather visits upon his grandchild, the grandchild returns in like coin; he would be led to believe that he failed in propriety if he did not give like for like. If the sister's son has right of access without leave to his mother's brother's possessions, the mother's brother has such rights also to the child's possessions. They share reciprocal privileges and obligations which in our society can develop only between age mates.

From the point of view of our present discussion, such kinship conventions allow the child to put in practice from infancy the same forms of behavior which it will rely upon as an adult; behavior is not polarized into a general requirement of submission for the child and dominance for the adult.

It is clear from the techniques described above, by which the child is conditioned to a responsible status role, that these depend chiefly upon arousing in the child the desire to share responsibility in adult life. To achieve this, little stress is laid upon obedience but much stress upon approval and praise. Punishment is very commonly regarded as quite outside the realm of possibility, and natives in many parts of the world have drawn the conclusion from our usual disciplinary methods that white parents do not love their children. If the child is not required to be submissive, however, many occasions for punishment melt away; a variety of situations which call for it do not occur. Many American Indian tribes are especially explicit in rejecting the ideal of a child's submissive or obedient behavior. Prince Maximilian von Wied, who visited the Crow Indians over a hundred years ago, describes a father's boasting about his young son's intractability even when it was the father himself who was flouted; "He will be a man," his father said. He would have been baffled at the idea that his child should show behavior which would obviously make him appear a poor creature in the eyes of his fellows if he used it as an adult. Dr. George Devereux tells me of a special case of such an attitude among the Mohave at the present time. The child's mother was white and protested to its father that he must take action when the child disobeyed and struck him. "But why?" the father said, "he is little. He cannot possibly injure me." He did not know of any dichotomy according to which an adult expects obedience and a child must accord it. If his child had been docile, he would simply have judged that it would become a docile adult—an eventuality of which he would not have approved.

Child training which brings about the same result is common also in other areas of life than that of reciprocal kinship obligations between child and adult. There is a tendency in our culture to regard every situation as having in it the seeds of a dominance-submission relationship. Even where dominance-submission is patently irrelevant we read in the dichotomy, assuming that in every situation there must be one person dominating another. On the other hand some cultures, even when the situation calls for leadership do not see it in terms of dominance-submission. To do justice to this attitude, it would be necessary to describe their political and especially their economic arrangements, for such an attitude to persist must certainly be supported by economic mechanisms that are congruent with it. But it must also be supported by—or what comes to the same thing, express itself in —child training and familial situations.

Contrasted sexual role

Continuity of conditioning in training the child to assume responsibility and to behave no more submissively than adults is quite possible in terms of the child's physiological endowment if his participation is suited to his strength. Because of the late development of the child's reproductive organs, continuity of conditioning in sex experience presents a difficult problem. So far as their belief that the child is anything but a sexless being is concerned, they are probably more nearly right than we are with an opposite dogma. But the great break is presented by the universally sterile unions before puberty and the presumably fertile ones after maturation. This physiological fact no amount of cultural manipulation can minimize or alter, and societies, therefore, which stress continuous conditioning most strongly sometimes do not expect children to be interested in sex experience until they have matured physically. This is striking among American Indian tribes like the Dakota; adults observe great privacy in sex acts and in no way stimulate children's sexual activity. There need be no discontinuity, in the sense in which I have used the term, in such a program if the child is taught nothing it does not have to unlearn later. In such cultures, adults view children's experimentation as in no way wicked or dangerous, but merely as innocuous play which can have no serious consequences. In some societies such play is minimal and the children manifest little interest in it. But the same attitude may be taken by adults in societies where such play is encouraged and forms a major activity among small children. This is true among most of the Melanesian cultures of Southeast New Guinea; adults go as far as to laugh off sexual affairs within the prohibited class, if the children are not mature, saying that since they cannot marry there can be no harm done.

It is this physiological fact of the difference between children's sterile unions and adults' presumably fertile sex relations which must be kept in mind in order to understand the different mores which almost always govern sex expression in children and in adults in the same culture. A great many cultures with pre-adolescent sexual license require marital fidelity, and a great many which value pre-marital virginity in either male or female arrange their marital life with great license. Continuity in sex experience is complicated by factors which it was unnecessary to consider in the problems previously discussed.

The essential problem is not whether or not the child's sexuality is consistently exploited—for even where such exploitation is favored, in the majority of cases the child must seriously modify his behavior at puberty or at marriage. Continuity in sex expression means rather that the child is taught nothing it must unlearn later. If the cultural emphasis is upon sexual pleasure, the child who is continuously conditioned will be encouraged to experiment freely and pleasurably, as among the Marquesans; if emphasis is upon reproduction, as among the Zuñi of New Mexico, childish sex proclivities will not be exploited, for the only important use which sex is thought to serve in his culture is not yet possible to him. The important contrast with our child training is that, although a Zuñi child is impressed with the wickedness of premature sex experimentation, he does not run the risk as in our culture of associating this wickedness with sex itself rather than with sex at his age. The adult in our culture has often failed to unlearn the wickedness or the dangerousness of sex, a lesson which was impressed upon him strongly in his most formative years.

Discontinuity in conditioning

Even from this very summary statement of continuous conditioning, the economy of such mores is evident. In spite of the obvious advantages, however, there are difficulties in its way. Many primitive societies expect as different behavior from an individual as child and as adult as we do, and such discontinuity involves a presumption of strain.

Many societies of this type, however, minimize strain by the techniques they employ; and some techniques are more successful than others in ensuring the individual's functioning without conflict. It is from this point of view that age-grade societies reveal their fundamental significance. Age-graded cultures characteristically demand different behavior of the individual at different times of his life and persons of a like age-grade are grouped into a society whose activities are all oriented toward the behavior desired at that age. Individuals "graduate" publicly and with honor from one of these groups to another. Where age society members are enjoined to loyalty and mutual support, and are drawn not only from the local group but from the whole tribe, as among the Arapaho, or even from other tribes as among the Wagawaga of Southeast New Guinea, such an institution has many advantages in eliminating conflicts among local groups and fostering intratribal peace. This seems to be also a factor in the tribal military solidarity of the similarly organized Masai of East Africa. The point that is of chief interest for our present discussion, however, is that by this means an individual who at any time takes on a new set of duties and virtues is supported not only by a solid phalanx of age mates but by the traditional prestige of the organized "secret" society into which he has now graduated. Fortified in this way, individuals in such cultures often swing between remarkable extremes of opposite behavior without apparent psychic threat. For example, the great majority exhibit prideful and non-conflicted behavior at each stage in the life cycle, even when a prime of life devoted to passionate and aggressive head hunting must be followed by a later life dedicated to ritual and to mild and peaceable civic virtues.

Our chief interest here, however, is in discontinuity which primarily affects the child. In many primitive societies, such discontinuity has been fostered not because of economic or political necessity or because such discontinuity provides for a socially valuable division of labor, but because of some conceptual dogma. The most striking of these are the Australian and Papuan cultures where the ceremony of the "Making of Man" flourishes. In such societies it is believed that men and women have opposite and conflicting powers, and male children, who are of undefined status, must be initiated into the male role. In Central Australia the boy child is of the woman's side, and women are taboo in the final adult stages of tribal ritual. The elaborate and protracted initiation ceremonies of the Arunta, therefore, snatch the boy from the mother, dramatize his gradual repudiation of her. In a final ceremony he is reborn as a man out of the men's ceremonial "baby pouch." The men's ceremonies are ritual statements of a masculine solidarity, carried out by fondling one another's *churingas*, the material symbol of each man's life, and by letting out over one another blood drawn from their veins. After this warm bond among men has been established through the ceremonies, the boy joins the men in the men's house and participates in tribal rites. The enjoined discontinuity has been tribally bridged.

West of the Fly River in southern New Guinea, there is a striking development of this Making of Men cult which involves a childhood period of passive homosexuality. Among the Keraki it is thought that no boy can grow to full stature without playing the role for some years. Men slightly older take the active role, and the older man is a jealous partner. The life cycle of the Keraki Indians includes, therefore, in succession, passive homosexuality, active homosexuality, and heterosexuality. The Keraki believe that pregnancy will result from post-pubertal passive homosexuality and see evidences of such practices in any fat man, whom, even as an old man, they may kill or drive out of the tribe because of their fear. The ceremony that is of interest in connection with the present discussion takes place at the end of the period of passive homosexuality. This ceremony consists in burning out the possibility of pregnancy from the boy by pouring lye down his throat, after which he has no further protection if he gives way to the practice. There is no technique for ending active homosexuality, but this is not explicitly taboo for older men; heterosexuality and children, however, are highly valued. Unlike the neighboring Marindanim, who share their homosexual practices, Keraki husband and wife share the same house and work together in the gardens.

I have chosen illustrations of discontinuous conditioning where it is not too much to say that the cultural institutions furnish adequate support to the individual as he progresses from role to role or interdicts the previous behavior in a summary fashion. The contrast with arrangements in our culture is very striking, and against this background of social arrangements in other cultures the adolescent period of *Sturm und Drang* with which we are so familiar becomes intelligible in terms of our discontinuous cultural institutions and dogmas rather than in terms of physiological necessity. It is even more pertinent to consider these comparative facts in relation to maladjusted persons in our culture who are said to be fixated at one or another pre-adult level. It is clear that if we were to look at our social arrangements as an outsider, we should infer directly from our family institutions and habits of child training that many individuals would not "put off childish things"; we should have to say that our adult activity demands traits that are interdicted in children, and that, far from redoubling efforts to help children bridge this gap, adults in our culture put all the blame on the child when he fails to manifest spontaneously the new behavior or, overstepping the mark, manifests it with untoward belligerence. It is not surprising that in such a society many individuals fear to use behavior which has up to that time been under a ban and trust instead, though at great psychic cost, to attitudes that have been exercised with approval during their formative years. Insofar as we invoke a physiological scheme to account for these neurotic adjustments, we are led to overlook the possibility of developing social institutions which would lessen the social cost we now pay; instead, we elaborate a set of dogmas which prove inapplicable under other social conditions.

CHAPTER 3 ⚙ THE MOTIVATION
OF BEHAVIOR ⚙

In searching to understand our own behavior and the behavior of others, we often ask the question, "Why did I do that?" In posing this question we are raising the problem of what motivates or moves us to certain actions. The term "motivation" itself reflects the nature of our problem in that it derives from the Latin verb moveo, *meaning "to move." In the development of all animals the earliest motives which arouse and sustain activity are physiologically based. The infant is activated primarily by such drives as hunger, thirst, and pain, and he continues to make his needs known until they are relieved by those around him. As adults we tend to take for granted that we feel hungry when our body needs food, but if we stop to examine the question, "How do I know when I need food?" we find that the solution is by no means obvious. A not uncommon response to this question might take this form: "I know I'm hungry when I feel hunger pangs [stomach contractions]."*

Such a reply represents a somewhat oversimplified statement of the view proposed some thirty years ago by the eminent physiologist Walter B. Cannon. In attempting to determine the critical mechanisms which instigate physiological drives, Cannon focused on peripheral factors such as stomach contractions. Although this peripheral theory of hunger motivation appeals to common sense experience, a wide variety of evidence indicates that it is faulty; for example, patients who have had their stomachs removed and thus cannot have stomach contractions seem to have normal hunger cycles. As a result, physiologists and psychologists began to look for mechanisms of motivation in portions of the central nervous system. In a paper entitled "Central Stimulation and Other New Approaches to Motivation and Reward," Selection 14, Dr. Neal Miller describes a variety of fascinating experiments which indicate that the critical mechanisms by which the organism "knows" that it is hungry, thirsty, etc., are to be found in subcortical regions of the brain. He points out that

the new science of psycho-pharmacology has great potential for fur-
thering our understanding of the biologically determined motivations
"of mice and men." We are just beginning to open an exciting new
chapter in the understanding of behavior!

There is no doubt that research such as Miller's greatly extends
our comprehension of the nature of physiological drives. However,
despite the importance of this type of research, such an approach is
incomplete since most of human behavior is aroused and sustained by
learned or social motives rather than physiological drives.[1] In his theory
of motivation, Selection 16, Dr. Abraham Maslow shows how human
motivations may be meaningfully arranged in a hierarchy of prepotency or urgency. The most basic, or urgent motives stem from
physiological needs and safety needs. However, if our society arranges
a benevolent environment, we are then freed to develop and satisfy
the higher order needs of self-esteem, love, and self-actualization.
Throughout his discussion Maslow notes social-interpersonal factors
which can facilitate or inhibit satisfaction of these basic needs. His
approach thus provides a synthesis of biological, psychological, and
social determinants of motivation. Some of the implications of this
way of thinking about the psychology of human motivation are ex-
panded in Dr. Maslow's more recent paper on "Deficiency Motivation
and Growth Motivation" (Selection 15). Physiological drives are
clear-cut examples of deficit motivations: the individual is reacting to
a physiological deficiency. However, Maslow emphasizes that we
"need" love just as surely as we "need" vitamin C. The person whose
primary efforts are expended in attempts to achieve a feeling of self-
esteem or to attain a sense of being loved is behaving out of deficiency
motivations just as surely as the "jungle savage" who expends his
efforts obtaining food. He suggests several ways in which the behavior
resulting from deficit motivation differs from that stemming from
growth motivation.

[1] In Selection 52 Dr. Robert Sears discusses the learning mechanisms by which
social drives could be developed out of the satisfaction of basic physiological
drives. The interested student may want to read this paper in the present
context.

selection 14 / central stimulation and other
new approaches to motivation and reward /
Neal E. Miller, Yale University

The focus of my paper will be that of determining how motivations
and rewards produce their effects. While the immediate practical im-

Abridged from Neal E. Miller, "Central Stimulation and Other New Approaches to Motivation and Reward," *American Psychologist*, 13:100–108,

plications will not be so obvious, it is a well-known fact that the deeper understanding of basic phenomena almost always leads to significant practical applications, frequently being the necessary foundation for radical innovations.

You are well aware that problems of motivation and reward, which incidentally shade off into mood and temperament, have wide clinical, social, and educational implications. I believe we are at last developing new techniques for getting inside of the organism, manipulating and measuring some of the simpler, more basic things that are going on there, and thus are laying the foundations for fundamental advances in our understanding of the mechanisms of motivation and reward.

COMBINATION OF BEHAVIORAL AND PHYSIOLOGICAL TECHNIQUES

The recent spurt of fruitful research on the mechanisms of motivations has emerged as a result of the convergence of two lines of development. Physiologists, pharmacologists, and biochemists have been developing new and subtler tools for radically affecting and measuring organic processes. At the same time, experimental psychologists have been developing a variety of more effective techniques for measuring drives. The combination of techniques from these two sources is beginning to yield results which have exciting potentialities.

In this brief presentation I can only sample a few of these results. I shall include some pictures to give you a firsthand impression of the work.

An early study of hunger

Using the improved electrolytic technique for making lesions deep in the more primitive structures of the brain, Hetherington and Ranson found that lesions in the region of the ventromedial nuclei of the hypothalamus would cause albino rats to overeat enormously so that, as Fig. 1 shows, they became very fat. But Bailey, Stevenson, and I used behavioral tests to show that these lesions do not necessarily always potentiate hunger. Although our rats would eat more, they would not work as hard for food. Furthermore, they were stopped by smaller doses of quinine. Thus the additional behavioral tests did not support the original inference of increased hunger drawn from the measure of amount of food consumed. It seemed more reasonable to assume that the lesion interfered with complete satiation.

In the foregoing study, the single test of amount of food consumed disagreed with the rate of bar pressing and a number of other behavioral measures. Other studies, summarized elsewhere, show that certain

1958. Reprinted by permission of the author and the American Psychological Association.

Fig. 1 Effects of overeating, produced by lesions in the region of the ventromedial nuclei of the hypothalamus.

circumstances can affect the rate of bar pressing, so the results of this test will disagree with those of a number of different tests. Discrepancies among tests purporting to measure the same thing raise important problems which the aptitude testers have long since explored: namely, problems of general versus specific factors, and of the purity of various measures of such factors. But our main point for the moment is that it is prudent and extremely fruitful to use a variety of behavioral tests in studying a drive such as hunger. We are just beginning to cash in on the potentialities of these tests; to date most studies of the physiological mechanisms of hunger are still limited to the single measure of the amount of food consumed.

Sample of other brain-lesion studies

Lesions in the same general region as those producing overeating can markedly change the temperament of the rat. Anand and Brobeck found that such lesions in the hypothalamus could make rats far more aggressive (a finding which Bailey, Stevenson, and I confirmed on our fingers) and that lesions in the region of the amygdala could abolish this hyperaggressiveness. Similarly, Brady and Nauta have shown that lesions in the septal region can produce heightened startle responses and, with the interesting exception of conditioned suppression (CER), a variety of other indications of increased emotionality. An abstract by King indicates that his paper shows that such emotionality can also be counteracted by lesions in the amygdaloid complex.

In addition to making the animals much tamer, lesions in the region of the amygdala can also produce marked hypersexuality. This is part of the classical Klüver-Bucy syndrome which has been one of the points of departure for many excellent studies of the effects of brain lesions on motivation.

In the past, the combination of the ablation technique with behavioral tests has been found to be a powerful method for studying sensory, perceptual, and motor functions of the brain. The same combination is becoming a powerful technique for studying also the motivational and emotional functions of the brain. I have cited only a small sample out of the increasingly impressive population of sophisticated studies by able men in this field.

Drive elicited by electrical stimulation

Electrical stimulation of specific points has been another classical technique for studying brain function. Originally, this technique was used to study motor effects on anaesthetized animals. In his classic work, Hess refined this technique by permanently implanting electrodes in the brains of cats so that they could be stimulated in the normal unanaesthetized state. In addition to eliciting complex motor and postural responses, which were less like reflexes and more like acts, Hess discovered that stimulation in the hypothalamus produced a variety of apparently motivational effects such as rage, flight, and eating. His trail-blazing results, which were limited to naturalistic observation, have provided an excellent point of departure for recent studies using a variety of more rigorous behavioral tests.

Turning now to some work in collaboration with E. E. Coons, we see in Fig. 2 a rat with electrodes placed in a region where stimulation elicits eating. This rat has been thoroughly satiated on food. Soon after stimulation is turned on, the rat starts to eat; soon after it is turned off, he stops. Again, the demonstration is very effective.

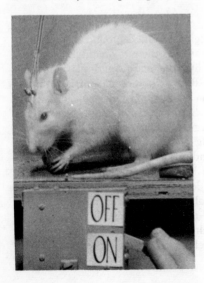

Fig. 2 Electrical stimulation of the brain causes a thoroughly satiated rat to eat.

Fig. 3 Stimulation in the hypo-thalamus elicits the learned response of bar pressing in a satiated rat. Each bar press moves the pen up a little. The rat has been trained on a variable-interval schedule; each spike below the record indicates when a bar press actually delivers food.

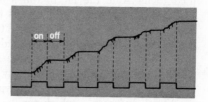

These rats, like Hess's cats, will sometimes also gnaw at inedible objects such as pieces of wood. Therefore, we wonder whether the centrally elicited eating has the properties of normal hunger or is mere reflex gnawing. As a test, we thoroughly trained rats, when thirsty, to get water from a spout above; and, when hungry, to get food by pushing aside a little hinged door below. Then, after thorough satiation, we tested the effects of electrical stimulation. The stimulation can cause a moderately thirsty rat to leave the water spout where he has been drinking and go to a different place to perform the instrumental response of pushing back the hinged door which he has learned as a means of getting food. The fact that the rat stops drinking shows that the effects of stimulation are not mere indiscriminate activation. The fact that the stimulation elicits the learned response of pushing aside the hinged door shows that it has at least some of the more general motivating properties of normal hunger.

In order to make the results completely official, we also trained the rats, when hungry, to secure food by pressing a Skinner bar which delivered small pellets on a variable-interval schedule. Fig. 3 shows the effects of brain stimulation on a thoroughly satiated rat. (Each time the rat presses the bar, the recording lever moves upwards slightly. Each time a bar press actually delivers food, the pen draws a downward spike.) Horizontal sections of the cumulative record show that the satiated rat did relatively little work at the bar during two-minute periods of nonstimulation. The upward steps show that, during the two minutes when the stimulation was on, the rat worked at the bar which occasionally delivered food. Thus we have further evidence that electrical stimulation in the areas that induce eating will also motivate the performance of learned instrumental responses that have been reinforced by food. The results are convincing pictorially; they also are statistically reliable.

Continuing our program of testing point-by-point whether the motivation elicited by the electrical stimulation of the brain has all of the properties of normal hunger, Coons and I found that its effects were not limited to the gnawing of solid foods; it caused a satiated rat to drink milk. In control tests the stimulation did not elicit similar sustained drinking of water. Furthermore, the stimulation could be used to motivate the rat to run a T maze with the termination of the stimulation serving as a reward to produce highly reliable choice of the endbox in which the stimulation was turned off. In short, the termination of centrally stimulated "hunger" by turning off the switch seems to have the same rewarding effects as the eating of food which ordinarily terminates normally elicited hunger.

Let us turn now to a different type of motivation: a pain–fear-like emotional disturbance which can be elicited by electrical stimulation in a number of regions deep in the brain. Does this emotional reaction have all of the functional properties of normally aroused pain and fear? Some of these properties are: (*a*) Pain and fear can motivate, and their termination reinforce, trial-and-error learning. (*b*) They can be used to establish a conditioned response. (*c*) They can serve as a punishment to establish an approach-avoidance conflict so that a hungry animal will avoid food.

The purpose of the experiments is to demonstrate point-by-point that central stimulation of the critical places in the brain has all of the foregoing properties.

Figure 4 illustrates the first of these experiments. It shows a cat with chronic Delgado-type electrodes ending in subminiature tube sockets into which are plugged the wires bearing the stimulation. This cat first learned to rotate a paddle wheel to turn off electric shock. Then he was tested with brain stimulation. As soon as the stimulation was delivered, the cat became active and, after a few irrelevant responses, rotated the wheel which turned off the stimulation and thus rewarded the response of rotating the wheel. After a few trials, facilitated by transfer from the previous training, the cat learned to rotate the wheel as soon as the stimulation was turned on. Fig. 4

Fig. 4 *Electrical stimulation of a pain-fear area in a cat's brain elicits a learned response: rotating a wheel which turns off the stimulation. Stimulation is turned on between the first and second pictures. [From a motion picture by Miller, Delgado, and Roberts, shown by the author at the 1953 meeting of the APA.]*

shows him performing this habit motivated by electrical stimulation of the brain.

In the next experiment, preliminary tests showed that a tone was a neutral stimulus which produced no obvious response. Then for a number of trials the tone was immediately followed by the brain stimulation which elicited wheel turning. After a few such trials, the wheel turning was conditioned: the tone alone, without brain stimulation, caused the cat to turn the wheel.

In the final experiment, we find that stimulation in the sensorimotor area of a hungry control cat, which was eating, produced a violent withdrawal from food; but even after repeated stimulation, the control animals promptly returned to eat. By contrast, experimental cats, stimulated once or twice with a lower voltage in the critical area of the brain, learned to avoid the food.

These experiments have shown that brain stimulation at critical points can have a number of the significant properties of normally elicited pain and fear. In addition to illustrating a general approach to the problem of investigating motivational factors elicited by electrical stimulation of the brain, experiments of the foregoing type may yield information which will help us in knowing where to place lesions in order to relieve certain hitherto hopeless patients from the acute misery of intractable pain.

Similar experiments on centrally aroused aggression have elicited a spectacular and relatively well-integrated cluster of symptoms of rage— hissing, spitting, clawing, etc.—which suggest that rage contains some integrated motor components different from fear. So far, however, Warren Roberts and I have confirmed Masserman's results in that we have not been able to condition such responses. This raises an interesting question. Is anger a distinctive drive whose mechanisms we have simply failed to date to locate, or are the motor components involved in rage organized without any separate, distinctive drive so that they must be motivated by other drives such as fear, hunger, or sex?

The results of these experiments are enough to illustrate that the combination of the physiological technique of electrical stimulation with various behavioral techniques for measuring the effects of such stimulation is turning out to be a powerful new tool for investigating the motivational functions of the brain.

Reward effects of electrical stimulation

The combination of the techniques for stimulating the brains of unanaesthetized animals with those of exact behavioral testing led Olds and Milner to a completely unexpected discovery. They found that electrical stimulation of certain areas of the brain would act as a powerful reward. This reward could be used to cause animals to choose the correct side of a T maze or to press a bar in a Skinner box. Often in the history of science, the unexpected discovery of a novel phenomenon, such as X-rays or radioactivity, has forced drastic revisions in current theory and ultimately led to important practical developments. While it is too early to be certain exactly how important will be the effects of this unexpected discovery by Olds and Milner, I suspect they will be considerable.

On the theoretical front, the rewarding effect of central stimulation tends to revive hedonistic theories of reinforcement. As I have pointed out elsewhere, however, the results known to date can be fitted in fairly well with any of the current theories of reinforcement, and the drive-reduction hypothesis suggests a number of interesting lines of investigation in the area of centrally rewarding effects. The important thing is that we have here a genuinely novel phenomenon and a completely new technique for investigating the mechanism of reward and its relationship to various drives.

This new discovery has touched off a flurry of research which is still mounting with positive acceleration. Olds has shown that there are certain regions of the hypothalamus where the rate of bar pressing increases with hunger much as it would if the animals were receiving a food reward. In a slightly different area, the rate of bar pressing varies positively with sex—being reduced by castration and increased by androgen therapy. Furthermore, different drugs, such as tranquilizers, seem to have differential effects on the reward phenomenon elicited by stimulation in different parts of the brain. Thus, we probably have here a technique for learning more about how drugs affect different parts of the brain and also for screening drugs in order to discover ones that have more specific psychological effects.

Motivational effects of drugs

One of my students, Robert Kirschner, used an apparatus having two bars diagonally across a corner from each other in order to equalize the skill and effort required to turn the stimulation on or off. Studying the effects of methamphetamine and chlorpromazine, he found that 2 mg/k of the former and 4 mg/k of the latter produced roughly equivalent reductions in the total number of bar presses.

But, when the rewarding and aversive effects were analyzed separately, these two drugs had strikingly different effects. The methamphetamine increased the time to turn the stimulation off while decreasing the time to turn it on. By contrast, the chlorpromazine produced a great increase in the time to turn the stimulation on and also some increase in the time to turn it off. One interpretation of these results is that methamphetamine was accentuating the positive rewarding effects and minimizing the negative punishing ones—a result congruent with its clinical euphoric effects. Chlorpromazine seemed to be reducing reward more than the aversion—a result congruent with the fact that it sometimes causes patients to feel depressed.

The organic chemists are turning out thousands of new compounds and are able to produce at will slight modifications in known drugs. Similarly, the biochemists are learning more about vital hormones, enzymes, enzyme inhibitors, and other powerful agents of metabolism. But one of the chief bottlenecks to the discovery of superior psychotropic drugs is the difficulty in efficiently and safely testing for the psychological effects of all these new compounds. Perhaps this test, along with many other ingenious ones recently devised by experimental psychologists, will help us in finding drugs which have more potent therapeutic effects with fewer harmful side effects. Although the current enthusiasm for the tranquilizing drugs may have the same rocketing rise and frustrating fall as other "wonder cures" for schizophrenia, I believe that the recent signs of vigorous growth of a new infant science of psychopharmacology afford a reasonable ground for eventual hope.

For the rapid growth of psychopharmacology to be healthy, however, I believe that it should soon advance beyond the stage where a single test is widely used for screening merely on the basis of its face validity. The standards and methods of modern aptitude testing should be adapted to this new area. Batteries of tests should be tried out and validated, first by the criterion of internal consistency and eventually by the criterion of predicting clinically useful effects. Both screening tests and drugs might eventually be factor analyzed. At the same time that we are refining our screening instruments, we should also be conducting pure-science studies to analyze how well-known drugs achieve their psychological effects. We need to discover fundamental laws to develop a basic science of psychopharmacology. Such a science should provide a rational basis for practical applications to mental hygiene in the same way that organic chemistry provides a basis for the analysis and synthesis of new compounds.

In connection with the problem of drugs, let me emphasize that there is no necessary incompatibility between organic and functional approaches to the problem of mental disease. As you know, I find it useful to describe neurosis and psychotherapy in terms of learning theory. But the book which Dollard and I wrote on this topic contains a chapter on drugs and brain lesions. It is entirely possible that people differ, for example, in the strength of the innate mechanisms for fear, guilt, and anxiety just as they vary in physical size and strength. A person with unusually strong emotional mechanisms of this kind would be especially susceptible to learning strong fears and guilts by traumatic incidents. These unusually strong fears and guilts might directly elicit certain psychosomatic symptoms, produce strong conflicts, or motivate the learning of functional symptoms. It is quite conceivable that chronic medication by suitable drugs could reduce this special susceptibility to irrationally strong fears and guilts much as insulin enables the diabetic to tolerate a diet containing more carbohydrates.

Furthermore, drug effects have the great advantage over certain other forms of organic intervention in that they are reversible. Some interesting results have already been secured by combining the use of barbiturates with psychotherapy. It is conceivable that a superior drug will be produced which will be a much more effective aid to emotional re-education. Indeed, it is conceivable that radically improved results with certain forms of mental disease may be achieved by an unconventional combination of drug therapy, individual therapy, group therapy, training in social skills, and temporary manipulation of the environment.

Biochemical stimulation

In addition to electrical techniques of stimulation, new biochemical techniques (which obviously have implications also for psychopharmacology) have recently been exploited. For example, Andersson has shown that minute injections of salt solution into the region of the third ventricle can cause excessive drinking in goats. Conversely, our group has shown that minute injections of water into the brain can cause a thirsty cat to stop drinking. Furthermore, we have shown that the minute salt injections increase, while the water ones decrease, the rate of performing a learned response to get water. Therefore, these minute injections into the brain have some of the more general effects of normal increases or reductions of thirst.

Similarly, Alan Fisher has shown that a minute injection of male hormone into a specific site in the brain can induce complex sexual, and in some instances maternal, behavior as though it had a motivating effect. Since similar effects were not produced by electrical stimulation of the same sites, there is reason to believe that, in some instances at least, the chemical stimulation may be more effective and selective than the electrical technique. Here again, we have a powerful new tool, the potentialities of which are just beginning to be explored.

Electrical recording of brain activity

The converse of the stimulation technique is that of recording electrical activity of the brain and other parts of the nervous system. This technique has been used with great success in tracing sensory systems and has recently produced some quite exciting results which may help to explain the mechanism for the relationship between motivation and attention. For example, it has been found that stimulation of the reticular system in the brain can actually reduce the transmission of sensory impulses from the end organs and through lower relay centers, thus partially shielding the brain from certain sources of stimulation. As Livingston has pointed out, this finding produces a radical change in our previous notions of sensory neurophysiology.

Can these new techniques be applied to other motivational phenomena? For example, Pavlov reports that, when a somewhat painful stimulus is made the conditioned stimulus for food, all of the obvious emotional responses to pain seem to drop out. By using suitable recording techniques, could we demonstrate that the pain impulses themselves are reduced before they reach the highest centers? Would we have an experimental method for producing and studying a phenomenon analogous to hysterical anaesthesia?

Although techniques for recording the electrical activity of the nervous system have been used very successfully in the study of sensory mechanisms, they have not been used much in the study of drive and reward. Here seems a promising new area of application, although there are technical difficulties to overcome. For example, if an animal's motor responses (which disturb electrical recording) were eliminated by one of the improved curare derivatives, such as flaxidil, would we find that the electrical activity in different tracts and centers of the brain is altered when the animal is hungry, thirsty, or suffering painful stimulation? What would be the effects of rewards such as water injected directly into the blood stream of a thirsty animal, if indeed it can be demonstrated that such injections function as a reward? Would there be any effects specific to stimulation of the brain at points where such stimulation is rewarding and different from those at points where it is neutral or aversive? Any such differences are likely to give us significant clues to the basic mechanisms of motivation and reward.

OTHER PROMISING APPROACHES

Now fasten your seat belts for a final spurt through a number of different approaches for which the brevity of listing does not mean any inferiority in merit.

Recently Roger Russell's group has been studying the effects of what might be called biochemical lesions of the brain, while David Krech and Mark Rosenzweig have been pursuing the relationships among brain chemistry, heredity, and behavior. While these new lines of work have been aimed chiefly at cognitive functions, they could easily turn up facts which would lead directly into problems of motivation and reward.

Most of the studies I have sampled thus far have involved relatively direct approaches to the brain. The combination of exact behavioral tests with various "intermediate" techniques has also proved fruitful. Some of the techniques used in this way have been a fistula into the stomach, a cannula into a vein, a subcutaneous saline injection, enzyme inhibitors, and unusual substances which are similar to a metabolite in one respect but different in others. Programs involving such work are well under way in Mayer's laboratory at Harvard, Stellar's at Pennsylvania, and our own laboratory at Yale. Similarly, Beach and his students are introducing a greater variety of behavioral techniques into the study of sex.

Thus far, various approaches usually have been used in relative isolation. Additional advances may be expected when more use is made of systematic combinations of these approaches. For example, appropriately placed lesions might be used in the analysis of the systems involved in the drive or reward effect of brain stimulation or of the different effects of distending the stomach with either food or a balloon.

Finally, a completely different and highly promising development has been the use of behavioral techniques to bring new drives into the laboratory: first fear, then curiosity, and most recently social deprivation. We can and should extend the range of drives experimentally studied. But that is another story.

selection 15 / deficiency motivation and growth motivation / Abraham Maslow, Brandeis University

Hans Zinsser has described the difference between philosophical and scientific theorizing by comparing the latter to a trellis which one builds out just ahead of the growing vine in the direction of its growth and for the sake of its future support. It is this latter task that I have set myself in this paper which is a portion of a larger systematic theory of general psychology. It is based mostly upon clinical and person-ological researches and experience, rather than upon formal experimentation but will soon be ready, I think, for the experimental test. I must warn you that the demands of system and of theory probably play a considerable role in what follows. To some extent, its existence and its particular shape are called for not only by data but also by theoretical, systematic considerations of which I cannot speak here,

Abridged from Abraham Maslow, "Deficiency Motivation and Growth Motivation," *Nebraska Symposium on Motivation*, Marshall R. Jones, ed., University of Nebraska Press, Lincoln, Nebraska, 1955, pp. 1–30. Reprinted by permission of the author and the publisher.

and which will be apparent only when the whole structure of theory is seen as a unity.

Another point that I must warn you about is this. This paper is very frankly in a different tradition from the ones you have heard in previous years in this series. For one thing, I am not *only* the disinterested and impersonal seeker for pure cold truth for its own sake. I am also very definitely interested and concerned with man's fate, with his ends and goals and with his future. I would like to help improve him and to better his prospects. I hope to help teach him how to be brotherly, cooperative, peaceful, courageous and just. I think science is the best hope for achieving this, and of all the sciences I consider psychology the most important to this end. Indeed I sometimes think that the world will either be saved by psychologists —in the very broadest sense—or else it will not be saved at all. It is this humanistic emphasis which is the source and the justification of what I consider to be the important questions which justify inexact and unreliable researches. They *must* be done; we don't *dare* turn away from them because we can't handle them well. We must do the best we can.

The concept "basic need" can be defined in terms of the questions which it answers and the operations which uncovered it. My original question was about psychopathogenesis. "What makes people neurotic?" My answer (a modification of and I think an improvement upon the analytic one) was, in brief, that neurosis seemed at its core, and in its beginning, to be a deficiency disease; that it was born out of being deprived of certain satisfactions which I called needs in the same sense that water and amino acids and calcium are needs, namely that their absence produces illness. Most neuroses involved, along with other complex determinants, ungratified wishes for safety, for belongingness and identification, for close love relationships and for respect and prestige. My "data" were gathered through twelve years of psychotherapeutic work and research and twenty years of personality study. One obvious control research (done at the same time and in the same operation) was on the effect of replacement therapy which showed, with many complexities, that when these deficiencies were eliminated, sicknesses tended to disappear. Still another necessary long-time control research was on the family backgrounds of both neurotic and healthy people establishing, as many others have since done, that people who are later healthy are not deprived of these essential basic-need-satisfactions, i. e., the prophylactic control.

The long-run deficiency characteristics are then the following. It is a basic or instinctoid need if:

1. Its absence breeds illness
2. Its presence prevents illness

3. Its restoration cures illness
4. Under certain (very complex) free choice situations, it is preferred by the deprived person over other satisfactions
5. It is found to be inactive, at a low ebb, or functionally absent in the healthy person

Two additional characteristics are subjective ones, namely, conscious or unconscious yearning and desire, and feeling of lack or deficiency, as of something missing on the one hand, and, on the other, palatability, ("It tastes good").

One last word on definition. Many of the problems that have plagued the writers in this series as they attempted to define and delimit motivation are a consequence of the exclusive demand for behavioral, externally observable criteria. The original criterion of motivation and the one that is still used by all human beings except behavioral psychologists is the subjective one. I am motivated when I feel desire or want or yearning or wish or lack. No objectively observable state has yet been found that correlates decently with these subjective reports, i. e., no good behavioral definition of motivation has yet been found.

Now of course we ought to keep on seeking for objective correlates of subjective states. On the day when we discover such a public and external indicator of pleasure or of anxiety or of desire, psychology will have jumped forward by a century. But *until* we find it we ought not make believe that we have. Nor ought we neglect the subjective data that we do have. It is unfortunate that we cannot ask a rat to give subjective reports. Fortunately, however, we *can* ask the human being, and I see no reason in the world why we should refrain from doing so until we have a better source of data. If the "objective" psychologists trying to define motivation sometimes seem to be staggering about in the dark, perhaps it is because they have voluntarily blindfolded themselves.

It is these needs which are essentially deficits in the organism, empty holes, so to speak, which must be filled up for health's sake, and furthermore must be filled from without by human beings *other* than the subject that I shall call deficits or deficiency needs for purposes of this exposition and to set them in contrast to another and very different kind of motivation.

There is not a person in this room to whom it would occur to question the statement that we "need" iodine or vitamin C. I remind you that the evidence that we "need" love is of exactly the same type.

In recent years more and more psychologists have found themselves compelled to postulate some tendency to growth or self-perfection to supplement the concepts of equilibrium, homeostasis, tension-reduction, defense and other conserving motivations. This was so for various reasons.

Psychotherapy　The pressure toward health makes therapy possible. It is an absolute *sine qua non*. If there were no such trend, therapy would be inexplicable to the extent that it goes beyond the building of defenses against pain and anxiety.

Brain injured soldiers　Goldstein's work is well known to all. He found it necessary to invent the concept of self-actualization to explain the reorganization of the person's capacities after injury.

Psychoanalysis　Some analysts, notably Fromm, and Horney, have found it impossible to understand even neuroses unless one postulates an impulse toward growth, toward perfection of development, toward the fulfillment of the person's possibilities.

Creativeness　Much light is being thrown on the general subject of creativeness by the study of healthy growing and grown people, especially when contrasted with sick people. Especially does the theory of art and art education call for a concept of growth and spontaneity.

Child psychology　Observation of children shows more and more clearly that healthy children *enjoy* growing and moving forward, gaining new skills, capacities and powers. This is in flat contradiction to that version of Freudian theory which conceives of every child as hanging on desperately to each adjustment that it achieves and to each state of rest or equilibrium. According to this theory, the reluctant and conservative child has continually to be kicked upstairs, out of its comfortable, preferred state of rest *into* a new frightening situation.

While this Freudian conception is continually confirmed by clinicians as largely true for insecure and frightened children, and while it is a little bit true for all human beings, in the main it is *untrue* for healthy, happy, secure children. In these children we see clearly an eagerness to grow up, to mature, to drop the old adjustment as outworn, like an old pair of shoes. We see in them with special clarity not only the eagerness for the new skill but also the most obvious delight in repeatedly enjoying it, the so-called *Funktionslust* of Karl Buhler.

For the writers in these various groups, notably Fromm, Horney, Jung, C. Buhler, Angyal, Rogers, and G. Allport, and recently some Catholic psychologists, growth, individuation, autonomy, self-actualization, self-development, productiveness, self-realization, are all crudely synonymous, designating a vaguely perceived area rather than a sharply defined concept. In my opinion, it is *not* possible to define this area sharply at the present time. Nor is this desirable either, since a definition which does not emerge easily and naturally from well-known facts is apt to be inhibiting and distorting rather than helpful, since it is quite likely to be wrong or mistaken if made by an act of the will on *a priori* grounds. We just don't know enough about growth yet to be able to define it well.

In any case, the psychological life of the person, in very many of its aspects, is lived out differently when he is deficiency-need-gratification-bent and when he is growth-dominated or "metamotivated" or growth-motivated or self-actualizing. The following differences make this clear.

Attitude toward impulse: impulse-rejection and impulse-acceptance

Practically all historical and contemporary theories of motivation unite in regarding needs, drives and motivating states in general as annoying, irritating, unpleasant, undesirable, as something to get rid of. Motivated behavior, goal seeking, consummatory responses are all techniques for reducing these discomforts. This attitude is very explicitly assumed in such widely used descriptions of motivation as need reduction, tension reduction, drive reduction, and anxiety reduction.

To put it as succinctly as possible, these people all find desire or impulse to be a nuisance or even a threat and therefore will try generally to get rid of it, to deny it or to avoid it.

This contention is sometimes an accurate report of what is the case. The physiological needs, the needs for safety, for love, for respect, for information are in fact often nuisances for many people, psychic trouble makers, and problem-creators, especially for those who have had unsuccessful experiences at gratifying them and for those who cannot now count on gratification.

Even with these deficiencies, however, the case is very badly overdrawn: one can accept and enjoy one's needs and welcome them to consciousness if (a) past experience with them has been rewarding, and (b) if present and future gratification can be counted on. For example, if one has in general enjoyed food and if good food is now available, the emergence of appetite into consciousness is welcomed instead of dreaded. ("The trouble with eating is that it kills my appetite.") Something like this is true for thirst, for sleepiness, for sex, for dependency needs and for love needs. However, a far more powerful refutation of the "need-is-a-nuisance" theory is found in the recently emerging awareness of, and concern with, growth (self-actualization) motivation.

The multitude of idiosyncratic motives which come under the head of "self-actualization" can hardly be listed since each person has different talents, capacities, potentialities. But some characteristics are general to all of them. And one is that these impulses are desired and welcomed, are enjoyable and pleasant, that the person wants more of them rather than less, and that if they constitute tensions, they are *pleasurable* tensions. The creator welcomes his creative impulses, the talented person enjoys using and expanding his talents.

It is simply inaccurate to speak in such instances of tension-reduction, implying thereby the getting rid of an annoying state. For these states are not annoying.

Differential effects of gratification

Almost always associated with negative attitudes toward the need is the conception that the primary aim of the organism is to get rid of the annoying need and thereby to achieve a cessation of tension, an equilibrium, a homeostasis, a quiescence, a state of rest, a lack of pain.

Charlotte Buhler has pointed out that the theory of homeostasis is different from the theory of rest. The latter theory speaks simply of removing tension which implies that zero tension is best. Homeostasis means coming not to a zero but to an optimum level. This means sometimes reducing tension, sometimes increasing it, e. g., blood pressure may be too low as well as too high.

In either case the lack of constant direction through a lifespan is obvious. In both cases, growth of the personality, increase in wisdom, self-actualization, strengthening of the character, and the planning of one's life are not and cannot be accounted for. Some long-time vector, or directional tendency, must be invoked to make any sense of development through the lifetime.

This theory must be put down as an inadequate description even of deficiency motivation. What is lacking here is awareness of the dynamic principle which ties together and interrelates all these separate motivational episodes. The different basic needs are related to each other in a hierarchical order such that gratification of one need and its consequent removal from the center of the stage brings about not a state of rest or Stoic apathy, but rather the emergence into consciousness of another "higher" need; wanting and desiring continues but at a "higher" level. Thus the coming-to-rest theory isn't adequate even for deficiency motivation.

However, when we examine people who are predominantly growth-motivated, the coming-to-rest conception of motivation becomes completely useless. In such people gratification breeds increased rather than decreased motivation, heightened rather than lessened excitement. The appetites become intensified and heightened. They grow upon themselves and instead of wanting less and less, such a person wants more and more of, for instance, education. The person rather than coming to rest becomes more active. The appetite for growth is whetted rather than allayed by gratification. Growth is, *in itself*, a rewarding and exciting process, e. g., the fulfilling of yearnings and ambitions, like that of being a good doctor; the acquisition of admired skills, like playing the violin or being a good carpenter; the steady increase of understanding about people or about the universe, or about oneself; the development of creativeness in whatever field, or, most important, simply the ambition to be a good human being.

Partly this intrinsic validity of living comes from the pleasurableness inherent in growing and in being grown. But it also comes from the ability of healthy people to transform means-activity into end-experience, so that even instrumental activity is enjoyed as if it were end activity. Growth motivation may be long-term in character. Most of a lifetime may be involved in becoming a good psychologist or a good artist. All equilibrium or homeostasis or rest theories deal only with short-term episodes, each of which have nothing to do with each other. Allport particularly has stressed this point. Plan-fulness and looking into the future, he points out, are of the central stuff of healthy human nature. He agrees that "Deficit motives do, in fact, call for the reduction of tension and restoration of equilibrium. Growth motives, on the other hand, maintain tension in the interest of distant and often unattainable goals. As such they distinguish human from animal becoming, and adult from infant becoming."

Clinical effects of gratification

Deficit-need gratifications and growth-need gratifications have differential subjective and objective effects upon the personality. If I may phrase what I am groping for here in a very generalized way, it is this: Satisfying deficiencies avoids illness; growth satisfactions produce positive health. I must grant that this will be difficult to pin down for research purposes at this time. And yet there is a real clinical difference between fending off threat or attack and positive triumph and achievement, between protecting, defending and preserving oneself and reaching out for fulfillment, for excitement and for enlargement. I have tried to express this as a contrast between living fully and *preparing* to live fully, between growing up and being grown.

Different kinds of pleasure

Erich Fromm has made an interesting and important effort to distinguish higher from lower pleasures, as have so many others before him. This is a crucial necessity for breaking through subjective ethical relativity and is a prerequisite for a scientific value theory.

He distinguishes scarcity-pleasure from abundance-pleasure, the "lower" pleasure of satiation of a need from the "higher" pleasure of production, creation and growth of insight. The glut, the relaxation, and the loss of tension that follows deficiency-satiation can at best be called "relief" by contrast with the *Funktionslust*, the ecstasy, the serenity that one experiences when functioning easily, perfectly and at the peak of one's powers—in overdrive, so to speak.

"Relief," depending so strongly on something that disappears, is itself more likely to disappear. It must be less stable, less enduring, less constant than the pleasure accompanying growth, which can go on forever.

Attainable and unattainable goal states

Deficiency-need gratification tends to be episodic and climactic. The most frequent schema here begins with an instigating, motivating state which sets off motivated behavior designed to achieve a goal-state, which, mounting gradually and steadily in desire and excitement, finally reaches a peak in a moment of success and consummation. From this peak curve of desire, excitement and pleasure fall rapidly to a plateau of quiet tension-release, and lack of motivation.

This schema, though not universally applicable, in any case contrasts very sharply with the situation in growth-motivation, for here characteristically there is no climax or consummation, no orgasmic moment, no end-state, even no goal if this be defined climactically. Growth is instead a continued, more or less steady upward or forward development. The more one gets, the more one wants so that this kind of wanting is endless and can never be attained or satisfied.

It is for this reason that the usual separation between instigation, goal-seeking behavior, the goal object and the accompanying affect breaks down completely. The behaving is itself the goal, and to differentiate the goal of growth from the instigation to growth is impossible. They too are the same.

Species-wide goals and idiosyncratic goals

The deficit-needs are shared by all members of the human species and to some extent by other species as well. Self-actualization is idiosyncratic since every person is different. The deficits, i. e., the species requirements, must ordinarily be fairly well satisfied before real individuality can develop fully.

Just as all trees need sun, water, and foods from the environment, so do all people need safety, love and status from *their* environment. However, in both cases this is just where real development of individuality can begin, for once satiated with these elementary, species-wide necessities, each tree and each person proceeds to develop in his own style, uniquely, using these necessities for his own private purposes. In a very tangible sense, development then becomes more determined from within rather than from without.

Dependence and independence of the environment

The needs for safety, belongingness, love relations and for respect can be satisfied only by other people, i. e., only from outside the person. This means considerable dependence on the environment. A person in this dependent position cannot really be said to be governing himself, or in control of his own fate. He *must* be beholden to the sources of supply of needed gratifications. Their wishes, their whims, their rules and laws govern him and must be appeased lest he jeopardize his sources of supply. He *must* be to an extent "other-directed" and *must* be sensitive to other people's approval, affection and good will. This is the same as saying that he must adapt and adjust by being flexible and responsive and by changing himself to fit the external situation. *He* is the dependent variable; the environment is the fixed, independent variable.

Because of this, the deficiency-motivated man must be more afraid of the environment, since there is always the possibility that it may fail or disappoint him. We now know that this kind of anxious dependence breeds hostility as well. All of which adds up to a lack of freedom, more or less, depending on the good fortune or bad fortune of the individual.

In contrast, the self-actualizing individual, by definition gratified in his basic needs, is far less dependent, far less beholden, far more autonomous and self-directed. Far from needing other people, growth-motivated people may actually be hampered by them. I have already reported their special liking for privacy, for detachment and for meditativeness.

Such people become far more self-sufficient and self-contained. The determinants which govern them are now primarily inner ones, rather than social or environmental. They are the laws of their own inner nature, their potentialities and capacities, their talents, their latent resources, their creative impulses, their needs to know themselves and to become more and more integrated and unified, more and more aware of what they really are, of what they really want, of what their call or vocation or fate is to be.

Since they depend less on other people, they are less ambivalent about them, less anxious and also less hostile, less needful of their praise and their affection. They are less anxious for honors, prestige and rewards.

Autonomy or relative independence of environment means also relative independence of adverse external circumstances, such as ill fortune, hard knocks, tragedy, stress, deprivation. As Allport has stressed, the notion of the human being as essentially reactive, the S-R man we might call him, who is set into motion by external stimuli, becomes completely ridiculous and untenable for self-actualizing people. The sources of *their* actions are internal rather than external. This relative independence of the outside world and its wishes and pressures, does not mean of course lack of intercourse with it. It means only that in these contacts, the self-actualizer's wishes and plans are the primary determiners, and that the environment becomes more and more a means to his ends. This I have called psychological freedom, contrasting it with geographical freedom.

Deficiency-motivated and growth-motivated perception

What may turn out to be the most important difference of all is the greater closeness of deficit-satisfied people to the realm of Being. Psychologists have never yet been able to claim this vague jurisdiction of the philosophers, this area dimly seen but nevertheless having undoubted basis in reality. But it may now become feasible through the study of self-fulfilling individuals to have our eyes opened to all sorts of basic insights, old to the philosophers but new to us.

For instance, I think that our understanding of perception and therefore of the perceived world will be very much changed and enlarged if we study carefully the distinction between need-interested and need-disinterested or desireless perception. Because the latter is so much more concrete and less abstracted and selective, it is possible for such a person to see more easily the intrinsic nature of the percept. He can perceive simultaneously the opposites, the dichotomies, the polarities, the contradictions and the incompatibles. It is as if less developed people lived in an Aristotelian world in which classes and concepts have sharp boundaries and are mutually exclusive and incompatible, e. g., male-female, selfish-unselfish, adult-child, angel-devil, kind-cruel, good-bad. A is A and everything else is not A in the Aristotelian logic, and never the twain shall meet. But seen by self-actualizing people is the fact that A and not-A interpenetrate and are one, that any person is simultaneously good *and* bad, male *and* female, adult *and* child. One can not place a whole person on a continuum, only an abstracted aspect of a person.

Because self-actualizing people ordinarily do not have to abstract need-gratifying qualities nor see the person as a tool, it is much more possible for them to take a non-valuing, non-judging, non-interfering, non-condemning attitude towards others, a desirelessness, a "choiceless awareness." This permits much clearer and more insightful perception and understanding of what is there. This is the kind of untangled, uninvolved, detached perception that surgeons and therapists are supposed to try for and which self-actualizing people attain *without* trying for.

Especially when the structure of the person or object seen is difficult, subtle and not obvious is this difference in style of perception most important. Especially then must the perceiver have respect for the nature of the object. Perception must then be gentle, delicate, unintruding, undemanding, able to fit itself passively to the nature of things as water gently soaks into crevices. It must *not* be the need-motivated kind of perception which *shapes* things in a blustering, over-riding, exploiting, purposeful fashion, in the manner of a butcher chopping apart a carcass.

The most efficient way to perceive the intrinsic nature of the world is to be more passive than active, determined as much as possible by the intrinsic organization of that which is perceived and as little as possible by the nature of the perceiver. This kind of detached, Taoist, passive, non-interfering awareness of all the simultaneously existing aspects of the concrete, has much in common with some descriptions of the aesthetic experience and of the mystic experience. The stress is the same. Do we see the real, concrete world or do we see our own system of rubrics, motives, expectations and abstractions which we have projected onto the real world? Or, to put it very bluntly, do we see or are we blind?

selection 16 / a theory of human motivation / A. H. Maslow, Brandeis University

THE BASIC NEEDS

The "physiological" needs The needs that are usually taken as the starting point for motivation theory are the so-called physiological drives. Two recent lines of research make it necessary to revise our customary notions about these needs, first, the development of the concept of homeostasis, and second, the finding that appetites (preferential choices among foods) are a fairly efficient indication of actual needs or lacks in the body.

Homeostasis refers to the body's automatic efforts to maintain a constant, normal state of the blood stream. Cannon has described this process for (1) the water content of the blood, (2) salt content, (3) sugar content, (4) protein content, (5) fat content, (6) calcium content, (7) oxygen content, (8) constant hydrogen-ion level (acid-base balance) and (9) constant temperature of the blood. Obviously this list can be extended to include other minerals, the hormones, vitamins, etc.

Young in a recent article has summarized the work on appetite in its relation to body needs. If the body lacks some chemical, the individual will tend to develop a specific appetite or partial hunger for that food element.

Thus it seems impossible as well as useless to make any list of

Abridged from A. H. Maslow, "A Theory of Human Motivation," *Psychological Review*, 50:370–396, 1943. Reprinted by permission of the author and the American Psychological Association.

fundamental physiological needs for they can come to almost any number one might wish, depending on the degree of specificity of description. We can not identify all physiological needs as homeostatic. That sexual desire, sleepiness, sheer activity and maternal behavior in animals, are homeostatic, has not yet been demonstrated. Furthermore, this list would not include the various sensory pleasures (tastes, smells, tickling, stroking) which are probably physiological and which may become the goals of motivated behavior.

In a previous paper it has been pointed out that these physiological drives or needs are to be considered unusual rather than typical because they are isolable, and because they are localizable somatically. That is to say, they are relatively independent of each other, of other motivations and of the organism as a whole, and secondly, in many cases, it is possible to demonstrate a localized, underlying somatic base for the drive. This is true less generally than has been thought (exceptions are fatigue, sleepiness, maternal responses) but it is still true in the classic instances of hunger, sex, and thirst.

Undoubtedly these physiological needs are the most prepotent of all needs. What this means specifically is, that in the human being who is missing everything in life in an extreme fashion, it is most likely that the major motivation would be the physiological needs rather than any others. A person who is lacking food, safety, love, and esteem would most probably hunger for food more strongly than for anything else.

If all the needs are unsatisfied, and the organism is then dominated by the physiological needs, all other needs may become simply non-existent or be pushed into the background. But what happens to man's desires when there *is* plenty of bread and when his belly is chronically filled?

At once other (and "higher") needs emerge and these, rather than physiological hungers, dominate the organism. And when these in turn are satisfied, again new (and still "higher") needs emerge and so on. This is what we mean by saying that the basic human needs are organized into a hierarchy of relative prepotency.

One main implication of this phrasing is that gratification becomes as important a concept as deprivation in motivation theory, for it releases the organism from the domination of a relatively more physiological need, permitting thereby the emergence of other more social goals. The physiological needs, along with their partial goals, when chronically gratified cease to exist as active determinants or organizers of behavior. They now exist only in a potential fashion in the sense that they may emerge again to dominate the organism if they are thwarted. But a want that is satisfied is no longer a want. The organism is dominated and its behavior organized only by unsatisfied needs.

If hunger is satisfied, it becomes unimportant in the current dynamics of the individual.

The safety needs If the physiological needs are relatively well gratified, there then emerges a new set of needs, which we may categorize roughly as the safety needs. All that has been said of the physiological needs is equally true, although in lesser degree, of these desires. The organism may equally well be wholly dominated by them. They may serve as the almost exclusive organizers of behavior, recruiting all the capacities of the organism in their service, and we may then fairly describe the whole organism as a safety-seeking mechanism. Again we may say of the receptors, the effectors, of the intellect and the other capacities that they are primarily safety-seeking tools. Again, as in the hungry man, we find that the dominating goal is a strong determinant not only of his current world-outlook and philosophy but also of his philosophy of the future. Practically everything looks less important than safety, (even sometimes the physiological needs which being satisfied, are now underestimated). A man, in this state, if it is extreme enough and chronic enough, may be characterized as living almost for safety alone.

Although in this paper we are interested primarily in the needs of the adult, we can approach an understanding of his safety needs perhaps more efficiently by observation of infants and children, in whom these needs are much more simple and obvious. One reason for the clearer appearance of the threat or danger reaction in infants, is that they do not inhibit this reaction at all, whereas adults in our society have been taught to inhibit it at all costs. Thus even when adults do feel their safety to be threatened we may not be able to see this on the surface. Infants will react in a total fashion and as if they were endangered, if they are disturbed or dropped suddenly, startled by loud noises, flashing light, or other unusual sensory stimulation, by rough handling, by general loss of support in the mother's arms, or by inadequate support.

The central role of the parents and the normal family setup are indisputable. Quarreling, physical assault, separation, divorce or death within the family may be particularly terrifying. Also parental outbursts of rage or threats of punishment directed to the child, calling him names, speaking to him harshly, shaking him, handling him roughly, or actual physical punishment sometimes elicit such total panic and terror in the child that we must assume more is involved than the physical pain alone. While it is true that in some children this terror may represent also a fear of loss of parental love, it can also occur in completely rejected children, who seem to cling to the hating parents more for sheer safety and protection than because of hope of love.

The healthy, normal, fortunate adult in our culture is largely satis-fied in his safety needs. The peaceful, smoothly running, "good" so-ciety ordinarily makes its members feel safe enough from wild animals, extremes of temperature, criminals, assault and murder, tyranny, etc. Therefore, in a very real sense, he no longer has any safety needs as active motivators. Just as a sated man no longer feels hungry, a safe man no longer feels endangered. If we wish to see these needs directly and clearly we must turn to neurotic or near-neurotic individuals, and to the economic and social underdogs. In between these extremes, we can perceive the expressions of safety needs only in such phenomena as, for instance, the common preference for a job with tenure and protection, the desire for a savings account, and for insurance of various kinds (medical, dental, unemployment, disability, old age).

Some neurotic adults in our society are, in many ways, like the unsafe child in their desire for safety, although in the former it takes on a somewhat special appearance. Their reaction is often to unknown, psychological dangers in a world that is perceived to be hostile, over-whelming and threatening. Such a person behaves as if a great catas-trophe were almost always impending, *i.e.*, he is usually responding as if to an emergency. His safety needs often find specific expression in a search for a protector, or a stronger person on which he may depend, or perhaps, a Fuehrer.

The love needs If both the physiological and the safety needs are fairly well gratified, then there will emerge the love and affection and belongingness needs, and the whole cycle already described will repeat itself with this new center. Now the person will feel keenly, as never before, the absence of friends, or a sweetheart, or a wife, or children. He will hunger for affectionate relations with people in general, namely, for a place in his group, and he will strive with great intensity to achieve this goal. He will want to attain such a place more than anything else in the world and may even forget that once, when he was hungry, he sneered at love.

In our society the thwarting of these needs is the most commonly found core in cases of maladjustment and more severe psychopa-thology. Love and affection, as well as their possible expression in sex-uality, are generally looked upon with ambivalence and are customarily hedged about with many restrictions and inhibitions. Practically all theorists of psychopathology have stressed thwarting of the love needs as basic in the picture of maladjustment. Many clinical studies have therefore been made of this need and we know more about it perhaps than any of the other needs except the physiological ones.

One thing that must be stressed at this point is that love is not synonymous with sex. Sex may be studied as a purely physiological need. Ordinarily sexual behavior is multi-determined, that is to say, determined not only by sexual but also by other needs, chief among which are the love and affection needs. Also not to be overlooked is the fact that the love needs involve both giving *and* receiving love.

The esteem needs   All people in our society (with a few pathological exceptions) have a need or desire for a stable, firmly based, (usually) high evaluation of themselves, for self-respect, or self-esteem, and for the esteem of others. By firmly based self-esteem, we mean that which is soundly based upon real capacity, achievement and respect from others. These needs may be classified into two subsidiary sets. These are, first, the desire for strength, for achievement, for adequacy, for confidence in the face of the world, and for independence and freedom. Secondly, we have what we may call the desire for reputation or prestige (defining it as respect or esteem from other people), recognition, attention, importance or appreciation. These needs have been relatively stressed by Alfred Adler and his followers, and have been relatively neglected by Freud and the psychoanalysts. More and more today however there is appearing widespread appreciation of their central importance.

Satisfaction of the self-esteem need leads to feelings of self-confidence, worth, strength, capability and adequacy of being useful and necessary in the world. But thwarting of these needs produces feelings of inferiority, of weakness and of helplessness. These feelings in turn give rise to either basic discouragement or else compensatory or neurotic trends. An appreciation of the necessity of basic self-confidence and an understanding of how helpless people are without it, can be easily gained from a study of severe traumatic neurosis.

The need for self-actualization   Even if all these needs are satisfied, we may still often (if not always) expect that a new discontent and restlessness will soon develop, unless the individual is doing what he is fitted for. A musician must make music, an artist must paint, a poet must write, if he is to be ultimately happy. What a man *can* be, he *must* be. This need we may call self-actualization.

This term, first coined by Kurt Goldstein, is being used in this paper in a much more specific and limited fashion. It refers to the desire for self-fulfillment, namely, to the tendency for him to become actualized in what he is potentially. This tendency might be phrased as the desire to become more and more what one is, to become everything that one is capable of becoming.

The specific form that these needs will take will of course vary greatly from person to person. In one individual it may take the form of the desire to be an ideal mother, in another it may be expressed athletically, and in still another it may be expressed in painting pictures or in inventions. It is not necessarily a creative urge although in people who have any capacities for creation it will take this form.

The clear emergence of these needs rests upon prior satisfaction of the physiological, safety, love and esteem needs. We shall call people who are satisfied in these needs, basically satisfied people, and it is from these that we may expect the fullest (and healthiest) creativeness. Since, in our society, basically satisfied people are the exception, we do not know much about self-actualization, either experimentally or clinically. It remains a challenging problem for research.

The preconditions for the basic need satisfactions There are certain conditions which are immediate prerequisites for the basic need satisfactions. Danger to these is reacted to almost as if it were a direct danger to the basic needs themselves. Such conditions as freedom to speak, freedom to do what one wishes so long as no harm is done to others, freedom to express one's self, freedom to investigate and seek for information, freedom to defend one's self, justice, fairness, honesty, orderliness in the group are examples of such preconditions for basic need satisfactions. Thwarting in these freedoms will be reacted to with a threat or emergency response. These conditions are not ends in themselves but they are *almost* so since they are so closely related to the basic needs, which are apparently the only ends in themselves. These conditions are defended because without them the basic satisfactions are quite impossible, or at least, very severely endangered.

CHAPTER 4 ✸ BEHAVIOR
AND EMOTION ✸

Surprisingly enough, the study of emotion has traditionally been rele-gated to a position secondary to that of motivation. However, it is at times quite difficult to differentiate emotion and motivation. As a result, we have recently begun to view emotions as special types of motives. The previous dearth of information and interest in the scientific study of emotions has stemmed in part from the difficulty inherent in investi-gating such a highly subjective phenomenon under controlled laboratory conditions. In addition, emotions have often been thought of as having a disorganizing effect on behavior. As a result, emotions have been pri-marily the concern of clinical psychologists who are typically more interested in the modification of a specific person's disorganized behavior, rather than in a scientific study of emotion per se.

Fortunately, in the last few years there has been an increased in-terest in understanding the physiological mechanisms underlying spe-cific emotional states. The work of Dr. Daniel H. Funkenstein, and his associates (Selection 17), has not only served to further our basic knowledge but promises to provide a new approach to the study of mental illness. On the basis of an extensive and diverse experimental program, Dr. Funkenstein presents evidence to indicate that under stress lower animals, normal human beings, and psychotics behave in one of three ways. They direct their anger outward, or they direct it inward and become depressed, or they become anxious. His meas-ures of the relative amounts of adrenalin and noradrenalin in the three cases support the generalization that the outward expression of anger is related to secretion of noradrenalin while anger-in and anxiety are associated with the secretion of adrenalin.

We have noted above that emotions have often been considered from the point of view of the disorganizing effects which they have on behavior. Dr. Robert Leeper was among the first psychologists to emphasize that emotions are not necessarily disintegrative. In Selection

18 Leeper and Madison conceive of emotions as special types of motives which have certain biological advantages over other physiological drives.

A common assumption of behavioristic psychology [cf. Selection 52] has been that complex learned or social motives and emotions are attached to neutral stimuli on the basis of being associated with reductions in a physiological drive such as hunger (secondary reinforcement) or with increases in a drive such as pain (secondary motivation). Also, Freud's psychoanalytic interpretation of the development of love assumed that a child's love for its mother was dependent on its satisfying an innate need for sucking in the presence of the mother. In his article on "The Nature of Love," Dr. Harry F. Harlow has made two major contributions. The first is in terms of method; he has perfected laboratory techniques for investigating the development of the emotion of love. The second is a substantive contribution; he has shown that love is much more dependent on satisfaction of the need for physical body contact than it is on satisfaction of the hunger drive or oral gratification.

In the process of socializing or training, our culture not only teaches the individual new ways to behave but also teaches him to delay or to inhibit his emotions. It is, of course, necessary for the welfare of the group that the individual learn to avoid the unbridled expression of such emotions as anger or the indiscriminate gratification of the sex-drive. However, the inhibition of expression and gratification is often over-learned. As a result, the individual often is left with a feeling of emptiness. He becomes aware of a lack of meaningfulness in his life. He often reacts to this condition of "emotional poverty" by seeking excessive gratification from external sources. In Selection 20 Leeper and Madison note that among other things excessive dependence on material comforts, on sexual gratification, and on other people are symptoms of this emotional deprivation. This tendency to throw oneself into excessive living when there is strong emotional insecurity is reminiscent of the sensuous orgies held by the Romans during the decadent period of the Empire. Leeper and Madison examine some of the facets of our own culture which tend to create an inability to satisfy emotional needs. Two cultural factors which operate all too often among college students are conformity pressures and the desire to obtain symbols of knowledge, such as grades, rather than knowledge itself. Leeper and Madison refer to this later tendency as "blue-ribbon motivation."[1]

[1] The student should also refer to Dr. Karen Horney's article on cultural factors in neurosis, Selection 56, to see how the tendency toward emotional poverty associated with blue-ribbon motivation may be related to the cultural emphasis on competition.

selection 17 / the physiology of fear and anger / Daniel H. Funkenstein, Boston Psychopathic Hospital

When the late Walter B. Cannon, by his historic experiments nearly half a century ago, showed a connection between emotions and certain physiological changes in the body, he opened a new frontier for psychology and medicine. His work, coupled with that of Sigmund Freud, led to psychosomatic medicine. It also made the emotions accessible to laboratory measurement and analysis. Within the last few years there has been a keen revival of interest in this research, because of some important new discoveries which have sharpened our understanding of specific emotions and their bodily expressions. It has been learned, for instance, that anger and fear produce different physiological reactions and can be distinguished from each other. The findings have given us a fresh outlook from which to study mental illnesses.

The best way to begin the account of this recent work is to start with Cannon's own summary of what he learned. Cannon found that when an animal was confronted with a situation which evoked pain, rage or fear, it responded with a set of physiological reactions which prepared it to meet the threat with "fight" or "flight." These reactions, said Cannon, were mobilized by the secretion of adrenalin: when the cortex of the brain perceived the threat, it sent a stimulus down the sympathetic branch of the autonomic nervous system to the adrenal glands and they secreted the hormone. Cannon graphically described the results as follows:

"Respiration deepens; the heart beats more rapidly; the arterial pressure rises; the blood is shifted away from the stomach and intestines to the heart and central nervous system and the muscles; the processes in the alimentary canal cease; sugar is freed from the reserves in the liver; the spleen contracts and discharges its content of concentrated corpuscles, and adrenin is secreted from the adrenal medulla. The key to these marvelous transformations in the body is found in relating them to the natural accompaniments of fear and rage—running away in order to escape from danger, and attacking in order to be dominant. Whichever the action, a life-or-death struggle may ensue.

"The emotional responses just listed may reasonably be regarded as preparatory for struggle. They are adjustments which, so far as

Daniel H. Funkenstein, "The Physiology of Fear and Anger," *Scientific American*, 192:74–80, 1955. Reprinted with permission.

possible, put the organism in readiness for meeting the demands which will be made upon it. The secreted adrenin cooperates with sympathetic nerve impulses in calling forth stored glycogen from the liver, thus flooding the blood with sugar for the use of laboring muscles; it helps in distributing the blood in abundance to the heart, the brain, and the limbs (*i.e.*, to the parts essential for intense physical effort) while taking it away from the inhibited organs in the abdomen; it quickly abolishes the effects of muscular fatigue so that the organism which can muster adrenin in the blood can restore to its tired muscles the same readiness to act which they had when fresh; and it renders the blood more rapidly coagulable. The increased respiration, the redistributed blood running at high pressure, and the more numerous red corpuscles set free from the spleen provide for essential oxygen and for riddance of acid waste, and make a setting for instantaneous and supreme action. In short, all these changes are directly serviceable in rendering the organism more effective in the violent display of energy which fear or rage may involve."

Cannon recognized that among all these physiological changes there were a few which could not be ascribed directly to the action of adrenalin. He therefore postulated that the hormone was supplemented by two additional substances from the sympathetic nerves. An active agent, distinguishable from adrenalin, was eventually identified in 1948, when B. F. Tullar and M. L. Tainter at length succeeded in preparing the optically active form of the substance. It proved to be a second hormone secreted by the adrenal medulla. Called nor-adrenalin, it differs markedly from adrenalin in its physiological effects. Whereas adrenalin elicits profound physiological changes in almost every system in the body, nor-adrenalin apparently has only one important primary effect: namely, it stimulates the contraction of small blood vessels and increases the resistance to the flow of blood.

An animal exhibits only two major emotions in response to a threatening situation: namely, rage and fear. A man, however, may experience three: anger directed outward (the counterpart of rage), anger directed toward himself (depression) and anxiety, or fear. In studies of physiological changes accompanying various emotional states among patients at the New York Hospital, H. G. Wolff and his coworkers noticed that anger produced effects quite different from those of depression or fear. For example, when a subject was angry, the stomach lining became red and there was an increase in its rhythmic contractions and in the secretion of hydrochloric acid. When the same subject was depressed or frightened, the stomach lining was pale in color and there was a decrease in peristaltic movements and in the hydrochloric acid secretion.

The experiments of Wolff, the evidence that the adrenal medulla secreted two substances rather than one and certain clinical observations led our group at the Harvard Medical School to investigate whether adrenalin and nor-adrenalin might be specific indicators which distinguished one emotion from another. The clinical observations had to do with the effects of a drug, mecholyl, on psychotic patients. We had been studying their blood-pressure responses to injections of adrenalin, which acts on the sympathetic nervous system, and mecholyl, which stimulates the parasympathetic system. On the basis of their blood-pressure reactions, psychotic patients could be classified into seven groups. This test had proved of value in predicting patients' responses to psychiatric treatments, such as electric shock and insulin: certain groups responded better to the treatments than others. But more interesting was the fact that psychotic patients with high blood pressure reacted to the injection of mecholyl in two distinctly different ways. In one group there was only a small drop in the blood pressure after the injection, and the pressure returned to the usually high level within three to eight minutes. In the other group the blood pressure dropped markedly after the injection and remained below the pre-injection level even after 25 minutes. Not only were the physiological reactions quite different, but the two groups of patients also differed in personality and in response to treatment. Thirty-nine of 42 patients whose blood pressure was sharply lowered by mecholyl improved with electric shock treatment, whereas only three of 21 in the other group improved with the same treatment. Further, the two groups showed distinctly different results in projective psychological tests such as the Rorschach.

All this suggested that the two groups of patients might be differentiated on the basis of emotions. Most psychotic patients in emotional turmoil express the same emotion constantly over a period of days, weeks or months. Psychiatrists determined the predominant emotion expressed by each of 63 patients who had been tested with mecholyl, without knowing in which physiological group they had been classified. When the subjects' emotional and physiological ratings were compared, it turned out that almost all of the patients who were generally angry at other people fell in Group N (a small, temporary reduction of blood pressure by mecholyl), while almost all those who were usually depressed or frightened were in Group E (sharp response to mecholyl). In other words, the physiological reactions were significantly related to the emotional content of the patients' psychoses.

The next step was to find out whether the same test could distinguish emotions in normal, healthy people, using medical students as subjects. They were studied at a time when they were under stress— while they were awaiting the decisions of hospitals on their applications for internships. As the competition among the students for the hospitals of their choice is keen, the period just prior to such announcements is a time of emotional turmoil for the men. A group of students who responded to this situation with elevated blood pressure was given the standard dose of mecholyl. The results were the same as for the psychotic patients: students who were angry at others for the situation in which they found themselves had a Type N physiological reaction; those who felt depressed (angry at themselves) or anxious showed a Type E physiological reaction. The reaction was related only to their temporary emotional state; after the internships were settled and their blood pressures had returned to pre-stress levels, all the students reacted the same way to the injection of mecholyl.

It was at this point that we undertook to investigate the comparative effects of adrenalin and nor-adrenalin. A group of workers at the Presbyterian Hospital in New York had shown that injections of nor-adrenalin and adrenalin produced two different types of rise in blood pressure, one due to contraction of blood vessels and the other to faster pumping by the heart. Upon learning of this work, we designed experiments to test the hypothesis that the two types of elevated blood pressure, differentiated by us on the basis of mecholyl tests, indicated in one instance excessive secretion of nor-adrenalin and in the other excessive secretion of adrenalin. Healthy college students were first given a series of intravenous injections of salt water to accustom them to the procedure so that it would not disturb them. Then each subject was tested in the following way. He was given an injection of nor-adrenalin sufficient to raise his blood pressure by 25 per cent. Then, while his blood pressure was elevated, he received the standard dose of mecholyl, and its effects on the blood pressure were noted. The next day the subject was put through the same procedure except that adrenalin was given instead of nor-adrenalin to raise the blood pressure.

Ten students were studied in this way, and in every instance the effect of nor-adrenalin was different from that of adrenalin. When the blood pressure was elevated by nor-adrenalin, mecholyl produced only a small drop in pressure, with a return to the previous level in seven to 10 minutes. This reaction was similar to the Type N response in psychotic patients and healthy students under stress. In contrast, when the blood pressure was elevated by adrenalin, mecholyl produced the Type E response: the pressure dropped markedly and did not return to the previous level during the 25-minute observation period.

These results suggested, in the light of the earlier experiments, that anger directed outward was associated with secretion of nor-adrenalin, while depression and anxiety were associated with secretion of adrenalin. To check this hypothesis, another series of experiments was carried out.

A group of 125 college students were subjected to stress-inducing situations in the laboratory. The situations, involving frustration, were contrived to bring out each student's habitual reaction to stresses in real life; that the reactions actually were characteristic of the subjects' usual responses was confirmed by interviews with their college roommates. While the subjects were under stress, observers recorded their emotional reactions and certain physiological changes—in the blood pressure, the pulse and the so-called IJ waves stemming from the action of the heart. This test showed that students who responded to the stress with anger directed outward had physiological reactions similar to those produced by injection of nor-adrenalin, while students who responded with depression or anxiety had physiological reactions like those to adrenalin.

There remained the question: Does the same individual secrete unusual amounts of nor-adrenalin when angry and of adrenalin when frightened? Albert F. Ax, working in another laboratory in our hospital, designed experiments to study this question. He contrived laboratory stressful situations which were successful in producing on one occasion anger and on another occasion fear in the same subjects. His results showed that when a subject was angry at others, the physiological reactions were like those induced by the injection of nor-adrenalin; when the same subject was frightened, the reactions were like those to adrenalin. This indicated that the physiology was specific for the emotion rather than for the person.

In all these experiments the evidence for excessive secretion of nor-adrenalin and adrenalin was based on the physiological changes being similar to those which can be produced by the intravenous injection of nor-adrenalin and adrenalin. Since the substances involved have not been identified chemically, and the evidence is entirely physiological, at the present time we prefer to limit ourselves to the statement that the reactions are *like* those to the two hormones. However, nothing in our experiments would contradict the hypothesis that these substances are actually adrenalin and nor-adrenalin.

What is the neurophysiological mechanism whereby different emotions evoke different adrenal secretions? Although no conclusive work in this area is yet available, some recent investigations suggest a possible answer. U. S. von Euler in Sweden found that stimulation of certain areas of the hypothalamus caused the adrenal gland to secrete nor-adrenalin, whereas stimulation of other areas caused it to secrete adrenalin. These areas may correspond to those which the

Nobel prize winner W. R. Hess of Zurich stimulated to produce aggressive behavior and flight, respectively, in animals. The experiments suggest that anger and fear may activate different areas in the hypothalamus, leading to production of nor-adrenalin in the first case and adrenalin in the second. Until more experiments are made, these possibilities must remain suppositions.

Some of the most intriguing work in this field was recently reported by von Euler. He compared adrenal secretions found in a number of different animals. The research material was supplied by a friend who flew to Africa to obtain the adrenal medullae of wild animals. Interpreting his findings, J. Ruesch pointed out that aggressive animals such as the lion had a relatively high amount of nor-adrenalin, while in animals such as the rabbit, which depend for survival primarily on flight, adrenalin predominated. Domestic animals, and wild animals that live very social lives (*e.g.*, the baboon), also have a high ratio of adrenalin to nor-adrenalin.

These provocative findings suggest the theory that man is born with the capacity to react with a variety of emotions (has within him the lion and the rabbit), and that his early childhood experiences largely determine in which of these ways he will react under stress. Stated in another way, the evolutional process of man's emotional development is completed in the bosom of the family. We have found in other studies that individuals' habitual emotional reactions have a high correlation with their perceptions of psychological factors in their families.

This entire series of experiments yielded data which can be understood in the frame of reference of psychoanalytical observations. According to theory, anger directed outward is characteristic of an earlier stage of childhood than is anger directed toward the self or anxiety (conflicts over hostility). The latter two emotions are the result of the acculturation of the child. If the physiological development of the child parallels its psychological development, then we should expect to find that the ratio of nor-adrenalin to adrenalin is higher in infants than in older children. Bernt Hokfelt and G. B. West established that this is indeed the case: at an early age the adrenal medulla has more nor-adrenalin, but later adrenalin becomes dominant.

Paranoid patients show a greater degree of regression to infantile behavior than do patients with depression or anxiety neurosis. And it will be recalled that in our test paranoid patients showed signs of excessive secretion of nor-adrenalin, while depressed and anxious patients exhibited symptoms of adrenalin secretion.

These parallels between psychological and physiological development suggest further studies and some theories for testing. Standing on the shoulders of Cannon and Freud, we have extended our view of human behavior and discovered fertile new fields for exploration.

selection 18 / the biological advantages of emotional motives / Robert Ward Leeper, University of Oregon, and Peter Madison, Swarthmore College

Ever since Charles Darwin published his book, *Expression of the Emotions in Man and Animals,* in 1872, psychologists have granted that emotional responses have certain limited biological advantages. Many animals respond in ways that make them look more dangerous when they are attacked, just as house-cats snarl and make their hair stand on end and so look bigger and stronger. The internal physiological effects of anger, rage, and fear frequently have biological value. A man or animal running away from an enemy can run faster and longer because certain of his emotional processes accelerate his heart beat, drive the blood supply from his digestive organs to the large muscles of the body, and release extra blood sugar, which is a source of energy, from the liver. Physiologists and psychologists have long recognized the advantages in these so-called emergency responses.

This is an instance, however, of the point that we were making near the start of the chapter—that people develop an understanding of relatively tangible matters long before they come to understand other more subtle relationships. Thus, in the present instance, the physiological by-products that appear with such emotional processes are much less important in the whole economy of the organism than is the fact that emotional processes are motives—that they influence the other parts of the *psychological* functioning of the individual in ways that also are characteristic of physiologically-based motives.

Emotional motives have the following four special advantages as compared with physiologically-based motives:

1. *There are advantages in the fact that the emotional motives do not possess the strongly cyclical characteristic so typical of many, though not all, physiologically-based motives.* This cyclical character is appropriate for many physiologically-based motives. Thus, after hunger has been satisfied, it is appropriate that the organism should pass through a period of quiescence before becoming hungry again. In the case of the sex motive, a period of quiescence permits replenishment of the glandular products involved in a renewal of sex activity.

But in matters related to emotional activity, there is typically no

Abridged from Robert Ward Leeper and Peter Madison, *Toward Understanding Human Personalities,* Appleton-Century-Crofts, Inc., New York, 1959, pp. 210–214. Reprinted by permission of the authors and Appleton-Century-Crofts, Inc.

such advantage in this cyclical phenomenon. Thus, if a hen has frightened away one cat that threatened her chicks, this does not mean that she can safely abandon, even for a short period, her readiness to respond in the same way to any other prowling cat. The hen is dealing with needs created by *environmental* factors rather than by any developments within her own body. Consequently, a kind of motivation that may operate continuously for long periods is needed, one that also may remain latent during other long periods merely because, under other environmental conditions, this motivation is not needed.

2. *Emotional motives can be touched off by much more delicate stimuli, and by much more precisely differentiated stimuli, than are required for the arousal of physiologically-based motives.* This is obviously true with regard to situations that are emotionally significant because of past learning. In these cases, it is easy to see that emotional processes can be excited by stimuli as slight as anything that the organism can differentiate perceptually, as in cases where deer have learned to respond with fear to the scent of cougars. But this principle is also seen in cases of unlearned emotional responses. If animals did not have such unlearned emotional responses, they would have to start their learning from some experience in which they actually received physical injuries from an enemy. But with unlearned emotional responses, much slighter cues can operate. Thus, Tinbergen has shown that young goslings will hide when they see a cardboard model with the silhouette of a hawk soaring overhead, but are not disturbed when something with the silhouette of a goose soars above them. Anyone who has observed quail knows that the warning cry of the mother bird causes her young to scatter and "freeze" and remain so quiet that, with their protective coloration, it is almost impossible to find them in the dried leaves and grass, even right at your feet.

3. *Emotional motives constitute the sort of motives that are developed by learning, and they are the ones, consequently, that can be elaborated for the particular circumstances of the given individual's life.* It is important, particularly in the case of the more complex organisms, and outstandingly in the case of man, that motivation should be highly variable from one individual to another. Thus, in a highly specialized civilization, there would be a lot of discontent if it were not possible for different persons to take delight in quite different sorts of vocational activity. It is because of this that the surgeon, the coal miner, and the political leader may each love his own work, despite the enormous differences of activity. Because of their susceptibility to learned modification, emotional motives also get shaped to suit slightly different situations, so that a beekeeper, for instance, can work comfortably with bees under conditions where

it is sensible for him to open up the hive, though he stays adequately motivated *not* to disturb the bees at other times when they would really "give him the works."

4. *Emotional motives have the advantages of operating as positive feedback mechanisms.* Perhaps you have encountered the phenomenon of *positive feedback* that is heard when the loudspeaker of a public-address system is too close to the microphone. The person speaks into the microphone, and the loudspeaker amplifies his voice; the increased sound comes back to the microphone, and is intensified still further. Once such a vicious spiral is started, the howl can get worse and worse, right to the upper limit of sound-production by the system.

The occurrence of such a phenomenon is a nuisance in most physical systems. Therefore, when engineers build complex systems that are intended to operate in self-regulating ways, they build them with a *negative feedback* or *reverse feedback,* instead. In these physical devices, however, there is some supply of energy already present in more or less optimal amount. The only thing that needs to be done is to increase or decrease the utilization of this energy to suit the changing conditions. But an organism is not like that. The organism does not have its different motivational energies already mobilized and pressing for expression. There isn't one "head of steam" that corresponds to "aggressive energy" and another "head of steam" that corresponds to "sex energy." Within the organism, instead, although there are potentialities for arousing any number of emotional processes in very strong form, these potentialities remain latent most of the time. At most moments, the potentially-intense emotional processes are like smouldering fires that have been carefully banked.

It would be wasteful for an organism to function otherwise. Energies would be unnecessarily squandered to maintain a considerable number of different emotional processes at full strength when only one or two were appropriate to the immediate situation. But at the same time it is true that an organism needs to be able to mobilize quickly any one of these energies when it really is relevant. When a deer approaches a water hole, it may be fairly quiet and unfearful at the moment (though probably, as a wild animal, never entirely devoid of some active fear). But when a sound is heard that indicates possible danger, there is a quick focusing of the eyes and of the perceptual processes generally on the spot from which the sound came, rather than on the water ahead. By this focusing the deer sees a cougar or hunter that otherwise would not have been perceived. And this perception will arouse an even more intense emotional response than that stirred up by the original sound.

In such situations we have the essentials of a positive-feedback system. Emotional processes seem to do the very sort of thing that engineers try to avoid in their mechanical devices. Emotional processes are a means—through such successively clarified representational processes, and through the working of reintegrative mechanisms—of quickly developing a strong motive out of what was merely a latent potentiality a moment before.

In each of these four respects, then, we see that emotional processes are not luxuries or frills from the standpoint of the fundamental life-needs of the organism. They sometimes create problems, of course, just as it is true that a person's struggles to obtain the air he needs may cause him to drown, whereas had it not been for this motive, he could have reached the surface before his need for air became too desperate. However, we ought not to derive our general picture of emotional processes only from situations in which emotions work disadvantageously, any more than we should regard fire or winds or rainfall as basically harmful because of the damage they can do. We need to see that, on the contrary, emotional processes are efficient mechanisms for the energizing and regulating of activity with reference to long-range objectives. They are indispensable in complex organisms. Human beings have survived, in the long course of evolution, partly because they are such emotionally sensitive and responsive creatures.

selection 19 / the nature of love / Harry F. Harlow, University of Wisconsin

Love is a wondrous state, deep, tender, and rewarding. Because of its intimate and personal nature it is regarded by some as an improper topic for experimental research. But, whatever our personal feelings may be, our assigned mission as psychologists is to analyze all facets of human and animal behavior into their component variables. So far as love or affection is concerned, psychologists have failed in this mission. The little we know about love does not transcend simple observation, and the little we write about it has been written better by poets and novelists. But of greater concern is the fact that psychologists tend to give progressively less attention to a motive which pervades our entire lives. Psychologists, at least psychologists who write textbooks, not only show no interest in the origin and development of love or affection, but they seem to be unaware of its very existence.

The apparent repression of love by modern psychologists stands in

Abridged from Harry F. Harlow, "The Nature of Love," *American Psychologist*, 13:673–685, 1958. Reprinted by permission of the author and the American Psychological Association. This paper was presented as the address of the President at the sixty-sixth annual convention of the American Psychological Association, Washington, D.C., August 31, 1958.

sharp contrast with the attitude taken by many famous and normal people. The word "love" has the highest reference frequency of any word cited in Bartlett's book of *Familiar Quotations*. It would appear that this emotion has long had a vast interest and fascination for human beings, regardless of the attitude taken by psychologists; but the quotations cited, even by famous and normal people, have a mundane redundancy. These authors and authorities have stolen love from the child and infant and made it the exclusive property of the adolescent and adult.

Thoughtful men, and probably all women, have speculated on the nature of love. From the developmental point of view, the general plan is quite clear: The initial love responses of the human being are those made by the infant to the mother or some mother surrogate. From this intimate attachment of the child to the mother, multiple learned and generalized affectional responses are formed.

Unfortunately, beyond these simple facts we know little about the fundamental variables underlying the formation of affectional responses and little about the mechanisms through which the love of the infant for the mother develops into the multifaceted response patterns characterizing love or affection in the adult. Because of the dearth of experimentation, theories about the fundamental nature of affection have evolved at the level of observation, intuition, and discerning guesswork, whether these have been proposed by psychologists, sociologists, anthropologists, physicians or psychoanalysts.

The position commonly held by psychologists and sociologists is quite clear: The basic motives are, for the most part, the primary drives—particularly hunger, thirst, elimination, pain, and sex—and all other motives, including love or affection, are derived or secondary drives. The mother is associated with the reduction of the primary drives—particularly hunger, thirst, and pain—and through learning, affection or love is derived.

It is entirely reasonable to believe that the mother through association with food may become a secondary-reinforcing agent, but this is an inadequate mechanism to account for the persistence of the infant-maternal ties. There is a spate of researches on the formation of secondary reinforcers to hunger and thirst reduction. There can be no question that almost any external stimulus can become a secondary reinforcer if properly associated with tissue-need reduction, but the fact remains that this redundant literature demonstrates unequivocally that such derived drives suffer relatively rapid experimental extinction. Contrariwise, human affection does not extinguish when the mother ceases to have intimate association with the drives in question. Instead, the affectional ties to the mother show a lifelong, unrelenting persistence and, even more surprising, widely expanding generality.

Oddly enough, one of the few psychologists who took a position counter to modern psychological dogma was John B. Watson, who believed that love was an innate emotion elicited by cutaneous stimulation of the erogenous zones. But experimental psychologists, with their peculiar propensity to discover facts that are not true, brushed this theory aside by demonstrating that the human neonate had no differentiable emotions, and they established a fundamental psychological law that prophets are without honor in their own profession.

The psychoanalysts have concerned themselves with the problem of the nature of the development of love in the neonate and infant, using ill and aging human beings as subjects. They have discovered the overwhelming importance of the breast and related this to the oral erotic tendencies developed at an age preceding their subjects' memories. Their theories range from a belief that the infant has an innate need to achieve and suckle at the breast to beliefs not unlike commonly accepted psychological theories. There are exceptions, as seen in the recent writings of John Bowlby, who attributes importance not only to food and thirst satisfaction, but also to "primary object-clinging," a need for intimate physical contact, which is initially associated with the mother.

As far as I know, there exists no direct experimental analysis of the relative importance of the stimulus variables determining the affectional or love responses in the neonatal and infant primate. Unfortunately, the human neonate is a limited experimental subject for such researches because of his inadequate motor capabilities. By the time the human infant's motor responses can be precisely measured, the antecedent determining conditions cannot be defined, having been lost in a jumble and jungle of confounded variables.

Many of these difficulties can be resolved by the use of the neonatal and infant macaque monkey as the subject for the analysis of basic affectional variables. It is possible to make precise measurements in this primate beginning at two to ten days of age, depending upon the maturational status of the individual animal at birth. The macaque infant differs from the human infant in that the monkey is more mature at birth and grows more rapidly; but the basic responses relating to affection, including nursing, contact, clinging, and even visual and auditory exploration, exhibit no fundamental differences in the two species. Even the development of perception, fear, frustration, and learning capability follows very similar sequences in rhesus monkeys and human children.

Three years' experimentation before we started our studies on affection gave us experience with the neonatal monkey. We had separated more than 60 of these animals from their mothers 6 to 12 hours after birth and suckled them on tiny bottles. The infant mortality was only a small fraction of what would have obtained had we let the monkey mothers raise their infants. Our bottle-fed babies were healthier and heavier than monkey-mother-reared infants. We know that we are better monkey mothers than are real monkey mothers thanks to synthetic diets, vitamins, iron extracts, penicillin, chloromycetin, 5% glucose, and constant, tender, loving care.

During the course of these studies we noticed that the laboratory-raised babies showed strong attachment to the cloth pads (folded gauze diapers) which were used to cover the hardware-cloth floors of their cages. The infants clung to these pads and engaged in violent temper tantrums when the pads were removed and replaced for sanitary reasons. Such contact-need or responsiveness had been reported previously by Gertrude van Wagenen for the monkey and by Thomas McCulloch and George Haslerud for the chimpanzee and is reminiscent of the devotion often exhibited by human infants to their pillows, blankets, and soft, cuddly stuffed toys.

We had also discovered during some allied observational studies that a baby monkey raised on a bare wire-mesh cage floor survives with difficulty, if at all, during the first five days of life. If a wire-mesh cone is introduced, the baby does better; and, if the cone is covered with terry cloth, husky, healthy, happy babies evolve. It takes more than a baby and a box to make a normal monkey. We were impressed by the possibility that, above and beyond the bubbling fountain of breast or bottle, contact comfort might be a very important variable in the development of the infant's affection for the mother.

At this point we decided to study the development of affectional responses of neonatal and infant monkeys to an artificial, inanimate mother, and so we built a surrogate mother which we hoped and believed would be a good surrogate mother. In devising this surrogate mother we were dependent neither upon the capriciousness of evolutionary processes nor upon mutations produced by chance radioactive fallout. Instead, we designed the mother surrogate in terms of modern human-engineering principles. We produced a perfectly proportioned, streamlined body stripped of unnecessary bulges and appendices. Redundancy in the surrogate mother's system was avoided by reducing the number of breasts from two to one and placing this unibreast in an upper-thoracic, sagittal position, thus maximizing the natural and known perceptual-motor capabilities of the infant operator. The surrogate was made from a block of wood, covered with sponge rubber, and sheathed in tan cotton terry cloth. A light bulb behind her radiated heat. The result was a mother, soft, warm, and tender, a mother with infinite patience, a mother available twenty-four hours a day, a mother that never scolded her infant and never struck or bit her baby in anger. Furthermore, we designed a mother-machine with maximal maintenance efficiency since failure of any system or function could be resolved by the simple substitution of black boxes and new component parts. It is our opinion that we engineered a very superior monkey mother, although this position is not held universally by the monkey fathers.

Before beginning our initial experiment we also designed and constructed a second mother surrogate, a surrogate in which we deliberately built less than the maximal capability for contact comfort. This surrogate mother is illustrated in Figure 1. She is made of wire-mesh, a substance entirely adequate to provide postural support and nursing capability, and she is warmed by radiant heat. Her body differs in no essential way from that of the cloth mother surrogate other than in the quality of the contact comfort which she can supply.

In our initial experiment, the dual mother-surrogate condition, a cloth mother and a wire mother were placed in different cubicles attached to the infant's living cage as shown in Figure 1. For four newborn monkeys the cloth mother lactated and the wire mother did not; and, for the other four, this condition was reversed. In either condition the infant received all its milk through the mother surrogate as soon as it was able to maintain itself in this way, a capability achieved within two or three days except in the case of very immature infants. Supplementary feedings were given until the milk intake from the mother surrogate was adequate. Thus, the experiment was designed as a test of the relative importance of the variables of contact comfort and nursing comfort. During the first 14 days of life the

Fig. 1   Wire and cloth mother surrogates.

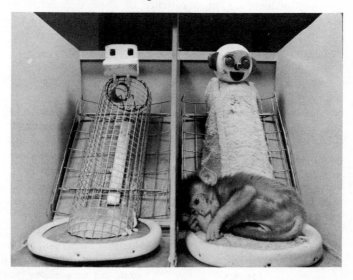

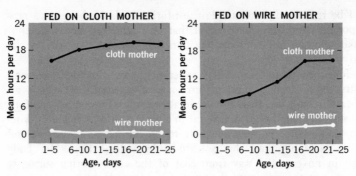

Fig. 2   Time spent on cloth and wire mother surrogates.

monkey's cage floor was covered with a heating pad wrapped in a folded gauze diaper, and thereafter the cage floor was bare. The infants were always free to leave the heating pad or cage floor to contact either mother, and the time spent on the surrogate mothers was automatically recorded. Figure 2 shows the total time spent on the cloth and wire mothers under the two conditions of feeding. These data make it obvious that contact comfort is a variable of overwhelming importance in the development of affectional responses, whereas lactation is a variable of negligible importance. With age and opportunity to learn, subjects with the lactating wire mother showed decreasing responsiveness to her and increasing responsiveness to the nonlactating cloth mother, a finding completely contrary to any interpretation of derived drive in which the mother-form becomes conditioned to hunger-thirst reduction. The persistence of these differential responses throughout 165 consecutive days of testing is evident in Figure 3.

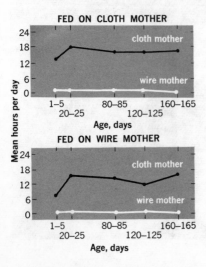

Fig. 3   Long-term contact time on cloth and wire mother surrogates.

One control group of neonatal monkeys was raised on a single wire mother, and a second control group was raised on a single cloth mother. There were no differences between these two groups in amount of milk ingested or in weight gain. The only difference between the groups lay in the composition of the feces, the softer stools of the wire-mother infants suggesting psychosomatic involvement. The wire mother is biologically adequate but psychologically inept.

We were not surprised to discover that contact comfort was an important basic affectional or love variable, but we did not expect it to overshadow so completely the variable of nursing; indeed, the disparity is so great as to suggest that the primary function of nursing as an affectional variable is that of insuring frequent and intimate body contact of the infant with the mother. Certainly, man cannot live by milk alone. Love is an emotion that does not need to be bottle- or spoon-fed, and we may be sure that there is nothing to be gained by giving lip service to love.

A charming lady once heard me describe these experiments; and, when I subsequently talked to her, her face brightened with sudden insight: "Now I know what's wrong with me," she said, "I'm just a wire mother." Perhaps she was lucky. She might have been a wire wife.

We believe that contact comfort has long served the animal kingdom as a motivating agent for affectional responses. Since at the present time we have no experimental data to substantiate this position, we supply information which must be accepted, if at all, on the basis of face validity.

One function of the real mother, human or subhuman, and presumably of a mother surrogate, is to provide a haven of safety for the infant in times of fear and danger. The frightened or ailing child clings to its mother, not its father; and this selective responsiveness in times of distress, disturbance, or danger may be used as a measure of the strength of affectional bonds. We have tested this kind of differential responsiveness by presenting to the infants in their cages, in the presence of the two mothers, various fear-producing stimuli. A typical response to a fear stimulus is shown in Figure 4, and the data on differential responsiveness are presented in Figure 5. It is apparent that the cloth mother is highly preferred over the wire one, and this differential selectivity is enhanced by age and experience. In this situation, the variable of nursing appears to be of absolutely no importance: the infant consistently seeks the soft mother surrogate regardless of nursing condition.

Similarly, the mother or mother surrogate provides its young with a source of security, and this role or function is seen with special clarity when mother and child are in a strange situation. At the present time we have completed tests for this relationship on four

Fig. 4 Typical response to cloth mother surrogate in fear test.

of our eight baby monkeys assigned to the dual mother-surrogate condition by introducing them for three minutes into the strange environment of a room measuring six feet by six feet by six feet (also called the "open-field test") and containing multiple stimuli known to elicit curiosity-manipulatory responses in baby monkeys. The subjects were placed in this situation twice a week for eight weeks with no mother surrogate present during alternate sessions and the cloth mother present during the others. A cloth diaper was always available as one of the stimuli throughout all sessions. After one or two adaptation sessions, the infants always rushed to the mother surrogate when she was present and clutched her, rubbed their bodies against her, and frequently manipulated her body and face. After a few additional sessions, the infants began to use the mother surrogate as a source of security, a base of operations. They would explore and manipulate a stimulus and then return to the mother before adventuring again into the strange new world. The behavior of these infants was quite different when the mother was absent from the room. Frequently they would freeze in a crouched position, as illustrated in Figure 6. Emotionality indices such as vocalization, crouching, rock-

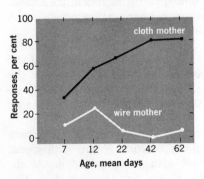

Fig. 5 Differential responsiveness in fear tests.

Fig. 6 *Response in the open-field test in the absence of the mother surrogate.*

ing, and sucking increased sharply. Total emotionality score was cut in half when the mother was present. In the absence of the mother some of the experimental monkeys would rush to the center of the room where the mother was customarily placed and then run rapidly from object to object, screaming and crying all the while. Continuous, frantic clutching of their bodies was very common, even when not in the crouching position. These monkeys frequently contacted and clutched the cloth diaper, but this action never pacified them. The same behavior occurred in the presence of the wire mother. No difference between the cloth-mother-fed and wire-mother-fed infants was demonstrated under either condition.

We have already described the group of four control infants that had never lived in the presence of any mother surrogate and had demonstrated no sign of affection or security in the presence of the cloth mothers introduced in test sessions. When these infants reached the age of 250 days, cubicles containing both a cloth mother and a wire mother were attached to their cages. There was no lactation in these mothers, for the monkeys were on a solid-food diet. The initial reaction of the monkeys to the alterations was one of extreme disturbance. All the infants screamed violently and made repeated attempts to escape the cage whenever the door was opened. They kept a maximum distance from the mother surrogates and exhibited a considerable amount of rocking and crouching behavior, indicative of emotionality. Our first thought was that the critical period for the development of maternally directed affection had passed and that these macaque children were doomed to live as affectional orphans. Fortunately, these behaviors continued for only 12 to 48 hours and then gradually ebbed, changing from indifference to active contact on, and exploration of, the surrogates. The home-cage behavior of these control monkeys slowly became similar to that of the animals raised with the mother surrogates from birth. Their manipulation and play on the cloth mother became progressively more vigorous to the point of actual mutilation, particularly during the morning after the cloth mother had been given her daily change of terry covering. The control subjects were now actively running to the cloth mother when frightened and had to be coaxed from her to be taken from the cage for formal testing.

Objective evidence of these changing behaviors is given in Figure 7, which plots the amount of time these infants spent on the mother surrogates. Within 10 days mean contact time is approximately nine hours, and this measure remains relatively constant throughout the next 30 days. Consistent with the results on the subjects reared from birth with dual mothers, these late-adopted infants spent less than one and one-half hours per day in contact with the wire mothers, and this activity level was relatively constant throughout the test sessions. Although the maximum time that the control monkeys spent on the cloth mother was only about half that spent by the original dual mother-surrogate group, we cannot be sure that this discrepancy is a function of differential early experience. The control monkeys were about three months older when the mothers were attached to their cages than the experimental animals had been when their mothers were removed and the retention tests begun. Thus, we do not know what the amount of contact would be for a 250-day-old animal raised from birth with surrogate mothers. Nevertheless, the magnitude of the differences and the fact that the contact-time curves for the mothered-from-birth infants had remained constant for almost 150

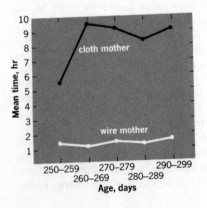

Fig. 7 *Differential time spent on cloth and wire mother surrogates by monkeys started at 250 days of age.*

days suggest that early experience with the mother is a variable of measurable importance.

That the control monkeys develop affection or love for the cloth mother when she is introduced into the cage at 250 days of age cannot be questioned. There is every reason to believe, however, that this interval of delay depresses the intensity of the affectional response below that of the infant monkeys that were surrogate-mothered from birth onward. In interpreting these data it is well to remember that the control monkeys had had continuous opportunity to observe and hear other monkeys housed in adjacent cages and that they had had limited opportunity to view and contact surrogate mothers in the test situations, even though they did not exploit the opportunities.

During the last two years we have observed the behavior of two infants raised by their own mothers. Love for the real mother and love for the surrogate mother appear to be very similar. The baby macaque spends many hours a day clinging to its real mother. If away from the mother when frightened, it rushes to her and in her presence shows comfort and composure. As far as we can observe, the infant monkey's affection for the real mother is strong, but no stronger than that of the experimental monkey for the surrogate cloth mother, and the security that the infant gains from the presence of the real mother is no greater than the security it gains from a cloth surrogate. Next year we hope to put this problem to final, definitive, experimental test. But, whether the mother is real or a cloth surrogate, there does develop a deep and abiding bond between mother and child. In one case it may be the call of the wild and in the other the McCall of civilization, but in both cases there is "togetherness."

In spite of the importance of contact comfort, there is reason to believe that other variables of measurable importance will be discovered. Postural support may be such a variable, and it has been suggested that, when we build arms into the mother surrogate, 10 is the minimal number required to provide adequate child care. Rocking motion may be such a variable, and we are comparing rocking and stationary mother surrogates and inclined planes. The differential responsiveness to cloth mother and cloth-covered inclined plane suggests that clinging as well as contact is an affectional variable of importance. Sounds, particularly natural, maternal sounds, may operate as either unlearned or learned affectional variables. Visual responsiveness may be such a variable, and it is possible that some semblance of visual imprinting may develop in the neonatal monkey. There are indications that this becomes a variable of importance during the course of infancy through some maturational process.

Since we can measure neonatal and infant affectional responses to mother surrogates, and since we know they are strong and persisting, we are in a position to assess the effects of feeding and contactual schedules; consistency and inconsistency in the mother surrogates; and early, intermediate, and late maternal deprivation. Again, we have here a family of problems of fundamental interest and theoretical importance.

If the researches completed and proposed make a contribution, I shall be grateful: but I have also given full thought to possible practical applications. The socioeconomic demands of the present and the threatened socioeconomic demands of the future have led the American woman to displace, or threaten to displace, the American man in science and industry. If this process continues, the problem of proper child-rearing practices faces us with startling clarity. It is cheering in view of this trend to realize that the American male is physically endowed with all the really essential equipment to compete with the American female on equal terms in one essential activity: the rearing of infants. We now know that women in the working classes are not needed in the home because of their primary mammalian capabilities; and it is possible that in the foreseeable future neonatal nursing will not be regarded as a necessity, but as a luxury—to use Veblen's term —a form of conspicuous consumption limited perhaps to the upper classes. But whatever course history may take, it is comforting to know that we are now in contact with the nature of love.

selection 20 / emotional riches and emotional poverty / Robert Ward Leeper, University of Oregon, and Peter Madison, Swarthmore College

We are likely to react with surprised disbelief to the idea that modern living may often leave us emotionally starved. We so habitually evaluate the adequacy of a culture in terms of its industrial development or of material wealth that we are sure anyone who disputes this self-evident goodness must have some peculiar and cranky streak in his nature making him want to belittle what we have achieved.

One does not need to belittle the material accomplishments of our society (incidentally, these are *not* our personal accomplishments, yours and mine) to see that there can be intense motivational satisfactions in ways of living that look extremely meager to sophisticated eyes. Nor do we need naively to urge man to return to the life of Rousseau's noble savage. In fact, in primitive life, the very lack of

Abridged from Robert Ward Leeper and Peter Madison, *Toward Understanding Human Personalities*, Appleton-Century-Crofts, Inc., New York, 1959, pp. 249–267. Reprinted by permission of the authors and Appleton-Century-Crofts, Inc.

material resources must often have resulted in an existence dominated by fears and bitter frustrations. Our material achievements are not to be depreciated. They conceivably can yet give us the means of a life richer, even in most emotional respects, than any primitive could ever have known.

To say that such a thing is possible is not the same as conceding, however, that we have achieved this result so far. Great numbers of people brought up in modern civilized surroundings are showing, either directly or indirectly, that something is wrong.

Some indirect expressions of this feeling of emotional poverty

Right now a lot more effort might be directed toward meeting this need for emotionally rich experience if more people saw clearly, and admitted, that there is something lacking in modern life. But, most often, the feeling of lack does not express itself in clearly conscious form. The discontent shows up more in indirect ways. It may be worthwhile looking into some of the indirect forms that emotional poverty may take. Let us examine six of these, even though this list is surely far from complete.

Pseudo-hungers for food as an expression of emotional poverty One of the simplest indirect expressions of emotional poverty is a craving for food that the individual does not really need and would not eat were it not for his emotional hungers. Thus, one college teacher observed this about himself:

It's not very long after Jane is gone that I often get intensely hungry. I wander around the house for a while, maybe, and get my desk organized for an evening's work. Sometimes, then, I feel suddenly tired. Other times I get hungry for cornflakes and milk. It's absurd. I've had a good dinner; but that insistent craving starts, and I can't get to work until I pour myself a huge bowl of the stuff and eat it while arranging my work. Once I get started, the work carries itself along, and time passes quickly. But, particularly if the work is a bit of a chore, or something I can't too well see my way through, I'm likely to get hungry, no matter how recently I've eaten.

Here you have only one case, but what it reports is typical of a good many persons—in short, it is a good instance of an expression of emotional deprivation.

An exorbitantly increased demand for closer human relationships as one effect of emotional poverty Emotional hungers may find an outlet through our dependence upon and demand for more satisfaction from our close human relationships than we can reasonably expect. In marriage and in other close relationships, some people tend to want others almost to revere them and to share with them all their ideals, ideas, and interests. Such a demand is exceedingly egotistical, not wholly unlike that of a small child who feels that his mother should think only of him. In all soberness we have no right even to imagine that any other person would respect us on some matters, love us for some reasons, or share some of our activities, because each of us is complex and each of us inevitably will differ somewhat from every other person. One wonders if it is not some unfulfilled emotional hunger on our part that makes us expect more from a marriage or from any other relationship than it can be expected to yield except under the rarest circumstances—except when both persons involved are of the most unusual fineness and when their natures are complementary in some fullest sense.

Overdependence on sexual satisfactions as a consequence of emotional poverty No one would think of denying that the sex motive is a strong one simply in its own right. The satisfactions of sex are vital in themselves, just as the satisfaction of hunger is vital in itself. Given its proper development and place in relation to all the other components of a full life, the sex motive becomes part of an enduring and profound love-relationship. As such it is part of a complex of motives that is anything but simple.

Because the sex motive has a strong physiological basis, it is a rare person who, as an adolescent and adult, has not depended to some considerable extent either on sexual relations with others or, if his upbringing and social ideals or his situation have made that sort of expression inappropriate, on autoerotic satisfactions. One fact tending to work in this direction is that, unlike many other motives such as the enjoyment of music that requires long training to develop adequately, the sex motive provides intensely pleasurable effects even when the richer forms of satisfaction of this motive—its fusion with the rich emotional elements of shared lives—have not been achieved.

However, even when all this is recognized, it must be definitely recorded that the sex motive is not as imperiously strong as it sometimes seems to be when its expression occurs under those conditions we have termed conditions of emotional poverty, or when it is accompanied by fear, sense of guilt, or some other intense and negative motive.

Many psychotherapists have come to the conclusion that most of what appears as excessively strong sexual motivation in human beings must be similarly explained. Karen Horney was expressing the views of many of such workers when she wrote as follows:[1]

. . . just as "all is not gold that glitters," so also "all is not sexuality that looks like it." A great part of what appears as sexuality has in reality very little to do with it, but is an expression of the desire for reassurance. If this is not taken into consideration one is bound to overestimate the role of sexuality.

The individual whose sexual needs are enhanced under the unrecognized

[1] Karen Horney, *The Neurotic Personality of Our Time*, W. W. Norton & Company, Inc., New York, 1937, pp. 157–159. Reprinted by permission of the publisher.

stress of anxiety is inclined naïvely to ascribe the intensity of his sexual needs to his innate temperament, or to the fact that he is free from conventional taboos . . . an individual who needs sexuality as an outlet for the sake of allaying anxiety will be particularly incapable of enduring any abstinence, even of short duration.

. . . a great deal of sexual activity today is more an outlet for psychic tensions than a genuine sexual drive, and is therefore to be regarded more as a sedative than as genuine sexual enjoyment or happiness. . . .

It is one of the great achievements of Freud that he contributed so much to giving sexuality its due importance. In detail, however, [within psychoanalytic views] many phenomena are accepted as sexual which are really the expression of complex neurotic conditions, mainly expressions of the neurotic need for affection.

It is not surprising, then, that the research of Kinsey on sex behavior in human beings should show, in a somewhat similar vein, that the socially and economically underprivileged classes in our society are more sexually active than is, for example, the professional class. The difference may not lie in the greater virility of lower class groups, or in some supposed repression of sex in professional groups, but in the over-all differences with respect to emotional satisfactions that their everyday lives provide.

The powerful and insistent demands for material comforts and material products that characterize our society may be an expression of emotional deprivation in other respects Many persons who study our society come to feel that our interest in the material products of our technology far exceeds their value as the means to a fuller life. Material goods, they feel, come to be wanted with an irrational intensity bewildering to the detached onlooker.

There is, for instance, our tremendous itch to own the newest, biggest, most powerful, and showiest car, an urge that goes far beyond any simple need for going places. One automobile executive remarked that if sales appeal were the sole basis for deciding what next year's car was to be like, it would have 500 horsepower and be made of solid chrome.

No one denies that a car is what most people need for getting quickly to work; it may allow a family to live in beautiful country though the breadwinner works a long distance away. It is wonderful for a trip to the coast or mountains on weekends, for vacation exploring. Going up 12,000 feet over Trail-Ridge Road in Rocky Mountain National Park, or over Tioga Pass in Yosemite, can be a never-to-be-forgotten thrill—an experience alive with adventure and beauty. But why must one have a car loaded with expensive chrome? Why must one have 285 horsepower rather than a mere 250 or 150? Why a new car every second year?

Often it seems that people are misled in judging how much emotional value they can get from the ownership of material goods—

cars and other things—acquired at great sacrifice. Some questions need looking into. Is it true, for example, that we especially enjoy and like people who own luxury homes and big cars? Do we feel any unusual sense of warm human interest in them when we are with them? Can it make a difference in the quality of friendship they extend to us if we arrive in the latest and biggest model of a car?

Or do we remember and like those people who are most human, friendly, and interested in us, and who are unpretentious, and warmly and simply welcoming and hospitable? Isn't it likely that if we go in for exaggerated material ostentation, it will arouse envy and competitive counterreactions rather than the kind of humanness we really want from others—despite the reactions that advertisers lead us to feel we will surely get if we arrive in a Cadillac?

Here, it would seem, is a fine instance of how basic, unfilled human hungers for companionship and appreciation, for being wanted, liked, valued, for feeling close to others, get sidetracked and replaced by a need for material things that we want so desperately as supposed means of gratifying these basic desires. But somehow the supposed means turn out to separate us even further from the kind of fundamental human responsiveness we want from others.

Much interest in violence (directly or through phantasy) may be an expression of emotional poverty   It is sobering to look at the activities of many teen-age gangs in cities such as New York and Philadelphia. One news item told about a teen-age youth, the leader of a street gang, who had shot and killed an innocent boy. He had mistaken the boy for the leader of a rival teen-age gang that his group were fighting over the question of whether the other group could wear jackets colored like their own. As he was led away by police, a group of teen-agers followed him, cheering him loudly. The girls in the group shouted, "We love you, Tarzan!" Several days later they assembled at the funeral of the innocent victim and booed and threatened the police there, loudly defending the act of their leader. That he had killed someone added to his stature in their eyes. Another report told of an unbelievable incident in which some boys drenched a child with gasoline and set fire to their screaming victim. One youth, arrested for knifing a perfectly innocent person, was asked why he had done such a horrible thing. He replied that he wanted to feel the thrill of his knife going through bone! Unbelievable? One need only read the newspaper reports to find similar incidents every week among teen-age gangs in our cities.

It may even be that war appeals to us because we are emotionally starved in peacetime   Many writers have pointed out that it is not the whole truth to say we fear and hate war; in many ways we like it. Some of them have concluded, as Freud did, that man is equipped with a fundamentally aggressive need that is almost bound at times to find an outlet in war if it cannot be successfully drained off by less horrible substitutes. Another possibility may be, though, that wars come partly from other indirect emotional sources. In war some men attain their deepest emotional experiences—in heroism, generosity, companionship, courage, and self-sacrifice. One need only read Winston Churchill's account of the "finest hour" of the British people subjected to Hitler's all-out bombardment of London in World War II to realize what wars can bring in the way of emotional values that continue to be celebrated in movies and fiction for long afterwards. When people so docilely support the aggressive military programs of their countries, it may not be entirely from a feeling of helplessness in the face of such a waste of treasure, but rather because the idea of a struggle for national survival has its positive emotional appeal, particularly in view of the dearth of meaning in much of peacetime existence. If so, the transforming of modern life to make it emotionally more rich is not something of merely individual concern, but is one of the major social needs of our modern world!

It would be possible to mention a number of other indications of emotional poverty in modern life. The high frequency of alcoholism may be one such indicator. The increasing reliance on cocktail parties as a means of making social life "sufficiently interesting" may be another. Sensationalistic newspapers may be still another.

The problem is extensive and serious enough, at any rate, that it is well worth our asking about the factors that produce emotional poverty in modern life and about the resources that we might use to foster emotionally rich experiences, instead.

Factors productive of emotional poverty

Conformity pressures In a country founded in part on a belief in rugged individualism, it is a curious fact that, with every passing year, it seems to become more difficult to be one's own individual self. It is commonly pointed out that we have been moving rapidly toward an "organizational" society where the individual tends to become lost in the large-scale unit such as a corporation, union, bureaucratic government, university, or church. The structure of such organizations is designed to meet the goals of the group, and before he knows it the individual finds himself falling in line with group pressures regardless of whether it is in his own fundamental interest to do so or not.

The young executive may want to live in New England where he grew up and where he deeply enjoys living, but he knows he has to take the offered transfer to Kansas if his career is not to be blocked. He wants to spend his evenings and week ends with his wife and children, but instead brings home a brief case full of work in order to meet the pressures that come down on him from above. He enjoys good literature and the theater, but the circle of associates who hold the reins to his future favor evenings of canasta, bridge, and social drinking. He dislikes parties, but knows that not to be seen at the organizational gatherings would be fatal.

The scientist is subject to the same forces. We may have always thought that research flourishes in proportion as the individual genius is free and that the fundamental premise of the laboratory is that the inquirer must be his own judge of what he considers the most promising line of work. But it is the relatively rare scientist who can do just what he wants. He too must conform to views of the large foundation or government bureau as to what deserves research funds. Too often our scientists find themselves offered large grants to work on something considered valuable by someone else but are unable to get a few thousand dollars for research on their own ideas.

These influences tend to dry up the wells of rich emotional living. It is the essence of such full living that the particular nature of each person and his interests serve as the basis for decision in choosing what he should do or not do. This does not mean that we are each to develop without contact or influence from others. But it does mean that we must have freedom to be attracted to this or that work or person in accord with the character of our own selves, rather than according to the dictates of conformity to an external value-standard set up by authority.

Blue-ribbon motivation and emotional poverty The following conversation was reported by a father of a girl who was near the end of her first grade in school:

"Daddy," she said, "you have to get me some books that I can read myself."

The father, pleased at such an early interest in reading, smiled benignly, "Well, if you like reading that well, we'll certainly have to get you some books."

"Yes," little Marguerite went on, "Dorothy's already got five stars on her reading chart, and I haven't got any yet."

"Reading chart? Stars? What's that got to do with wanting books to read?"

"Well, you see Daddy, I'm in the fast reading group, along with Dorothy Harlan, Sally Evans, and Jeanie Scott—those three are the best readers—and they're in our 'sharp eye' group, which is the best in the first grade. This week the teacher put up a big chart on the wall. She said that now that we could read, we would all have to read books on our own, outside of class. Everytime we read a book, we tell her, and she marks another star by our name. Dorothy gets two or three stars every day, and I haven't got a one yet."

While this is a schoolroom example, the practice of giving recognition to those who are to be considered first in any activity is not limited to child education. In our culture the question too often is: "Are you *first*? Are you the *top* in your field? Are you the *best* there is?"

This is "blue-ribbon motivation." The character of the work itself, its interest for you, its importance to society, are all secondary, or not even asked about. The only question is whether, by some external, tangible criterion, you have, in some sense, won first, or at least ranked high, in competition against the rest of the field. To some extent, it doesn't even matter too much what the competition is about. It may be for making the best pie at the fair or the best model of a nineteenth-century sailing ship, for being president of the largest manufacturing plant in the whole country; or it may be that you came in first in a hamburger-eating contest.

Throughout our whole society it is remarkable to what extent such extrinsic, tacked-on, blue-ribbon evaluation is the main basis for undertaking what people do. Listen, sometime, to parents talking about their children who are away at the university. You will find them telling of their son's or daughter's being elected to class presidency, or some club presidency, or being on the honor roll, or getting a prize for being the best freshman engineering student, or what not. How rare it is, instead, to hear a parent rejoice because Mary or Ronnie has a brand new area of interest that fills her or his letters home— just that, and no blue ribbon!

It is very hard, in our society, to continue to like doing something for itself, for its intrinsic merits. Such an interest is regarded as an indulgence. Even hobbies too often become competitive. Sometimes we allow art to become an intrinsic interest, providing it is understood to be distinctly amateurish. But, most of us are a little mystified by the person who says he is doing something merely because it is interesting. He doesn't make money at it, he isn't very good at it, but he likes it—something surely a little odd about such a fellow!

Oversatiation of major interests   Pressures to conform and to succeed have another insidious effect. Even when they do not keep us from pursuing our major interests, they tend to produce an excessive concentration on one single activity and tend to have corrosive effects on the emotional satisfactions inherent in this activity.

Professional activities tend to be self-chosen, and when a person has gone into science, teaching, business, or the ministry as something he preferred to do above everything else in life, it is hard to imagine that doing it could have harmful side effects. In fact, if such activities were limited to a 40-hour week, they wouldn't. But whereas the 40-hour week is standard in working-class lives, the professional and business-managerial groups in our society are fortunate if they have less than a 60-hour or 65-hour week.

Any mother of three or four little children can tell you about satiation effects, though she may not call it by that name. For, in our contemporary kind of servantless middle-class society, where families live long distances from any relatives who could help, and where the husband typically is gone from breakfast time until the children's bedtime, the mother may find that she has spent well over 80 hours per week in caring for her children and running her home.

She loves her children. But still it is true that any activity, when engaged in too persistently, tends to lose its interest, except when a person has unusual emotional resources.

The neglect and belittling of concrete perceptual experiences is another source of emotional poverty in our culture Modern Western society is highly advanced in technology and scientific understanding. Our culture has laid stress upon abstract knowledge and standardization. These things have some real emotional value for us, and they are not solely the servants of material ends. But they fall far short of serving our emotional needs in a full way. Some of our emotional experience must spring from things around us that impinge directly, immediately, concretely upon us, that are perceived as having color, warmth, and vitality and are likely to be down-to-earth—as the play of color and form in the fireplace, the feel of the winds, and skies, the alternation of lights and shade in a forest, being surrounded with friends.

There is even a lot of tacit disapproval of living in the present in our middle-class culture. It is as if we had some leftovers from past religious prohibitions against investing too heavily in present earthly pleasures. Of course, we need abstractions, we need to have a future orientation, and so on, else we would be a nation of sensualists bent only on immediate pleasures. But we also ought to be able to shuck off regularly all these necessaries and immerse ourselves in fuller realities and concrete joys of life.

Emotional poverty may spring from the failure to develop the neural mechanisms for some satisfactions It is amazing how we seem to assume that our children will grow, without any special help on the part of the older generation, into adults who will have the motivational mechanisms for a resourceful and satisfying adult life. Here is the family of another vacationer whom one of the writers had a chance to observe:

They were a family of three staying in a cottage among the mountains for several weeks. The father was a college professor. He and his wife were never seen outside their cottage except as they emerged in order to get into their car periodically, drive into town, and back again.

On the first day, their 11-year-old boy appeared outside carrying three toy rifles, a cartridge belt, and two cap pistols. Each day he appeared, armed to the teeth, and proceeded to play, as best he could, with his guns.

Across the road there was an inviting-looking livery where even small children could learn to ride horses. There were plenty of fishing streams nearby, a lake, beautiful trails. Never once did the father take his boy out to sample any of these interesting activities. The boy happened to be playing among rocks that would have been fascinating to collect and study, with trees and flowers around that fairly begged to be observed in their beauty. The general scenery was awe-inspiring, or so it seemed until perhaps we chanced to remember that it isn't the eyes that see, but the habits of the beholder. As far as we, his neighbors, could see, those five guns were the sole interest that boy had.

What will such a boy be able to find deeply satisfying at age 30 or 40? What is he prepared for except to sit and watch some of those 588 killings and other crimes that the National Association for Better Radio and Television workers tallied in one week of watching seven TV stations?

How are people to be made less blind to their responsibilities for helping their children to develop, to *grow*, psychologically? Rich positive motives do not simply unfold by themselves without somebody's making the effort to care about them, to implant and foster them. The development of strong and diversified motives is one of society's main tasks and it requires stupendous efforts in comparison with what we as a people have done in the past.

CHAPTER 5 ✺ FRUSTRATION AND CONFLICT ✺

As a result of continued interactions with his environment, the individual learns to value and to want to obtain a wide variety of objects, activities, and symbols. When the possibility of attaining these goals is temporarily or permanently blocked, we speak of frustration. Common barriers to goal attainment are restrictions imposed by authorities, restricted socioeconomic opportunities, and inadequate personal ability. Since our wants are so diverse and heterogeneous, it is understandable that these wants often compete and are in conflict with each other. Such motivational conflict constitutes an especially important source of frustration. Whatever the source, frustration always involves an increase in emotionality, typically an arousal of anger, and fear or anxiety. Extensive investigations of experimentally induced conflicts in lower animals have been performed by Dr. Neal E. Miller and his colleagues at Yale University. His most recent experiments have focused on the effects of certain drugs in modifying the fear-motivated behavior resulting from approach-avoidance conflicts. Dr. Miller first demonstrated that sodium amytal appeared to have fear-reducing effects on rats similar to its effects on human beings. After establishing this basis for generalizing his results, he attempted to determine more precisely the mechanisms of the apparent fear-reducing property of the drug. In addition to his specific findings, the experimental program as a whole illustrates "a type of work which is needed on a variety of selected drugs each of which has well established, but different, psychological effects on the human subject."

So far we have indicated only one component of reactions to frustration—the emotional component. In Selection 22 Dr. S. Stansfeld Sargent outlines a hypothesis about the behavior resulting from frustration which attempts to take into account several additional determinants of the overt response. He states that the internal emotional response is the first stage in the reaction sequence; in fact, without the emotional reaction it does not seem meaningful to infer that frustration has occurred. The specific kind of emotion which occurs depends on how the person perceives the situation, especially his perception of the source of the frustration. Understanding of the overt response to frustration must also take into account the habits which the individual has built up in reacting to previous frustrations. It is at this stage of the sequence that learned mechanisms of defense come into play. The last stage, overt behavior, is determined by interaction of the intervening organismic factors of perception, emotion, and habit.

If it is necessary to take into account the processes of frustration and conflict in order to understand normal human behavior, it is even more necessary for the understanding of that portion of each person's behavior which could be described as neurotic. Although neurosis itself will be considered in more detail in Chapter 13, we can at this point make use of Dr. Karen Horney's insight into neurotic conflicts to help us understand conflicts in general. Horney emphasizes that the really important conflicts are generated by our interactions with other people, especially our parents or parent substitutes. From them we learn our basic attitudes about the world. If, as children, our interactions with parents are characterized by rejection, lack of warmth, inconsistency, etc., then a feeling of basic anxiety is generated. The child becomes hostile, but because the expression of hostility will cause further rejection, he tends to project this hostility out on to the external world and comes to perceive other people as basically untrustworthy. He thus feels isolated and estranged from others. The child may attempt to cope with this threatening environment in three ways: he "may move toward people, against them, or away from them. . . . In each of these attitudes one of the elements involved in basic anxiety is overemphasized: helplessness in the first, hostility in the second, and isolation in the third." In the normal person these three tendencies complement each other for effective behavior. In the neurotic these are irreconcilable and he is caught in a severe conflict. Horney contends that this type of conflict constitutes the core of neurosis. She calls it the basic conflict.

selection 21 / some recent studies of conflict behavior and drugs / Neal E. Miller, Yale University

Clinical studies of mental disease indicate the extreme importance of fear and conflict, two factors which usually are closely interrelated.

Abridged from Neal E. Miller, "Some Recent Studies of Conflict Behavior and Drugs," *American Psychologist*, 16:12–24, 1961. Reprinted by permission of the author and the American Psychological Association, Inc.

Studies of men in combat show clearly that practically all of the common symptoms of neuroses, and even psychoses, can be produced by intense fear and conflict. Similarly, experimental studies on animals show that fear and conflict can produce behavioral disturbances, and even psychosomatic symptoms such as stomach acidity, ulcers, cardiac symptoms, and increased susceptibility to infection. Even in normal life, fear and conflict contribute significantly to human physical and mental fatigue.

My earlier work on conflict behavior was closely integrated by theory. I started with principles which had been abstracted from results of experiments in the simplified conditioning situation, and made a few additional assumptions. First, very simple deductions from these principles were tested in very simple experimental situations. Then, step by step, attempts were made to apply the joint action of a number of principles to more complex situations with additional experimental checks at each successive stage of development. The studies I am talking about here are related to the same theory; but they also attempt to investigate new variables which ultimately should be incorporated into the theory, after we have enough data to formulate reasonably probable principles. Since I am investigating a variety of such variables, the studies are somewhat heterogeneous.

In both the former work and these studies, I have benefited greatly by interaction with my students. The work I report here is that of the entire group in my laboratory. It continues to be a great pleasure to work with such wonderful groups of students and collaborators.

EFFECTS OF SODIUM AMYTAL ON CONFLICT

First, I shall describe some studies of effects of drugs on fear and conflict done in collaboration with Herbert Barry III. One of our purposes is to study how performance in a number of experimental situations which presumably measure fear is changed by various drugs which presumably affect fear. We want to see whether fear behaves as a single unitary variable, or whether certain drugs have more effect on the crouching-freezing pattern, while others have more effect on startle and avoidance responses, or whether the results are still more complex.

In the course of this work, we have devised a number of techniques for getting repeated measures of conflict behavior, so that each animal can be used as his own control, and so that a variety of drugs can be tested with the same group of animals.

Another of our purposes (which is the basis of the work to be exemplified here) is to make analytical studies of the behavioral effects of certain drugs which are definitely known to have interesting effects on human behavior. I shall illustrate our work by presenting some results of an analytical series of experimental studies still in progress on one of the drugs with interesting clinical effects, amobarbital sodium, commonly called sodium amytal. I believe that in a modest and incomplete way the studies of this drug illustrate a type of work which is needed on a variety of selected drugs, each of which has well-established, but different, psychological effects on the human subject.

A decade ago, John Dollard and I advanced the hypothesis that the therapeutic effects of this drug, which are especially notable in combat neuroses, are produced by reducing the avoidance component of an approach-avoidance conflict more than the approach one. In fairly extensive exploratory work on rats, Bailey and I were unable to demonstrate such an effect, but we did readily get the fear-reducing effect in an experiment on cats. In the current experiments on rats under the supervision of Barry, this drug has produced unusually consistent effects in ameliorating approach-avoidance conflict. The unexplained discrepancy with the early exploratory results on rats is puzzling and indicates the danger of generalizing too widely from observations of drug effects in a single experimental situation.

Figure 1 shows the effects of an intraperitoneal injection of 20 mg/kg of amobarbital sodium, commonly called sodium amytal, on a

Fig. 1 *Effects of an intraperitoneal injection of 20 mg/kg of amobarbital sodium (sodium amytal) administered to Sprague-Dawley albino rats 20 minutes before testing in six experiments on fear and conflict by different techniques described in the text.*

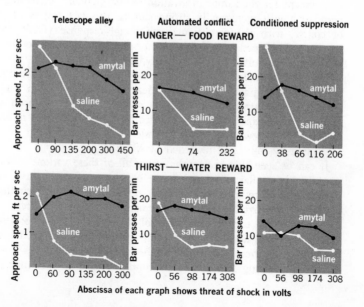

variety of experimental tests of fear and conflict in the albino rat. Let me briefly describe the tests.

In the *telescope alley* test, on the first trial, the rats run 1 foot to the reward, where they never receive electric shock. (Therefore this trial is labeled "0" on the ordinate which indicates threat of shock.) On each successive trial, the rats are required to run an additional foot and occasionally receive the shocks at the goal which, when they occur, are stronger the longer the distance to the goal. Incidentally, the shocks in all of our experiments are given through a series resistance of approximately 200,000 ohms, which accounts for the high voltages. The current is 60 cycle ac.

In this test the cues for danger are primarily proprioceptive and visual. The response, which is running, involves considerable movement and is rewarded every trial.

In the *automated conflict* test, the rats press a bar for a reward on a variable interval schedule. The first 2 minutes are safe, but after that, an increasingly loud tone signals unpredictable shocks on the bar which, when they occur, are increasingly strong the louder the tone. For the last 2 minutes, the tone and shock are turned off. The cues for danger are primarily auditory, the test chamber severely limits movement, and the response of standing on the hind legs and pressing a bar is rewarded on a variable interval schedule.

The *conditioned suppression* test is similar except that the shock is delivered via the grid floor and is inescapable, so that we are measuring conflict with "freezing," rather than with active withdrawal from the bar. Except for the minor innovation of the gradually increasing tone correlated with increasingly strong shocks, this last test is identical, of course, with the conditioned emotional response (CER) which has been developed out of Estes and Skinner's classic paper and has been extensively used by Hunt, Brady, and others.

On the test trials shown in Figure 1, no electric shocks were given, so we are dealing with the effects of fear, rather than of pain plus fear. In order to control for any effects specific to the approach drive, animals in the experiments represented in the top row were motivated by hunger and rewarded by food, while those in the bottom row were motivated by thirst and rewarded by water.

It can be seen that the results under all of these various conditions were highly similar. Looking at the beginning of each curve, which represents performance with little or no fear, it can be seen that, in general, the amytal reduced performance below the placebo level. This part of the test acts as a control to show that the effects of the amytal were not simply to produce an increase in the approach drive, or to act as a general stimulant. As the rats encountered cues to which increasingly strong fear had been conditioned, the performance following placebo was markedly reduced. But the performance under sodium amytal was not affected nearly as much by the fear-inducing cues. Thus, amytal improved the performance under fear.

The fact that so similar results appear in tests involving different cues, different responses, and different drives, makes it unlikely that the effects are specific to the peculiarities of a certain testing situation. The remarkable agreement in the results of the six different experiments makes it clear that sodium amytal definitely reduced the relative strength of fear in our different conflict situations.

Having experimentally demonstrated a striking effect on rats consonant with clinical observations on people, the next step is to determine how this effect is produced. More precise knowledge of the detailed behavioral effects of this drug is needed in order to know under what circumstances a fear-reducing effect can be expected to occur. It is also needed as a basis for relating behavioral effects to results secured with powerful new neurophysiological and biochemical techniques for studying the action of drugs on different parts of the brain.

Primacy of habit versus direct action on fear

In all of the preceding experiments, the amytal improved performance by reducing the relative strength of the fear-motivated habit. How was this effect achieved: directly by a selective action on the brain mechanisms involved in fear, or indirectly by other means? For example, in all of these experiments, as well as in all other experiments that I know of on the effects of drugs on conflict, the habit of approach was established first, and the habit of avoidance second. Perhaps the drug reduced the fear-motivated avoidance not because it has a selective effect on certain fear centers, but rather because it has a selective effect on the more recently established habit.

Perhaps there is something special about the first habit to be established in any situation that makes it more resistant to drug effects— and also to other interventions. In their trail blazing papers on primary inhibition, Szwejkowska, and Konorski and Szwejkowska have shown that whether a cue is first presented in an excitatory or inhibitory role makes a great deal of difference in the ease of subsequent excitatory or inhibitory conditioning, even after several reversals of the role. Perhaps primacy is more important than we have realized. How can we test for its effects in our experiments on drugs?

In the simplest of a series of experiments on this problem, we trained an animal first to go right in a T maze and then to go to the left. After the second habit was fairly well established, we tested with injections of drug or saline. The sodium amytal produced an increase in errors which would be consistent with the primacy hypothesis. Since the errors did not reliably exceed the 50% that would be expected by chance, we were unable to discriminate a differential resistance of the first-established habit to the drug from a mere increase in random behavior.

In another experiment, we tried establishing the fear of the tone in a Skinner box first before we trained the animal to press a bar to secure food there. In the hope of attaching the fear specifically to the tone, and avoiding too much fear of the whole situation, we started out with weak shocks first and gradually increased them after the animal had a chance to learn the discrimination. This procedure apparently was reasonably successful, because it was not extraordinarily difficult subsequently to train the animals to eat and then to press the bar during silent periods in the Skinner box. Then we tested for the effects of sodium amytal. If this drug primarily affects fear, results should be similar to our previous ones, but if it primarily affects the most recent habit, our results should be completely reversed.

Figure 2 shows the results. You can see that the results were similar to our previous ones; the sodium amytal had the greater effect on fear, even though it was the first-established habit. In this experiment we may have had some residual fear of the general testing situation. Such fear would account for the low initial rate of bar pressing and for the fact that the amytal had some beneficial effect on performance even before the fear-evoking tone was sounded.

In another experiment on the same topic, we used a technique analogous to our telescope alley. We used a shuttle alley 8 feet long with a light bulb at either end. Five seconds after the light at one end started flashing, an electric shock was delivered through the sections of the grid floor. This shock was strongest at the lighted end and progressively weaker in farther sections, with the one at the opposite end having no shock. In this way, we trained the rats to shuttle from one end of the alley to the other, always staying away from the flashing light. After they had learned this, we gave the hungry rats trials of being started at alternate ends of the darkened alley, and finding food pellets in tiny cups in the center of each

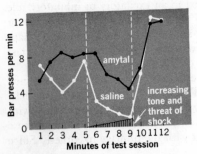

Fig. 2 *In the conditioned suppression test, sodium amytal affects the habit motivated by fear rather than the habit established most recently. (The rats had learned to fear the tone before they learned to press the bar.)*

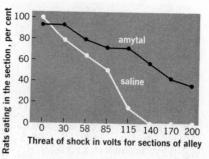

Fig. 3 *In the shuttle alley, sodium amytal reduces the strength of the originally learned habit of avoiding electric shock associated with a flashing light more than it does that of the subsequently learned habit of advancing to eat pellets of food found in cups spaced at 1 foot intervals.*

1-foot section. Then they were given trials with the light flickering at the far end from the start. On these trials shocks occurred on the grid at unpredictable times, being stronger, as before, nearer to the flashing light. The rat was taken out after he had been in the alley 2 minutes, or had taken the pellet in the section nearest the flashing light.

Following this training, the animals were given the drug and placebo tests. During these test trials, no shock was actually given. The results are presented in Figure 3. It can be seen that under amytal, the animals approached farther toward the flashing light into sections with a higher threat of shock than they did after a placebo. Since the habit of approaching was established after the fear of the sections near the flashing light, we would expect exactly the *opposite* results if the main effect of the amytal had been to weaken most the most recently established habit.

The results of these two different experiments indicate that the amytal did not produce its fear-reducing effects merely by weakening the more recently established habit.

Transfer of fear-reduction from drugged to sober state

If a drug produces a differential reduction in fear, by any one of a number of mechanisms, it may have some therapeutic usefulness as a chronic medication for people who need to have all of their fears reduced somewhat, or may help to tide a person over a transient situation which is producing too much general anxiety.

In many cases, however, it is necessary to reduce a specific unrealistic fear which is far too strong without producing an equivalent reduction in realistic fears, such as those of reckless driving. Since we cannot expect any drug to have such a discriminative action tailored to the needs of the culture at a given moment in history, the patient can only be helped by retraining, or, in other words, psychotherapy. Even here, a temporary use of the drug might theoretically be useful in order to help the person to become able to practice the responses he needs to learn. But as John Dollard and I

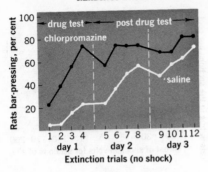

Fig. 4 The therapeutic effects of sodium amytal fail to transfer from the drugged to the nondrugged condition.

pointed out, such new learning under the influence of the drug will not be useful unless it ultimately can be transferred to the normal nondrugged state. Perhaps drugs differ in this significant aspect of their effectiveness. How can we test for this?

In one of the few studies on this problem, Hunt recently found that experimental extinction of fear under chlorpromazine did not transfer effectively to the normal state. But human patients usually are not merely extinguished on their fears; they also are rewarded for performing the correct response in spite of fear. Thus the approach-avoidance conflict situation seemed to me more relevant than simple experimental extinction. It also seemed more likely to show a positive transfer effect because the reward would be expected to add counter-conditioning to the extinction of fear.

Hungry albino rats were trained to press a bar with food as a reward on a 100% schedule. Then the bar was electrified for unpredictable brief periods approximately half of the time. The strength of these shocks was increased until such a strong conflict was established that the rats would not press the bar.

After this conflict had been set up, the rats were given a retraining session in the apparatus with the shock turned off. During this session half of them had received a dose of amytal, and the other half a placebo injection. Figure 4 shows the results. You can see that during the extinction session, labeled "Drug Test," more of the amytal than the control animals resumed pressing the bar. On another day, the rats were given post-drug tests to see whether the superiority during retraining with drug transferred to the normal nondrugged state. You can see that it did not. But the apparent inferiority of the drug group is not statistically reliable.

Figure 5 shows the results of a similar experiment with 2 mg/kg of chlorpromazine. Although the initial fear-reducing effects with this drug do not seem to be as striking as those with sodium amytal, there is less loss with transfer to the normal state. The superiority of the chlorpromazine group on the post-drug test approaches statistical reliability. We are performing dose-response studies essential to establish more definitely the apparent difference in transfer of the effects of these two drugs. If indeed there is less decrement in the transfer of training from the drugged to the normal state with chlorpromazine, this difference may be related to the fact that this drug has less extensive effects on the reticular formation than does sodium amytal.

Meanwhile, these experiments clearly show that it is unsafe to assume that therapeutic transfer will occur from the drugged to the nondrugged state. It is also unsafe to assume that the drug which produces the greatest effect on immediate performance will have the greatest ultimate effect on learning transferred to the normal state. Perhaps some drugs will be discovered which are markedly superior in this crucial respect. Such a drug could make a major contribution to psychotherapy.

NEED FOR BASIC STUDIES TO ESTABLISH A SCIENCE OF PSYCHOPHARMACOLOGY

The work I have just described is a progress report rather than a completed program. By now it should be clear that an adequate study of even certain aspects of the behavioral effects of a single drug is a major project. Nevertheless, I believe it is necessary for us to take the time to be analytical and precise in determining the exact behavioral effects of a variety of drugs already known in a general way to have interesting clinical effects. Then we should advance to the further step of trying to find lawful relationships between these behavioral effects and the action of the drug on different parts of the brain as determined by techniques of neurophysiology, biochemistry, and biophysics. Out of such work may come a better understanding of how the brain functions to control behavior. Out of such work may emerge a basic science of psychopharmacology. As I have said before, the principles of such a basic science should eventually supply a rational basis for practical applications to mental health in the same way that organic chemistry provides a rational basis for the synthesis of new compounds.

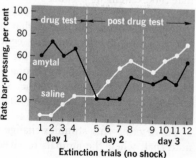

Fig. 5 While chlorpromazine (2 mg/kg administered intraperitoneally 45 minutes before the test) produces less initial improvement than does sodium amytal, more of the gain seems to persist during subsequent tests without drugs.

DOES FEAR BECOME CONSOLIDATED WITH TIME?

In lay and clinical experience there are two schools of thought which make different assumptions concerning the setting or forgetting of fear after a traumatic event. One school of thought recommends that a person suffering a fear-inducing accident when practicing an activity, such as flying an airplane or riding a horse, should go back to it immediately before the fear has a chance to become set. The opposite school of thought recommends an immediate rest to allow the fear to subside. Of course, these human examples may be complicated by the effects of verbal rehearsal during the intervening intervals. Nevertheless, the notion has been advanced by a number of different people that a basic physiological process of consolidation occurs shortly after a new learning experience. Thus it seemed worthwhile to Edgar Coons, James Faust, and me to investigate this problem with animals.

In the first experiment, hungry rats received 30 trials at the rate of 5 a day running down an elevated strip to food. Then they were divided into two matched groups. On the first trial of the next day, upon touching the food, each rat received a traumatic electric shock at the goal and then was immediately removed to its home cage. Thirty seconds later the rats in the first group were returned to the runway for a test, while those in the second group were tested 24 hours later. The time required to touch food was recorded with a 5-minute maximum limit. It can be seen from the left-hand side of Figure 6 that the rats tested 24 hours later required twice as long to go back to touch the food than those tested 30 seconds afterwards. Since the difference is highly reliable, we may conclude that the relative strength of avoidance, and hence presumably of fear, increased during the 24-hour interval immediately following the strong electric shock.

We have considered a number of hypotheses to explain these results. One is that the fear is consolidated during the interval. Another is that the excitement produced by the electric shock has a dynamogenic effect that increases the rat's tendency to run up to the goal immediately afterwards. Another is that under the particular conditions of this experiment, the stimulus conditions for the 30-second group differed more than did those for the 24-hour group from the ones immediately preceding the strong shock. Then it follows that the greater stimulus change for the 30-second group should produce a greater decrement in avoidance than in approach, so that this group would reach the goal sooner.

To describe this stimulus-change hypothesis in more detail, let us note that, when the animals received their shock, it was the first trial of the day, and they had not received any immediately preceding shock. For these animals tested 24 hours later, it was again the first trial of the day, and as before, they had not received any immediately preceding shock. But for the 30-second group the conditions were different in that it was the second trial of the day and they had just received an electric shock. Assuming that some sort of after-effects from the immediately preceding trial and/or shock persist, these would be expected to change the stimulus situation. These changes should produce a greater decrement in the avoidance motivated by fear than in the approach motivated by hunger. Therefore, these animals should show relatively less avoidance.

How can we test this hypothesis? Suppose we change the conditions so that the two factors—an immediately preceding trial and an immediately preceding shock—make the training and test conditions more similar for the 30-second group instead of for the 24-hour one. Then, we will expect the direction of the difference of the two groups to be reversed. The other two hypotheses would not predict such a reversal.

To test this prediction, we ran additional animals in another experiment exactly similar to the foregoing one, except that, instead of giving them their shock in the runway on the first trial of the day, we gave it to them on the third trial. We also gave them a shock in a quite different apparatus 30 seconds before their shock trial in the alley. When these animals were being trained to avoid the goal by being shocked there, they had the stimulus after-effects of an immediately preceding trial and shock. But when tested 24 hours later, they were in a somewhat different stimulus context of no immediately preceding trials and no immediately preceding shock. Therefore, we would expect their avoidance to be relatively weaker on this test 24 hours later, so that the results would be completely opposite to those of the preceding experiment.

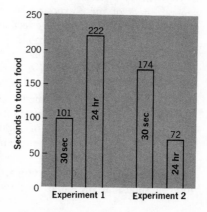

Fig. 6 *Whether or not a 24-hour interval produces consolidation or forgetting of fear depends upon details of the experimental situation, which were designed to affect the degree to which the interval of time restored or altered the pattern of cues present when the traumatic shock was received.*

The right-hand side of Figure 6 shows the results of the second experiment. It can be seen that the results are opposite to those in the first experiment. The difference is highly reliable ($p < .01$). Instead of being consolidated with time, the relative strength of fear was reduced in the second experiment. The stimulus-change hypothesis was confirmed. Under the conditions of these experiments, differences in the stimulus traces were shown to be more important than any setting or forgetting of fear with time.

The results of these two experiments impress us with the importance of trying to analyze the exact stimulus conditions under which the fear was originally established and those under which it is tested.

LEARNING RESISTANCE TO STRESS

The final experiments I shall describe have to do with learning resistance to pain and fear in an approach-avoidance conflict situation. Can resistance to stressful situations be learned? If such learning is possible, what are the laws determining its effectiveness and generality?

In one experiment on this topic, which is reported in more detail elsewhere, albino rats were trained to run down an alley for food. Their criterion task was to continue running in spite of 400-volt electric shocks administered through a 250,000-ohm series resistance for .1 second immediately after they reached the goal. Some of these animals were introduced to the shock suddenly, others were given special training to resist the shock by receiving first mild shocks at the goal, followed by trials with shocks of gradually increasing strength.

The results are presented in Figure 7. You can see that the animals that had been habituated to gradually increasing shocks in the alley continued to run much faster than those in the sudden groups which had not received the same type of training.

Was the superior performance of the gradually habituated group a general effect of mere exposure to the shocks, or, as our theoretical analysis demanded, was it an effect dependent upon specific rewarded training in the criterion situation? This was tested by giving another group the same gradual habituation to the same shocks administered at a different time of day in a distinctive box outside of the alley. You can see that this group was not appreciably helped. Apparently, mere exposure to tough treatments will not necessarily improve resistance to stress in a different criterion situation.

As a control for the effect of additional training trials in the alley, we ran one group which was suddenly exposed to 400-volt shocks at the goal on the same trial that the gradual group received its first mild shocks, and we ran another group which was suddenly exposed to the 400-volt shocks at the same time that the gradual group reached the

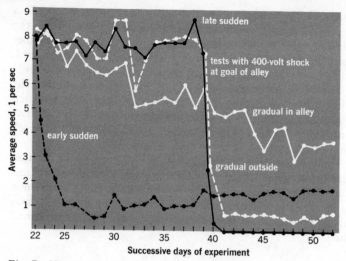

Fig. 7 *Hungry rats may be trained to resist stress by continuing to run down an alley to a goal where they receive both food and electric shock. Under these conditions, previous overlearning of the habit of running to food decreases, rather than increases, resistance to stress.*

level of 400 volts. As you have already seen, the performance of both of these groups was poorer than that of the rats receiving the gradually increasing shocks at the goal of the alley. But looking at the curves for these two groups immediately after the sudden shocks were introduced, we can see a surprising fact. The speed of the group shocked late in training falls off much more rapidly than that of the one shocked early in training. This difference, which is reliable at the .02 level of confidence, confirms earlier suggestive results in our laboratory by Eileen Karsh. It is directly contrary to the widely-held notion that overtraining will increase resistance to stress.

The results of the foregoing experiment suggest that it should be feasible and profitable to analyze further at both the animal and human level, the laws governing the learning of resistance to stresses, such as pain, fear, fatigue, frustration, noise, nausea, and extremes of temperature.

Two of my colleagues, David Williams and Herbert Barry III, have already performed an interesting experiment providing behavioral evidence for the counterconditioning of fear. Rats were trained on a variable interval schedule of food reward. On exactly the same variable interval schedule, they were given a gradually increasing series of electric shocks for pressing the bar. For one group the food and shock schedules were in phase, so that every time they got a shock, a pellet of food was promptly delivered; for the other group, the schedules were out of phase, so that they received the same number and distribution of shocks, but at times when food was not delivered. You should note that for each bar press in both groups, the probability of food or shock was equally great and equally unpredictable. Nevertheless, the correlation of shock with food apparently rendered shock less disrupting to the rat, because the animals in the in-phase group continued pressing through considerably higher levels of shock than those in the out-of-phase group.

At present we are trying to secure objective measures of the counter-conditioning of physiological responses to pain, a phenomenon suggested by Pavlov. If we succeed, we want to study this phenomenon in greater detail to determine how it is affected by factors such as strength of drive, amount and schedule of reward, and experimental extinction.

SUMMARY

In the first part of this paper I have described a series of experiments analyzing how a drug with well-established clinical effects on human behavior may act to achieve some of these effects. Amobarbital sodium, commonly called sodium amytal, was the drug selected for this first series of experiments. As the first step, we established that we could produce in experiments on rats, effects which appear to parallel the fear-reducing effects of this drug in human conflict situations. These effects were repeated in experiments in three different types of apparatus with the approach motivated by two different drives. We also found that it was not primarily due to a greater effect of the drug on the more recently established habit of avoidance; similar effects were secured when avoidance was learned first.

One series of experiments suggested that the fear-reducing effects of the drug in the Skinner box were not due merely to interference with the rat's ability to discriminate the tone used as a cue for danger in that situation. But another experiment in the alley situation showed that the drug either did interfere with discrimination, or produced recovery from experimental extinction. Thus, although a number of indirect modes of action have been ruled out, we have not yet decisively narrowed down the drug's fear-reducing effects to a direct action on the fear mechanism.

Finally, we found that the beneficial effects of the sodium amytal on relearning in a conflict situation did not generalize from the drugged to the normal state. Chlorpromazine yielded more promising results on this crucial test. Dose-response studies are in progress to determine the generality of the difference between the drugs in this respect.

We have also seen that some conditions can produce an apparent consolidation of fear with the passing of time, while other conditions produce an apparent forgetting of fear. In these experiments, the crucial factor seems to be the extent to which the elapsed time changes or restores the cues present immediately before the traumatic electric shock.

Finally, we have seen that it is possible to increase the resistance to the stress of pain and fear by appropriate training. But one of the most obvious methods, overlearning, can reduce, rather than improve, the resistance of the habit to disruption by fear.

selection 22 / reaction to frustration—a critique and hypothesis / S. Stansfeld Sargent, Columbia University

The problem of frustration has commanded considerable attention during the last decade. Not only psychiatrists and specialists in clinical and abnormal psychology, but also students of personality and social psychology have become interested in frustration. The *Frustration and Aggression* volume by the Yale collaborators, Dollard, Doob, Miller, Mowrer and Sears, has helped focus attention on the subject, as have papers by Maslow, Rosenzweig and others.

While dealing with the concept of frustration in a course in Social Psychology, I became convinced that current treatments of frustration still lack a systematic framework and a clear definition of terms. The major concepts which are used lack integration; for example, frustration, conflict, motives, emotions, defense mechanisms, habit patterns, personality factors of many kinds, and situational influences. Several instances might be cited to illustrate confusion in usage of terms. 'Frustration' usually refers to environmental blocking of motives, but sometimes to an unpleasant emotional state resulting from the blocking. At times 'hostility' seems to mean actual behavior; again it signifies a strong feeling underlying behavior. 'Inferiority,' 'insecurity,' 'anxiety,' 'guilt' and many other concepts are frequently employed in ways which are unclear psychologically. Probably the worst of all is 'aggression,' which sometimes seems to mean a motive, sometimes an emotional state akin to anger, sometimes a habit of mechanism, and sometimes a type of overt behavior!

I wish to propose a rather simple conceptual scheme for describing behavior resulting from frustration. It is presented as a hypothesis

From S. Stansfeld Sargent, "Reaction to Frustration—A Critique and Hypothesis," *Psychological Review*, 55:108–114, 1948. Reprinted by permission of the author and the American Psychological Association.

which seems reasonably consistent with clinical and experimental data and also with many of the theoretical formulations which have been advanced.

Briefly the hypothesis is this: frustration evokes a patterned sequence of behavior whose chief stages or aspects are indicated by the terms *frustration, emotion, habit or mechanism,* and *overt behavior.* The nature of each stage of the total process is determined by the interaction of two major factors: the individual's past experience, and the present situation as perceived or defined by the individual. Let us consider each of these in more detail.

It is well agreed that frustration involves the thwarting or blocking of a person's dominant motives, needs, drives, desires or purposes. However, some psychologists place greater stress upon the thwarting than upon the individual's reaction to it. For example, the Yale group defines frustration as "that condition which exists when a goal-response suffers interference." In his recent book Symonds defines it as "the blocking or interference of the satisfaction of an aroused need through some barrier or obstruction." Others emphasize not so much the thwarting, *per se,* as the significance of the thwarting to the individual. Maslow insists that frustration involves two concepts—deprivation, and threat to the personality. Sexual deprivation, for example, does not necessarily constitute frustration, but when such deprivation is felt by the individual to represent rejection by the opposite sex, inferiority, or lack of respect, it becomes seriously frustrating. Similarly, Rosenzweig distinguishes between 'need-persistive' and 'ego-defensive' reactions, the latter representing greater frustration. Zander maintains that frustration occurs only when there is interference with "a goal believed important and attainable by a given person." In all probability future studies of frustration will take into account such subjective individual differences as are mentioned by Maslow, Rosenzweig and Zander.

In any event, we turn next to the question, What is the immediate psychological consequence of frustration? It is definitely not aggression, as most readers of *Frustration and Aggression* might assume. Nor is it the adoption of some handy defense mechanism, as others might conclude. First in time, and foremost in significance, frustration arouses a *pronounced emotional reaction.*

Most students of frustration refer to concomitant emotional tensions, but they seldom make emotion a central aspect of the whole reaction pattern. According to the present hypothesis, emotion is the core of reaction to frustration. If no emotion is aroused, there is no frustration—at least not in any psychologically meaningful sense.

Furthermore, the emotion aroused may be broad and diffuse, like a generalized anger or fear, or it may be fairly specific, like hostility, jealousy, inferiority or shame. Whether the emotion is general or specific depends largely upon the nature of the whole precipitating situation as interpreted by the individual.

It is clearly established that strong emotional reactions upset the organism and tend to pass over into overt behavior. However, the form of the resultant behavior is not, *ipso facto*, determined by the kind and intensity of the emotion. Behavior is, of course, partly dependent upon the emotion which agitates the organism; anger is more likely to work itself out in aggressive behavior than is anxiety or shame. But the form of the overt reaction is importantly affected by the individual's adjustive habits or mechanisms, and by the way he interprets the situation.

The above analysis agrees rather well with Rosenzweig's interpretation. In studying reactions to frustration, according to Rosenzweig, we must be concerned not with what is objectively present, but instead with what the individual emphasizes or reads into the situation according to his personality needs and traits. He finds three main types of reaction to frustration. The 'extrapunitive' is an aggressive reaction toward others. It arises from anger and indignation and from the individual's judgment which blames others; "I'll get you!" is its thesis. Thus, if snubbed by a friend, the extrapunitive reaction is to regard him as ill-bred and ungrateful. The 'intropunitive' is an aggressive reaction directed toward the self. It comes from feelings of humiliation and guilt, and from judgments of self-blame. The intropunitive reaction to a snub is to regard oneself as inferior and unworthy. The 'impunitive' reaction is unaggressive. It arises from feelings of embarrassment and shame and from the judgment "It can't be helped." A friend's snub would be condoned or glossed over as an oversight.

More than any other interpreter of frustration, Rosenzweig stresses the importance of both emotional and 'apperceptive' or judgmental factors. I feel, however, that he has made the latter too conscious. According to my hypothesis there is a continuously operating, relatively unconscious perceptual process which may be called 'defining the situation.'

This term is taken from the sociologist, W. I. Thomas. It was used by him and by others to designate the process of perceiving and interpreting, and also of exploring the behavior possibilities of a social situation. It has elements in common with Lewin's 'psychological environment' and with Sherif's 'frames of reference.' But 'defining the situation' is more than perceiving; it is a kind of active perceiving, interpreting and sizing up a situation with reference to one's potential behavior in it. We cannot know how a given situation influences an individual unless we know how he defines it for himself.

Strong emotions, then, tend toward overt behavior, but always directed and limited by the individual's adjustive habits and by the way he defines the situation. He may customarily express his emotions freely, or he may repress them. Or he may be adept at utilizing substitute forms—*i.e.*, mechanisms—for expressing his strong emotions which are the essence of frustration. Generally speaking, the more stress or threat he reads into the immediate social situation, the more inhibited and disguised his expressive behavior will be.

Our analysis will be made clearer by the use of an example and a diagram [see Fig. 1]. An individual intent upon an important promotion in his business or profession learns the promotion has been won by another person, which produces real frustration. He becomes emotional—but how? If the event is unexpected and the cause unclear, the emotion is a generalized sort of anger. If he knows, or thinks he knows, whose efforts defeated him, his emotional reaction takes the more specific form of hostility or hatred, quite possibly with components of jealousy. Psychologically this is a different phenomenon from generalized anger (though it may be similar physiologically) since it is directed toward a particular individual.

Let us assume, however, that our individual has no detailed information about the events leading up to the loss of his expected promotion and that, therefore, he is in a state of generalized anger. Then what? If he characteristically expresses emotion in an uninhibited way, he may throw things, kick chairs around and curse vehemently. But he is less likely to do this if persons whose opinions he values are present. If they are, he might rather engage in some substitute type of expression, such as rationalizing or seeking sympathy.

On the other hand, he may be the kind of person who seldom gives free vent to his emotions. He may then displace his anger upon his wife and children if they are present. He might kick the dog or cat, or 'take it out' on a clumsy delivery boy, all depending upon who is present at the time and what his relationship to them happens to be. Or if he were a person of violent prejudices, he might displace his anger upon 'the Jews,' 'the Reds,' 'the Catholics' or some other handy scapegoat. Again, he might regress; if his mother were present he might burst into tears and put his face in her lap as he always did when a child. Or he might engage in one or another kind of comforting fantasy.

Actually he would probably utilize more than one kind of defense mechanism. Seldom does a single outlet relieve all of one's strong emotional tensions. An immediate emotional outburst might well be followed by rationalizing, fantasy, or some kind of compensatory behavior. Clinical data suggest that as children most of us acquire quite a repertory of forms of substitute expression. Hence the particu-

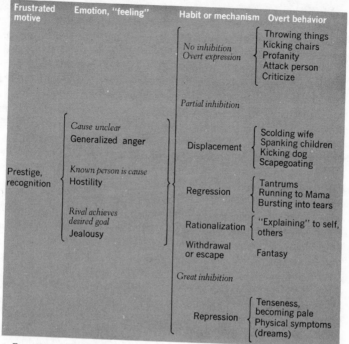

Fig. 1   Reaction to frustration.

lar one or ones we employ depend in large measure upon the social situation as we interpret it.

Another possibility is that, because of past training and/or a very stringent social situation, an individual may inhibit or repress nearly all overt behavior. If so, we would expect some sort of delayed overt expression, possibly in disguised form, as in dreams or physical symptoms of illness.

Does frustration eventuate in aggression? At the beginning of their book the Yale psychologists propose "that the existence of frustration always leads to some form of aggression." This thesis is hard to defend, as two of the authors, Miller and Sears, point out in subsequent articles.[1]

[1] The first part of the same proposition is "that the occurrence of aggressive behavior always presupposes the existence of frustration." We shall not discuss the subject here, except to suggest that it is also difficult to defend as a general statement. Certain kinds of behavior which are definitely aggressive seem to be the socially sanctioned ways of behaving in some communities (*e.g.*, a tough city slum area or a primitive culture). Such behavior may well be learned and practiced without having its origin, necessarily, in frustration.

Much behavior resulting from frustration is, of course, aggressive. Probably the Yale group arrived at their sweeping conclusion partly because the cases they considered were dramatic, short-time, anger-producing kinds of frustration—the young man who was bawled out by the traffic cop while driving with his girl, the boarders and the delayed dinner, and so on. Clinical data, however, suggest that frustration may produce different emotional reactions, such as fear, anxiety, inferiority or shame, sometimes without any trace of anger, hostility or jealousy. Symonds considers anxiety a very common reaction to frustration. In fact, he defines anxiety as a "mental distress with respect to some anticipated frustration." Rosenzweig, as already mentioned, notes that frustration may produce emotional reactions like humiliation and shame.

What kind of overt behavior occurs when frustration gives rise to other emotions than anger? Consider an example, diagrammed in Fig. 2. Here is a 'rejected' child—a child frustrated by denial of affection and social response. If the situation is unclear to him, his emotional reaction is one of general anxiety or insecurity. What does he do? He may, indeed, compensate and engage in bullying, boasting and other kinds of aggressive behavior. But he may instead compensate by making a friend of the teacher or by forming a strong attachment for an older boy or girl. He may seek satisfaction through identification—either by playing the role of a 'big shot,' or by joining some social group with prestige value. If he withdraws and daydreams, his fantasies may or may not be of an aggressive sort. In other words, we suggest that aggression is not necessarily present in the compensatory or other substitute behavior.

Here again, past experience and the prevailing social situation are both important. The child's behavior is partly a function of the kind of emotion aroused, partly of his training—whether or not he has learned to express himself aggressively, for example,—and partly of his interpretation of the situation, such as whether or not he defines it as containing a potentially sympathetic person.

What about the relation between 'frustration' and 'conflict'? Frustration is usually considered an objective or environmental kind of thwarting; conflict a subjective clash of incompatible motives. The current tendency seems to be to consider conflict a special case of frustration. Many psychologists, however, treat frustration and conflict separately and do not attempt to relate them. In terms of the present hypothesis the important point is that both frustration and conflict involve dynamic and highly upsetting emotional states which impel the organism toward some sort of overt behavior. Reaction to conflict, as to frustration, follows the same sequence: emotion, habit

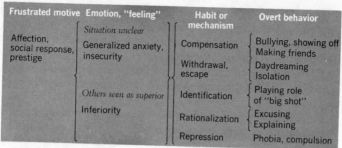

Frustrated motive	Emotion, "feeling"	Habit or mechanism	Overt behavior
Affection, social response, prestige	*Situation unclear* Generalized anxiety, insecurity	Compensation	Bullying, showing off Making friends
		Withdrawal, escape	Daydreaming Isolation
	Others seen as superior Inferiority	Identification	Playing role of "big shot"
		Rationalization	Excusing Explaining
		Repression	Phobia, compulsion

Fig. 2   Reaction to frustration.

or mechanism, and overt behavior. For instance, conflict arising from performance of an act considered immoral may arouse a feeling of generalized anxiety, or a more specific feeling of guilt, embarrassment or shame. Habits and mechanisms come into play. Through sublimation the emotional reaction may impel one toward religious or altruistic activity; through projection, toward gossip or scandal-mongering; through repression, toward phobia or compulsion; through a kind of displacement toward masochism or other self-directed aggression. The nature of the frustration largely determines the basic emotional reaction, and the resultant behavior depends upon existing habit-patterns operating in the individually defined social situation.

The above discussion has omitted many important aspects of the problem of frustration. It has not dealt with the efficacy of resultant behavior in reducing emotional tensions evoked by frustration. It has neglected the important matters, so ably treated by the Yale group, of the effects of differing degrees and strengths of instigation, or the effects of anticipated punishment. Nor has it dealt with the concept of 'frustration tolerance' which is taken up by Rosenzweig and others.

The critique and hypothesis presented above is a systematic contribution designed to fill in certain gaps and to fit loose ends together. Some psychologists may object to such an analysis, *per se*, as violating the essential unity or Gestalt-character of behavior. The only answer, I suppose, is that some kinds of behavior are too complex to be treated as a whole; they have to be analyzed, though efforts must be made to put the pieces together again. Other psychologists will undoubtedly object to certain of the statements and interpretations. The whole hypothesis needs, of course, to be verified by clinical or experimental methods.

In addition to setting up the four stage scheme of frustration-emotion-mechanism-overt behavior, the hypothesis proposes the following things:

It makes emotion the central dynamic factor in reaction to frustration, and distinguishes between generalized emotional states (*e.g.*, anger, anxiety) and more specific and directed states or 'feelings' (*e.g.*, hostility, jealousy, inferiority).

It stresses the interoperation of both past experience and present situations as determining the form and content of resulting overt behavior.

Furthermore, it emphasizes that the crucial present factor is not the situation as it exists in some objective sense, but rather as the individual defines and interprets it.

Most of all, perhaps, this paper represents a protest against what Leeper calls 'peripheralism' in psychology; that is to say, the description of behavior chiefly in terms of stimuli and overt responses, to the neglect of intervening organismic factors. Hence it is, in brief, an attempt to describe all the significant psychological variables which interoperate when a person is frustrated.

selection 23 / our inner conflicts / Karen Horney, New York City

Let me say to begin with: It is not neurotic to have conflicts. At one time or another our wishes, our interests, our convictions are bound to collide with those of others around us. And just as such clashes between ourselves and our environment are a commonplace, so, too, conflicts within ourselves are an integral part of human life.

An animal's actions are largely determined by instinct. Its mating, its care for its young, its search for food, its defenses against danger are more or less prescribed and beyond individual decision. In contrast, it is the prerogative as well as the burden of human beings to be able to exert choice, to have to make decisions. We may have to decide between desires that lead in opposite directions. We may, for instance, want to be alone but also want to be with a friend; we may want to study medicine but also to study music. Or there may be a conflict between wishes and obligations: we may wish to be with a lover when someone in trouble needs our care. We may be divided between a desire to be in accord with others and a conviction that would entail expressing an opinion antagonistic to them. We may be in conflict, finally, between two sets of values, as occurs when we believe in taking on a hazardous job in wartime but believe also in our duty to our family.

From Karen Horney, *Our Inner Conflicts*, W. W. Norton & Company, Inc., New York, 1945. Reprinted by permission of the publisher.

The kind, scope, and intensity of such conflicts are largely determined by the civilization in which we live. If the civilization is stable and tradition bound, the variety of choices presenting themselves are limited and the range of possible individual conflicts narrow. Even then they are not lacking. One loyalty may interfere with another; personal desires may stand against obligations to the group. But if the civilization is in a stage of rapid transition, where highly contradictory values and divergent ways of living exist side by side, the choices the individual has to make are manifold and difficult. He can conform to the expectations of the community or be a dissenting individualist, be gregarious or live as a recluse, worship success or despise it, have faith in strict discipline for children or allow them to grow up without much interference; he can believe in a different moral standard for men and women or hold that the same should apply for both, regard sexual relations as an expression of human intimacy or divorce them from ties of affection; he can foster racial discrimination or take the stand that human values are independent of the color of skin or the shape of noses—and so on and so forth.

When conflicts center about the primary issues of life, it is all the more difficult to face them and resolve them. But provided we are sufficiently alive, there is no reason why in principle we should not be able to do so. Education could do much to help us to live with greater awareness of ourselves and to develop our own convictions. A realization of the significance of the factors involved in choice would give us ideals to strive for, and in that a direction for our lives.[1]

The difficulties always inherent in recognizing and resolving a conflict are immeasurably increased when a person is neurotic. Neurosis, it must be said, is always a matter of degree—and when I speak of "a neurotic" I invariably mean "a person to the extent that he is neurotic." For him awareness of feelings and desires is at a low ebb. Often the only feelings experienced consciously and clearly are reactions of fear and anger to blows dealt to vulnerable spots. And even these may be repressed. Such authentic ideals as do exist are so pervaded by compulsive standards that they are deprived of their power to give direction. Under the sway of these compulsive tendencies the faculty to renounce is rendered impotent, and the capacity to assume responsibility for oneself all but lost.

Neurotic conflicts may be concerned with the same general problems as perplex the normal person. But they are so different in kind

[1] To normal persons merely dulled by environmental pressures, a book like Harry Emerson Fosdick's *On Being a Real Person* would be of considerable profit.

that the question has been raised whether it is permissible to use the same term for both. I believe it is, but we must be aware of the differences. What, then, are the characteristics of neurotic conflicts?

Conflicts play an infinitely greater role in neurosis than is commonly assumed. To detect them, however, is no easy matter—partly because they are essentially unconscious, but even more because the neurotic goes to any length to deny their existence. What, then, are the signals that would warrant us to suspect underlying conflicts? In the examples cited [in an earlier chapter] their presence was indicated by two factors, both fairly obvious. One was the resulting symptoms—fatigue in the first case, stealing in the second. The fact is that every neurotic symptom points to an underlying conflict; that is, every symptom is a more or less direct outgrowth of a conflict. We shall see gradually what unresolved conflicts do to people, how they produce states of anxiety, depression, indecision, inertia, detachment, and so on. An understanding of the causative relation here helps direct our attention from the manifest disturbances to their source—though the exact nature of the source will not be disclosed.

The other signal indicating that conflicts were in operation was inconsistency. In the first example we saw a man convinced of a procedure being wrong and of injustice done him, making no move to protest. In the second a person who highly valued friendship turned to stealing money from a friend. Sometimes the person himself will be aware of such inconsistencies; more often he is blind to them even when they are blatantly obvious to an untrained observer.

Inconsistencies are as definite an indication of the presence of conflicts as a rise in body temperature is of physical disturbance. To cite some common ones: A girl wants above all else to marry, yet shrinks from the advances of any man. A mother oversolicitous of her children frequently forgets their birthdays. A person always generous to others is niggardly about small expenditures for himself. Another who longs for solitude never manages to be alone. One forgiving and tolerant toward most people is oversevere and demanding with himself.

I see the basic conflict of the neurotic in the fundamentally contradictory attitudes he has acquired toward other persons. Before going into detail, let me call attention to the dramatization of such a contradiction in the story of Dr. Jekyll and Mr. Hyde. We see him on the one hand delicate, sensitive, sympathetic, helpful, and on the other brutal, callous, and egotistical. I do not, of course, mean to imply that neurotic division always adheres to the precise line of this story, but merely to point to a vivid expression of basic incompatibility of attitudes in relation to others.

To approach the problem genetically we must go back to what I have called basic anxiety,[2] meaning by this the feeling a child has of being isolated and helpless in a potentially hostile world. A wide range of adverse factors in the environment can produce this insecurity in a child: direct or indirect domination, indifference, erratic behavior, lack of respect for the child's individual needs, lack of real guidance, disparaging attitudes, too much admiration or the absence of it, lack of reliable warmth, having to take sides in parental disagreements, too much or too little responsibility, over-protection, isolation from other children, injustice, discrimination, unkept promises, hostile atmosphere, and so on and so on.

The only factor to which I should like to draw special attention in this context is the child's sense of lurking hypocrisy in the environment: his feeling that the parents' love, their Christian charity, honesty, generosity, and so on may be only pretense. Part of what the child feels on this score is really hypocrisy; but some of it may be just his reaction to all the contradictions he senses in the parents' behavior. Usually, however, there is a combination of cramping factors. They may be out in the open or quite hidden, so that in analysis one can only gradually recognize these influences on the child's development.

Harassed by these disturbing conditions, the child gropes for ways to keep going, ways to cope with this menacing world. Despite his own weakness and fears he unconsciously shapes his tactics to meet the particular forces operating in his environment. In doing so, he develops not only *ad hoc* strategies but lasting character trends which become part of his personality. I have called these "neurotic trends."

If we want to see how conflicts develop, we must not focus too sharply on the individual trends but rather take a panoramic view of the main directions in which a child can and does move under these circumstances. Though we lose sight for a while of details we shall gain a clearer perspective of the essential moves made to cope with the environment. At first a rather chaotic picture may present itself, but out of it in time three main lines crystallize: a child can move *toward* people, *against* them, or *away from* them.

When moving *toward* people he accepts his own helplessness, and in spite of his estrangement and fears tries to win the affection of others and to lean on them. Only in this way can he feel safe with them. If there are dissenting parties in the family, he will attach

[2] Karen Horney, *The Neurotic Personality of Our Time*, W. W. Norton, 1937.

himself to the most powerful person or group. By complying with them, he gains a feeling of belonging and support which makes him feel less weak and less isolated.

When he moves *against* people he accepts and takes for granted the hostility around him, and determines, consciously or unconsciously, to fight. He implicitly distrusts the feelings and intentions of others toward himself. He rebels in whatever ways are open to him. He wants to be the stronger and defeat them, partly for his own protection, partly for revenge.

When he moves *away from* people he wants neither to belong nor to fight, but keeps apart. He feels he has not much in common with them, they do not understand him anyhow. He builds up a world of his own—with nature, with his dolls, his books, his dreams.

In each of these three attitudes, one of the elements involved in basic anxiety is overemphasized: helplessness in the first, hostility in the second, and isolation in the third. But the fact is that the child cannot make any one of these moves wholeheartedly, because under the conditions in which the attitudes develop, all are bound to be present. What we have seen from our panoramic view is only the predominant move.

From the point of view of the normal person there is no reason why the three attitudes should be mutually exclusive. One should be capable of giving in to others, of fighting, and of keeping to oneself. The three can complement each other and make for a harmonious whole. If one predominates, it merely indicates an over-development along one line.

But in neurosis there are several reasons why these attitudes are irreconcilable. The neurotic is not flexible; he is driven to comply, to fight, to be aloof, regardless of whether the move is appropriate in the particular circumstance, and he is thrown into a panic if he behaves otherwise. Hence when all three attitudes are present in any strong degree, he is bound to be caught in a severe conflict.

Another factor, and one that considerably widens the scope of the conflict, is that the attitudes do not remain restricted to the area of human relationships but gradually pervade the entire personality, as a malignant tumor pervades the whole organic tissue. They end by encompassing not only the person's relation to others but also his relation to himself and to life in general. If we are not fully aware of this all-embracing character, the temptation is to think of the resulting conflict in categorical terms, like love *versus* hate, compliance *versus* defiance, submissiveness *versus* domination, and so on. That, however, would be as misleading as to distinguish fascism from democracy by focusing on any single opposing feature, such as their difference in approach to religion or power. These are differences certainly, but exclusive emphasis upon them would serve to obscure the point that democracy and fascism are worlds apart and represent two philosophies of life entirely incompatible with each other.

It is not accidental that a conflict that starts with our relation to others in time affects the whole personality. Human relationships are so crucial that they are bound to mold the qualities we develop, the goals we set for ourselves, the values we believe in. All these in turn react upon our relations with others and so are inextricably interwoven.[3]

My contention is that the conflict born of incompatible attitudes constitutes the core of neurosis and therefore deserves to be called *basic*. And let me add that I use the term *core* not merely in the figurative sense of its being significant but to emphasize the fact that it is the dynamic center from which neuroses emanate. This contention is the nucleus of a new theory of neurosis whose implications will become apparent in what follows. Broadly considered, the theory may be viewed as an elaboration of my earlier concept that neuroses are an expression of a disturbance in human relationships.[4]

[3] Since the relation to others and the attitude toward the self cannot be separated from one another, the contention occasionally to be found in psychiatric publications, that one or the other of these is the most important factor in theory and practice, is not tenable.

[4] This concept was first presented in *The Neurotic Personality of Our Time* and elaborated in *New Ways in Psychoanalysis* and *Self-Analysis*.

CHAPTER 6 ✸ PERCEPTION
AND BEHAVIOR ✸

The term "perception" refers to the complex processes which begin with the stimulation of a sense organ and end with an interpretation of the resulting neural activity by the organism, that is, with the "meaning of the stimulus." However, since this inner meaning is entirely personal and subjective, it cannot be observed directly by another person; therefore, the psychologist must infer the characteristics of these intervening processes from the behavior of the individual.

Even casual analysis of the perceptual process reveals that the meaning of a stimulus pattern depends on such biological characteristics as the capacities of the receptor organs through which we are sensitive to stimulation. Some 300 years ago a British philosopher, John Locke, made explicit the position that there is nothing in the mind which was not first in the senses. Thus, in attempting to understand man's behavior we must know something about the characteristics of his receiving mechanisms, that is, his sense organs. Certainly our world would be a quite different one if we were not able to be sensitive to light waves via our visual receptors; similarly our behavior would undoubtedly be different if we were able to be directly sensitive to radio waves! However, the ability of our receptors to be excited by external stimuli is not the whole story. Sensory stimulation is modified greatly by the characteristics of our nervous system. The nerve fibers do not conduct a miniature image of an external object to the brain; rather, this information is coded into a series of neural impulses. In Selection 24 Dr. Clifford T. Morgan, a physiological psychologist, helps us to understand some of the structural factors which influence our perception.[1] Morgan points out that our ability to differentiate

[1] Since Morgan's discussion assumes some familiarity with the "basic physics of stimuli, the anatomy of our sense organs and the neurology of sensory systems . . . ," the student would be well-advised to read this selection after

sensory qualities such as red from blue, and pain from touch, is not dependent simply on which receptor organ is stimulated. Rather, the receptor organs such as the eye contain millions of specific receptor elements which respond differentially to certain types of stimuli, that is, they serve as analysers. He goes on to show that several receptor elements often attach to the same individual nerve fiber, and thus, perception depends on "very complex patterns of signals coming from receptors."

Morgan briefly alludes to inhibitory mechanisms which operate in the nervous system to prevent some nerve fibers from firing. It is this inhibitory capacity which seems to serve as the basic physiological correlate of the psychological process of attention. Clearly, the organism does not perceive all of the potential stimuli which surround it from moment to moment. The term "attention" refers to the selection process whereby some stimuli are "let through" and others "cut out." Hernández-Peón and his associates have demonstrated (Selection 25) that when an animal is attending to stimuli in one sense modality, such as vision, there is considerable inhibition of transmission in the auditory pathways. (Thus perhaps the daydreaming student who is unable to answer his instructor's question is being truthful when he says, "I didn't hear you.")

Perception not only depends on functioning sense organs and the neural mechanisms of attention, but is extensively determined by the previous experiences that the individual has had with similar stimuli. In other words, our ability to extract "meaning" from raw stimulation depends on the previous transactions that we have had with the stimulus. In Selection 26 Drs. Ittelson and Kilpatrick show that seemingly simple perceptions such as object size are based on a variety of cues. The organism seems to implicitly weigh these cues in coming up with a prediction about (perception of) object size.

Several important generalizations about perception are suggested by Ittelson and Kilpatrick's paper: (1) Perception is predictive (probabilistic); (2) perception is functional; (3) the results of the perceptual processes vary with previous experience; (4) perception is organismic; and (5) perception defines for the individual the nature of external reality.

The two major classes of factors which influence perception have been variously emphasized by different explanations of specific perceptual phenomena. Those theories which give primary weight to sensory and neural functions have been called nativistic, while those which em-

---

he has mastered the discussion of the senses and neural transmission in his text. He will then be in a better position to understand some of the complexities of the problem of how we experience different sensory qualities.

phasize previous experiences are empiricistic. *Allport and Pettigrew (Selection 27) report an experiment in which they studied the effects of different previous experience on the perception of movement. They made use of the revolving trapezoid illusion, which, although actually revolving through 360°, is typically perceived as oscillating or "wig-wagging." Their results indicate that under conditions which had previously been demonstrated to give the maximum illusory effect (monocular viewing from 20 feet), differences in previous experiences do not greatly influence perception. However, when the illusion is viewed under conditions which ordinarily do not yield such a strong illusion, previous experience does seem to influence perception. This experiment suggests a generalization which is supported by other investigations also:* whenever the features of the stimulus are made optimal, perception will be heavily influenced by sensory and neural factors; however, when the stimulus is suboptimal, impoverished, or ambiguous, then organismic characteristics related to previous experience become increasingly important in determining our perception.

selection 24 / some structural factors in perception / Clifford T. Morgan, University of Wisconsin

Perception has its substrate in structure. We can only see and feel what our sense organs and nervous system let us sense. It is natural, therefore, that this chapter should deal with anatomical and structural factors in perception. It will provide a background of the facts and present conception of how physiological structures function in perception.

In setting out on this task there is obviously no point in repeating the many details of anatomy, physiology, and psychology that can be found in the various textbooks. In fact, acquaintance with the basic physics of stimuli, the anatomy of our sense organs, and the neurology of sensory systems must be assumed. Having these fundamentals in mind, however, it is possible to work toward two goals in this chapter.

One is to bring the discussion up to date on the results of recent research. Many of these results really upset our old ideas and make us take new views of the anatomy of perception.

Abridged from Clifford T. Morgan, "Some Structural Factors in Perception," *Perception: An Approach to Personality*, Robert R. Blake and Glenn V. Ramsey, eds., The Ronald Press Company, New York, 1951, pp. 23–37. Copyright 1951 by The Ronald Press Company.

The second goal will be to look at perceptual mechanisms as a whole. When we study some one part of a sensory system, say the retina, we often "cannot see the woods for the trees." If we stand off a bit, however, and look at all the senses together, we begin to be able to make some general rules and principles about the mechanisms of perception.

That will be attempted in this chapter—at the risk sometimes of suggesting ideas that not everyone will agree with.

THE QUALITIES OF EXPERIENCE

We see with our eyes, hear with our ears, and feel with our skins, and it is obvious in each case that the structure of the sense organ has a lot to do with what we perceive through it. More than a hundred years ago, however, Müller carried the anatomical approach far beyond the obvious and gave us his now famous doctrine of specific nerve energies. We see red or blue, hear high tones or low tones, feel pain or heat, he said, only because each of these perceptions involves different sensory paths. Thus he gave us an anatomical explanation for qualities of experience.

Hardly any suggestion could have been taken so seriously by so many persons for so many years. Even today some physiologists take it as an axiom, rather than a hypothesis, and try to prove other notions by it. Many specific theories of sensory functions have been based upon it, and a good many of them have been wrong. Müller's general idea, however, still looks like a good one. We have simply had to revise again and again our specific notions of how the idea works in practice.

The shape of receptors

Take the question of structure of receptors. It would have been very handy not only for Müller's doctrine to prove right but for every receptor to have some unusual shape or color that would let us tell it from other receptors for other experiences. Our wishful thinking on this score has made us waste a lot of research time and peddle some bad notions. They tell us in the elementary textbooks, for example, that we have two kinds of receptors in our eyes, one for twilight vision and the other for color vision. We have been taught, too, that there are different kinds of receptors for skin perception—Meissner corpuscles for touch, Krause end-bulbs for cold, Ruffini cylinders for warmth, and free nerve endings for pain. It would indeed be nice if anatomy were that good to us—if each receptor had its trade-mark of experience on it—but we are gradually learning to be wary of such notions.

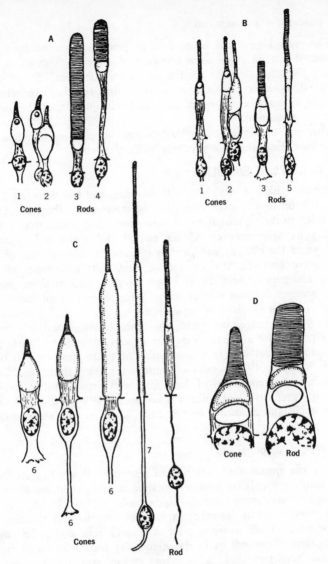

Fig. 1   Rods and cones found in the eyes of different vertebrates: A, the leopard frog; B, the house sparrow; C, man;
and D, the mud puppy; 1, typical cones; 2, so-called twin
cone; 3, typical red rod; 4, green rod; 5, rod from the central
area; 6, cones from different regions of the periphery of the
retina; and 7, cone from the fovea. [Based on the work of
L. B. Arey and G. L. Walls. From E. N. Willmer, Retinal
Structure and Colour Vision, Cambridge, Cambridge University Press, 1946, p. 2. By permission of the publisher.]

Visual receptors   Take as an example the matter of visual receptors. In Figure 1 you see drawings of the photoreceptors of four different vertebrate animals. In A are those of the frog, and they divide themselves fairly well into cones and rods, just as the classical doctrine says they should. In B are the rods and cones of the house sparrow. Again they look somewhat as they are supposed to, but the rods look something like cones and the cones look like rods. In C we meet a disturbing situation, for these are the receptors of man. Many of the cones from the peripheral retina look like cones and the rods look like rods, but notice what is supposed to be a cone from the fovea centralis—the all-cone area of our fovea. It outdoes the rods in being long, cylindrical, and rodlike. The best excuse for calling it a cone is that our theory of duplicity says that it should be a cone. Anatomy certainly does not justify the label.

These are just a few examples of the problem. There are other animals in which it is hard to make out rods and cones. In some cases, like that of the lizard *Gecko*, the animal seems to have all rods in its eye, yet reacts to visual objects as though it had only cones. In other cases, histologists have a hard time deciding whether there are any cones in an animal's eye, when electrical records of the eye's behavior make it quite certain that "cones" are there. Finally, some vision scientists have reason to believe that our perception of the color blue may rest not upon the cones, as we have so long thought, but rather upon some kind of rod.

So the duplicity theory seems to be passing on toward its death. It gave us a kind of anatomical explanation for one aspect of perception which would have been very nice if true. Indeed, we may even go on teaching students this theory for years to come as a sort of teaching device that may be partly true. It is not true enough, however, to depend on to make correct guesses about perception. We cannot tell about the color perception of an animal by the looks of the receptors in its eyes.

Skin receptors   We are being even more rudely disappointed by the skin senses. The physiologists and psychologists used to assign these receptors to different experiences. Some in fact still do. The common scheme is to assign the Meissner corpuscle to the experience of touch or pressure, the Krause end-bulb to cold, the Ruffini cylinder to warmth, and the free nerve ending to pain. The reason for this kind of scheme is that one kind of receptor seems to be in greater numbers in regions of the skin where one experience may be more prominent. Other arguments can and have been made with great vigor.

The only trouble—and the big trouble—is that these receptors are not always present where they ought to be. It is, of course, a simple matter to make a map of the skin, marking just where we feel various experiences. When a spot seems to give one experience much more than another, we can do a biopsy on the spot, that is, cut out a piece of skin and see what receptors we have been able to trap. Such experiments have often been done in the last seventy years, and the result all too often is that the receptors our anatomical scheme calls for are missing. We do not always find Meissner corpuscles under pressure spots, Krause end-bulbs under cold spots, and so on. We can swear in fact that they very often are not there.

What scientists always do find when they make biopsies is a network of nerve fibers and blood vessels. This is not strange, of course, because our skin needs blood and so do the nerve fibers. Nerve fibers are also needed to control the dilation and contraction of blood vessels. More than that, however, these networks obviously supply the skin with a good many free nerve endings. These endings, in fact, are about the only possible receptors in many areas of the skin. We can be very sure that they serve as pain receptors and as pressure receptors. The experiments leave little doubt about that. They strongly suggest, too, even if they do not prove, that we can experience cold and warmth with free nerve endings. Perhaps some of the fancier corpuscles also get involved in our experiences of touch and temperature, but they are certainly not the sole receptors.

We should not get into too many details here. The upshot of the matter is that one cannot tell much about perception from the anatomy of receptors in the skin. A free nerve ending is just as likely to give one kind of experience as another. The beautifully designed corpuscles such as the Meissner or Krause bodies do not stand for a particular experience. It would have been very nice—in fact, it would often be very helpful—if each receptor in the skin had a different function. Alas, it is not so.

The receptors as analyzers

Even though the receptors do not wear uniforms that tell us their duties, Müller could still be right. Which receptor gets stimulated could still decide what we perceive. The differences in receptors might be chemical or electrical rather than anatomical. There may very well be a receptor in the eye for red, another for blue, and so on without our being able to tell it by looking at them. So, too, with the skin receptors. All the receptors have to do is respond differently to different stimuli, and then make the proper connections in the sensory pathways so that the brain can keep their identities straight. If they do that, then Müller's theory is right.

Specificity vs. pattern As we know, research workers have divided into two camps on this issue. Natanson, Helmholtz, Von Frey, Hecht,

Stevens, and Dallenbach—to mention but a few—have stood by Müller. Lotze, Hering, Goldscheider, Wever, and Nafe are some who departed a little or a lot from the anatomical point of view. They have held that receptors can send in to the nervous system different kinds of messages and that these messages, and not just the receptors that sent them, affect our experiences. Wever used to say, for example, that the frequency of impulses in the auditory nerve had something to do with whether we hear a high tone or a low tone. Hering believed that the same receptor could make us see red acting in one way and, sending in another kind of message, could make us see green. Nafe has been saying that what receptors *do*, not just which ones they are, determines our perception.

When people argue long and loud about something, there is a fair chance that both sides are partly right, partly wrong. So it seems to be in this case. Research has been telling us enough lately to let us make some decisions about these issues, and it looks more and more as though both camps are partly right. With very small electrodes and the right electrical systems, physiologists have been finding out just what receptors do when they are stimulated. Many facts of great interest have come out of their work. Let us spend just a little time hitting their high points.

Kinds of receptors It looks as though we have two kinds of receptors in all the senses. One kind responds in about the same way as does the sense organ as a whole. The eye, for example, can see wave lengths of light as long as 760 mμ and as short as 380 mμ. Some of the individual receptors in the eye do exactly the same thing. When plotted on a graph, their response looks about the same as the over-all response of the eye. In hearing, too, some of the receptors of the ear are aroused by about the same range of stimuli as is the whole ear, namely, 20 cps to 20 kcps. In taste, too, there are receptors that give impulses to almost any kind of chemical stimulus, whether it be sour, salt, or bitter. Receptors such as these may be very good for telling us about the intensity of a stimulus and are thus of help in perception. They cannot tell us much, however, about the nature of a stimulus. A receptor that reacts just as does the eye as a whole, or the ear, or the tongue, is not good for quality of perception. It does not let us perceive different colors or pitches or tastes.

Besides these broad-band receptors, however, we have some narrow-band receptors—cells that pick out only some of the spectrum of stimuli that hit the receptors. Granit, for example, has put his electrodes in the retinas of various animals and gotten the records shown in Figure 2. Some of the nerve cells he records from have peak responses at 600 mμ, and he calls them red elements. Some have peaks at 530 mμ in the green, 580 mμ in the yellow, and 450 mμ

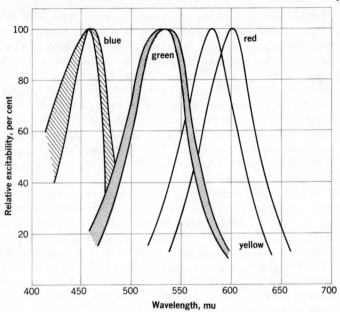

Fig. 2 Relative excitability of four types of receptors found by Granit in different mammalian eyes. The cross-hatched and stippled portions of the "blue" and "green" receptors indicate variability in the exact forms of these curves. [From C. T. Morgan, and E. Stellar, Physiological Psychology, 2d ed., New York, McGraw-Hill Book Company, Inc., 1950. By permission of the publisher.]

in the blue. Galambos, making the same kind of experiments in a cat, finds nerve cells that react to a small part of the acoustic spectrum. And from the cat's tongue, Pfaffmann has picked up cells that respond more to bitter than to salt or more to salt than to bitter. Those are the only experiments we have now, but we shall probably hear before long of similar results in smell or the skin senses.

Physiology is now giving us an answer to the long debated question whether receptors are at the root of the different qualities of experience we have. Müller was at least partly right. Receptors are analyzers. One receptor picks out some stimuli to respond to more than others, and they somehow or other keep themselves identified upstream in the nervous system. We can perceive different colors, tones, tastes, and probably odors because different anatomical receptors send in messages. There is little doubt about that.

Patterns for messages The story, however, is not as simple as it might seem at first glance. We do not have receptor A sending in its private message over line A, and receptor B talking to the nervous system over line B. The notion of private lines from receptors to the brain is simple and attractive. Unfortunately, however, it is not true. Instead, receptors get hooked up with each other, so different receptors are talking to the nervous system at the same time. Their talk makes a complex pattern that must be uncoded by the nervous system before we can perceive their meaning.

To make this point clear, let us turn to some examples. Take first Pfaffmann's study of the taste receptors of the cat. All the fibers that he got under his microelectrodes would respond to acids. They were, one might say, sour receptors. Some of the fibers would respond only to acid. Another type of fiber, however, responded to both acid and bitter stimuli. Still a third class reacted to acid and salt. So there are at least three classes of taste receptors in the cat. They let the cat perceive different tastes, but not in the simple way we might expect. Instead, the cat tastes "salt" when fiber A is sending in messages, "bitter" when fiber B is signaling, but "sour" when all three fibers— A, B, and C, are firing. Thus it is a pattern of impulses that comes into the nervous system and that makes the basis for perceiving different tastes.

Coupling of receptors Pfaffmann's records of taste receptors come from fibers heading into the nervous system which have not yet made synapses. At the first synapse, there are a lot of possibilities for matters to get more mixed up. Perhaps the different classes of taste fibers— A, B, and C—make connections at these synapses that make the pattern much more complicated. Certainly that happens in the eye and the ear. For example, the records of Galambos and of Granit, referred to above, probably come from nerve cells that have had synapse since the messages left the eye and ear. Granit's records probably come from the third order ganglion cells of the eye, and Galambos' from second order neurons of the cochlear nucleus. Both scientists report complex patterns of response in the nerve cells that gave them their records.

Fig. 3 Activity of three types of ganglion cells distinguished in the vertebrate eye by Hartline. [From S. H. Bartley, "Some Factors in Brightness Discrimination," Psychological Review, 46:340, 1939. By permission of the author and the publisher.]

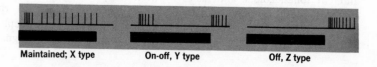

Maintained; X type   On-off, Y type   Off, Z type

In the eye we see receptors getting coupled together in various ways. Receptors, each responding to a narrow band of the spectrum, hook into the same neurons after one or two synapses are passed. Sometimes a green and a blue receptor are coupled together, sometimes a blue and a yellow, and sometimes there are other combinations. There are certainly cases in which many are ganged together in different ways. That can be proved by bleaching out some receptors with one wave length of light and then seeing what records the remaining receptors give. Some day, with the right facts in hand, we may be able to say exactly how the coupling of receptors makes us see different colors. So far we know only that the receptors are coupled in many ways.

Inhibition by receptors Life would be simple if receptors were coupled together in only one way, so that their responses added up. Thus it would be nice if a red and a green receptor were so hooked onto the same bipolar or ganglion cell that their responses simply added together. Sadly enough, though, receptors not only add together, they also subtract from each other's effects. That is to say, when receptors are coupled together, one receptor sometimes inhibits or stops the effects of the other.

We find this sort of coupling turning up in other kinds of experiments with the eye. From electrodes in the optic nerve or in the ganglion cells of the retina, we can see several kinds of reactions to light. As is shown in Figure 3, some nerve cells "go on," that is, give impulses, when a light comes on. Some are in spontaneous activity while the eye is in the dark and stop firing when a light comes on. Still others go on when the light goes on, then stop while the light is on, and finally start firing again when the light goes off. The main point is that turning on a light can inhibit or stop impulses that have been started by other lights or in some other way. Thus we are led to believe that receptors are coupled not only by adding but also by subtracting, that is, by inhibiting arrangements of various sorts.

We do not understand just how the receptors add and subtract in perception. We are starting to get the general idea though, and we are making progress year by year. As matters now stand, we know this much: One cannot tell what a receptor does by the way it is built or how it looks. Receptors have different features that do not meet the eye. Some act like the sense organ as a whole, but others pick out only part of the sensory gamut of stimuli to react to. We can perceive different tones, colors, and tastes by what receptors signal that they are responding to. The signals, however, are not simple. In the synapses between the receptors and the brain, receptors get coupled to the same nerve cells. Sometimes this coupling adds up to signals

from different receptors. Sometimes it causes a nerve cell to be inhibited by a receptor. Our perception thus rests on very complex
patterns of signals coming from receptors.

selection 25 / modification of electric activity in cochlear nucleus during "attention" in unanesthetized cats / Raúl Hernández-Peón, Harold Scherrer, and Michel Jouvet, School of Medicine, University of California, Los Angeles

Attention involves the selective awareness of certain sensory messages
with the simultaneous suppression of others. Our sense organs are
activated by a great variety of sensory stimuli, but relatively few evoke
conscious sensation at any given moment. It is common experience
that there is a pronounced reduction of extraneous sensory awareness
when our attention is concentrated on some particular matter. During
the attentive state, it seems as though the brain integrates for consciousness only a limited amount of sensory information, specifically,
those impulses concerned with the object of attention.

An interference with impulses initiated by sensory stimuli other
than those pertaining to the subject of attention seems to be an
obvious possibility. It is clear that this afferent blockade might occur
at any point along the classical sensory pathways from receptors to the
cortical receiving areas, or else perhaps in the recently disclosed extra-
classical sensory paths that traverse the brain-stem reticular system.

Recent evidence indicates the existence of central mechanisms that
regulate sensory transmission. It has been shown that appropriate
stimulation of the brain-stem reticular system will inhibit afferent con-
duction between the first- and second-order neurons in all three
principal somatic paths. During central anesthesia, the afferent-evoked
potentials in the first sensory relays are enhanced. This appears to be
due to the release of a tonic descending inhibitory influence that
operates during wakefulness and requires the functional integrity of
the brain-stem reticular formation.

The possibility that a selective central inhibitory mechanism might

From Raúl Hernández-Peón, Harold Scherrer, and Michel Jouvet, "Modification of Electric Activity in Cochlear Nucleus During 'Attention' in Unanesthetized Cats," *Science*, 123:331–332, 1956. Reprinted by permission of the
authors and the publisher.

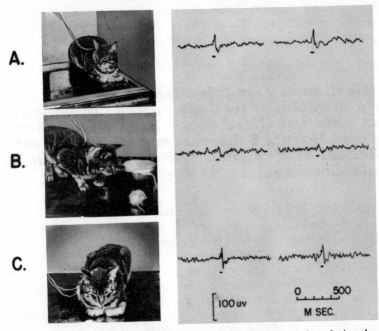

Fig. 1   *Direct recording of click responses in the cochlear nucleus during three periods; the photographs were taken simultaneously. Top and bottom: cat is relaxed; the click responses are large. Middle: while the cat is visually attentive to the mice in the jar, the click responses are diminished in amplitude.*

operate during attention for filtering sensory impulses was tested by studying afferent transmission in the second- or third-order neurons of the auditory pathway (cochlear nucleus) in unanesthetized, unrestrained cats during experimentally elicited attentive behavior. Bipolar stainless steel electrodes with a total diameter of 0.5 mm were implanted stereotaxically in the dorsal cochlear nucleus through a small hole bored in the skull. The electrodes was fixed to the skull with dental cement. A minimum of 1 week elapsed between the operation and the first electroencephalographic recordings. Electric impulses in the form of short bursts of rectangular waves (0.01 to 0.02 sec) at a frequency of 1000 to 5000 cy/sec were delivered to a loudspeaker near the cats at an intensity comfortable to human observers in the same environment.

Three types of sensory modalities were used to attract the animal's attention: visual, olfactory, and somatic. As is illustrated in Fig. 1, during presentation of visual stimuli (two mice in a closed bottle), the auditory responses in the cochlear nucleus were greatly reduced in comparison with the control responses; they were practically abolished as long as the visual stimuli elicited behavioral evidence of attention. When the mice were removed, the auditory responses returned to the same order of magnitude as the initial controls. An olfactory stimulus that attracted the animal's attention produced a similar blocking effect. While the cat was attentively sniffing tubing through which fish odors were being delivered, the auditory potential in the cochlear nucleus was practically absent. After the stimulus had been removed and when the cat appeared to be relaxed once more, the auditorily evoked responses in the cochlear nucleus were of the same magnitude as they had been prior to the olfactory stimulation. Similarly, a nociceptive shock delivered to the forepaw of the cat— a shock that apparently distracted the animal's attention—resulted in marked reduction of auditorily evoked responses in the cochlear nucleus.

If this sensory inhibition during attentive behavior, as demonstrated in the auditory pathway, occurs in all other sensory paths except the ones concerned with the object of attention, such an inhibitory mechanism might lead to favoring of the attended object by the selective exclusion of incoming signals. It is conceivable not only that such a selective sensory inhibition might operate simultaneously for various sensory modalities, leaving one or more unaffected but that the selectivity could extend to some discriminable aspects of any single modality—for example, to one tone and not to others. This suggestion finds support in the recent demonstration that sensory "habituation" may occur to a particular tone—that is, a slowly developing inhibitory effect on auditorily evoked potentials observed in the cochlear nucleus on prolonged repetition of a given tone, an influence that does not affect other frequencies that are novel to the animal. The pathway by which this inhibitory influence acts on incoming auditory impulses remains to be determined, but experiments now in progress have shown that during electric stimulation of the midbrain reticular formation, the auditory potential in the cochlear nucleus is depressed.

The present observations suggest that the blocking of afferent impulses in the lower portions of a sensory path may be a mechanism whereby sensory stimuli out of the scope of attention can be markedly reduced while they are still in their trajectory toward higher levels of the central nervous system. This central inhibitory mechanism may, therefore, play an important role in selective exclusion of sensory messages along their passage toward mechanisms of perception and consciousness. In a recent symposium on brain mechanisms and consciousness, Adrian pointed out that "the signals from the sense organs must be treated differently when we attend to them and when we do not, and if we could decide where and how the divergence arises we should be nearer to understanding how the level of consciousness is reached."

selection 26 / experiments in perception / W. H. Ittelson, Brooklyn College, and F. P. Kilpatrick, Princeton University

What is perception? Why do we see what we see, feel what we feel, hear what we hear? We act in terms of what we perceive; our acts lead to new perceptions; these lead to new acts, and so on in the incredibly complex process that constitutes life. Clearly, then, an understanding of the process by which man becomes aware of himself and his world is basic to any adequate understanding of human behavior. But the problem of explaining how and why we perceive in the way we do is one of the most controversial fields in psychology. We shall describe here some recent experimental work which sheds new light on the problem and points the way to a new theory of perception.

The fact that we see a chair and are then able to go to the place at which we localize it and rest our bodies on a substantial object does not seem particularly amazing or difficult to explain—until we try to explain it. If we accept the prevailing current view that we can never be aware of the world as such, but only of the nervous impulses arising from the impingement of physical forces on sensory receptors, we immediately face the necessity of explaining the correspondence between what we perceive and whatever it is that is there.

An extremely logical, unbeatable—and scientifically useless—answer is simply to say there is no real world, that everything exists in the mind alone. Another approach is to postulate the existence of an external world, to grant that there is some general correspondence between that world and what we perceive and to seek some understandable and useful explanation of why that should be. Most of the prominent theories about perception have grown out of the latter approach. These theories generally agree that even though much of the correspondence may be due to learning, at some basic level there exists an absolute correspondence between what is "out there" and what is in the "mind." But there is a great deal of disagreement

W. H. Ittelson and F. P. Kilpatrick, "Experiments in Perception," *Scientific American*, 185:50–55, 1952. Reprinted with permission. Copyright © 1952 by Scientific American, Inc. All rights reserved.

concerning the level at which such innately determined correspondence occurs. At one extreme are theorists who believe that the correspondence occurs at the level of simple sensations, such as color, brightness, weight, hardness, and so on, and that out of these sensations are compounded more complex awarenesses, such as the recognition of a pencil or a book. At the other extreme are Gestalt psychologists who feel that complex perceptions such as the form of an object are the result of an inherent relationship between the properties of the thing perceived and the properties of the brain. All these schools seem to agree, however, that there is some perceptual level at which exists absolute objectivity; that is, a one-to-one correspondence between experience and reality.

This belief is basic to current thinking in many fields. It underlies most theorizing concerning the nature of science, including Percy W. Bridgman's attempt to reach final scientific objectivity in the "observable operation." In psychology one is hard put to find an approach to human behavior which departs from this basic premise. But it leads to dichotomies such as organism v. environment, subjective v. objective. Stimuli or stimulus patterns are treated as though they exist apart from the perceiving organism. Psychologists seek to find mechanical relationships or interactions between the organism and an "objectively defined" environment. They often rule out purposes and values as not belonging in a strictly scientific psychology.

The experiments to be described here arose from a widespread and growing feeling that such dichotomies are false, and that in practice it is impossible to leave values and purposes out of consideration in scientific observation. The experiments were designed to re-examine some of the basic ideas from which these problems stem.

During the past few years Adelbert Ames, Jr., of the Institute for Associated Research in Hanover, N. H., has designed some new ways of studying visual perception. They have resulted in a new conception of the nature of knowing and of observation. This theory neither denies the existence of objects nor proposes that they exist in a given form independently, that is, apart from the perceiving organism. Instead, it suggests that the world each of us knows is a world created in large measure from our experience in dealing with the environment.

Let us illustrate this in specific terms through some of the demonstrations. In one of them the subject sits in a dark room in which he can see only two star points of light. Both are equidistant from the observer, but one is brighter than the other. If the observer closes one eye and keeps his head still, the brighter point of light looks nearer than the dimmer one. Such apparent differences are related not only to brightness but also to direction from the observer. If two points of light of equal brightness are situated near the floor, one about a foot above the other, the upper one will generally be perceived as farther away than the lower one; if they are near the ceiling, the lower one will appear farther away.

A somewhat more complex experiment uses two partly inflated balloons illuminated from a concealed source. The balloons are in fixed positions about one foot apart. Their relative sizes can be varied by means of a lever control connected to a bellows, and another lever controls their relative brightness. When the size and brightness of both balloons are the same, an observer looking at them with one eye from 10 feet or more sees them as two glowing spheres at equal distances from him. If the brightnesses are left the same and the relative sizes are changed, the larger balloon appears to nearly all observers somewhat nearer. If the size lever is moved continuously, causing continuous variation in the relative size of the balloons, they appear to move dramatically back and forth through space, even when the observer watches with both eyes open. The result is similar when the sizes are kept equal and the relative brightness is varied.

With the same apparatus the effects of size and brightness may be combined so that they supplement or conflict with each other. When they supplement each other, the variation in apparent distance is much greater than when either size or brightness alone is varied. When conflict is introduced by varying size and brightness in opposition to each other, the relative change in distance is considerably less than when they act in combination or alone. Most people, however, give more weight to relative size than they give to brightness in judging distance.

These phenomena cannot be explained by referring to "reality," because "reality" and perception do not correspond. They cannot be explained by reference to the pattern in the retina of the eye, because for any given retinal pattern there are an infinite number of brightness-size-distance combinations to which that pattern might be related. When faced with such a situation, in which an unlimited number of possibilities can be related to a given retinal pattern, the organism apparently calls upon its previous experiences and assumes that what has been most probable in the past is most probable in the immediate occasion. When presented with two star-points of different brightness, a person unconsciously "bets" or "assumes" that the two points, being similar, are probably identical (*i. e.*, of equal brightness), and therefore that the one which seems brighter must be nearer. Similarly the observed facts in the case of two star-points placed vertically one above the other suggest that when we look down we assume, on the basis of past experience, that objects in the lower part of the visual field are nearer than objects in the upper part; when we look up, we assume the opposite to be true. An analogous explanation can be made of the role of relative size as an indication of relative distance.

Why do the differences in distance seem so much greater when the relative size of two objects is varied continuously than when the size difference is fixed? This phenomenon, too, apparently is based on experience. It is a fairly common experience, though not usual, to find that two similar objects of different sizes are actually the same distance away from us. But it is rare indeed to see two stationary objects at the same distance, one growing larger and the other smaller; almost always in everyday life when we see two identical or nearly identical objects change relative size they are in motion in relation to each other. Hence under the experimental conditions we are much more likely to assume distance differences in the objects of changing size than in those of fixed size. In other words, apparently we make use of a weighted average of our past experience in interpreting what we see. It seems that the subject relates to the stimulus pattern a complex, probability-like integration of his past experience with such patterns. Were it not for such integrations, which have been labeled assumptions, the particular perceptual phenomenon would not occur. It follows from this that the resulting perceptions are not absolute revelations of "what is out there" but are in the nature of probabilities or predictions based on past experience. These predictions are not always reliable, as the demonstrations make clear.

Visual perception involves an impression not only of *where* an object is but of *what* it is. From the demonstrations already described we may guess that there is a very strong relationship between localization in space ("thereness") and the assignment of objective properties ("thatness"). This relationship can be demonstrated by a cube experiment.

Two solid white cubes are suspended on wires that are painted black so as to be invisible against a black background. One cube is about 3 feet from the observer and the other about 12 feet. The observer's head is in a headrest so positioned that the cubes are almost in line with each other but he can see both, the nearer cube being slightly to the right. A tiny metal shield is then placed a few inches in front of the left eye. It is just big enough to cut off the view of the far cube from the left eye. The result is that the near cube is seen with both eyes and the far cube with just the right eye. Under these conditions the observer can fix the position of the near cube very well, because he has available all the cues that come from the use of the two eyes. But in the case of the far cube seen with only one eye, localization is much more difficult and uncertain.

Now since the two cubes are almost in line visually, a slight movement of the head to the right will cause the inside vertical edges of the cubes to coincide. Such coincidence of edge is strongly related to an assumption of "togetherness." Hence when the subject moves his head in this way, the uncertainly located distant cube appears to have moved forward to a position even with the nearer cube. Under these conditions not only does the mislocated cube appear smaller, but it appears different in shape, that is, no longer cubical, even though the pattern cast by the cube on the retina of the eye has not changed at all.

The same point can be illustrated most dramatically by experiments in which the subject wears a pair of glasses fitted with so-called aniseikonic lenses, which are ground in such a way that they give images of different size and shape to the two retinas. This produces very marked distortions of any objects which the subject visualizes mainly through the use of two-eyed stereoscopic vision. In an ordinary environment there are generally enough one-eye cues, such as shadow, overlay, familiar objects of known size, and so on, to suppress the binocular cues and hold the visual world "in shape." But in an environment poor in one-eye cues the observer is forced to rely on binocular cues, and under these circumstances the distortion is enhanced for anyone wearing such glasses. It has been found that if an ordinary square room is lined with tree leaves, which reduce monocular cues to a minimum by covering the flat wall spaces, most observers looking through aniseikonic lenses perceive a great deal of distortion of the room and the leaves. To an observer looking at the room as a whole through certain glasses of this type the walls appear to slant inward from floor to ceiling, the ceiling seems much lower than it is and its leaves look very small. The floor, which is the object of interest in this particular analysis, appears to be much farther away than its true position, and the leaves covering it look huge. Now, if the observer wearing the same glasses looks at just the floor instead of the room in general, the floor changes markedly in appearance. It appears to be much nearer than before, and instead of being level it seems to rise from front to back at a pitch of about 45 degrees. The leaves, however, now look more nearly normal in size.

These perceptions can be explained in terms of the geometry of stereoscopic vision. The stimulus patterns on the retinas of the eyes are the geometric projections of an external surface. But identical projections may be produced by surfaces of different kinds. In this case a distant surface that is nearly horizontal, a closer surface that is slightly tipped and a very near surface that is sharply tipped all produce the same stereoscopic stimulus patterns. When the observer looks at the whole room, he "chooses" the nearly horizontal faraway floor surface as the focus of perception, probably because he cannot make a room out of the pattern if the floor is sharply tipped up. When he limits his gaze to the floor, he no longer needs to make a room of what he is looking at, and he sees the floor sharply tipped, perhaps because the leaves now appear more nearly the size he assumes them to be.

In the everyday environment outside the laboratory the wearing of these glasses produces similarly interesting illusions. For example, a large body of water such as a lake appears horizontal and farther away than its real position, but a large expanse of level lawn looks tipped and nearer than its real position. Presumably this happens because the observer brings to these occasions the assumptions, based on past experience, that the probability of a lake surface being other than horizontal is almost zero, while the probability of a grass surface being a slope is fairly high.

The most reasonable explanation of these visual phenomena seems to be that an observer unconsciously relates to the stimulus pattern some sort of weighted average of the past consequences of acting with respect to that pattern. The particular perception "chosen" is the one that has the best predictive value, on the basis of previous experience, for action in carrying out the purposes of the organism. From this one may make two rather crucial deductions: (1) an unfamiliar external configuration which yields the same retinal pattern as one the observer is accustomed to deal with will be perceived as the familiar configuration; (2) when the observer acts on his interpretation of the unfamiliar configuration and finds that he is wrong, his perception will change even though the retinal pattern is unchanged.

Let us illustrate with some actual demonstrations. If an observer in a dark room looks with one eye at two lines of light which are at the same distance and elevation but of different lengths, the longer line will look nearer than the shorter line. Apparently he assumes that the lines are identical and translates the difference in length into a difference in position. If the observer takes a wand with a luminous tip and tries to touch first one line and then the other, he will be unable to do so at first. After repeated practice, however, he can learn to touch the two lines quickly and accurately. At this point he no longer sees the lines as at different distances; they now look, as they are, the same distance from him. He originally assumed that the two lines were the same length because that seemed the best bet under the circumstances. After he had tested this assumption by purposive action, he shifted to the assumption, less probable in terms of past experience but still possible, that the lines were at the same distance but of different lengths. As his assumption changed, perception did also.

There is another experiment that demonstrates these points even more convincingly. It uses a distorted room in which the floor slopes up to the right of the observer, the rear wall recedes from right to left and the windows are of different sizes and trapezoidal in shape. When an observer looks at this room with one eye from a certain point, the room appears completely normal, as if the floor were level, the rear wall at right angles to the line of sight and the windows rectangular and of the same size. Presumably the observer chooses this particular appearance instead of some other because of the assumptions he brings to the occasion. If he now takes a long stick and tries to touch the various parts of the room, he will be unsuccessful, even though he has gone into the situation knowing the true shape of the room. With practice, however, he becomes more and more successful in touching what he wants to touch with the stick. More important, he sees the room more and more in its true shape, even though the stimulus pattern on his retina has remained unchanged.

By means of a piece of apparatus called the "rotating trapezoidal window" it has been possible to extend the investigation to complex perceptual situations involving movement. This device consists of a trapezoidal surface with panes cut in it and shadows painted on it to give the appearance of a window. It is mounted on a rod connected to a motor so that it rotates at a slow constant speed in an upright position about its own axis. When an observer views the rotating surface with one eye from about 10 feet or more or with both eyes from about 25 feet or more, he sees not a rotating trapezoid but an oscillating rectangle. Its speed of movement and its shape appear to vary markedly as it turns. If a small cube is attached by a short rod to the upper part of the short side of the trapezoid, it seems to become detached, sail freely around the front of the trapezoid and attach itself again as the apparatus rotates.

All these experiments, and many more that have been made, suggest strongly that perception is never a sure thing, never an absolute revelation of "what is." Rather, what we see is a prediction—our own personal construction designed to give us the best possible bet for carrying out our purposes in action. We make these bets on the basis of our past experience. When we have a great deal of relevant and consistent experience to relate to stimulus patterns, the probability of success of our prediction (perception) as a guide to action is extremely high, and we tend to have a feeling of surety. When our experience is limited or inconsistent, the reverse holds true. According to the new theory of perception developed from the demonstrations we have described, perception is a functional affair based on action, experience and probability. The thing perceived is an inseparable part

of the function of perceiving, which in turn includes all aspects of
the total process of living. This view differs from the old rival theories:
the thing perceived is neither just a figment of the mind nor an
innately determined absolute revelation of a reality postulated to exist
apart from the perceiving organism. Object and percept are part and
parcel of the same thing.

This conclusion of course has far-reaching implications for many
areas of study, for some assumption as to what perception is must
underly any philosophy or comprehensive theory of psychology, of
science or of knowledge in general. Although the particular investigations involved here are restricted to visual perception, this is only a
vehicle which carries us into a basic inquiry of much wider significance.

selection 27 / cultural influence of the perception of movement: the trapezoidal illusion among zulus / Gordon W. Allport and Thomas F. Pettigrew, Harvard University

Traditionally, theories of the visual perception of movement—with
which the present study deals—have been divided into two classes:
(1) The *nativistic*, i.e., theories emphasizing the role of retinal and
cortical functions relatively unaffected by learning, habit, experience,
or meaning; and (2) The *empiricistic*, i.e., theories giving primary
weight to the role of experience and learning.

For our purposes it is essential to subdivide empiricistic theories
into two groups:

Cumulative habit Stressing the effects of many types of early, remote,
and generalized experience which by transfer or cross conditioning became a
major determinant of the perception of movement. Toch and Ittelson state
that "contemporary empiricism" favors this type of approach, offering its
explanations of perceived movement in terms of "weighted averages of experiential sediments of all kinds acting inseparably."

Object connotation (meaning) Explaining perceived movement largely in
terms of familiar objects. One sees continuous wing motion in an electric sign
representing a bird in flight, although the stimulus actually occurs discon-
tinuously in two or in three fixed positions. This theory would hold that our

Abridged from Gordon W. Allport and Thomas F. Pettigrew, "Cultural
Influence of the Perception of Movement: The Trapezoidal Illusion Among
Zulus," *Journal of Abnormal and Social Psychology*, 55:104–113, 1957. Reprinted by permission of the authors and the American Psychological Association.

familiarity with birds in flight causes us to fill the gaps with perceived motion. A good statement of this theory of stroboscopic movement may be found in James. This author insisted that "perception is of definite and probable things." In explaining illusions, James leaned heavily upon their resemblance to familiar objects. In so doing he was merely rendering more concrete and specific Helmholtz's theory of "unconscious inferences" and Wundt's "assimilation" theory.

THE CROSS-CULTURAL APPROACH

To gain light on this dispute psychologists have often asked, "How about primitive peoples?" If we can find a tribe or a culture where relevant past experience can be ruled out, we could then determine whether the perception resembles that of western peoples. If it does so, then the argument for nativism is presumably stronger. The first extensive attempt to apply this test was made by W. H. R. Rivers during the Torres Strait expedition in 1898. Rivers presented to the island natives a whole array of visual illusions and compared their reports with western norms. For some of the illusions there were no appreciable differences; for others, the natives seemed on the whole less susceptible than westerners. While Rivers himself does not make the point clearly, his results seem to show that illusions involving object connotation (e.g., a European street scene) are far less compelling to the natives than are illusions having no such object connotation (e.g., the rotating spiral).

It is not easy for western psychologists to visit primitive tribes, nor to conduct among them adequately controlled experiments. The present article, however, deals with one such attempt. But before we describe it, the theoretical point at issue should be made entirely clear: *We do not claim to be testing the merits of the nativist or empiricist positions directly.* For reasons that will appear in the course of our discussion, we do not believe that comparative perceptual studies on western and on primitive peoples can solve this particular riddle. *We claim only to have illuminated the part played by object connotation (meaning) in the perception of motion as over and against the part played by either nativistic determinants or cumulative habit.* Our experiment is *not* able to distinguish between the role of these last two factors.

The rotating trapezoidal window

Before the days of Gestalt psychology it was customary to regard visual illusions as oddities, as exceptional experiences to be accounted for either in terms of nativistic or experiential constraints. Today, however, we make little distinction between illusions and veridical perceptions, since no illusion lacks veridical elements and no veridical perception is devoid of subjective shaping. So-called illusions are simply instances of perception where the discrepancy between impression and knowledge (whether the knowledge be the subject's or the experimenter's) is relatively striking. It is in such "looser" conditions of perception that theorists often seek to obtain light on the relative weight of factors entering into the normal perceptual process. The reasoning is not unlike that which leads psychologists to study exaggerated functions in psychopathology in order to obtain light on the same but less exaggerated functions of the normal mind.

Our experiment follows this logic, making use of the rotating trapezoidal window described by Ames—a device that has been called "a dramatic masterpiece of ambiguous stimulation." The window is so proportioned that as it rotates, the length of the longer edge is always longer on the retina than is the shorter edge (even when the shorter edge is nearer). The resulting perception is normally one of oscillation or sway; the observer apparently tending to keep the longer edge nearer to him. Instead of seeming to rotate, as it actually does, the window is seen to sway back and forth in an arc of 90 to 180 degrees.

An appended cube and rod add great interest to the illusion, since the perceived *rotating* of these objects conflicts sharply with the perceived *sway* of the window. In consequence, the cube is usually seen to detach itself and swing without support in a ghostly fashion in front of the window (for that period of time when the shorter edge, to which it is attached, is in fact nearer to the subject). Similarly, the rod bends, twists or "cuts through" the mullions in order to accommodate itself to the phenomenal oscillation. The observer finds the bizarre effect both amusing and inexplicable.

The explanation Ames gives for the illusion maintains (a) that the observer, owing to familiarity with rectangular windows assumes *this* window to be rectangular; and (b) that owing to long experience with doors, windows, and similar objects, the observer has learned to interpret longer retinal stimulations as coming from nearer objects. Hence, the longer edge of the window is interpreted as being nearer, and the window is seen to oscillate rather than to rotate.

Ames gives a clearly empiricistic explanation with a leaning toward the object connotation version:

In his past experience the observer, in carrying out his purposes, has on innumerable occasions had to take into account and act with respect to rectangular forms, e.g., going through doors, locating windows, etc. On almost all such occasions, except in the rare case when his line of sight was normal to the door or window, the image of the rectangular configuration formed on his retina was trapezoidal. He learned to interpret the particularly characteristic retinal images that exist when he looks at doors, windows, etc., as rectangular forms. Moreover, he learned to interpret the particular degree of trapezoidal distortion of his retinal images in terms of the positioning of the rectangular form to his particular viewing point. These interpretations do not occur at the conscious level, rather, they are unconscious and may be characterized as *assumptions* as to the probable significance of indications received from the environment.

It should be added that Ames does not insist that object connotation ("windowness") is the sole determinant of the illusion. He himself employed a variety of trapezoidal figures and discovered that even a plane surface of trapezoidal shape arouses the illusion of sway, though to a much less degree than does a "window frame."

The hypothesis

In order to test the "object connotation" theory, we studied various groups of Zulu children (10–14 years old) in Natal whose own culture is virtually devoid not only of windows, but, to a surprising extent, of angles, straight lines, and other experiential cues that would presumably "cause" the illusion if it were wholly a product of experience. Our hypothesis therefore is:

Zulu children, provided they are unacculturated (amabinca) *will report the illusion of sway in the trapezoidal window less often than will urbanized acculturated Zulu children* (amabunguka) *or than white ("European") children.*

The Zulu culture

Zulu culture is probably the most spherical or circular of all Bantu cultures, possibly the most spherical of all native African cultures (though it would be difficult to prove this contention). The word "zulu" means heavens or firmament, and the aesthetic ideal of round rather than angular styles affects native art, architecture, and speech.

Huts are invariably round (rondavels) or else beehive shaped, whereas in other Bantu tribes they are sometimes square or rectangular. Round huts arranged in a circular form with round stockades to fence in animals, constitutes a typical African homestead (kraal). Fields follow the irregular contours of the rolling land, and never seem to be laid out in the neat rectangular plots so characteristic of western culture.

The typical Zulu hut has no windows, and no word for such an aperture exists. In the more primitive beehive grass huts, doors are merely round entrance holes; in the round mud huts doors are amorphous, seldom if ever neatly rectangular. Cooking pots are round or gourd shaped. In his studies among Zulus, L. Doob finds that the less acculturated natives, relative to westernized natives, show a statistically significant preference for circles over squares when they are asked to choose between designs drawn in these shapes (personal communication to the authors).

It is commonly said in Natal that Zulus fresh from reserves cannot plow a straight furrow and are unable to lay out a rectangular flower bed. Such inability is of course overcome with experience and training, but the initial defect would seem clearly related to the circularity that is characteristic of life on the reserves and to the lack of familiarity with straight layouts.

Linguistically, the same bias towards circularity is seen. While it is possible to say "round" in Zulu, there is no word for "square." There is a word for "circle" but not for "rectangle." To speak of window, of square, or of rectangle at all, a Zulu is forced to borrow these terms from Afrikaans or from English—provided he is able to do so.

The subjects

The experiment required the use of two contrasting groups of subjects (Ss): those who had lived all or most of their lives in western culture, and those who were unacculturated. Even in the Bantu reserves or in Zululand itself it is not possible to make certain that a resident does not know what a window is like. While schools, churches, and health centers are few and far between, they are nevertheless within the possible range of visitation by most native inhabitants, even children. Our experiments at Polela and Ceza took place in health centers, at Nongoma in a court house. The Ss, to be sure, were brought in from remote parts of the reserves by lorry, or came on foot; but they had at least this one-time acquaintance with a rectangular building and windows.

Still, it is possible to say that the experiment dealt with two widely contrasting groups in respect to the degree of experience they had had with western architecture and ways of life. Some members of the more primitive groups, for example, may never have seen windows with rectangular panes of glass prior to the actual experimental situation.

By using herd boys as Ss—mostly between 10 and 14 years of age (few of them knew their age exactly)—we were able to make certain that they had never been off the reserves and had never attended school. Boys of the same age comprised our urban control groups: one group of European boys at Greyville Community Center; another group of Bantu boys at the Lamontville Community Center in Durban. Most of these urban boys were attending school.

Our major experiment thus involved the following groups:

Group A	Urban European boys	(20 cases)
Group B	Urban African boys	(20 cases)
Group C	Polela Rural Africans	(20 cases)
Group D	Nongoma Rural Africans	(20 cases)

A rough indication of the cultural differences between the rural and urban groups lies in answers to the question asked at the end of the experiment about the rectangular window, "What does this look like?" The percentage saying "window" or "window frame" among the urban children was 88; among the rural, 45.

Procedure

The procedure involves four conditions, varying two factors bearing on the perception of the illusion: monocular vs. binocular viewing and distance from the stimulus object. Each S saw first the rectangular, and then the trapezoidal window in at least 3 full revolutions under each of the following conditions.

First trial: 10 ft.   binocular
Second trial: 10 ft.   monocular
Third trial: 20 ft.   binocular
Fourth trial: 20 ft.   monocular

It was thought that this order would impose the "hardest" condition first and therefore minimize the effects of suggestion. One might fear that if at 20 feet with one eye a subject easily perceived the illusion he might become accustomed to expecting oscillation in the trapezoidal window at closer distances and under binocular conditions. Conversely, of course, it might be argued that a subject who cannot perceive the illusion at ten feet binocularly would form an expectation that might prevent his obtaining it under easier conditions. We shall refer later to a control experiment (starting at 20 feet monocularly) designed to check on any suggestive effect that might arise from our order of presentation.

The experimenter (E) required the assistance of a second psychologist who kept records of the Ss' reports, also of an interpreter with all African Ss. Care was taken to prevent Ss who had finished the experiment from communicating with Ss who had not.

After being put at ease, the S gave his age (if he knew it) and his degree of education (if any). The S then sat in a chair placed at the proper distance from the window and was told to watch carefully the movement that he would see. After approximately three revolutions the E asked, "How does it seem to you to be moving?" Often the S spontaneously used his hands to indicate the motion until the E was satisfied whether a full rotation or a fluctuation was intended. The use of hand motion by the S proved to be fully convincing, for when he reversed the hand at precisely the right moment for the illusion to occur there could be no question concerning his experience. This device gave a useful check on the accuracy of the translator's report of the S's verbal statements.

After obtaining a report for the rectangular window in each of the positions, the trapezoidal window was inserted in place of the rectangular, and the same method of report employed. In addition, the S was asked to tell whether the motion of the trapezoidal window was "like" that of the first window. This procedure served as a further check on the verbal description and hand report. In nearly all cases it was possible to record a clear and unequivocal judgment of the S's perception. Less than three per cent of all judgments were listed by the E as "uncertain."

Whenever the illusion was reported for the first condition, the bar was inserted and the S asked, "How does the bar move?" and "Does the bar stay straight?" On occasional trials when the S had reported both the sway of the window and the bending of the bar, the cube was attached and the S asked to describe its motion. In these cases there was usually laughter (as with American Ss) and considerable confusion and difficulty manifested in describing so unreal and "spooky" a motion. Because of the difficulty of communicating concerning these complex phenomena we make no further systematic use of the cube and rod in the present study.

At the conclusion of the experiment, the S was asked what the rectangular window "looked like." He also stated his preference for one of two geometrical drawings presented to him in pairs (a circle, square, trapezoid). He then received a slight payment for his services (usually one pound of sugar or a candy bar and six pence).

RESULTS

General results Table 1 gives the results for the two unacculturated groups (Nongoma and Polela Reserves) and for the two districts within metropolitan Durban, African (Lamontville), and European (Greyville).

Combining all four conditions, there is a very significant tendency for the urban groups to report the illusion more often than the rural groups (corrected 2×2 $\chi^2 = 15.34$; $p < .001$). This difference is

TABLE 1 NUMBER REPORTING ILLUSION (BOYS 10–14 YRS. OF AGE, $N = 20$ IN EACH GROUP)

Condition	Nongoma rural			Polela rural			African urban			European urban		
	Yes	No	Uncertain	Yes	No	Uncertain	Yes	No	Uncertain	Yes	No	Uncertain
First condition (10', both eyes)	3	17	0	4	14	2	13	7	0	11	9	0
Second condition (10', one eye)	14	6	0	16	4	0	19	1	0	19	1	0
Third condition (20', both eyes)	8	12	0	17	1	2	16	3	1	16	4	0
Fourth condition (20', one eye)	18	2	0	17	2	1	18	2	0	19	0	1
Totals	43	37	0	54	21	5	66	13	1	65	14	1

TABLE 2   DISTRIBUTION OF SCORES

Sample	Number of yes's					Average
	4	3	2	1	0	
Nongoma	2	4	10	3	1	2.15
Polela	4	10	3	2	1	2.70
Urban African	12	4	2	2	0	3.30
Urban European	11	5	3	0	1	3.25
Total (N = 80)	29	23	18	7	3	2.85

most marked with the first condition (corrected 2×2 $\chi^2 = 12.38$; $p < .001$). There is also a significant trend with the second condition (corrected 2×2 $\chi^2 = 4.80$; $p < .05$) and a slight tendency with the third condition (corrected 2×2 $\chi^2 = 1.87$; $p < .20$) for the rural children to observe the illusion less often than the urban children. Virtually no difference exists with the fourth, 20 feet and one eye condition.

Table 2 expresses the results in an alternative way. Since four conditions of presentation were used we can determine in how many of these four conditions on the average each of the cultural groups reported the illusion. For the two unacculturated groups combined, the illusion is reported in 2.425 of the four conditions, while for the acculturated groups the average is 3.275. This mean difference has high statistical significance ($t = 3.51$; $p < .001$).

It is evident from Tables 1 and 2 that city dwellers, whether Zulu or European, find the illusion somewhat more compelling than do rural ("primitive") natives. This tendency is especially pronounced at 10 feet with binocular vision—a condition when binocular cues of true depth (in this case, true rotation) are most plentiful. The reader will also note that the results for Polela (rural) stand somewhat between those for the city children and those from Nongoma (rural). At ten feet binocularly, they resemble those of Nongoma; at twenty feet binocularly, those of the city boys. Polela is, in fact, one hundred miles closer to Durban than is Nongoma which lies in the heart of Zululand. There is no doubt that the children in Polela have somewhat more familiarity with western architecture (specifically with windows) than do the children of Nongoma. The results (Table 2) correspond to a continuum of cultures: city children having a maximum of familiarity with western architecture, Nongoma children the least.

Preference for circles   Following the experiment, all Ss were shown drawings of a square, a trapezoid, and a circle (in pairs), and asked to express a preference. Table 3 indicates that those who expressed a preference for the circle (at least once in the two pairings) tend in the African groups to report the illusion *less* often. This tendency holds for all experimental conditions for all three African groups. The relationship is statistically significant, however, for only the binocular conditions. Circle-preferring Zulu children report the illusion significantly less often than the angle-preferring Zulus in Conditions 1 and 3 (corrected 2×2 $\chi^2 = 3.89$; $p < .05$), but the difference in the monocular, second and fourth, conditions is not significant (corrected 2×2 $\chi^2 = 0.18$, *n.s.*). There are no differences approaching significance between the circle and noncircle-preferring European Ss.

Let us assume that the aesthetic preference for circles may provide an index of the subjective closeness of the individual to Zulu culture (since it is, as we have seen, overwhelmingly a circular culture). If we do so we may say that this subjective closeness seems to predispose the S to resist the illusion. Stated in terms of transactional theory, rectangles and trapezoids have less functional significance for him. His perception of the window's rotation is accordingly more frequently veridical.

We have noted that this influence is significant only in the conditions involving *binocular* perception. A reasonable interpretation would be that cultural effects cannot easily change the basic demand character of the illusion monocularly perceived, but may do so when binocular conditions leave more latitude for choice and for interpretation among a greater number of cues.

This result then, so far as it goes, lends some weight to the contention that "cultural significance" is playing an appreciable part in determining the results.

Illusion with rectangle   Before viewing the trapezoidal window,

TABLE 3   PERCENTAGE OF CASES REPORTING ILLUSION AMONG SUBJECTS PREFERRING AND NOT PREFERRING CIRCLE

| Condition | Combined African groups N = 60 | | European group N = 20 | |
	Preferring circle N = 39	Not preferring circle N = 21	Preferring circle N = 12	Not preferring circle N = 8
10' binocular	28	43	58	50
10' monocular	79	86	100	88
20' binocular	59	86	83	75
20' monocular	87	90	100	88
All conditions	63	76	85	75

every S in all four conditions first saw the rectangular window rotating. The purpose was to make sure that the sway (oscillation) reported for the trapezoid was judged to be *different* from the motion of the rectangular window. In most cases, indeed, the S was able to make the distinction clearly, indicating by gesture and by words that the rectangular window went "round and round" whereas the trapezoid oscillated.

There were cases, however, where the rectangular window was reported as oscillating. In fact, nearly one-third of the 80 Ss reported such a phenomenon at one or more of the four conditions. The actual percentage reporting sway in the *rectangular* window at each of the four conditions is:

First condition	0
Second condition	8
Third condition	16
Fourth condition	28

It is conceivable that this curious and somewhat unwelcomed finding may be a result of a "suggestive" order of presentation. Thus, no S seeing the rectangle before the trapezoid under the first condition (10 feet binocularly) reported the phenomenon. And, with the exception of 3 cases, no S reported the rectangular illusion in the second, third, or fourth condition *unless* he had previously reported the trapezoidal illusion. Altogether, 81 per cent of our Ss reported the illusion monocularly at 20 feet for the trapezoidal window, but only 28 per cent did so for the rectangular window under the same condition. In virtually all these cases the Ss had grown accustomed to seeing oscillation at some previous stage with the trapezoid.

Pastore, however, finds that more than half of his 58 American college Ss reported sway with the rectangle during a three-minute exposure, and at considerable distance from the window (where the retinal angle subtended by the two shapes may be subliminal). He does not tell whether the Ss had grown accustomed to the sway of the trapezoid before they reported sway in the rectangle. We must leave this problem for the time being unsolved.

DISCUSSION

Our most striking finding is that under optimal conditions (monocularly at 20 feet) virtually as many primitive Zulus report the trapezoidal illusion as do urban Zulus or Europeans. Taking this one partial result by itself we can say that the experiment supports either the nativistic or the cumulative habit theory. It does not by itself give us grounds for choosing between them.

Nativists might argue, for example, that whenever a longer and a shorter projection on the retina occur simultaneously the longer will assume a figure character and therewith a frontal position in the perception (other conditions being equal). Thus, some form of isomorphism obtains between retinal-cortical processes and the perception itself.

An empiricist with a "cumulative habit" preference might say that myriad ocular-motor adjustments from infancy have built up a dependable expectancy that longer projections on the retina will betoken nearer objects. One learns through repeated experience that longer retinal images of trees, cattle, people, stand for *nearer* objects (provided, of course, that one assumes such objects to be of equal size whether far or near from the eyes). It is not necessary for the S to have acquaintance with specific objects (in this case a window) in order to make a similar inference. The transfer effect is wide. Even the shadows painted on the rotating window are reminiscent of the S's experience with shadows in nature. Old experiences automatically condition novel experiences even though the latter are only analogous.

One assumption that may play a decisive part in this case is the assumption of "right angularity." From earliest life the child is conditioned to the fact that perpendicular objects best withstand the force of gravity. Circular though his culture is, his basic frame of reference is still one of verticals and horizontals. Seeing an entirely new object (the trapezoidal window) he assumes unconsciously (no less than do people who are familiar with windows) that its shape is rectangular. Just like people in western culture he may make this assumption even if he "knows" that the object is not in reality rectangular. This assumption, together with the assumption that longer objects on the retina are usually nearer objects, would predispose him to perceive that the longer edge of the window is always nearer (thus inducing the perceived oscillation). No less than people in western culture he would fail to "correct" his assumptions of right-angularity and of long-edges being-near-edges by his "knowledge" of the trapezoidal shape of the stimulus.

Our major result is clearly not compatible with a narrowly conceived object-connotation theory. It is not necessary for the S consciously to assume that the object is a window in order to experience the illusion. True, the specific object connotation seems somewhat to favor the illusion, but it is clearly not the decisive determinant. Thus, for example, 88 per cent of those who did not consciously recognize the frame as a "window" nevertheless experienced the illusion at 20' monocularly.

Yet, at the same time, our results show that object connotation cannot be disregarded. It also plays a part. Let us review the evidence:

1. Under all *suboptimal* conditions, as we see in Tables 1 and 4

(10 feet monocularly, and binocularly at 10 or 20 feet) there is a tendency for unacculturated Ss to report the illusion less frequently than do the acculturated.

2. The Ss who recognize the "windowness" of the stimulus object tend to report the illusion somewhat more frequently especially at 10 feet binocularly.

3. African Ss expressing a preference for circles (assumed here to indicate a subjective closeness to the rotund Zulu culture) tend to report the illusion less often than those expressing preference for angular figures.

We conclude that experience with, and identification with, western culture make it more likely that the illusion will be perceived under marginal (suboptimal) conditions.

One fact reported by Ames, and mentioned above, supports our interpretation. He finds that a plane trapezoidal frame yields appreciable oscillation, but that the addition of mullions, panes, and shadows enhances the illusion. In other words, specific "thingness" contributes to the experience though it does not account for it wholly. And we may again allude to von Schiller's contention that expectancy is effective in determining perceived movement under marginal (*alternative*) conditions.

May Brenner likewise makes the point that when marginal conditions obtain, the S is forced to depend on stimulus *meaning*. On the other hand, when optimal stimulus conditions obtain, even brain-damaged cases report apparent movement to much the same degree as do normal cases.

Several other experiments have dealt with the effects of meaning on apparent movement. Thus, Jones and Bruner report that in a stroboscopic experiment the line drawing of a man is seen to be in motion more actively than is a nonsense figure. De Silva had previously established this same fact. Jones and Bruner conclude that "the more probable and practiced the movement, the more adequately will the movement experience maintain itself under suboptimal conditions." This conclusion is in agreement with our own.

Toch and Ittelson report an experiment in which drawings of a bomb stroboscopically presented are seen in a downward (falling) motion, whereas drawings of an airplane presented in an identical fashion are seen in an upward (rising) motion. Though this experiment taken by itself favors an object-connotation theory, the authors argue in general for the cumulative-habit theory. They contend, rightly no doubt, that the nativist position cannot be adequately tested short of a longitudinal study of infants from birth. They believe that generalized past experience accounts for our major dispositions to perceive stroboscopic or other illusory movement, but allow that under conditions of ambiguity or equivocation specific meaning connotations will enter to determine the direction and nature of the movement. Here, too, our findings are concordant.

If we leave the field of experimental testing for a moment, we can find many familiar instances of the role of object connotation in resolving perceptual ambiguities. A streak of light in the night sky may be seen as a shooting star, as distant fireworks, or as a jet plane, depending largely on one's expectations. Bartlett tells of the Swazi chieftain who perceived all traffic policemen in London as friendly beings, because in Swazi culture the upraised arm is an amiable greeting. A child in a dentist's chair, more familiar with space-ships than with nitrous oxide, perceives the inhalator as a spaceship toy. Every projective test assumes that ambiguous (multivalent) stimuli will receive subjective structuring on the basis of need, set, expectancy, or habit.

Our experiment does not introduce factors of need or of set, but deals only with the relevance of past experience (meaning) as a determinant of perceived movement. It may, however, be pointed out that among sophisticated observers of the trapezoidal illusion under marginal conditions (e.g., at 10 feet binocularly) a voluntary effort to see or not to see the window as oscillating (or as rotating) can also be effective, especially if the observer picks out some detail of the window to watch during the rotation, thus inhibiting the impression as a whole. Meaning is not the only determinant entering into the resolution of perceptual ambiguity, but it is one of them.

Returning to James's statement that, "Perception is of definite and probable things," we may say that under optimal conditions of stimulation definite structure is conferred by physiological conditions or by deeply ingrained functional habits of spatial adjustment, or by both. But when marginal conditions prevail, an association with the most "probable" object is often called upon to provide the definiteness that is otherwise lacking.

What we have called "marginal" conditions should receive a further word of explanation. We use the term in our experiments to indicate that perceptual conflict is present. Under binocular conditions (especially at 10') there are many cues that "give away" the true rotation; at the same time there are operating also the assumptions that the window is rectangular and that longer objects are nearer. Under such a condition of conflict our finding is that urban children resolve the conflict with the aid of the supplementary assumption of "windowness." Not being able to draw on this supplementary assumption, the rural children as a rule resolve the conflict in favor of the binocular (or true) evidence. In this particular case, therefore, one might say that the primitive children see things "as they are" more often than do the children of civilization.

CONCLUSION

The perception of motion as represented in the rotating trapezoidal window is governed, under *optimal* conditions, by nativistic determinants or by the unconscious utilization of residual (but not immediately relevant) experience, or by both. (Our experiment does not enable us to decide this issue.) At the same time, object connotation (meaning) based on closely relevant cultural experience helps to determine the nature of the perceived movement under *marginal* conditions.

An adequate theory of perceived movement must therefore allow a place for the subject's specific assumptions of meaning even though it cannot be based solely on this foundation.

CHAPTER 7 ✸ THE LEARNING PROCESS ✸

In our previous selections we have seen that development of complex motivations and of even rudimentary perceptions is dependent on the ability of the organism to be modified by interactions with its environment, that is, to learn from experience. In this chapter we are concerned with the nature of the modification process per se. When we observe a change in behavior over time which we call learning, we make the assumption that the behavioral change reflects some more or less permanent modification of the central nervous system. Even though this assumption seems eminently reasonable, we are in the unfortunate position of having relatively little empirical knowledge concerning the nature of this neurological change. In Selection 28 Dr. R. W. Sperry notes that "the physical nature of the residual effects or lasting traces left in the brain remains a matter of pure speculation." However, at this stage of our knowledge, "educated guesses" appear to be not only permissible but highly desirable. Sperry proposes that conditioning does not involve "connecting" the neural correlates of a conditioned stimulus directly to the motor neurons responsible for the conditioned response. Rather, what is probably involved in conditioning is that an intermediate pattern of neural excitation is established. This formulation implies that when a subject is returned to the experimental situation in which he was previously conditioned, the stimulus pattern of the laboratory sensitizes or reactivates this intermediate pattern of brain circuits. When the conditioned stimulus is then presented, it is the neural "facilitory set" which elicits the conditioned response. Thus, even though a human subject were conditioned in the laboratory to blink his eye at the onset of a tone, it is not likely that this response would occur to the same stimulus outside of the laboratory. Psychologically he would not have the "anticipatory set" or "expectancy" to respond; neurologically, the relevant "central facilitory set" would not have been activated.

Despite the experimental difficulties involved in investigating the neurophysiological conditions for learning, encouraging results are being obtained. In the 1957 Annual Review of Psychology, Stellar *describes an experiment by Galambos, Sheatz, and Vernier as "a significant breakthrough in the physiology of learning." This experiment, reported as Selection 29, demonstrates that neural responses in the cochlear nucleus can be conditioned and extinguished. You will recall from Selection 25 that Hernández-Peón et al., showed that neural responses to a "click" auditory stimulus are inhibited when the subject is attending to other stimuli. Could it be that the neural response conditioned by Galambos et al., is the physiological correlate of the psychological process of learning to attend to certain stimuli and not to others?*

At the psychological level there is no lack of experiments exploring those variables which influence learning. In fact, probably more papers are published every year on the topic of learning than on any other basic psychological process. Despite the vast amount of data, there is still no basic agreement on such fundamental questions as, "What is it that is learned when learning takes place?" In general, there are two major theoretical positions: the stimulus-response theories (as represented by Clark Hull) hold that what is learned is an association between a stimulus and the response which the subject makes; the cognitive theories (represented by Edwin C. Tolman) hold that the making of an overt response is not necessary for learning, but rather the organism is said to learn the relationship between two sets of stimuli, that is, "what leads to what." In an experiment reported as Selection 30, McNamara, Long, and Wike attempt to determine if lower animals can learn the locus of food without actually making the instrumental response required to come in contact with the food. The results indicate that rats can learn without overt performance, but only if they have the stimulus-support of extra maze cues.

Too often the student of introductory psychology completes his assigned reading on the learning process with the feeling that the material has little relevance to everyday practical problems of learning. It is in part the purpose of the next three selections to dispel such doubts. In Selection 31 Professor William S. Verplanck shows how the principles of operant conditioning, which have been derived from the experimental study of rats and pigeons, may be generalized to complex forms of human verbal behavior under both laboratory and "natural" conditions. A further application of these same principles has exciting implications for new techniques of teaching. In Selection 32 Professor B. F. Skinner points out that the usual classroom learning situation falls short of the ideal conditions in several respects, especially in terms of the lack of control over the relationship between the responses and the reinforcement. He argues that in order to obtain

the necessary response-reinforcement contingencies we must use me-
chanical devices which have come to be known as "teaching machines."
In addition to indicating the basic principles which must be imple-
mented by such a machine, he also replies to some questions which
have been raised about their use. In Selection 33 Dr. Carl Williams
shows how the principle of extinction of a response by removal of the
reinforcement may be applied to the practical problem of eliminating
undesirable behavior in children.

As we have previously seen, socio-cultural factors determine in large
part the specific behaviors, attitudes, and motivations which we learn,
that is to say, "culture is a gigantic conditioning machine." We may
raise the question of how strong are these cultural conditionings?
What are the conditions which are necessary to modify deeply en-
grained cultural attitudes and beliefs? During the Korean War, a
few American prisoners dramatically changed their culturally learned
beliefs and value systems and accepted the indoctrination program of
the Communists. The paper by Farber, Harlow, and West, Selection
34, examines some of the determinants of the behavioral modification
resulting from this "brain washing" process.

selection 28 / on the neural basis of the conditioned response / R. W. Sperry, California Institute of Technology

A bell sounds and the conditioned dog lifts its forepaw. Although the physiological explanation of this seemingly simple sequence of events has been sought intensively ever since conditioned responses were first discovered more than a quarter of a century ago (Pavlov, 1927), we still lack today a satisfactory picture of the underlying neural mechanism. Even the broadest outlines of the neural events remain obscure.

It was first thought that the repeated association of bell and paw movement opened new pathways between the auditory and response centres of the brain. The repeated firing of the two brain centres in association was presumed to leave some kind of residual effect on the interconnecting nerve pathways making it easier for future impulses to travel these same routes. Although now regarded as being much too simple in its original form, this explanation continues to survive with various modifications and qualifications. In particular it is now agreed that the new cerebral associations are more than the direct trans-cortical linkages earlier supposed, and must involve devious and highly complex pathways.

From R. W. Sperry, "On the Neural Basis of the Conditioned Response," *The British Journal of Animal Behavior*, 3:41–44, 1955. Reprinted by permission of the author and the publisher.

The physical nature of the residual effects or lasting traces left in the brain remains a matter of pure speculation. Among the wide range of possibilities that continue to receive consideration are the following: growth of new fibre connections, i.e. of axonal and dendritic collaterals and new synaptic endfeet, alteration of transmission resistance at synapses as by expansion and contraction of endfeet or by changes in synaptic membrane permeability, adjustments of excitation threshold within nerve cells or in local portions of their dendritic expansions, specific chemical sensitization of neurons to qualitatively distinct modes of excitation, chemical changes in the neurofibrils and in the neuronal proteins, selective sensitization of neurons to specific spatial patterns of activation, and even structural and chemical changes within the glia.

As an alternative to the notion of the brain traces or engrams as static changes in brain tissue, it has been suggested that the traces might take the form of perseverating eddies of active discharge maintained in self-reexciting circuits. However, the fact that conditioned responses ordinarily survive deep anesthesia, electro-convulsive shock, epileptic seizures and other disruptions of functional continuity has seemed to rule out any explanation expressed entirely in these dynamic terms.

There remain, nevertheless, certain explanatory advantages in the dynamic form of brain trace, and in a recent advance in learning theory a dual form hypothesis has been proposed, that incorporates the benefits of both the older static and the newer dynamic type of memory trace. In this dual scheme, self-maintained reverberatory excitation is held responsible for the rapid short-term effects in learning and conditioning. In time the continued reverberatory activity is presumed to lead to permanent micro changes in brain morphology that make possible long-term retention of conditioned responses and their survival through states of deep coma, electro-convulsive shock, and the like.

In general the physiological theories have thus far tended to neglect a factor that long has been recognized in psychological studies to be an important element in conditioning, namely, the so-called "anticipatory set" or "expectancy." The incorporation of this factor into the physiological picture leads directly to significant revisions in our thinking about the underlying neural mechanism and to a modified hypothesis which, though somewhat increased in complexity, appears nevertheless to fit better the whole complexity of the conditioned response including some of its more paradoxical features.

Following this approach we are led to postulate as an important aspect of the conditioning process the intermediation of complex high level patterns of central nervous facilitation, i.e. the neural counterparts and derivatives of the psychological expectancies and anticipatory sets. The pattern of central excitation aroused in the brain by the conditioned stimulus can then be assumed to be governed by an intermediate pattern of transient facilitation, rather than being channelled directly by neural engrams or traces as traditionally conceived. Unlike the dynamic traces of earlier theory, the central facilitory pattern or "set" is not a simple vestige or trace of cerebral excitation involved in an earlier pairing of conditioned stimulus and response. It represents rather, a novel and relatively independent organization arising out of high level cerebral activity such as insight, expectancy and the like. In this hypothesis, the permanent structural changes for long-term retention do not help directly to form new associations between sensory and motor centres. Instead they reinforce the intermediary expectancy or facilitory set.

The concept of the central facilitory set and its role in conditioning is best illustrated perhaps with reference to a simple voluntary reaction in man. Let us suppose that electrodes have been taped to the hand of a human subject and that the person has been instructed to lift the hand promptly when a bell sounds, on the penalty of receiving otherwise a severe electric shock. At the sound of the bell, his hand jerks upward instantly, just as quickly as does the paw of the conditioned dog. In the human subject this withdrawal response at the sound of the bell involves a novel pattern of central excitation, which is not the product of any long training, or repeated pairing of bell and shock stimuli. There is no grooving of the fibre pathways between receptor and effector centres of the cortex. In fact, the particular train of central excitation set off by the bell may never have occurred previously in the person's lifetime.

Under these circumstances we say that the human subject gets himself physiologically set to make the proper response at the sound of the bell. The brain pathways for arm flexion become temporarily opened while those for innumerable other possible reactions are temporarily closed. In other words, the prevailing distribution of excitation and inhibition in the brain circuits opens the way for the bell stimulus to release instantly that specific response for which the circuits are adjusted. Once the circuits are properly set, extraneous sensory excitation tends to be absorbed without effect and incompatible reactions are excluded. The novel motor effect of the bell stimulus derives in this case, not from any new pattern of structural pathways but rather, from a new pattern of central excitation and facilitation.

We note that the human subject could just as easily set himself to make the reverse response (i.e., to depress the hand instead of lifting it) in which case the excitatory sequence initiated by the bell discharges with equal rapidity into the antagonist muscles. The transient brain set could be patterned likewise for a reaction with the foot, or with the opposite hand. In each case, the specific and immediate motor effect of the incoming auditory impulse is determined by the particular facilitory set that dominates or prevails in the brain at the time the sensory excitations enter.

These governing facilitory sets may be generalized or specific in their organization on both sensory and motor side. For example, a person could set himself to respond only to a bell of low pitch and not to one of high pitch. Or, his set might be quite nonspecific such that any loud noise would set off the reaction; even a sudden tactile stimulus might suffice. Similarly on the motor side, a single response may be rigidly predetermined, or a choice of two responses made possible, or any of a given category.

The main point to be emphasized is that a purely transient, dynamic setting of the brain circuits, in terms of active facilitation and inhibition, is quite capable by itself of causing the bell stimulus to set off a particular limb movement. There is no need here for any new fibre pathways, chemical traces in the neuroplasm, or new synaptic associations. It is evident, furthermore, that *the same response, or other responses, could be coupled functionally in a similar manner to any neutral stimulus (of the type employed in conditioning) simply by an appropriate adjustment in the cerebral facilitory set.* (In referring to these transient adjustments of the brain mechanism as *facilitory* sets, it should be recognized that the central *inhibitory* phase of the process may be fully as important as the facilitory.)

There is much to suggest that the coupling of bell and forepaw response in the dog during conditioning is achieved through the development of a comparable cerebral facilitory set. The bell-shock expectancy that it takes only a moment to convey to the brain of man with the aid of language, may require hours or days to develop in the brain of the dog by the more roundabout method of example and experience. Eventually as a result of training, the dog comes to expect the shock at the sound of the bell. More than this the dog comes to anticipate both the bell and shock so that by the time the bell sounds, the dog already is actively prepared in advance (like the human subject) to make the correct forelimb response.

We may thus suppose that in the brain of the conditioned animal a well-organized facilitory set appears prior to the incidence of the conditioned stimulus. It is this special pattern of central facilitation— absent before training and developed through training—that is directly responsible for channelling the sensory impulses into the proper motor response.

The activity of these cerebral facilitory sets is not confined to conditioning and voluntary reaction. They operate continually in behaviour and constitute a prime factor in the control of all brain function. Thinking, perceiving, recognizing, imagining, reasoning, reflex activity, learning, and remembering, as well as conditioning and voluntary activity, have all been found in the laboratory to be profoundly affected by the so-called "mental set." It is by means of differential facilitory sets that the brain is able to function as many machines in one, setting and resetting itself dozen of times in the course of a day, now for one type of operation, now for another. In short, a great deal of the plasticity in vertebrate behaviour, including that of conditioning, is made possible, not through structural remodelling of the fibre pathways but through dynamic readjustments in the background of central facilitation.

To account for the long-term retention of conditioned responses, one must infer further that the facilitory sets and associated dynamic readjustments become reinforced by some permanent type of neural trace, or engram. In considering the problem of the patterning of the brain engrams, it is all-important that one does not lose sight of the primary role played by the above dynamic factors. Even after a long rest interval, or electroshock treatment, the conditioned response is still dependent upon a preliminary rearousal of the anticipatory set. If the proper pattern of central facilitation has not been established by the time the bell sounds, the conditioned forepaw response fails to occur.

A number of implications regarding the nature of the static engram are incorporated in this approach to conditioning, some of which may be stated briefly as follows: (a) The engrams for a conditioned response do not take the form merely of new associations between the receptor and effector centres of the brain, however complex. A different type of engram pattern is implied, namely, a pattern so designed as to facilitate, at the proper time and place, the establishment of the correct expectancy and facilitory set. (b) With much of the burden of the detailed patterning of the conditioned response relegated to the dynamics of cerebral facilitation, the engrams themselves need be much less extensive and complete than is otherwise necessary. Relatively small changes at critical points may be sufficient to reactivate a given anticipatory set in the proper dynamic background. (c) The static engrams on the one hand and the dynamic facilitory patterns on the other are regarded as co-functions, i.e. the operation of the two factors in long-term retention becomes mutually dependent with the conditioned response being a product of the combined action. (d) Since the engrams reinforce higher level cerebral activity, they are believed to be complex and diffused rather than localized in nature even in the very simplest conditioned responses. (e) The engram patterning is further complicated by the fact that the engrams must function in large part to support the transitions between the expectancies and sets as well as the facilitory patterns per se.

There are definite advantages from the engineering standpoint in having the permanent alterations of the brain designed to reinforce the higher level intermediary facilitation, instead of having them affect the sensory-motor associations directly. This makes it possible, to mention just one advantage, for different (even antagonistic) motor responses to be linked simultaneously to the same sensory stimulus, something that may be desirable to suit different circumstances. This scheme also provides much more readily for that class of phenomena included under the terms "sensory and motor equivalence." In general, with this kind of arrangement, the sensory and response mechanisms of the brain do not become tied down nor selectively modified for specific habits, but remain free to be used in various ways and in various combinations in all categories of behaviour.

This description of the neural events also accounts more readily than earlier theories for findings like those of Lashley and others on the effects of brain extirpation. Consider the difficulty, on this basis of trying to ablate even so simple a habit as the conditioned paw movement mentioned above for illustration. One might eliminate the conditioned response by extirpating enough of the auditory centres of the brain to prevent the stimulus from reaching the anticipatory set. However, if the facilitory set is strongly organized, very little stimulus is needed to trigger off the response. In fact, it is known that the response may occur spontaneously under certain conditions without any outside stimulus. Any small remnant of the primary sensory area that would permit the impulses from the bell to filter through to the central facilitory set would be enough to trigger off the conditioned response.

Similarly on the motor side, any undamaged motor mechanisms by which the animal can achieve the desired effect will be sufficient. The ability to switch quickly from one motor pattern to another to accomplish an end (motor equivalence) is already an intrinsic property of the brain. Once the dog learns that contact with the shock electrode must be broken immediately after the bell sounds, any remaining means available is automatically called into play to accomplish this end. Consequently extensive and widely paralyzing lesions in the motor cortex are required to prevent an animal from making a conditioned response in one way or another. For some learning situations any residual ability to move at all may be enough to carry out the learned performance.

To effectively destroy by surgery the engrams themselves or the expectancies, insights, and sets which they reinforce is equally difficult. According to the foregoing, the constellation of engrams for even the simplest conditioned response tends to be complex in design and diffused through the brain, and thus highly resistant to local ablation. Further, the intermediary central facilitation is reinforced from all sides by a great mass of stimuli, associated not only with the conditioning chamber, but also with the situations leading to it, with the experimenter's person, even with the home cage and with various related events in the diurnal cycle. To eliminate by brain damage the channels for all these reminders of the conditioning experience would be prohibitive.

selection 29 / electrophysiological correlates of a conditioned response in cats / Robert Galambos, Guy Sheatz, and Vernon G. Vernier, Walter Reed Army Medical Center

The search for neurophysiological correlates for psychological phenomena such as learning and emotion has a long history that cannot profitably be treated here. This report presents a brief account of some electric changes that are observable in the brain when animals are conditioned and extinguished to an auditory stimulus.

The animals under study lived in a box measuring 0.5 by 1.0 by 0.5 m that contained a loud-speaker through which clicks (at constant intensity) were delivered at a rate of 1 click/3 sec along with noise generated by a thermionic noise generator. The noise intensity was adjusted at the outset so that it was sufficient to mask most ambient sounds. Recording from brain structures was achieved through electrodes of the Delgado type that were implanted stereotaxically at sterile operation some weeks or months prior to the testing; as many as 14 separate brain locations were thus made available for study in each animal. To date, ten cats with implantations in or on auditory and visual cortex, cochlear nucleus, hippocampus, caudate nucleus, septal area, and amygdala have been examined in the conditioning process. The electrodes were directly connected through a plug to the amplifiers of a Grass EEG machine and thereafter, alternately or simultaneously, to inkwriters and a cathode-ray oscilloscope. The cats also wore a harness bearing two metal brushes, each making contact with one side of the thorax; the output of a Grass stimulator could be delivered to these brushes, and thus shocks could be applied, at will, across the chest of the animal.

The plan and results of the experiments are as follows. The animals were placed in the box for periods of many days or weeks, clicks being delivered continuously day and night throughout. From time to time

Abridged from Robert Galambos, Guy Sheatz, and Vernon G. Vernier, "Electrophysiological Correlates of a Conditioned Response in Cats," *Science*, 123:376–377, 1956. Reprinted by permission of the authors and the publishers.

COCHLEAR NUCLEUS

Extinguished   Conditioned

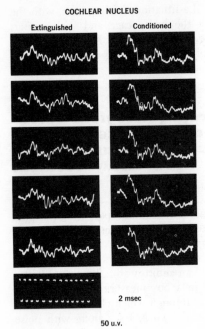

2 msec

50 u.v.

Fig. 1   Cochlear nucleus responses to successive identical click stimuli before ("extinguished") and after ("conditioned") application of three shocks to a cat. The increase in response magnitude after shocks as noted here has been observed eight times in this animal, two of them previous to the instance given here.

their electrodes were connected to the recording devices, and the activity evoked by the clicks was visualized. The report that under such conditions the response at the cochlear nucleus becomes, with time, much reduced in size ("habituation," "adaptation") was readily confirmed; in addition, we found that responses evoked in various other brain loci diminished in a similar manner. Responses so attenuated in the cochlear nucleus can be seen in the left column of Fig. 1.

After an animal had been in the box for hours or days, the tracings from its brain showed small, absent, or irregular evoked potentials caused by the clicks, and consistent behavior toward the stimuli was absent. At this point single strong shocks were given across the chest contiguously with randomly selected clicks. After these shocks had been discontinued—perhaps some 10 or 20 having been given—the behavior in response to the click stimuli was noticeably different. The animals crouched, appeared alert, and most of them twitched, snarled, or otherwise responded to many individual clicks. When exhibiting this behavior, the animals were considered to have been "conditioned" to the auditory stimulus; records from the cochlear nucleus of such an animal are shown in the right column of Fig. 1. As the click continued without shock reinforcement, both motor and electric responses tended to disappear (motor long before electric), and the "extinguished" condition invariably returned after hours or days. In most of our animals, the cycle of conditioning and extinction thus defined has been repeated many times.

From the data, only some of which have been presented here, the following general statements appear to be justified. When cats with indwelling electrodes are subjected to a relatively simple auditory conditioning technique, changes in electric activity of the brain apparently related to conditioning and extinction can be reliably recorded. Evoked auditory responses are larger and are seen more frequently and in more numerous locations when a given animal is in the conditioned as opposed to the extinguished state. Such changes occur near the origin of the classical auditory pathway (cochlear nucleus) as well as at its termination (auditory cortex), in portions of such limbic system structures as the hippocampus and septal area and in the head of the caudate nucleus.

selection 30 / learning without response under two conditions of external cues / Harold J. McNamara, John B. Long, and Edward L. Wike, University of Kansas

In 1946 Thorndike critically examined Tolman's concept of expectancy and proposed a number of experiments to evaluate this viewpoint. Bugelski and his co-workers mention some unpublished research, using Thorndike's situations, which failed to provide support for the expectancy interpretation. More recently, Gleitman has demonstrated place learning without performance in an elevated T maze with rats that had been drawn along a path in a "cable car" and shocked during transit. Learning was observed only when the locus of the T maze coincided with the path which the Ss had traversed.

The first situation suggested by Thorndike was:

. . . put the rat in a little wire car, in the entrance chamber of a maze, run it through the correct path of a simple maze and into the food compartment. Release it there and let it eat the morsel provided. Repeat 10 to 100 times according to the difficulty of the maze under ordinary conditions. The rat had an opportunity to form expectancies that presence in the food compartment is followed by food, that the correct turn is followed by the food chamber, and so on. Then put it in the entrance chamber free to go wherever it is inclined and observe what it does. Compare the behavior of such rats with that of rats run in the customary manner.

From Harold J. McNamara, John B. Long, and Edward L. Wike, "Learning without Response under Two Conditions of External Cues," *Journal of Comparative and Physiological Psychology*, 49:477–480, 1956. Reprinted by permission of the authors and the American Psychological Association.

The present experiments follow rather closely Thorndike's suggested procedure except that the performance on a number of extinction trials is utilized as an indicant of learning. In addition, each S in the experimental ("basket") group is matched with a control S in terms of the number and pattern of rewarded and nonrewarded responses; and, instead of a complex maze, the learning task is a single-unit elevated T maze.

Thus, the experimental question becomes: Is execution of running and turning responses necessary in order for rats to learn the locus of food in an elevated T maze? If learning involves the establishment of S-R connections by means of drive-reduction, then we should expect that the Ss that are conveyed about the maze in a wire basket would show little or no learning, since the running and turning responses are not made contiguously with the eliciting cues and reinforcement. On the other hand, if the learning consists of the development of field expectancies, then there is no obvious reason why the conveyed animals should not acquire a *representation* of the situation if there are sufficient differential cues to serve as environmental supports and the Ss frequently have access to these discriminanda. Accordingly, in experiment I, it is anticipated that Ss which have been transported about an elevated T maze in a basket will go to the correct side as often on the extinction trials as control Ss which have previously learned the maze under normal running conditions.

The purpose of Experiment II is to determine the influence of an extensive reduction in the extra-maze cues upon the learning of a basket-transported group and a normally run group of Ss. With the extramaze cues at a minimum, it is expected that the control Ss will select the formerly rewarded side more frequently in extinction than the transported Ss. With decreased external cues the learning is probably dependent to a greater degree on internal, response-produced cues, and since these cues are not available to the conveyed Ss, their extinction performance should be inferior.

Experiment I: method

Subjects Twenty-four experimentally naive Long-Evans strain hooded male rats were used. They were bred in the University of Kansas laboratory and were four to five months of age at the start of the experiment.

Apparatus The elevated T maze, which was constructed of 3.75-in. black wooden strips, had a 51-in. stem, 31-in. side arms, and stood 30-in. from the floor. A flat black metal tray, 3.75 in. by 3.75 in. by .25 in. served as a food dish. It was clipped to either side arm and was not visible from the choice point.

The basket, which was used to transport the Ss of the experimental group along the maze, had a floor consisting of a 9-in. by 4-in. sheet of transparent plastic. A piece of .5-in.-sq. hardware cloth bent in the shape of a half-cylinder was fastened to the basket floor so as to make a cage with 6-in. walls.

The ends of the basket were also constructed of .5-in.-sq. hardware cloth, and one end was hinged to permit the entrance and exit of S.

The maze was placed in the center of a room measuring 10 ft. by 10 ft. by 8.5 ft. Although the walls and ceiling were uniformly white, differential cues were provided by a radiator and window opposite the left arm and a large, black multicelled cage opposite the right arm. The floor of the room provided the possibilities for other gross visual cues since the left half was unpainted while the right half was black. The room was illuminated by the sunlight from the window on the left and by a fluorescent lamp with two 90-w. bulbs which was attached to the ceiling directly over the center of the maze and aligned with the stem.

Procedure The Ss were placed on a 22-hr. hunger cycle five days before the beginning of maze adaptation by limiting them to a daily 1-hr. feeding session in the living cages. Water was always available in these cages, and Purina Layena pellets were employed as the maintenance food and as an incentive in the maze. During this period, each S was handled for several minutes per day.

In the adaptation phase the Ss were accustomed to the elevated apparatus. The starting half of the stem was detached from the T and aligned in the direction of the stem proper. The purpose of this arrangement was to provide rewarded adaptation without the concurrent induction of directional habits. The reward tray was attached to the end of the stem section, and S was permitted to explore the stem and eat freely for 5 min. daily. After seven days the adaptation was terminated because the Ss ate and moved along the stem without timidity. Four Ss were discarded in this phase when they displayed continued emotionality, leaving a total of 10 Ss in each treatment.

The maze training extended over four days until a group criterion of 95 per cent correct was attained by the control Ss. The control Ss learned a position response by running the maze in the traditional, noncorrection fashion. Four trials were given each day with a 30-sec. intertrial interval. Half the Ss in each group found food on the right side and half on the left. When an S placed all four paws on either side arm, it was prevented from retracing by E's blocking the choice with a wooden paddle. A correct choice resulted in 30-sec. feeding at the food tray, and an incorrect turn led to 60-sec. confinement on that arm of the maze.

The Ss in the experimental group were placed in the basket at the start of the stem, the basket was gently slid along the top of the maze, and they were released from the basket at the end of the side arm. Each experimental S was given the same experiences of right and wrong choices, reward, and confinement, and was rewarded on the same side of the maze as its matched control S. Both groups were subjected to a 30-min. waiting period following the completion of the last trial before being fed their daily ration.

On the following day, extinction trials were administered to both groups in the same manner. The S was placed at the start of the stem, and the direction of choice was recorded. Retracing was again prevented by blocking off the choice point, the same response criterion was utilized, and the Ss were confined on the selected side arm for a 60-sec. period. Whenever S failed to make a choice within 300 sec., it was placed on a side arm by E for the regular confinement period, and the trial was scored as an error. The S was arbitrarily placed on the right arm after the first no-choice trial, on the left arm after the second, and so on. The Ss received eight extinction trials on the first day and eight more trials the second. The intertrial interval of 30 sec. was maintained throughout extinction.

Experiment II: method

Subjects There were three replications with 10 Wistar albino rats, six males and four females, in the first, 12 male hooded rats in the second, and 14 male hooded rats in the third. The albino rats were purchased from a local vender, and the Long-Evans strain Ss were from the University of Kansas laboratory. The Ss had not been used in an experiment previously and were three to five months of age.

Apparatus The T maze described above was employed. To decrease the extra-maze cues, the total room was painted flat black. The window on the left side of the room was covered completely by a plywood sheet and sealed to prevent the passage of light. The maze was enclosed in a rectangular wooden framework, 8 ft. by 6 ft. by 8.5 ft., and black cheesecloth was fastened to the frame. To reduce the illumination, the overhead fluorescent light was covered by a black cheesecloth panel. The light intensities, as measured by a photo-electric photometer, were 14.4 ft.-c. at the start of the stem, 13.5 ft.-c. at the choice point, 8.8 ft.-c. at the end of the left arm, and 8.5 ft.-c. at the end of the right arm. The greatest intensity difference between corresponding points on the side arms was 0.8 ft.-c. which was present at the mid-point of the side arm.

Procedure The procedure was almost identical to that of Experiment I except that the Ss in the third replication received three additional days of training after attaining the criterion of 95 per cent correct, and Ss in all replications had only eight extinction trials. One pair of Ss was discarded from the third replication when a control S failed to learn the maze.

Results

The percentages of correct responses for the successive quarters of extinction in experiment I are shown in Table 1. The average percentage correct was 66.25 for the experimental group and 64.38 for the control group. The difference between these two values was evaluated by the sign test and was not significant ($p > .30$). In addition, none of the tests at the separate quarters of extinction was significant at less than the .30 level. We may conclude that, with the number of correct responses in extinction serving as a measure of previous

TABLE 1   PERCENTAGES OF CORRECT RESPONSES DURING EXTINCTION IN EXPERIMENT I

Group	N	*Trials* 1–4	5–8	9–12	13–16
C (run)	10	65	60	67.5	65
E (carry)	10	60	65	65	75

TABLE 2   PERCENTAGES OF CORRECT RESPONSES DURING EXTINC-
TION IN EXPERIMENT II

Group	N	Trials			
		1–2	3–4	5–6	7–8
C (run)	17	85	62	50	59
E (carry)	17	44	59	56	32

learning, there were no reliable differences between the Ss that ran the maze and those that traversed the maze in a basket.

A further question which can be raised is: Did the performance of the groups in extinction differ from chance? To answer this question, the number of Ss in the combined groups which ran to the correct side more than eight times and the number of Ss that ran to the correct side equal to, or less than, eight times were found. On an a priori basis, if no learning occurred, we should expect 10 Ss in each category. Actually there were 17 Ss in the "above" category and 3 Ss in the "below." The resulting x^2 of 8.45 is significant at less than .01 level of confidence—the Ss manifested a significant preference for the formerly rewarded side in extinction.

The three replications of Experiment II were tested for homogeneity of their means and variances. Since the differences among the replications were within the limits of sampling, they were pooled. The combined extinction data in the form of the percentages of correct turns for the four quarters of extinction are presented in Table 2. When the external cues were reduced, the transported Ss scored 47.75 per cent correct choices in extinction, and the regularly run Ss made 64 per cent correct turns. Eleven of the Ss in the latter condition went to the correct side more often than their matched mates, one regularly run S was inferior to its mate, and in five instances there were no differences between Ss in the two treatments. Disregarding the ties, the probability of such an outcome is .01.

It is clear from Table 2 that the experimental Ss did not deviate from chance on the extinction trials. If assignment is made at random of the 5 control Ss that ran to the correct side on half the trials, there were 14 Ss in the above-chance category and 3 Ss in the below-chance category. The significance of this outcome is less than the .02 level of confidence. In summary, then, in Experiment II the regularly run animals gave evidence, in extinction, of learning, whereas the transported Ss did not.

Discussion

The results of Experiment I confirm Gleitman's finding that place learning in an elevated T maze can occur without performance. However, when the extramaze cues are reduced (Experiment II), performance appears to be necessary for place learning. The finding that place learning without performance is demonstrable is congruent with *our* interpretation of Tolman's system as given in the introduction.

This same finding is not readily reconcilable with those aspects of Hull's system which conceive of learning as habit formation via drive reduction. For, in the case of the basket Ss, the response component of the cue pattern-response-reinforcement paradigm is not present. To encompass these findings, the Hullian theorist must, as in some latent learning studies, call upon fractional antedating goal reactions and/or secondary reinforcement to account for the results. To us, at present, the linkages of these constructs with independent and dependent variables seem to be as programmatic as the coordinating definitions of cognitive map, expectancy, etc. The hopeful feature of this situation is, as Hilgard points out, that with an increased emphasis in S-R theory on secondary reinforcement the differences between field and association theory become more blurred and the possibilities for a fruitful *rapprochement* may be seen.

Summary

Two experiments were performed to determine whether or not place learning is possible without performance. In Experiment I ten Ss were regularly run in an elevated T maze, and ten Ss were transported about the maze in a basket. In the extinction trials there were no reliable differences between the two groups in the frequency of correct choices. In Experiment II, carried out under the conditions of reduced external cues, the run Ss displayed significantly more learning than the transported Ss. It was concluded that: (*a*) Gleitman's finding that place learning can occur without performance was confirmed; and (*b*) when the extramaze cues are minimized, performance is necessary for learning.

selection 31 / the operant, from rat to man: an introduction to some recent experiments on human behavior / William S. Verplanck, Harvard University

Virtually all psychologists accept the premise that human behavior is orderly. The order that they see, however, varies considerably from group to group, and the aspects of behavior in which these orders

From William S. Verplanck, "The Operant, from Rat to Man: An Introduction to Some Recent Experiments on Human Behavior," *Transactions of the New York Academy of Sciences*, 17:594–601, 1955. Reprinted by permission of the author and publisher.

appear differ as well. The clinician and the personality psychologist observe their fellow men and see need-presses, repressions, and aggressive drives. The experimental psychologist finds his order in the rates at which nonsense syllables are learned, or at which conditioned eyelid reflexes are acquired. If he is physiologically oriented, he is apt to concern himself with muscle twitches and even with the secretion of saliva. It is in terms of such variables that psychologists have set their descriptions of, and their predictions about, the actions of people.

All of us, whether psychologists or not, observe people acting. We learn rules of "practical psychology." Some of us, especially the novelists and playwrights, do a remarkably good job of giving plausible accounts of behavior, often in terms that seem pertinent. These writers, however, do not employ the language used by psychologists at either end of the spectrum. They describe ordinary, everyday behavior, and describe it well, but not by using the conceptualizations that psychologists seem to have found useful, nor even terms that can be readily translated into such conceptualizations.

The psychologist's efforts tend to be limited in their usefulness to the description and prediction of the behavior of people whose behavior is awry, or of people who are engaged in the strange and unusual activities demanded of them in a laboratory of experimental psychology. Dale Carnegie, practical politicians, and, perhaps, everybody *but* psychologists, concern themselves with simple, ordinary, everyday behavior. One reason for this situation is, perhaps, the lack of methods of conceptualizing behavior, or of abstracting relevant aspects of behavior for study that are not clinic- or laboratory-bound. This lack of methods is due, perhaps, to a conviction that ordinary behavior is too complex and is determined by too many variables to make possible the discovery of any order except by the application of theory.

What I desire to do here is to introduce some concepts, and to describe some experiments derived from them, that suggest that the orderliness of human behavior may be more accessible than has been hitherto assumed. These experiments may accordingly suggest new directions for research on human behavior.

A number of years ago, in a series of articles that were summarized in his book, *The Behavior of Organisms*, B. F. Skinner introduced two new concepts into the behavioral sciences. These concepts had familiar names, but their experimental and theoretical content represented a sharp break with the past, a break that had been foreshadowed only in the writings of Kantor.

The first of these concepts is that of the operant response, defined as a part of behavior (*a*) that is recurrently identifiable and hence enumerable; and (*b*) whose rate of occurrence can be determined as a systematic function of certain classes of environmental variables. These

parts of behavior, or actions, are what we can see an animal perform repeatedly. They are not simple muscle twitches or limb movements. Rather, they are meaningful, repeated actions. They constitute bar presses rather than leg extensions, the picking up of food rather than digital flexions, the speaking of words rather than laryngeal contractions. One class of environmental variable of which such responses are functions represents the second new concept. This is the reinforcing stimulus, defined as a recurrently identifiable and experimentally manipulable part of the environment that has the property of modifying the rate of occurrence of those operant responses that have produced it. Like responses, they are parts of the environment that are meaningful to the animal, not abstract physical events. They are doors, spoken words, food, not the energy patterns that concern sense physiologists. The two concepts are closely related to one another, so much so, in fact, that many writers, including Skinner himself, often state that operant responses are defined by their consequences, that is, by their production of a given reinforcement. Without going into detail on the experimental and theoretical questions involved in this statement, let me single out for elaboration certain properties of these concepts that distinguish them sharply from those other concepts of stimulus and response that have been widely understood—and even more widely misunderstood—by both psychologists and laymen.

The first of these properties is this: it is not possible to determine arbitrarily and a priori what recurrently identifiable parts of behavior will prove to be responses—that is, what parts of behavior will obey the empirically established laws of behavior. True, within limits, an experimenter may "shape" a part of behavior by differential reinforcement, and thus may be able to introduce a new response into the animal's repertoire, but his ability to do so is sharply limited by the animal itself. Animals of each species, each with its own individual history, come to the experimenter with a repertoire of operant responses that the experimenter can analyze and, within limits, modify. By and large, however, the experimenter must work with those responses that he finds in the animal's behavior. Not all recurrently identifiable behaviors are responses. After observation, the sophisticated experimenter will often be able to guess which identifiable parts of the animal's behavior will prove to be responses, that is, will vary as particular functions of reinforcing stimuli.

Similarly, the experimenter does not have unlimited latitude in determining a priori what environmental events he can use as reinforcing stimuli for an animal. As with responses, he can convert, to a limited degree, originally neutral events into reinforcing stimuli. To do this, he must follow certain experimental procedures. There still

remains, however, the empirical problem of determining the whole class of events that will reinforce an already identified response of his experimental subject. Again, as with response, the sophisticated experimenter often will be able to guess which of the environmental events that he can make dependent on a response will produce changes in the rate of occurrence of that response in the period following the occurrence of the environmental event.

With some reason, operant responses have been characterized as "spontaneous" or "voluntary." They are what the animal does "by himself." This is not to say that operants are independent of the ordinary laws of elicitation (and hence of our usual conceptions of causality in behavior) but rather that, for all practical purposes, the only control the experimenter has over them is the one he exerts by the operation of reinforcement, that is, by presenting the animal with a reinforcing stimulus following the occurrence of the response.

In tackling any new piece of behavior experimentally, or in starting to study the behavior of a previously uninvestigated species, the experimenter has a double problem. He must find responses, and he must find reinforcing stimuli that control their occurrence. More often than not, he designs experiments that involve the simultaneous identification both of the operant responses and of the reinforcing stimuli by demonstrating orderly changes in the rate of some part of behavior that are contingent upon the association between that part of behavior and a specific environmental change. A bar press is a response, and food is a reinforcing stimulus, because when bar presses produce food, the rat presses the bar more frequently. By the same rules, water is a reinforcing stimulus for a thirsty rat, whose response may be the sticking of its nose in one corner of the cage.

In view of these systematic restrictions, one is not surprised that almost all studies of operant conditioning have been made on two responses and on two species. The bar pressing of hungry rats and the key-pecking of hungry pigeons, both with reinforcement by food, have been experimentally studied on a scale that, to put it mildly, is intensive. A few other responses from a few other species, involving a few other reinforcing stimuli, have been studied, but not very extensively. In any case, a very large body of experimental evidence has been amassed on the operant, and behavioral psychologists may take some pride in the number of stimulus-response laws that have been found.

The problem arises, however, of the relationship of this body of experimental data, and the laws derived from it, to human behavior. For those investigators interested in men, wherein lies the relevance of these laws? Several kinds of attempts have been made to exhibit such relevance. The first of these may be termed "extrapolation by analogy." The theorist hypothesizes that certain kinds of human be-

havior are responses and that certain kinds of events are reinforcing stimuli for humans. The rat- and pigeon-derived laws are then assumed to apply, and a set of statements about human behavior are generated that satisfy the writer and his friends, and that horrify others or (what is worse) leave them cold. This has been the history of Skinner's *Walden Two*, and of his *Science and Human Behavior*.

The second tactic is to elaborate a rather complex theoretical structure and then to spell out predictions of human behavior that may or may not be experimentally testable. This, too, has produced books (*e.g.*, Miller and Dollard) that edify or horrify, depending on the reader.

A third procedure is an experimental one. In this, one studies human behavior in the laboratory under conditions that parallel as closely as possible the experimental procedures followed for the lower animals. Very simple responses are studied, and very simple reinforcers are used. In 1942, Warren and Brown conditioned children to press a lever, using candy as a reinforcing stimulus. Since then, a number of responses have been conditioned, usually involving tapping a telegraph key or the like as response and, with food, the registration of a number, or the playing of music as reinforcer. The studies have shown clearly the reproducibility in human subjects of the laws of operant conditioning found to obtain in rats. These methods, however, leave something to be demanded. The relevance of pressing-a-key-for-a-piece-of-candy to most everyday human behavior may be questioned, and the vexing problem of "awareness" enters, so that a variety of "interpretations of the results" are possible. It may reasonably be questioned whether a human subject, under observation and engaged in unfamiliar activities in a laboratory, will behave as he would if he were not in such a special situation.

The fourth tactic is the one that is the subject of this paper. This is the identification of responses and of reinforcing stimuli, and the verification and eduction of laws relating them to one another in human behavior under conditions where the subject is acting as naturally as possible, and where, insofar as possible, he is not "aware" of what is going on. The approach is characterized by a broad increase in the classes of both responses and reinforcing stimuli investigated, and by a controlled relaxation of the rigorous (and very probably irrelevant) environmental controls exerted in the laboratory.

The first such investigation was that of Greenspoon. From his observations of "nondirective" therapy, Greenspoon suspected that the therapist's "mmm-hmm" was a reinforcing stimulus and, hence, that it modified the verbal behavior of the client undergoing therapy. He proceeded to test this notion in the laboratory by instructing each of his large (separately run) number of subjects to say as many dif-

ferent words as they could. He further assumed that *saying plural nouns* was a response, and proceeded to show that the relative frequency of plural nouns in the subject's verbal behavior was a function of the experimenter's manipulations in reinforcing the subject by casually murmuring "mmm-hmm" each time he said one. Greenspoon went on to discover several other reinforcing stimuli. In the data he reported, none of his subjects was aware that his behavior had changed as a function of reinforcement. None seemed to notice the experimenter's "mmm-hmm's," even though his behavior changed as a function of them.

In 1951, we tried to repeat the Greenspoon experiment in a class at Harvard. The experimenters had had very little previous work with human conditioning. They were game, however, and cornered their subjects in a variety of places. The results were interesting and instructive. A few experimenters obtained unequivocally positive results, but not always without the subject becoming aware of the reinforcements. The successful experimenters were the most prestigeful, socially adept individuals, and the unsuccessful ones tended to be those of what might be termed lower prestige. At the same time, attempts were made to condition simple motor behavior, using reinforcers such as "mmm-hmms," smiles, and "good." The results, as with verbal behavior, were indifferent.

Therefore, a new tack in the research was taken. In an attempt to pin down the relevant variables, we reverted to the study of simple motor behavior, and modified the procedure to ensure that subjects responded to the reinforcing stimuli (the experiments described here are more fully reported in a paper now in press: Verplanck). Subjects were instructed explicitly as to the environmental changes that the experimenter would manipulate, although no information was given them as to the behavior the experimenter would reinforce. After finding a fellow student who was willing to be a subject, the experimenter instructed him as follows: "Your job is to work for points. You get a point every time I tap the table with my pencil. As soon as you get a point, record it on your sheet of paper. Keep track of your own points." With these instructions, it seemed likely that a pencil tap, a "point," would prove to be a reinforcing stimulus. The method worked very well. Indeed, the experimenters were now able to condition a wide variety of simple motor behaviors, such as slapping the ankle, tapping the chin, raising an arm, picking up a fountain pen, and so on. They were further able to differentiate out, or shape, more complex parts of behavior, and then to manipulate them as responses. The data they obtained included the results on the manipulation of many of the variables whose effects were familiar in operant conditioning of rats and pigeons. Despite the fact that the experiments were carried out in a variety of situations, the experimenters were able to obtain graphical functions that could not be distinguished from functions obtained on the rat or the pigeon in a Skinner box.

To be sure, the responses studied in humans were very different from the key pecking of a pigeon, or the bar pressing of a rat, and a point is a very different event from the arrival of a pellet of food in a food hopper. But the general laws relating those parts of behavior demonstrated to be responses to those environmental events shown to be reinforcing stimuli were the same.

More interesting, there appeared to be no fixed relationship between the conditioning effects and the subject's ability to state verbally the response that the experimenter was reinforcing. That is, the subjects were responding in a lawful and orderly way without necessarily being aware of what they were doing. They were not necessarily "figuring it out."

With these results, we were encouraged to proceed in two directions. First, we returned to the Greenspoon experiment and repeated it with certain refinements of design, and with experimenters who had acquired considerable experience in the conditioning of human motor behavior. These results are reported elsewhere, but they may be summarized briefly here: experienced experimenters had no difficulty in reproducing the changes in rate of saying words of particular classes that Greenspoon reported. The experimenters' "mmm-hmm," although uttered without instructions and introduced as if unintentionally, modified the subjects' behavior, whether or not the subject noticed it. Subjects usually were aware of the reinforcing stimuli, however, and, at the end of the experiment, would tend to report something such as, "I noticed that you seemed to like nouns for a while, and that then you didn't care."

The second direction was forward, and it took a long step beyond the chin tappings and word sayings that had been shown to be responses. For a number of reasons (not the least of which was a set of encouraging results from an exploratory experiment), we hypothesized that in an ordinary conversation, saying sentences of a particular class would act as a response, and that agreement by a hearer, or paraphrasing back to the speaker by a hearer, would prove to be reinforcing stimuli to the speaker.

Two experiments were done. In the first, the response reinforced was *stating opinions*, where opinions were defined as sentences beginning "I think that," "I believe that," and the like. In the second, the response reinforced was *making any statement on a preselected topic*, the topic being chosen by the experimenter and introduced into the conversation by him in a sentence requiring no answer.

The experiments were carried out in a series of 44 conversations that took place on a wide variety of topics and in a variety of circumstances. The sole restriction on the experimenter was that he carry out the experiment with only himself and the subject present, and under conditions where he could keep accurate but camouflaged records of the subject's behavior. He was also under instructions to terminate the experiment if the subject gave any indication that he suspected that this was anything other than an ordinary conversation.

The results of these experiments were unequivocal. In the first experiment, on opinion-statements, every one of 23 subjects showed a higher rate of giving opinion-statements during the 10-minute period when the experimenter reinforced each of them by agreeing with it, or by repeating it back to him in paraphrase, than he showed in the first 10-minute period, when the experimenter did not reinforce. In a final 10-minute period, 21 of 23 subjects showed the converse effect, termed extinction, that is, they decreased in their rate of stating opinions when reinforcement was withdrawn. Irrespective of topic of conversation, or of the situation in which the conversation took place, the expected changes in rate occurred, under conditions where not one subject gave any indication, at any time, that he was "aware" of the experimental manipulation. The subjects' behavior, an orderly function of the experimenters' actions, followed the laws of reinforcement without any awareness by the subject, even of the fact that he was in an experiment.

In the second experiment, the experimenter introduced the experimental topic at the end of the first 10 minutes of conversation. Some subjects ($N = 6$) were controls, and were not reinforced through the following 10-minute period. The others ($N = 15$) were regularly reinforced. Under these conditions, every subject but one replied to the experimenter's sentence introducing the topic. Those who were not reinforced dropped the topic quickly (within 2 or 3 minutes), whereas those who were reinforced shifted their speech so that almost everything they said through the next 10 minutes of conversation fell into the specified response-class. In all cases, on the withdrawal of reinforcement, and without respect to whether statements on other topics were reinforced, the subjects dropped to a rate of zero on the previously introduced and reinforced topic.

Again, no subject gave evidence of being aware in any way that this was not an ordinary conversation.

These experimental results indicate that our hypotheses with respect to the analysis of conversational speech into response and reinforcing stimuli were justified. One example of complicated, superficially variable human behavior proves simple under experimental analysis. Order is readily demonstrable. The time may hence be ripe for an extension of experimental analysis into other areas of human behavior that have been considered unsusceptible to direct experimental investigation.

Orderly, significant data *can* be collected in situations devoid of the elaborate environmental controls exerted in the laboratory if significant variables are manipulated, if measures of that behavior are possible, and if experimental designs are clear-cut. Experiments can be performed on human subjects "in the field" and under conditions where the subject will not be able to discriminate either his own or the experimenter's behavior as dependent on an experimental procedure. Hence we can study human behavior with good reason to hope that the mere fact that it is being investigated will not modify it. This alone has seriously limited the generality of the many results of laboratory experiments.

One can now conceive of a broad experimental program designed to determine what other parts of behavior have the functional properties of responses, and how broad a class of environmental events will prove to be reinforcing stimuli for one or another subject. The conceptual tools are at hand. The experimental methodology, involving a number of sophisticated and skilled experimenters, is at hand. A very rapid development in this field may be expected. We may hope for an experimental, rather than an "intuitive," understanding of many of the things that people do.

selection 32 / the science of learning and the art of teaching / B. F. Skinner, Harvard University

Some promising advances have recently been made in the field of learning. Special techniques have been designed to arrange what are called "contingencies of reinforcement"—the relations which prevail between behavior on the one hand and the consequences of that behavior on the other—with the result that a much more effective control of behavior has been achieved. It has long been argued that an organism learns mainly by producing changes in its environment, but it is only recently that these changes have been carefully manipulated. In traditional devices for the study of learning—in the serial maze, for example, or in the T-maze, the problem box, or the familiar discrimination apparatus—the effects produced by the organism's behavior are left to many fluctuating circumstances. There is many a slip between the turn-to-the-right and the food-cup at the end of the alley. It is not surprising that techniques of this sort have yielded only very rough data from which the uniformities demanded by an experimental science can be extracted only by averaging many cases.

Abridged from B. F. Skinner, "The Science of Learning and the Art of Teaching," *Harvard Educational Review*, 24:86–97, 1954. Reprinted by permission of the author and the publisher.

In none of this work has the behavior of the individual organism been predicted in more than a statistical sense. The learning processes which are the presumed object of such research are reached only through a series of inferences. Current preoccupation with deductive systems reflects this state of the science.

Recent improvements in the conditions which control behavior in the field of learning are of two principal sorts. The Law of Effect has been taken seriously; we have made sure that effects *do* occur and that they occur under conditions which are optimal for producing the changes called learning. Once we have arranged the particular type of consequence called a reinforcement, our techniques permit us to shape up the behavior of an organism almost at will. It has become a routine exercise to demonstrate this in classes in elementary psychology by conditioning such an organism as a pigeon. Simply by presenting food to a hungry pigeon at the right time, it is possible to shape up three or four well-defined responses in a single demonstration period—such responses as turning around, pacing the floor in the pattern of a figure-8, standing still in a corner of the demonstration apparatus, stretching the neck, or stamping the foot. Extremely complex performances may be reached through successive stages in the shaping process, the contingencies of reinforcement being changed progressively in the direction of the required behavior. The results are often quite dramatic. In such a demonstration one can *see* learning take place. A significant change in behavior is often obvious as the result of a single reinforcement.

A second important advance in technique permits us to maintain behavior in given states of strength for long periods of time. Reinforcements continue to be important, of course, long after an organism has learned *how* to do something, long after it has acquired behavior. They are necessary to maintain the behavior in strength. Of special interest is the effect of various schedules of intermittent reinforcement. Charles B. Ferster and the author are currently preparing an extensive report of a five-year research program, sponsored by the Office of Naval Research, in which most of the important types of schedules have been investigated and in which the effects of schedules in general have been reduced to a few principles. On the theoretical side we now have a fairly good idea of why a given schedule produces its appropriate performance. On the practical side we have learned how to maintain any given level of activity for daily periods limited only by the physical exhaustion of the organism and from day to day without substantial change throughout its life. Many of these effects would be traditionally assigned to the field of motivation, although the principal operation is simply the arrangement of contingencies of reinforcement.

These new methods of shaping behavior and of maintaining it in strength are a great improvement over the traditional practices of professional animal trainers, and it is not surprising that our laboratory results are already being applied to the production of performing animals for commercial purposes. In a more academic environment they have been used for demonstration purposes which extend far beyond an interest in learning as such. We have trained two pigeons to coordinate their behavior in a cooperative endeavor with a precision which equals that of the most skillful human dancers. In a more serious vein these techniques have permitted us to explore the complexities of the individual organism and to analyze some of the serial or coordinate behaviors involved in attention, problem solving, various types of self-control, and the subsidiary systems of responses within a single organism called "personalities." Some of these are exemplified in what we call multiple schedules of reinforcement. In general a given schedule has an effect upon the rate at which a response is emitted. Changes in the rate from moment to moment show a pattern typical of the schedule. The pattern may be as simple as a constant rate of responding at a given value, it may be a gradually accelerating rate between certain extremes, it may be an abrupt change from not responding at all to a given stable high rate, and so on. It has been shown that the performance characteristic of a given schedule can be brought under the control of a particular stimulus and that different performances can be brought under the control of different stimuli in the same organism. At a recent meeting of the American Psychological Association, Dr. Ferster and the author demonstrated a pigeon whose behavior showed the pattern typical of "fixed-interval" reinforcement in the presence of one stimulus and, alternately, the pattern typical of the very different schedule called "fixed ratio" in the presence of a second stimulus. In the laboratory we have been able to obtain performances appropriate to *nine* different schedules in the presence of appropriate stimuli in random alternation. When Stimulus 1 is present, the pigeon executes the performance appropriate to Schedule 1. When Stimulus 2 is present, the pigeon executes the performance appropriate to Schedule 2. And so on. This result is important because it makes the extrapolation of our laboratory results to daily life much more plausible. We are all constantly shifting from schedule to schedule as our immediate environment changes, but the dynamics of the control exercised by reinforcement remain essentially unchanged.

One of the most dramatic applications of these techniques has recently been made in the Harvard Psychological Laboratories by Floyd Ratliff and Donald S. Blough, who have skillfully used multiple and serial schedules of reinforcement to study complex perceptual processes in the infrahuman organism. They have achieved a sort of psychophysics without verbal instruction. In a recent experiment by Blough, for example, a pigeon draws a detailed dark-adaptation curve showing the characteristic breaks of rod and cone vision. The curve is recorded continuously in a single experimental period and is quite comparable with the curves of human subjects. The pigeon behaves in a way which, in the human case, we would not hesitate to describe by saying that it adjusts a very faint patch of light until it can just be seen.

In all this work, the species of the organism has made surprisingly little difference. It is true that the organisms studied have all been vertebrates, but they still cover a wide range. Comparable results have been obtained with pigeons, rats, dogs, monkeys, human children, and most recently, by the author in collaboration with Ogden R. Lindsley, human psychotic subjects. In spite of great phylogenetic differences, all these organisms show amazingly similar properties of the learning process. It should be emphasized that this has been achieved by analyzing the effects of reinforcement and by designing techniques which manipulate reinforcement with considerable precision. Only in this way can the behavior of the individual organism be brought under such precise control. It is also important to note that through a gradual advance to complex interrelations among responses, the same degree of rigor is being extended to behavior which would usually be assigned to such fields as perception, thinking, and personality dynamics.

From this exciting prospect of an advancing science of learning, it is a great shock to turn to that branch of technology which is most directly concerned with the learning process—education. Let us consider, for example, the teaching of arithmetic in the lower grades. The school is concerned with imparting to the child a large number of responses of a special sort. The responses are all verbal. They consist of speaking and writing certain words, figures, and signs which, to put it roughly, refer to numbers and to arithmetic operations. The first task is to shape up these responses—to get the child to pronounce and to write responses correctly, but the principal task is to bring this behavior under many sorts of stimulus control. This is what happens when the child learns to count, to recite tables, to count while ticking off the items in an assemblage of objects, to respond to spoken or written numbers by saying "odd," "even," "prime," and so on. Over and above this elaborate repertoire of numerical behavior, most of which is often dismissed as the product of rote learning, the teaching of arithmetic looks forward to those complex serial arrangements of responses involved in original mathematical thinking. The child must acquire responses of transposing, clearing fractions, and so on, which modify the order or pattern of the original material so that the response called a solution is eventually made possible.

Now, how is this extremely complicated verbal repertoire set up? In the first place, what reinforcements are used? Fifty years ago the answer would have been clear. At that time educational control was still frankly aversive. The child read numbers, copied numbers, memorized tables, and performed operations upon numbers to escape the threat of the birch rod or cane. Some positive reinforcements were perhaps eventually derived from the increased efficiency of the child in the field of arithmetic and in rare cases some automatic reinforcement may have resulted from the sheer manipulation of the medium— from the solution of problems or the discovery of the intricacies of the number system. But for the immediate purposes of education the child acted to avoid or escape punishment. It was part of the reform movement known as progressive education to make the positive consequences more immediately effective, but any one who visits the lower grades of the average school today will observe that a change has been made, not from aversive to positive control, but from one form of aversive stimulation to another. The child at his desk, filling in his workbook, is behaving primarily to escape from the threat of a series of minor aversive events—the teacher's displeasure, the criticism or ridicule of his classmates, an ignominious showing in a competition, low marks, a trip to the office "to be talked to" by the principal, or a word to the parent who may still resort to the birch rod. In this welter of aversive consequences, getting the right answer is in itself an insignificant event, any effect of which is lost amid the anxieties, the boredom, and the aggressions which are the inevitable by-products of aversive control.

Secondly, we have to ask how the contingencies of reinforcement are arranged. When is a numerical operation reinforced as "right"? Eventually, of course, the pupil may be able to check his own answers and achieve some sort of automatic reinforcement, but in the early stages the reinforcement of being right is usually accorded by the teacher. The contingencies she provides are far from optimal. It can easily be demonstrated that, unless explicit mediating behavior has been set up, the lapse of only a few seconds between response and reinforcement destroys most of the effect. In a typical classroom, nevertheless, long periods of time customarily elapse. The teacher may walk up and down the aisle, for example, while the class is working on a sheet of problems, pausing here and there to say right or wrong. Many seconds or minutes intervene between the child's response and the teacher's reinforcement. In many cases—for example, when papers are taken home to be corrected—as much as 24 hours may intervene. It is surprising that this system has any effect whatsoever.

A third notable shortcoming is the lack of a skillful program which moves forward through a series of progressive approximations to the final complex behavior desired. A long series of contingencies is necessary to bring the organism into the possession of mathematical behavior most efficiently. But the teacher is seldom able to reinforce at each step in such a series because she cannot deal with the pupil's responses one at a time. It is usually necessary to reinforce the behavior in blocks of responses—as in correcting a work sheet or page from a workbook. The responses within such a block must not be interrelated. The answer to one problem must not depend upon the answer to another. The number of stages through which one may progressively approach a complex pattern of behavior is therefore small, and the task so much the more difficult. Even the most modern workbook in beginning arithmetic is far from exemplifying an efficient program for shaping up mathematical behavior.

Perhaps the most serious criticism of the current classroom is the relative infrequency of reinforcement. Since the pupil is usually dependent upon the teacher for being right, and since many pupils are usually dependent upon the same teacher, the total number of contingencies which may be arranged during, say, the first four years, is of the order of only a few thousand. But a very rough estimate suggests that efficient mathematical behavior at this level requires something of the order of 25,000 contingencies. We may suppose that even in the brighter student a given contingency must be arranged several times to place the behavior well in hand. The responses to be set up are not simply the various items in tables of addition, subtraction, multiplication, and division; we have also to consider the alternative forms in which each item may be stated. To the learning of such material we should add hundreds of responses concerned with factoring, identifying primes, memorizing series, using short-cut techniques of calculation, constructing and using geometric representations or number forms, and so on. Over and above all this, the whole mathematical repertoire must be brought under the control of concrete problems of considerable variety. Perhaps 50,000 contingencies is a more conservative estimate. In this frame of reference the daily assignment in arithmetic seems pitifully meagre.

The result of all this is, of course, well known. Even our best schools are under criticism for their inefficiency in the teaching of drill subjects such as arithmetic. The condition in the average school is a matter of wide-spread national concern. Modern children simply do not learn arithmetic quickly or well. Nor is the result simply incompetence. The very subjects in which modern techniques are weakest are those in which failure is most conspicuous, and in the wake of an ever-growing incompetence come the anxieties, uncertainties, and aggressions which in their turn present other problems to the school. Most pupils soon claim the asylum of not being "ready" for arithmetic at a given level or, eventually, of not having a mathematical mind. Such explanations are readily seized upon by defensive teachers and parents. Few pupils ever reach the stage at which automatic reinforcements follow as the natural consequences of mathematical behavior. On the contrary, the figures and symbols of mathematics have become standard emotional stimuli. The glimpse of a column of figures, not to say an algebraic symbol or an integral sign, is likely to set off—not mathematical behavior—but a reaction of anxiety, guilt, or fear.

There would be no point in urging these objections if improvement were impossible. But the advances which have recently been made in our control of the learning process suggest a thorough revision of classroom practices and, fortunately, they tell us how the revision can be brought about. This is not, of course, the first time that the results of an experimental science have been brought to bear upon the practical problems of education. The modern classroom does not, however, offer much evidence that research in the field of learning has been respected or used. This condition is no doubt partly due to the limitations of earlier research. But it has been encouraged by a too hasty conclusion that the laboratory study of learning is inherently limited because it cannot take into account the realities of the classroom. In the light of our increasing knowledge of the learning process we should, instead, insist upon dealing with those realities and forcing a substantial change in them. Education is perhaps the most important branch of scientific technology. It deeply affects the lives of all of us. We can no longer allow the exigencies of a practical situation to suppress the tremendous improvements which are within reach. The practical situation must be changed.

There are certain questions which have to be answered in turning to the study of any new organism. In the first place, what reinforcements are available? What does the school have in its possession which will reinforce a child? We may look first to the material to be learned, for it is possible that this will provide considerable automatic reinforcement. Children play for hours with mechanical toys, paints, scissors and paper, noise-makers, puzzles—in short, with almost anything which feeds back significant changes in the environment and is reasonably free of aversive properties. The sheer control of nature is itself reinforcing. This effect is not evident in the modern school because it is masked by the emotional responses generated by aversive control. It is true that automatic reinforcement from the manipulation of the environment is probably only a mild reinforcer and may need to be carefully husbanded, but one of the most striking principles to emerge from recent research is that the *net* amount of reinforcement is of little significance. A very slight reinforcement may be tremendously effective in controlling behavior if it is wisely used.

If the natural reinforcement inherent in the subject matter is not enough, other reinforcers must be employed. Even in school the child is occasionally permitted to do "what he wants to do," and access to reinforcements of many sorts may be made contingent upon the more immediate consequences of the behavior to be established. Those who advocate competition as a useful social motive may wish to use the reinforcements which follow from excelling others, although there is the difficulty that in this case the reinforcement of one child is necessarily aversive to another. Next in order we might place the good will and affection of the teacher, and only when that has failed need we turn to the use of aversive stimulation.

In the second place, how are these reinforcements to be made contingent upon the desired behavior? There are two considerations here—the gradual elaboration of extremely complex patterns of behavior and the maintenance of the behavior in strength at each stage. The whole process of becoming competent in any field must be divided into a very large number of very small steps, and reinforcement must be contingent upon the accomplishment of each step. This solution to the problem of creating a complex repertoire of behavior also solves the problem of maintaining the behavior in strength. We could, of course, resort to the techniques of scheduling already developed in the study of other organisms but in the present state of our knowledge of educational practices, scheduling appears to be most effectively arranged through the design of the material to be learned. By making each successive step as small as possible, the frequency of reinforcement can be raised to a maximum, while the possibly aversive consequences of being wrong are reduced to a minimum. Other ways of designing material would yield other programs of reinforcement. Any supplementary reinforcement would probably have to be scheduled in the more traditional way.

These requirements are not excessive, but they are probably incompatible with the current realities of the classroom. In the experimental study of learning it has been found that the contingencies of reinforcement which are most efficient in controlling the organism cannot be arranged through the personal mediation of the experimenter. An organism is affected by subtle details of contingencies which are beyond the capacity of the human organism to arrange.

If our current knowledge of the acquisition and maintenance of verbal behavior is to be applied to education, some sort of teaching machine is needed.[1] Contingencies of reinforcement which change the behavior of lower organisms often cannot be arranged by hand; rather elaborate apparatus is needed. The human organism requires

[1] The remaining portion of this selection is abridged from B. F. Skinner, "Teaching Machines," *Science*, 128:969–977, 1958. Reprinted by permission of the author and the publisher.

even more subtle instrumentation. An appropriate teaching machine will have several important features. The student must *compose* his response rather than select it from a set of alternatives, as in a multiple-choice self-rater. One reason for this is that we want him to recall rather than recognize—to make a response as well as see that it is right. Another reason is that effective multiple-choice material must contain plausible wrong responses, which are out of place in the delicate process of "shaping" behavior because they strengthen unwanted forms. Although it is much easier to build a machine to score multiple-choice answers than to evaluate a composed response, the technical advantage is outweighed by these and other considerations.

A second requirement of a minimal teaching machine also distinguishes it from earlier versions. In acquiring complex behavior the student must pass through a carefully designed sequence of steps, often of considerable length. Each step must be so small that it can always be taken, yet in taking it the student moves somewhat closer to fully competent behavior. The machine must make sure that these steps are taken in a carefully prescribed order.

Several machines with the required characteristics have been built and tested. Sets of separate presentations or "frames" of visual material are stored on disks, cards, or tapes. One frame is presented at a time, adjacent frames being out of sight. In one type of machine the student composes a response by moving printed figures or letters. His setting is compared by the machine with a coded response. If the two correspond, the machine automatically presents the next frame. If they do not, the response is cleared, and another must be composed. The student cannot proceed to a second step until the first has been taken. A machine of this kind is being tested in teaching spelling, arithmetic, and other subjects in the lower grades.

For more advanced students—from junior high school, say, through college—a machine which senses an arrangement of letters or figures is unnecessarily rigid in specifying form of response. Fortunately, such students may be asked to compare their responses with printed material revealed by the machine. In the machine, material is printed in 30 radial frames on a 12-inch disk. The student inserts the disk and closes the machine. He cannot proceed until the machine has been locked, and, once he has begun, the machine cannot be unlocked. All but a corner of one frame is visible through a window. The student writes his response on a paper strip exposed through a second opening. By lifting a lever on the front of the machine, he moves what he has written under a transparent cover and uncovers the correct response in the remaining corner of the frame. If the two responses correspond, he moves the lever horizontally. This movement punches a hole in the paper opposite his response, recording the fact that he called it correct, and alters the machine so that the frame will not appear again when the student works around the disk a second time. Whether the response was correct or not, a second frame appears when the lever is returned to its starting position. The student proceeds in this way until he has responded to all frames. He then works around the disk a second time, but only those frames appear to which he has not correctly responded. When the disk revolves without stopping, the assignment is finished. (The student is asked to repeat each frame until a correct response is made to allow for the fact that, in telling him that a response is wrong, such a machine tells him what is right.)

The machine itself, of course, does not teach. It simply brings the student into contact with the person who composed the material it presents. It is a labor-saving device because it can bring one programmer into contact with an indefinite number of students. This may suggest mass production, but the effect upon each student is surprisingly like that of a private tutor. The comparison holds in several respects. (i) There is a constant interchange between program and student. Unlike lectures, textbooks, and the usual audio-visual aids, the machine induces sustained activity. The student is always alert and busy. (ii) Like a good tutor, the machine insists that a given point be thoroughly understood, either frame by frame or set by set, before the student moves on. Lectures, textbooks, and their mechanized equivalents, on the other hand, proceed without making sure that the student understands and easily leave him behind. (iii) Like a good tutor the machine presents just that material for which the student is ready. It asks him to take only that step which he is at the moment best equipped and most likely to take. (iv) Like a skillful tutor the machine helps the student to come up with the right answer. It does this in part through the orderly construction of the program and in part with techniques of hinting, prompting, suggesting, and so on, derived from an analysis of verbal behavior. (v) Lastly, of course, the machine, like the private tutor, reinforces the student for every correct response, using this immediate feedback not only to shape his behavior most efficiently but to maintain it in strength in a manner which the layman would describe as "holding the student's interest."

Can material be too easy?

The traditional teacher may view these programs with concern. He may be particularly alarmed by the effort to maximize success and minimize failure. He has found that students do not pay attention unless they are worried about the consequences of their work. The customary procedure has been to maintain the necessary anxiety by inducing errors. In recitation, the student who obviously knows the answer is not too often asked; a test item which is correctly answered by everyone is discarded as nondiscriminating; problems at the end of a section in a textbook in mathematics generally include one or two very difficult items; and so on. (The teacher-turned-programmer may be surprised to find this attitude affecting the construction of items. For example, he may find it difficult to allow an item to stand which "gives the point away." Yet if we can solve the motivational problem with other means, what is more effective than giving a point away?) Making sure that the student knows he doesn't know is a technique concerned with motivation, not with the learning process. Machines solve the problem of motivation in other ways. There is no evidence that what is easily learned is more readily forgotten. If this should prove to be the case, retention may be guaranteed by subsequent material constructed for an equally painless review.

The standard defense of "hard" material is that we want to teach more than subject matter. The student is to be challenged and taught to "think." The argument is sometimes little more than a rationalization for a confusing presentation, but it is doubtless true that lectures and texts are often inadequate and misleading by design. But to what end? What sort of "thinking" does the student learn in struggling through difficult material? It is true that those who learn under difficult conditions are better students, but are they better because they have surmounted difficulties or do they surmount them because they are better? In the guise of teaching thinking we set difficult and confusing situations and claim credit for the students who deal with them successfully.

The trouble with deliberately making education difficult in order to teach thinking is (i) that we must remain content with the students thus selected, even though we know that they are only a small part of the potential supply of thinkers, and (ii) that we must continue to sacrifice the teaching of subject matter by renouncing effective but "easier" methods. A more sensible program is to analyze the behavior called "thinking" and produce it according to specifications. A program specifically concerned with such behavior could be composed of material already available in logic, mathematics, scientific method, and psychology. Much would doubtless be added in completing an effective program. The machine has already yielded important relevant by-products. Immediate feedback encourages a more careful reading of programmed material than is the case in studying a text, where the consequences of attention or inattention are so long deferred that they have little effect on reading skills. The behavior involved in observing or attending to detail—as in inspecting charts and models or listening closely to recorded speech—is efficiently shaped by the contingencies arranged by the machine. And when an immediate result is in the balance, a student will be more likely to learn how to marshal relevant material, to concentrate on specific features of a presentation, to reject irrelevant materials, to refuse the easy but wrong solution, and to tolerate indecision, all of which are involved in effective thinking.

Part of the objection to easy material is that the student will come to depend on the machine and will be less able than ever to cope with the inefficient presentations of lectures, textbooks, films, and "real life." This is indeed a problem. All good teachers must "wean" their students, and the machine is no exception. The better the teacher, the more explicit must the weaning process be. The final stages of a program must be so designed that the student no longer requires the helpful conditions arranged by the machine. This can be done in many ways—among others by using the machine to discuss material which has been studied in other forms. These are questions which can be adequately answered only by further research.

No large-scale "evaluation" of machine teaching has yet been attempted. We have so far been concerned mainly with practical problems in the design and use of machines, and with testing and revising sample programs. Material has been prepared and tested with the collaboration of Lloyd E. Homme, Susan R. Meyer, and James G. Holland. Nearly 200 students completed 48 disks (about 1400 frames) prepared with the collaboration of Holland. The factual core of the course was covered, corresponding to about 200 pages of the text. The median time required to finish 48 disks was 14½ hours. The students were not examined on the material but were responsible for the text which overlapped it. Their reactions to the material and to self-instruction in general have been studied through interviews and questionnaires. Both the machines and the material are now being modified in the light of this experience, and a more explicit evaluation will then be made.

Meanwhile, it can be said that the expected advantages of machine instruction were generously confirmed. Unsuspected possibilities were revealed which are now undergoing further exploration. Although it is less convenient to report to a self-instruction room than to pick up a textbook in one's room or elsewhere, most students felt that they had much to gain in studying by machine. Most of them worked for an hour or more with little effort, although they often felt tired afterwards, and they reported that they learned much more in less time and with less effort than in conventional ways. No attempt was made to point out the relevance of the material to crucial issues, personal or otherwise, but the students remained interested. (Indeed, one change in the reinforcing contingencies suggested by the experiment is intended to *reduce* the motivational level.) An important advantage proved to be that the student always knew where he stood, without waiting for an hour test or final examination.

Some questions

Several questions are commonly asked when teaching machines are discussed. Cannot the results of laboratory research on learning be used in education without machines? Of course they can. They should lead to improvements in textbooks, films, and other teaching materials. Moreover, the teacher who really understands the conditions under which learning takes place will be more effective, not only in teaching subject matter but in managing the class. Nevertheless, some sort of device is necessary to arrange the subtle contingencies of reinforcement required for optimal learning if each student is to have individual attention. In nonverbal skills this is usually obvious; texts and instructor can guide the learner but they cannot arrange the final contingencies which set up skilled behavior. It is true that the verbal skills at issue here are especially dependent upon social reinforcement, but it must not be forgotten that the machine simply mediates an *essentially verbal* relation. In shaping and maintaining verbal knowledge we are not committed to the contingencies arranged through immediate personal contact.

Machines may still seem unnecessarily complex compared with other mediators such as workbooks or self-scoring test forms. Unfortunately, these alternatives are not acceptable. When material is adequately programmed, adjacent steps are often so similar that one frame reveals the response to another. Only some sort of mechanical presentation will make successive frames independent of each other. Moreover, in self-instruction an automatic record of the student's behavior is especially desirable, and for many purposes it should be fool-proof. Simplified versions of the present machines have been found useful—for example, in the work of Ferster and Sapon, of Porter, and of Gilbert—but the mechanical and economic problems are so easily solved that a machine with greater capabilities is fully warranted.

Will machines replace teachers? On the contrary, they are capital equipment to be used by teachers to save time and labor. In assigning certain mechanizable functions to machines, the teacher emerges in his proper role as an indispensable human being. He may teach more students than heretofore—this is probably inevitable if the world-wide demand for education is to be satisfied—but he will do so in fewer hours and with fewer burdensome chores. In return for his greater productivity he can ask society to improve his economic condition.

The role of the teacher may well be changed, for machine instruction will affect several traditional practices. Students may continue to be grouped in "grades" or "classes," but it will be possible for each to proceed at his own level, advancing as rapidly as he can. The other kind of "grade" will also change its meaning. In traditional practice a C means that a student has a smattering of a whole course. But if machine instruction assures mastery at every stage, a grade will be useful only in showing *how far* a student has gone. C might mean that he is halfway through a course. Given enough time he will be able to get an A; and since A is no longer a motivating device, this is fair enough. The quick student will meanwhile have picked up A's in other subjects.

Differences in ability raise other questions. A program designed for the slowest student in the school system will probably not seriously delay the fast student, who will be free to progress at his own speed. (He may profit from the full coverage by filling in unsuspected gaps in his repertoire.) If this does not prove to be the case, programs can be constructed at two or more levels, and students can be shifted from one to the other as performances dictate. If there are also differences in "types of thinking," the extra time available for machine instruction may be used to present a subject in ways appropriate to many types. Each student will presumably retain and use those ways which he finds most useful. The kind of individual difference which arises simply because a student has missed part of an essential sequence (compare the child who has no "mathematical ability" because he was out with the measles when fractions were first taken up) will simply be eliminated.

Conclusion

An analysis of education within the framework of a science of behavior has broad implications. Our schools, in particular our "progressive" schools, are often held responsible for many current problems —including juvenile delinquency and the threat of a more powerful foreign technology. One remedy frequently suggested is a return to older techniques, especially to a greater "discipline" in schools. Presumably this is to be obtained with some form of punishment, to be administered either with certain classical instruments of physical injury—the dried bullock's tail of the Greek teacher or the cane of the English schoolmaster—or as disapproval or failure, the frequency of which is to be increased by "raising standards." This is probably not a feasible solution. Not only education but Western culture as a whole is moving away from aversive practices. We cannot prepare young people for one kind of life in institutions organized on quite different principles. The discipline of the birch rod may facilitate learning, but we must remember that it also breeds followers of dictators and revolutionists.

In the light of our present knowledge a school system must be called a failure if it cannot induce students to learn except by threatening them for not learning. That this has always been the standard pattern simply emphasizes the importance of modern techniques. John Dewey was speaking for his culture and his time when he attacked aversive educational practices and appealed to teachers to turn to positive and humane methods. What he threw out should have been thrown out. Unfortunately he had too little to put in its place. Progressive education has been a temporizing measure which can now be effectively supplemented. Aversive practices can not only be replaced, they can be replaced with far more powerful techniques. The possibilities should be thoroughly explored if we are to build an educational system which will meet the present demand without sacrificing democratic principles.

selection 33 / the elimination of tantrum behavior by extinction procedures / Carl D. Williams, University of Miami

This paper reports the successful treatment of tyrant-like tantrum behavior in a male child by the removal of reinforcement. The subject (S) was approximately 21 months old. He had been seriously ill much of the first 18 months of his life. His health then improved considerably, and he gained weight and vigor.

S now demanded the special care and attention that had been given him over the many critical months. He enforced some of his wishes, especially at bedtime, by unleashing tantrum behavior to control the actions of his parents.

The parents and an aunt took turns in putting him to bed both at night and for S's afternoon nap. If the parent left the bedroom after putting S in his bed, S would scream and fuss until the parent returned to the room. As a result, the parent was unable to leave the bedroom until after S went to sleep. If the parent began to read while in the bedroom, S would cry until the reading material was put down. The parents felt that S enjoyed his control over them and that he fought off going to sleep as long as he could. In any event, a parent

From Carl D. Williams, "The Elimination of Tantrum Behavior by Extinction Procedures," *Journal of Abnormal and Social Psychology*, 59:269, 1959. Reprinted by permission of the author and the American Psychological Association.

was spending from one-half to two hours each bedtime just waiting in the bedroom until S went to sleep.

Following medical reassurance regarding S's physical condition, it was decided to remove the reinforcement of this tyrant-like tantrum behavior. Consistent with the learning principle that, in general, behavior that is not reinforced will be extinguished, a parent or the aunt put S to bed in a leisurely and relaxed fashion. After bedtime pleasantries, the parent left the bedroom and closed the door. S screamed and raged, but the parent did not re-enter the room. The duration of screaming and crying was obtained from the time the door was closed.

The results are shown in Fig. 1. It can be seen that S continued screaming for 45 min. the first time he was put to bed in the first extinction series. S did not cry at all the second time he was put to bed. This is perhaps attributable to his fatigue from the crying of Occasion 1. By the tenth occasion, S no longer whimpered, fussed, or cried when the parent left the room. Rather, he smiled as they left. The parents felt that he made happy sounds until he dropped off to sleep.

About a week later, S screamed and fussed after the aunt put him to bed, probably reflecting spontaneous recovery of the tantrum behavior. The aunt then reinforced the tantrum behavior by returning to S's bedroom and remaining there until he went to sleep. It was then necessary to extinguish this behavior a second time.

Figure 1 shows that the second extinction curve is similar to the first. Both curves are generally similar to extinction curves obtained with subhuman subjects. The second extinction series reached zero by the ninth occasion. No further tantrums at bedtime were reported during the next two years.

It should be emphasized that the treatment in this case did not involve aversive punishment. All that was done was to remove the reinforcement. Extinction of the tyrant-like tantrum behavior then occurred.

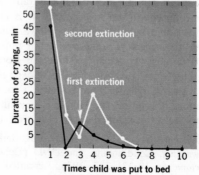

Fig. 1 Length of crying in two extinction series as a function of successive occasions of being put to bed.

No unfortunate side- or aftereffects of this treatment were observed. At three and three-quarters years of age, S appeared to be a friendly, expressive, outgoing child.

selection 34 / brainwashing, conditioning, and ddd (debility, dependency, and dread) / I. E. Farber, State University of Iowa, Harry F. Harlow, University of Wisconsin, and Louis Jolyon West, University of Oklahoma Medical School

Few aspects of Communism have been more puzzling and disturbing to the Western world than the widely publicized collaboration, conversion, and self-denunciation in individuals—communist and noncommunist, innocent and guilty alike—who have suffered Communist imprisonment. Such behavior in persons whose intelligence, integrity, or patriotism can scarcely be doubted has suggested to many a mysterious power or knowledge that enables Communists to manipulate the thoughts and actions of others in a manner ordinarily reserved to characters in the more lurid sorts of science fiction. Accordingly, such terms as "brainwashing," "thought control," "menticide," and so on, have been applied to the process or product of this manipulation. To lend some degree of scientific respectability to such concepts, attempts have been made to relate them to the psychiatric implications of Pavlovian conditioning procedures.

While these speculations have an undeniable romantic appeal, more sober analyses of factors influencing the behavior of prisoners under Communist control indicate that they are neither mysterious nor indicative of any unusual amount of psychiatric sophistication on the part of Communists. Indeed, considering the extraordinary degree of control the Communists maintain over the physical and social environments of their prisoners, it is rather surprising that their efforts to indoctrinate and convert have not been more successful. Contrary to the views of some writers in popular media, the record indicates that most American prisoners in Korea, for instance, showed remarkable "sales resistance," even under profound duress.

In the light of these findings, a complete analysis would concentrate more heavily on the factors that enabled the large majority of POW's to resist in some degree. However, it is not with these phenomena

Abridged from I. E. Farber, Harry F. Harlow, and Louis Jolyon West, "Brainwashing, Conditioning, and DDD (Debility, Dependency and Dread)," *Sociometry*, 19:271–285, 1956. Reprinted by permission of the authors and publisher.

that the present discussion is primarily concerned. Rather, we wish to discuss the basis for the success of techniques whereby false confessions, self-denunciations, and participation in propaganda activities were brought about. The Communists made special efforts to elicit these behaviors in flying personnel, particularly with regard to confessions of participation in bacteriological warfare. After their world-wide propaganda campaign went into high gear with accusations of "germ warfare" in Korea, beginning on February 21, 1952, a vigorous policy of coercive pressure was applied to a large number of American flying personnel captured during the Korean conflict. As a result, a number of flyers from the Air Force and Marine Corps signed false confessions of bacteriological warfare and participated to various extents in enemy propaganda activities. A detailed account of these events may be found elsewhere.

The objective intensity of noxious stimulation, injury, disease, malnutrition, deprivation, sleeplessness, fatigue, isolation, and threat suffered by many prisoners for a greater or lesser period was extreme. There were few, if any, who were not subjected to some of these conditions. Accounts of observations and experiments related to these various types of stress are now appearing in the literature in increasing numbers. The present discussion is concerned with the theoretical analysis of the psychological states and processes resulting from such objective conditions of stress.

DDD

Although the specific components of these states vary in intensity and pattern, in the case of the prisoner of war they contain at least three important elements: debility, dependency, and dread. They refer to the fact that individuals subjected to the kinds of environmental conditions listed above have reduced viability, are helplessly dependent on their captors for the satisfaction of many basic needs, and experience the emotional and motivational reactions of intense fear and anxiety. These components are separable, but it is evident that they also interact. Consequently it seems appropriate as well as convenient to conceive of these states and processes as though they were an entity or syndrome including debility, dependency, and dread, to be referred to as DDD. Among the POW's pressured by the Chinese Communists, the DDD syndrome in its full-blown form constituted a state of discomfort that was well-nigh intolerable.

Debility was induced by semi-starvation, fatigue, and disease. Chronic physical pain was a common feature. Loss of energy and inability to resist minor abuse, combined with the lack of proper facilities for the maintenance of personal hygiene, led to inanition and a sense of terrible weariness and weakness.

Dependency, produced by the prolonged deprivation of many of the factors, such as sleep and food, needed to maintain sanity and life itself, was made more poignant by occasional unpredictable brief respites, reminding the prisoner that it was possible for the captor to relieve the misery if he wished. If an individual was placed in prolonged isolation, as was so often the case with flyers pressed to confess to the bacteriological warfare charges, the deprivation of ordinary social stimulation and relations markedly strengthened the dependency. Although we shall not dwell on this aspect of the situation, the effectiveness of Communist methods was undoubtedly greatly enhanced by their control of the means for satisfying nuclear social needs for recognition, status, communication, and so on. The captors' condemnation and misunderstanding of American social values, in connection with the withdrawal of accustomed social supports, e.g., reliable sources of information and communication with others as a means of testing reality and of appraising moral standards, played a significant part in the dependency relationship.

Dread is the most expressive term to indicate the chronic fear the Communists attempted to induce. Fear of death, fear of pain, fear of nonrepatriation, fear of deformity or permanent disability through neglect or inadequate medical treatment, fear of Communist violence against loved ones at home, and even fear of one's own inability to satisfy the demands of insatiable interrogators—these and many other nagging despairs constituted the final component of the DDD syndrome.

The interrelations of these factors, carefully contrived and nurtured by the Communists, were of great importance in determining the total effect of DDD. Although there were some individuals who acceded to the demands of their captors fairly early in the game, it is clear that the Chinese realized the importance of preparing the resistant prisoner, through DDD, for the long, drawn-out process designed to bring about the desired goal—complete compliance.

Before considering in greater detail the specific mechanisms underlying the role of DDD in accomplishing this aim, three prefatory comments are in order. First, the present analysis lays no claim to comprehensiveness. It deals with only a few aspects of DDD occurring under certain conditions. We believe these aspects to be important, but they are not all that is important. In this connection, the present paper may be considered as an elaboration of portions of the comprehensive discussion of Communist "thought reform" by Hinkle and Wolff. It is gratifying that our conclusions, arrived at independently and on somewhat more theoretical grounds, are essentially in agreement with theirs.

Second, our use of the terminology of learning theory, broadly conceived, and our use of concepts derived from conditioning, does not imply that we consider learning theory uniquely competent to explain the effects of DDD. On the other hand, we do consider factors influencing behavior in DDD to have something in common with factors affecting behavior in learning situations generally, and, therefore, that it may be worth while attempting to analyze some aspects of behavior associated with DDD in terms of principles of classical and instrumental conditioning. But, as an eminent conditioning theorist has recently noted, the view that principles derived from conditioning might apply to more complex behavior does not at all imply that complex behavior can be explained solely in terms of the variables affecting conditioning. In this instance, it is particularly doubtful that the procedures used to influence the behavior of prisoners under Communism derived from the methods of Pavlov, or that the prisoners' reactions are generally understandable in purely Pavlovian terms. On the contrary, to the extent that such concepts apply at all, selective or instrumental (Thorndikean) learning was a more prominent feature than classical (Pavlovian) conditioning. Certainly, only limited aspects of the behavior of prisoners under Communism bear any resemblance to the generalized inhibitory or excitatory states characterizing some of Pavlov's dogs.

Finally, we should beware of the "psychologist's error." Although some of the behavior of prisoners under Communism may be susceptible to analysis in terms of learning and conditioning principles, it does not follow that the application of these principles by Communist captors was deliberate and self-conscious. Animal trainers and sideshow barkers are often extremely competent manipulators of behavior; this does not mean they are comparative or social psychologists.

Reinforcement of social communication

On the assumption that conditioning principles apply in part to the behavior of prisoners of war, it is important to analyze further the nature of the conditioned stimuli and the responses elicited by them. Careful consideration would seem to indicate that the situation contains features both of selective or instrumental learning and of classical conditioning. The instrumental (i.e., Thorndikean rather than Pavlovian) aspect is emphasized by the fact that an individual must acquire a particular set of responses in order to bring about a reinforcing state of affairs. It is our thesis that an alleviation in the state of DDD provides the reinforcement for much of the behavior desired by the enemy. In other words, DDD does not, in and of itself, produce the desired behavior. DDD merely provides the occasion for the selective reinforcement of certain modes of response.

The role of DDD in the reinforcement process depends on the fact that it is not constant. Instead, it may be assumed to fluctuate in time, partly as a result of spontaneous psychophysiological processes, and partly as a result of deliberate manipulations designed to maintain its intermittent nature, thus preventing its fall to a baseline of permanent depression and hopelessness. Those individuals who were reduced to complete apathy undoubtedly represented failures from the point of view of their Communist captors.

At the risk of considerable oversimplification, one may conceive of two consequences of the occasional mitigation of DDD. First is the conditioning of the "expectancy" that DDD will be alleviated. (This constitutes the actual classically conditioned anticipatory goal response.) Relief, whether due to spontaneous factors or deliberate manipulations, is intermittent, temporary, and unpredictable. Far from weakening the expectancy of relief, however, this tends to maintain the expectancy and renders it less susceptible to extinction. In nontechnical terms, this process serves to keep hope alive, permitting some degree of adaptive behavior, and inhibiting self-destructive tendencies, which would frustrate the enemy's purpose.

This aspect of the learning process throws some light on the frequent practice in Communist prisons of having prisoners "punish themselves." Thus, a captive might be instructed to stand or kneel in a certain position until he should decide to cooperate. This emphasis on the self-inflicted nature of the prisoner's punishment, and his ability to mitigate his condition "voluntarily," is clearly calculated to increase the intensity of expectancies of the possibility of relief. At the same time, it is evident that the prisoner's belief that he actually exercises control is delusory, so far as the objective facts are concerned, since the captor may select any behavior he chooses as the condition for relieving a prisoner's distress.

The alleviation of DDD at the time of occurrence of the desired behavior leads to the second consequence—the learning of instrumental acts. This is not so difficult to arrange as one might suppose and is certainly not the result of any mysterious power of the manipulator. Very often, the desired behavior is verbal in nature. Verbal behavior is in a general way already strongly conditioned to DDD in all human adults. One learns from infancy to use verbal behavior as a means of relieving or avoiding many of the components of DDD. And, as the foregoing discussion indicates, the aperiodic and unpredictable nature of the selective reward of particular language responses may be one of its chief strengths. If one may extrapolate from the results of numerous laboratory experiments, this is the very procedure calculated to produce the maximum number of responses and also to make them highly resistant to extinction, even in the absence of rewards.

The nature of the rewards used needs no elaboration. Relief of hunger, fatigue, isolation, or pain, even temporarily, serves as an automatic reward. Even the verbal and empty promise of alleviation of DDD leads to appropriate anticipatory goal responses, keeping hope alive. Paradoxically, interrogation, harangues, threats, and contumely may also have a rewarding aspect, so great is the acquired reinforcement value of social communication and speech under conditions of isolation, dependency, and physical debility.

Since the habits of social communication associated with DDD are initially strong, and are further strengthened by selective reinforcement, it is not strange that prisoners often show considerable social responsiveness in the presence of their captors. Despite the impoverishment of the self-concept and primitivization of thinking referred to earlier, prisoners could enjoy in some degree a much needed social relationship in the interrogation and indoctrination situations. It may be hypothesized that some prisoners became the victims of the very socialization process that under ordinary circumstances is regarded as a desirable and, indeed, essential aspect of civilized living. It is of interest in this connection to record the finding of Lifton, who explicitly noted among a group of repatriated prisoners who had most aggressively resisted collaboration with the Communists, a large portion of individuals with significant antisocial tendencies. We do not suggest that collaboration and confession by prisoners under Communism are signs of desirable social attitudes. We do suggest that socialization training facilitates the tendency to engage in social communication, even with a recognized enemy, particularly under conditions in which the behavior is reinforced by the satisfaction of powerful drives while at the same time interfering or inhibitory tendencies are markedly reduced.

Retention of prison experiences and behavior

What is the aftermath of such experiences? The evidence clearly indicates that, except in the case of organic brain damage such as might result from avitaminosis, the behavior of the typical returnee from Communist prisons is "normal," in the special and important sense that he behaves in a manner that would be predicted on the basis of ordinary laws of behavior. There is not the slightest evidence for the necessity of postulating new or unknown factors or conditions. This does not mean the experience of imprisonment leaves no trace. Such a circumstance would in itself be abnormal, i.e., inconsistent with the known principles of behavior. In terms of normative criteria, many ex-prisoners are more than ordinarily anxious, defensive, dependent, suspicious, insecure. Pressed to explain any possibly discreditable acts, they often exhibit a very considerable degree of hesitancy, vagueness, paramnesia, and rationalization. In a word, they behave exactly as one would expect of any individual required to explain and defend his behavior, many determinants of which he is not aware.

Most returnees remember a great deal of what occurred during their imprisonment. They do not remember everything and may be unable to give a very clear account of their own behavior. Some behavior may appear as strange and inexplicable to the person concerned as to anyone else. The explanation of whatever impairment of memory occurs may be found in the laws of forgetting, deriving from both clinic and laboratory. There is no need to expatiate here on the role of repression in forgetting when the material to be recalled elicits anxiety and guilt. But it may be useful to note briefly some of the factors that would influence retention even in the absence of these emotions.

In an earlier section, it was pointed out that the state of DDD produces responses that actively compete with ordinary responses to environmental stimuli. By the same process, the comforting and familiar stimuli of home and friends are associated with a wholly different set of responses from those produced by DDD. The changed context may actively inhibit recall of the prison experiences. This phenomenon is nothing more than the familiar psychological explanation of forgetting in terms of associative interference.

Among the most important of these competing responses are the affective ones. The returnee simply does not feel as he did as a prisoner. He may be able to talk about how he felt, although this too offers difficulties because our terminology for describing emotional states is woefully inadequate and vague, but he does not currently respond affectively in the same way. Similarly, the familiar stimuli of home reinstate different verbal responses, both overt and implicit, that affect recall. The returnee feels different, talks differently, and thinks differently than he did in the former context. Since, like all of us, he is unaware of many of the cues to his former behavior (as well as his current behavior), it is as useless to ask him to explain his earlier reactions as it is to ask a person why he once disliked olives or is for the moment unable to recall the name of an old acquaintance.

The particular reactions and attitudes constituting patriotism, bravery, loyalty, and so on, depend on the appearance of particular cues, symbolic or other. Such qualities are tendencies to respond positively or negatively, in varying degrees and combinations, in the presence of certain combinations of cues. From this point of view, unwonted reactions occurring under DDD do not represent a different attitude; rather, the habitual attitude does not appear because the appropriate cues have been removed. Back home in the presence of adequate cues, the returnee tends to act and feel as he did prior to imprisonment.

Finally, one must consider the effect on retention of the adequacy of the original impression. Occasionally the returnee does not remember much because he did not observe much. The impoverished stimulation, impaired responsiveness, reduced symbolic activity, and disorganization of time-spanning characteristic of DDD reduce the clarity and strength of impressions at the time of the original experience, and thus decrease ability to recall.

In the light of all these factors, whose pejorative influence on retention is well known by students of human learning, it is clearly to be expected that the recall of returnees would be something less than complete and wholly accurate as regards their actual prison experiences and behavior.

Resistance to effects of DDD

It is evident that there are great individual differences in susceptibility to DDD even under conditions in which the level of DDD itself could reasonably be regarded as constant, i.e., not a differential factor. To state the point somewhat differently, there are unquestionably a number of variables, whose values differ from person to person, affecting the degree of resistance to the effects of DDD. The question may then be raised whether the potency of these variables might not be increased in any given individual. We believe they can.

The statement, "Every man has his breaking point," contains a germ of truth, but like other bromides, is liable to misinterpretation. It does not mean the "breaking point" is fixed for any given individual, so that nothing can affect it. Such a view is scientifically indefensible, if not meaningless, since it implies that some kinds of behavior are unlawful, i.e., not affected by variations in any kinds of antecedent conditions. Furthermore, the term "breaking point" is itself misleading. Susceptibility to DDD or any other stressful condition is not an all-or-none affair. We are discussing behavior, and behavior varies in degree and in kind. It may be possible to define "breaking" in the manner that one defines a right or wrong response in arithmetic, but it should be recognized that such a definition would be arbitrary at best and of doubtful conceptual significance. As Biderman has pointed out, a prisoner's physical and moral strength may be sapped by Communist coercive methods to a degree that resistance appears insignificant. But, however feeble his performance, motivation to resist usually persists and shows itself as circumstances permit.

It is not the purpose of the present discussion to consider all the possible personal or social variables of which resistance to the effects of DDD may be a function, or indeed to consider any of them in detail. We mention two, not because they are necessarily of particular importance, but because they throw further light on the nature of the *DDD* state. First, there is the factor of physical health. Other things equal, there is probably a negative relation between degree of physical health and vigor on the one hand and susceptibility to *DDD* on the other. Debility can be postponed longer, dependency fought against, and the self-concept maintained more easily if bodily well-being obtains. Second, there is the factor of initial or chronic anxiety. No matter what anxiety is due to, the higher the anxiety level, the greater is the possibility of rewarding behavior by its momentary reduction. Contrariwise, a low level of initial anxiety should retard the growth of the "dread" component of *DDD*, and at least indirectly affect some of its antecedents, e.g., the reactivity to pain.

Thus, techniques for promoting health and decreasing anxiety in those who may become prisoners are probably of great importance. Nevertheless, one should not expect factors such as these to block the effects of *DDD* indefinitely. Physical health, for instance, may be of utmost value over the short haul, e.g., during early interrogation. But on a long-term basis it may be relatively insignificant. Health can be broken down by a determined and informed enemy in a very short time. And although a healthy individual can better resist the effects of debilitating variables, there is no evidence that, once illness and physical debility occur, previously healthy individuals can tolerate this condition better than those who might have become habituated to it. In some cases, indeed, the reverse might obtain.

A somewhat similar reservation may be expressed concerning procedures calculated to reduce initial anxiety, i.e., training individuals to be generally nonanxious. The fear component of *DDD*, unlike neurotic anxiety or neurotic fears (phobias), is quite realistic for the most part. Realistic fears are not easily extinguishable and, if they were, the desirability of extinguishing such fears is not altogether certain. For instance, fear of punishment for displaying hostility toward one's captors is adaptive. Wolf and Ripley quote one prisoner of the Japanese in World War II in this regard: "I had to make a conscious effort not to resent things because I realized that my bones are brittle."

On the other hand, certain anticipatory fears may be modified through training procedures. Alleviation of unrealistic fears of the unknown (through accurate indoctrination regarding enemy methods) undoubtedly improves the ability of the individual to deal with those fears that are realistic. It may make it possible for him to admit his fear to himself, as a reasonable and expected reaction, thus modifying its influence as a covert force toward compliance. Furthermore, an expectation of the probable psychophysiological effects of stress may rob them of some of their "shock" value. Finally, a certain amount of transfer may be expected from stressful training experiences in which adaptive modalities have been learned, thus permitting the prisoner to conceptualize his current stressful experience in terms of previous (and at least partly successful) transactions under stress.

Though many of the behavioral consequences of *DDD* are not innately determined, the conditioning of certain types of responses desired by the enemy may eventually occur, even in the face of superlative resistance. One of the conclusions that may legitimately be drawn from the present analysis of the circumstances of imprisonment under Communism is that, if a prisoner's state of *DDD* reaches a truly extreme degree of severity (and it cannot now be predicted whose ability to resist will be the most effective in combating *DDD*), and *if he lives*, he probably cannot be expected to resist indefinitely. This prediction does not require the assumption that Communists have mysterious powers, or that their prisoners are subjected to some strange process of "brainwashing" negating the effects of their previous training and attitudes. It is based, rather, on the assumption that under the physical, social, and emotional conditions of extreme *DDD*, some degree of ultimate compliance may be considered a natural consequence of the operation of ordinary principles of human behavior.

Summary

Although the behavior of some prisoners under Communism, including collaboration, conversion, and self-denunciation, appears to suggest that Communists are able to "brainwash" their prisoners in a mysterious way, a consideration of the physical, emotional, and social conditions of the prisoner in conjunction with the ordinary principles of human behavior reveals that such behavior may be readily explained. The state of the prisoner may be described in terms of the concepts of debility, dependency, and dread (*DDD*), and some of the behavioral principles explaining the effects of the *DDD* state derive from learning and conditioning phenomena.

It is assumed that *DDD* operates in part to produce a generalized state of hyporesponsiveness, disrupting time-spanning processes and disorganizing the self-concept. Another consequence of *DDD* is the impairment of symbolic processes, perhaps rendering the prisoner susceptible to relatively simple conditioning techniques. The intermittent nature of *DDD* leads both to the expectancy of relief (i.e., hope) and to the reinforcement of specific kinds of verbal behavior. The latter effect is facilitated by the fact that social communication is already strongly conditioned to cues such as those produced by *DDD*, as a result of normal socialization training.

The typical prisoner returnee exhibits no extraordinary peculiarities of memory. The degree of forgetting of prison experiences is such as would be expected as a result of the inhibition of anxiety-producing thoughts (repression), change of situational context during recall, and the inadequacies of original impressions during imprisonment.

Resistance to the undesirable consequences of *DDD* is a matter of degree and may be modified by such factors as physical health and level of initial anxiety. Nevertheless, factors such as these cannot reasonably be expected to provide more than temporary respite. Through various defenses, a prisoner may postpone the development of extreme *DDD* for a long time, perhaps indefinitely. But if a prisoner's state of *DDD* is extreme, and if he lives, he probably cannot resist indefinitely. Far from furnishing proof of the operation of some unnatural process of "brainwashing," this eventuality is a predictable consequence of the operation of laws of normal human behavior.

CHAPTER 8 ✳ THINKING, REASONING, AND PROBLEM SOLVING ✳

Although the experimental evidence indicates that lower animals are capable of rudimentary representational processes, man is superior to his mammalian relatives in his ability to manipulate symbols of objects and relationships in his environment, that is, to think. Defining thinking as the covert manipulation of symbols makes the term inclusive of a wide variety of mental activity ranging from the visual imagery characteristic of dreams and fantasy to the manipulation of verbal symbols involved in problem solving. In this chapter we are concerned primarily with the latter type of thinking. Such thinking makes use of the results of previous learning (engrams or "traces," cf. Selection 28) so that certain neural correlates of symbols are activated in sequences. In the case of concept formation and other creative thinking, the symbols are put together in new and unique ways. As was pointed out in our chapter on learning processes, the neurological basis for learning remains a matter for speculation.

The neurophysiological correlates of thinking and reasoning are even more obscure. In Selection 35 Dr. John Gaito presents a speculative formulation regarding some aspects of the neurophysiology of thinking. Although he admits that the theory is still far from complete, he presents a good deal of evidence to support his major premise that the integrative function of the central nervous system is related to the frequency of the spontaneous electrical activity of the brain. He points out, for example, that the quality of thinking decreases in lowered levels of consciousness such as sleeping, and at the same time slow brain waves make their appearance in electrical recordings of brain activity.

Since an integral part of most problem solving situations is assumed to be the manipulation of verbal symbols, the experimental investigation of the role of verbal responses in problem solving is of considerable importance. Professor Charles N. Cofer has extensively explored this problem. He describes, in Selection 36, a series of experiments which helps us to understand the role played by verbal mediators in problem solving. These intervening verbal associations give "direction" to our thought processes. They serve to make one class of thought processes more likely than another. They seem to serve the same function for potential internal stimuli (neural traces) that other "gating" or "screening" mechanisms serve for external stimuli (cf. Hernández-Peón et al. on the neural correlates of attention, Selection 25). In his paper on the influence of mental set, Selection 37, Dr. Ian M. L. Hunter presents evidence which shows that specific sets facilitate solution in anagram problems. It is likely that this facilitation is dependent on the activation of verbal mediators discussed by Cofer. Thus, if you tell a person that the anagram spells the name of an animal, he no longer has to try out and discard possible solutions regarding plants, trees, etc.

In many actual problem solving situations, the solution is not attained or is greatly retarded because the correct general category of ideas or associations is not emitted. Sometimes the person tends to block, to run dry of possible solutions, or to become fixated on a wrong approach. His "guessing" or hypothesizing becomes prematurely narrowed to a small set of ideas which excludes the category of ideas which, if explored, might lead to successful solution. In such problem situations a reasonable approach would seem to be to rely on a group of persons rather than a single individual. We would thus expect that there would be a better chance of "getting in the right ball park." A particular approach to group problem solving which has received considerable attention in business and industry has been called "brainstorming." Consistent with the above analysis, Taylor, Berry, and Block (Selection 38) note that the basic assumption of brainstorming is that the larger the number of ideas produced, the greater the probability of achieving an effective solution.

Taylor et al. point out that common sense and informal experience with this technique seem to indicate that groups do produce more ideas and are thus more effective than individuals. However, a scientifically adequate evaluation of brainstorming requires more adequately controlled experimentation and statistical evaluation. They also note that it is not adequate simply to compare average group performance to average individual performances, since by virtue of being composed of several individuals the group should most certainly produce more ideas than the average individual. Thus, they make use of a "nominal group" control procedure in which persons who have actually worked on the problems alone are combined at random to form a "group" of a size equal to the real groups which performed together. Their results indicate that, as expected, the real groups produced more ideas than individuals. However, when the real groups are compared with the "nominal groups," the results were contrary to expectation, that is, the nominal groups produced significantly more ideas than real groups. Further, analysis of the results indicated that the real groups were also inferior to the nominal groups in terms of uniqueness and quality of ideas. The authors conclude that to the extent that the results may be generalized, brainstorming inhibits rather than facilitates creative thinking. They further suggest that the inhibition may be due to a reduction of the variety of ideas produced. The curious student may wonder if this factor of reduction of the variety of ideas was not, in fact, especially important in this experiment since the subjects were a relatively homogeneous group. It may well be that in a setting where individuals with a wide variety of backgrounds (for example, electrical engineers, aeronautical engineers, physicists, and psychologists) are composed into groups to solve an applied problem, the brainstorming technique may facilitate problem solution. The answer to this question awaits further research.

selection 35 / a neuropsychological approach to thinking / John Gaito, Kansas State University

The study of thinking presents a prominent and interesting problem in human behavior but it has not been investigated experimentally extensively, until recently. Prior to this decade relatively few important studies on the thinking process were reported. The dearth of research in this area possibly may be attributed to the experimental psychologist's desire to be objective and to circumvent any processes which are covert. Whatever the reason may be for the retardation, it seems apparent that to understand human behavior it will be necessary to understand the process of thinking. However, more emphasis has been devoted recently to thinking, as indicated by an increase in the number of relevant books and articles.

Thinking has sometimes been defined narrowly, sometimes broadly. Those who define it narrowly separate it from such phenomena as learning, problem solving, and reasoning, whereas the broad definition would consider these as different aspects of the same problem. It seems appropriate to maintain a distinction between learning and thinking but to consider thinking, reasoning, and problem-solving behavior as involving the same set of operations. The distinction between learning and thinking is based on the difference between content and process. Learning always involves the "residue" or "trace"

From John Gaito, "A Neuropsychological Approach to Thinking," *Psychological Reports*, 4:323–332, 1958. Reprinted by permission of the Southern Universities Press, Missoula, Montana.

of previous experience whereas thinking is a process in which the "residues" are manipulated. However, this distinction is of academic interest only inasmuch as thinking and learning are so intimately intertwined that it is difficult to investigate one irrespective of the other. It is postulated that thinking is a process which is common to learning and so-called problem-solving and reasoning situations and is practiced by the organism through all waking states, even though sometimes on a very low habitual level. It even appears in dreams but at a very low level wherein the neurophysiological substratum which is responsible for integrated thinking and behavior is usually functioning well below the optimum level.

Even though it seems certain that some modification of the brain is involved in behavior, there has been great reluctance on the part of most psychologists to incorporate neurological concepts in theory building. However, the stimulating neuropsychological theory propounded by Hebb, research on the brain stem reticular activation system, and further advances in the recording of electrical activity of brain tissue in the last decade have served to dispel some of the mistrust of neurology. During this period the number of "neurologizing" studies has increased tremendously.

In his neuropsychological theory of behavior, Hebb included an interesting treatment of thinking based on results concerning the spontaneous activity of nerve cells as indicated by electroencephalographic (EEG) studies. He maintained that thinking involved the interaction of cell assemblies and phase sequences. The purpose of this paper is to present another neuropsychological approach to thinking based on EEG studies. Even though results of studies are disappointingly vague, some relationships appear to be clear.

Theoretical formulation

Thinking may be conceived as a covert process of coordinating, integrating, and manipulating information received and stored within the central nervous system and maintained by the neural electrochemical functions; a continuous process which never abates except in death. It can be scaled from very low level thinking which requires minimal or no monitoring to the constant monitoring and unique reorganization and modification required in complex thinking. In the thinking process man makes use of symbols and other shorthand measures and rarely describes the problem completely in language. Even though the process is covert it can be externalized through operations. The important behavioral variable on which the level of thinking continuum is based is that of amount of monitoring of thought by the thinker. The continuum can be viewed experimentally as an ordinal scale and the level of thinking in two or more situations can be ranked by means of behavioral aspects such as latency, smoothness, or continuity of performance, etc. In this context monitoring is defined as the active guiding or the giving of direction to the thought process, i.e., imposing controls on the thought process at various points in the sequence. During the waking state the thinking process may be monitored very actively and thus thinking will be characterized by greatest integration. Habitual, low-level but integrated thought may occur also during the waking state when little or no monitoring is involved. However, guiding of the thought process may be imposed intermittently so that thinking and behavior is integrated. During sleeping thinking may continue in the form of dreams, but the level of thinking and integrative capacity is usually low because little or no active monitoring can be imposed unless the individual awakens.

From a review of a substantial amount of neurophysiological and psychological literature it appears that various logical predictions about thinking can be made. Therefore, various statements in postulate form will relate neurophysiological data to psychological phenomena. The empirical data relevant to these postulates (or to deductions from these postulates) then will be presented where possible to indicate the basis for the postulates.

1. *The basic function of the central nervous system is integration.* Integration may be defined as the function which combines and relates distinct internal or external cues in order that unified, coordinated overt or covert behavior may occur. Different levels of the hierarchy of the central nervous system contribute to integration. However, complete integration in complex activities requires the cerebral cortex. Integration is on a continuum varying from low to high levels. A high level is required in complex problem-solving behavior; a simple behavior requires a lower level. However, even simple behavior involves a complex interaction of multiple neurophysiological units.

Integration is not a new concept. It has been proposed or implied by many.

2. *An intact cerebrum is considered to be the neurophysiological basis for optimal levels of integration.* Lesions of the cerebrum affect the integrative function to a greater or lesser degree, depending on their nature, size, and location. Lesions may also interfere with specific performances (other than a general integrative defect) if specialized tissue is affected.

The effects of lesions on behavior have been considered to be nonexistent in some psychological complex processes, e.g., intelligence. However, others have reported contrary results. It appears that some intelligence test items rely heavily on knowledge attained by the individual during his premorbid life and thus the lesion has no effect on this knowledge. However, it is reasonable to assume that if sensitive indicators are available for testing psychological processes and that the individual's premorbid performance is known, any lesion will produce some decrement in performance.

3. *Thinking is the main aspect of, and a basic instrumentality for, integration.* It is the sensory aspect of integration. The other aspect of integration involves the motor sphere, that of coordinated motor behavior.

If thinking is distorted, integration should decrease in degree. However, thinking which may appear distorted to an observer (e.g., as in schizophrenia) may be considered integrated if viewed within the frame of reference of the thinker. In this case the thinker may be operating logically with concepts which are regarded as faulty by the observer.

If integration decreases, thinking should be affected adversely. However, low level thinking of an habitual nature may occur without affecting the degree of integration inasmuch as habitual coordinated motor behavior may be involved.

4. *The electrical activity recorded in electroencephalograms arises from the electro-chemical processes of neural tissues (metabolism) and indicates the state of the neural substratum.*

The nerve cell may be considered a chemical battery in which the chemical products of metabolism give rise to electrical reactions. Therefore, it is obvious that dead cells will show neither metabolic activity nor electrical reactions. Furthermore, the electrical activity of live cells near dead cells may be modified because of inhibitory or irritating effects of the dead cells. This latter aspect was expounded clearly by von Monakow years ago under the concept of "diaschisis."

5. *A certain level of metabolism and of accompanying electrical activity is necessary for learning to occur.* This storing of information is by means of "traces." No mechanism for the "traces" need be hypothesized. However, present thinking seems to indicate two possible mechanisms: (*a*) reverberatory circuits, to provide for short-term memory; and (*b*) neural growth, for long-term memory ("engrams").

6. *A measure of the degree of neurophysiological integration is the frequency of the spontaneous electrical activity of the brain during the resting state. This activity may be considered roughly as an indication of integrated behavior.*

Empirical data indicates that the aspect of electrical activity of the cortex which correlates best with behavioral changes is frequency. Thus, changes in level of awareness (which may be defined operationally as the ability to respond to external stimulation) are associated with changes in the frequency of the cortical rhythms, as discussed below. Furthermore, level of awareness may be considered necessary to the concept of integration. For example, at low levels of awareness integration will be seriously impaired. Therefore, inasmuch as level of awareness is correlated with changes in frequency of electrical activity,

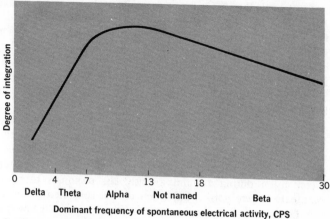

Fig. 1   Gradient of integration.

and since level of awareness may be considered to be a necessary condition in integration, the degree of integration should be correlated with changes in frequency.

A gradient of integration, measured by the frequency of the spontaneous electrical activity of the organism, i.e., during rest or sleep, when external stimulation is minimized, is implied by empirical data as shown in Fig. 1. The degree of integration is optimal within the alpha range, and possibly slightly above or below. At frequencies above alpha, decline is slow but below alpha there is a rapid decline. This treatment must be considered as a rough sketch of the gradient inasmuch as normal EEGs for adults show much variation but comprise frequencies mainly in the alpha and beta bands. There are also small variations in intra-subject frequencies. Likewise, the optimal point would probably vary slightly between individuals. Thus, a gradient such as proposed above has value in considering only the extreme portions at this stage of our knowledge inasmuch as the experimental error is large. In a recent paper on drive, Hebb presents a similar gradient based on the level of arousal function. The level of cue function directing or guiding behavior varies with the level of arousal function (non-specific cortical bombardment). When the level of arousal is low, an increase in cortical bombardment will tend to strengthen concurrent cortical activity. When the level is high the greater bombardment may interfere with behavioral patterns requiring delicate adjustment. In between these two portions of the arousal dimension there is an optimal level of arousal for effective behavior.

Some of the evidence to support a gradient of integration based on the frequency pattern of the electrical activity of neural tissue is as follows.

a. At birth the EEG is irregular, asymmetrical, and rather formless. However, what rhythm is present is in the slow delta band. During the first year the delta activity becomes more regular. From then on there is a gradual increase in the dominant frequency from 3 cps until at 10 yr. of age the alpha band is reached. By 16 the normal pattern is seen. Paralleling this gradual development of a dominant frequency is an increase in the integrative capacity of the organism as indicated by his behavior.

b. During petit mal seizures, when a wave and spike pattern (delta band) occurs, the organism is unable to respond to stimulation, indicating decreased integration. For example, Schwab reports the case of a naval officer who denied all episodes of epilepsy even after having a convulsion during a training class. His responses to neurological examination were normal but when he was subjected to hyperventilation, he showed the typical burst of wave and spikes at low frequency. When the wave and spike pattern occurred he was given a command but was unable to respond. This was repeated on four occasions with similar results. Thus, within this low frequency range he was oblivious to his external environment.

c. Davis and Wallace found amnesia, confusion, and vagueness for stimuli given to their Ss while delta activity was apparent.

d. The spontaneous electrical activity of an individual in a state of delirium decreases and the mental functions deteriorate; however, some fast activity also appears. Engel and Romano report that accompanying the physiological impairment of cerebral metabolism in delirium is a reduced level of awareness, and the dominant EEG frequency is below the alpha range.

e. In severe mental deterioration, low frequency diffuse waves predominate and decreased integration and decreased quality of thinking occurs. Weiner and Schuster report that nonfocal, diffuse slowing of the EEG accompanies dementia due to organic brain damage and that the greater the degree of dementia the more pronounced is the slowing. Likewise, Mundy-Castle, et al. state that there is a significant decrease in the EEG frequencies in senile dementia and that the characteristic abnormalities of senile psychoses are diffuse delta and theta waves or diffuse theta.

f. In a series of experiments, Kennard, et al. attempted to determine if the EEG frequency patterns of groups of individuals having different personality characteristics showed significant differences and if these patterns could be correlated with specific personality attributes. It was indicated that normal Ss show more order and synchrony in EEG pattern and have a greater concentration of the dominant frequency pattern in the alpha range (with little spread of energy beyond this portion of the spectrum) than a group of mental patients composed mostly of schizophrenics. This latter group showed much fast activity. A group of psychopaths from a penal institution showed a high incidence of alpha rhythm similar to normals but the records of the former included much theta activity as well. This group had a greater spread of energy and less order and synchrony. A longitudinal study with mental patients and normals indicated that the EEGs of patients who recovered clinically had accompanying changes in the frequency pattern; the later EEG frequency graphs more nearly resembled normals than the record taken on entry. This change in frequency pattern was not apparent for persons who became more disturbed or showed no improvement, however.

g. Bexton, Heron, and Scott report that concentration, ability to carry on organized thinking, and various intellectual tasks are adversely affected when an individual is confined to a small space and sensory stimulation is greatly reduced. Ss in this study wore goggles which prevented pattern vision as entrance of diffuse light only was possible, and cuffs extending below the finger tips (as well as gloves) to greatly diminish tactual sensitivity. Auditory stimulation was minimized by the continuous hum of a fan, an air conditioner, and an amplifier. In a later study Heron, Doane, and Scott reported behavior decrements under the same conditions. Also EEGs of the Ss were obtained. The records showed a slowing of the alpha frequencies and marked delta wave activity. These two studies taken together lend support to the gradient proposed here.

h. The degree of integration during the waking stage would decrease if the spontaneous activity were modified by pharmacological or activation methods. Thus, for example, if the organism's dominant pattern was 11 cps and hypoxia occurred, the dominant frequency would shift toward the delta band; both thinking and integrated behavior would deteriorate. This has been reported and is common to individuals at high altitudes if oxygen is not supplied.

i. Phenomena during sleep, which will be discussed below, also appear to support the proposed gradient.

7. *Level of potential thinking is indicated by the spontaneous electrical activity during the resting state or sleep.* The resting potentials may be modified by sensory stimulation or active thought which redistributes the pattern of energy concentration; likewise, electrical activity during sleep may be modified by external stimulation. The latter event is less apt to occur than the former because the threshold for central reactivity increases with decreases in electrical activity of the neural tissue. Thus, the spontaneous electrical activity can be considered as an indicator of the level of potential thought. If the frequency is low, especially in the delta range, only low level thinking can occur. If the frequency is within the alpha range, then there is a greater possibility for the occurrence of higher level thinking.

As previously stated, thinking reflects an aspect of the integrative state of the organism. When a decrease in integration accompanies a decrease or increase in frequency of spontaneous electrical activity beyond the alpha range, the quality of thinking decreases. Thus in the instances reported above, thinking would decrease in quality in all cases showing a shift of the dominant frequency outside the alpha band.

8. *Decreased integration and decreased quality of the thinking process occur in sleep.* Dreams occur and these are an indication of the sensory aspect of integration, thinking. The motor portion of integration is relatively absent because, as a rule, dreams involve mainly sensory contents.

In sleep, the normal alpha rhythm disappears, followed by a short period of 14-cps rhythm in the post-frontal regions, and then by decreased frequencies until delta waves as slow as 1 cps appear on both sides. As metabolism and electrical activity of the brain decrease in sleep, the integrative process is also depressed. However, the thinking process continues but the capacity for complex thinking is decreased. The results of the thinking process during sleep are dreams, which are "traces" reactivated by some mechanism or which persist from the waking state. Dreams usually consist of illogical and incongruent phenomena; many spatial and temporal incongruities occur, e.g., many individuals may be associated together even though in previous experience there may have been no temporal or spatial association; events of different temporal periods may occur together, etc. (observations by the author). However, not all dreams need be of an illogical nature, but depend on the frequency of the spontaneous activity during the dream period. The most illogical dreams (or no dreams) should occur when frequency is the lowest.

9. *Dreams are not easily remembered because the electrical activity of the brain is depressed.* During waking states the electrical activity and metabolism are at the usual level and "traces" are easily formed. But during dreams electrical activity is at a low ebb, and "traces" formed during "reproduction" and "modification" of previous experiences are not stable. If electrical activity is very low they may not be formed at all. However, if one awakens in the midst of a dream he should be able to recall much better than at some other time.

Ramsey, in a review of studies of dreaming, reports some results which are in accord with the above statements. He states that Blake and Gerard found the presence of delta waves to be related either to the inability to recall having dreamed or to dreamless sleep. Berrien found that sudden awakening of the sleeper resulted in recall of a greater number of dreams than more gentle techniques which allow a lapse of time to occur. Calkins, DeSanctis, Bentley, and Berrien each report that more dreams are recalled during the hours just before morning waking. Calkins, Weed and Hallam, and DeSanctis note that dreams occurring nearer the morning were much more vivid than those occurring earlier in the night. The above investigators awakened their Ss at various hours during the night and asked them if they were dreaming. These results should be considered relevant to evidence which indicates that deepest sleep, with low electrical activity, occurs early in the sleeping period.

From the above considerations it is apparent that the significance attached to sequential inconsistencies and illogicalities in dream analysis is unfounded. The contents of dreams require an explanation but the illogicalities and incongruities that occur should be treated as normally expected because of the depression of the integrative function and the thinking process.

Concluding remarks

The above formulation is not a complete system. It is merely a suggested treatment of thinking at the neuropsychological level and appears to be most appropriate for the extremes of the frequency spectrum. It certainly contains many gaps. For example, the spontaneous electrical activity of some schizophrenic patients may be similar to the normal pattern but the thinking process can involve illogicalities, incongruities, and may be quite bizarre (as defined by external criteria). However, this does not necessarily indicate that the mechanism controlling the quality of potential thought is not the frequency of the spontaneous electrical activity. The schizophrenic may be responding with rules of thinking which are as logical as those governing normal thinking but which are based on faulty premises. Likewise, our technique may not be precise enough to detect differences that exist, i.e., the recording and observation techniques give rise to a large experimental error which may mask differences. Furthermore, as in prediction with psychological tests, prediction of individual cases is less successful than prediction of group characteristics. However, a fruitful approach to the problem of the relationship of thinking to the frequency of electrical activity might be to study the same individual under different conditions in which frequency is shifted. This procedure would allow each S to serve as his own control and, thus, reduce the magnitude of experimental error. It would appear that each S would have an optimal level of thinking over a range of frequencies, within or just outside the alpha band.

Summary

A neuropsychological approach to thinking is presented. Level of potential thinking is related to the dominant frequency of the spontaneous electrical activity of the brain. A gradient of integration, indicating that highest level thinking should occur during the presence of alpha (or near alpha) frequencies, is suggested. Thinking deteriorates as frequencies deviate from this band. Relevant supporting literature is cited.

selection 36 / reasoning as an associative process: III. the role of verbal responses in problem solving / Charles N. Cofer, University of Maryland

INTRODUCTION

In this paper I shall begin by describing some studies of verbal behavior and problem solving, studies which I believe to bear directly on my topic. The summary of these investigations will be followed by a discussion of some aspects of mediational processes in human behavior, in which will be cited in particular a number of studies of verbal mediational processes. Then, I should like to suggest some relationships of verbal processes to stages in human problem solving, citing additional relevant evidence. Lastly, I wish to make some general remarks concerning the verbal control of behavior.

Before proceeding to the first point in the outline, I should like to offer a word on one of the hoary issues in the problem solving area. For probably 2,000 years or more it has been suggested that perhaps thought is but the operation of implicit speech. As a stimulus-response type of psychologist, I find this doctrine attractive, but also I find it difficult or impossible to conceive any operations by which the assertion can be convincingly tested once and for all. I also suspect that non-verbal responses may serve mediational functions in some cases, just as may verbal responses in others. Hence, I shall avoid the bald assertion of the identity of thought and speech, believing that debate upon this point will be endless and not fruitful.

INVESTIGATIONS OF VERBAL PROCESSES AND PROBLEM SOLVING

Since 1949 my students and I have carried out several studies designed to explore the utility of conceiving "direction" in problem solving as consisting of response systems or perhaps habit families, capable of influence by the external stimulating conditions (the problem) and by reinforcement. We also hypothesized that if classes of such response systems had reached a high degree of strength in our

Abridged from Charles N. Cofer, "Reasoning as an Associative Process: III. The Role of Verbal Responses in Problem Solving," *The Journal of General Psychology*, 57:55–68, 1957. Reprinted by permission of The Journal Press, Provincetown, Massachusetts.

Ss before the experiment then such systems would "control" or "direct" the course of problem solving under ordinary conditions. Because we believed that verbal processes are of great significance in human reasoning, we decided to employ verbal problems. Some of the problems we used were extremely simple; perhaps some of them do not qualify as materials for studying reasoning or problem solving.

The first set of observations I wish to report was made with respect to what we have called the "Four Word Problem." What we wished to use was a simple problem, with alternative solutions, in which the stimulus pattern could be readily manipulated. We were interested in testing the hypothesis that solution might be determined by which response system was activated first; this hypothesis may perhaps be most readily tested by using different arrangements of the same problem.

The Four Word Problem may be illustrated by the following item:

Add　　　　*Subtract*　　　　*Multiply*　　　　*Increase*

S's task, with this and the other items, is to select the word that "does not belong." But there are two ways in which the words may be classified, as arithmetic operations and as indicators of growing magnitude. Depending on which classification S uses, he will exclude as not belonging either "increase" or "subtract." In the above item "increase" and "subtract" may be designated as unambiguous words, whereas "add" and "multiply" may be designated as ambiguous words.

In using this type of item, we have asked, essentially, what is the effect of varying the order of the words of the problem? The answer is clear. The unambiguous word chosen as not belonging is most frequently the one which appears second in the problem. Thus it would appear as if the *first* unambiguous stimulus to impinge on S in the Four Word Problem has a major influence on problem solution; presumably this influence is mediated by the activation of some response family, category or "concept" which becomes dominant either because of prior entry as such or because of increments of strength which it picks up from the ambiguous words or both. The results here are clearly relevant to the problem of the influence of verbal context, and the Four Word Problem is essentially a problem in verbal context.

We have performed a number of studies with this technique, described elsewhere. Suffice it to say that further studies have more systematically and thoroughly explored and confirmed the word order effects just described. One finding of importance, recently confirmed in an unpublished thesis at Catholic University by Eileen Kelly, is that if a verbal concept is consistent with a strongly held attitude or value, the behavior of an S who has such an attitude will resist the influence of word order changes, and S will tend consistently to exclude the word which does not agree with the attitude congruent concept.

Because the Four Word Problem is a strictly verbal and very simple problem, its study may well contribute more to the understanding of language than to reasoning. Judson and later Gelfand investigated two of the problems used by Maier. Our methods for studying these problems have emphasized verbal rather than manipulative solutions, however.

In these studies, the problem was to determine whether increasing the strength or the availability of relevant verbal responses would influence solution of a problem. One problem used was Guetzkow's group form of the Maier two-string problem. The problem is that two strings are suspended from the ceiling and S is to tie them together. The strings, however, are too short for S to grasp one, walk to the other, and tie them. There are several possible solutions to the problem, and we decided to attempt to increase the proportion of solutions by the pendulum method by means of pre-problem verbal experience.

To provide this verbal experience, we asked Ss to learn lists of words prior to working on the two-string problem. One of the lists learned by one group was as follows: rope, swing, pendulum, time, clock. This list was embedded among seven others, and none of the other groups learned these particular words, or any other problem relevant words, in this associative pattern. Theoretically, after this training, the Ss of Group A on seeing the strings of the problem would have more available than would the Ss of the other groups the words "pendulum" and "swing" because of generalization from rope to string and because of the specific associations to rope learned in the list. Therefore, Group A should produce more pendulum solutions than the other groups, but there should be no differences for the other methods.

For male Ss the results confirmed these expectations. Female Ss, however, produced relatively few pendulum solutions, and the differences among the groups for females were not significant. A third run by Gelfand of the experiment with this problem again produced results consistent with theoretical expectation, although none of the differences reached a satisfactory level of statistical significance.

Gelfand conducted a similar experiment with Maier's hat rack problem. The words associated in one of the lists for Group A and not the others were plank, prop, reach, ceiling, floor. These were selected on the supposition that they would "direct" S to wedge the two boards between the ceiling and floor, a step necessary to the solution as Maier has described it. Thirty-nine per cent of the men in Group A produced solutions in which the structures contacted both ceiling and floor, as compared with 19 per cent and 15 per cent in control groups. The males of the several groups did not differ in the frequencies with which they gave other solutions, and females produced hardly any ceiling to floor solutions. These data support the conclusion that setting up a pattern of verbal associations relevant to problem solution will influence the course of problem solving. It is assumed in this case that the relevant pattern of associations occurs to the Ss of Group A if they call the boards of the problem planks or if the associations transfer to the boards.

In summary, we think that problem solving is carried on by response systems which become temporarily dominant because of (a) activation by the stimuli in the problem situation, (b) their high strength and wide availability as in the case of strongly held attitudes or other habits, or (c) their being subjected to special conditions of reinforcement or non-reinforcement with consequent changes in strength either before or during the course of problem solving itself.

MEDIATIONAL PROCESSES

I have referred occasionally to mediational processes, and it is now appropriate to attempt a description of what this phrase means. What I mean is similar to Hull's notion of "pure stimulus acts" and to Dollard and Miller's concept of "response produced cues." The essence of these concepts is that a response or a fractional part of a response occurs with concomitant stimulational consequences. If these response produced stimuli have in the past been associated with other responses, the latter can occur, depending on their relative strengths, as a consequence of the occurrence of the response produced stimuli, even though the direct stimuli of the problem or of the situation have not been associated with these other responses.

I think it is important to consider that mediating functions may be the primary contribution of verbal processes to problem solving. Two points may be mentioned here. Mediating verbal processes need not conform to the formal structure of oral speech or written language, and it well may be necessary for the thinker to "translate" the outcomes of such operations into forms suitable for communication with others. The second point is that Ss may be unable to report on the mediational processes, verbal or otherwise, which they undergo. Thus the Ss in the Judson-Gelfand experiments did not report any relationships between the pre-problem verbal experience and the processes of solving the two-string and the hat rack problems. Nor did the Ss "catch on" to the nature of things in the Russell-Jenkins experiments to be discussed in a moment. What this probably means is that verbal report or introspective methods are inadequate to get at verbal or other mediating processes and that experimental procedures will have to be carefully designed so that legitimate inferences about such processes can be made.

An interesting and complex instance of mediation in the area of learning has been demonstrated in recent experiments by Russell and Storms, and I cite this work here because I suspect that similar effects occur in problem solving. Their Ss first learned pairs in which the stimulus members (A) were nonsense syllables and the response members (B) were stimulus words from the Kent-Rosanoff list. Following this, they learned new pairs in which the stimulus members were the same nonsense syllables (A) and in which the response members (C) were frequent association responses to the Kent-Rosanoff stimulus words (B) as shown in normative data. These new pairs $(A-C)$ were learned more rapidly than control pairs. In addition, an advantage was found for learning $A-D$ pairs, i.e., pairs in which the nonsense syllable (A) was now combined with a word (D) which was the associate of another word (C) in turn the associate of the Kent-Rosanoff stimulus word (B). The effects of mediate association as shown in these studies are considerably greater than those found in the experiments of Peters and Bugelski and Scharlock. It is probable that the associative linkages in the Russell-Storms experiments were much stronger than they were in the earlier studies.

It would appear from the Russell-Storms data that learning the $A-B$ pairs must raise the availability of those words associatively linked with B as a stimulus. Latency measurements were not made in these studies, so that it is not possible to say whether these processes occur simultaneously or require a temporal delay. A similar effect was studied in the case of verbal problem solving in another experiment by Judson.

These investigations clearly demonstrate that mediating processes can function in situations other than those involving direct conditioning procedures, but they constitute only a small beginning in our understanding of the extent to which and the variety of ways in which mediating processes operate. In the verbal area a basic problem is to get at meaningful dimensions of similarity of mediating responses. The semantic differential developed by Osgood offers some promise in this direction, and Osgood says of it, ". . . degrees of semantic generalization should be predictable from meaningful similarity as measured on the differential . . ."

VERBAL PROCESSES AND THE STAGES OF PROBLEM SOLVING

I should like now to attempt to specify something of the rôle of verbal processes in problem solving, separating the process of problem solving into three stages, following Johnson's account. The three stages are (a) recognition of or orientation to the problem, (b) producing relevant material or elaborating relevant hypotheses, (c) judging and verification, often involving selection of particular hypotheses for separate trial. It is recognized that, practically speaking, it is difficult to separate these stages from one another. However, it seems to me to be worthwhile to do so if for no other reason than to show how little specific information we have concerning the rôle of verbal processes in problem solving.

Recognition of and orientation to the problem

Although occasionally laboratory studies of problem solving require S to discover for himself what the problem is, typically the verbal instructions to S set up the problem for him. I have already indicated by citing the work of Duncker, Weaver and Madden, Sells and Woodworth, and Heidbreder that the form of the verbal instructions and verbal characteristics of the problem itself may significantly influence the course of problem solving and the kind of solution developed. But we know very little about this matter, and I can only offer the hypothesis, tested in a limited way by studies with the Four Word Problem, that the verbal characteristics of the problem or of the instructions have their effect through the constraints which they impose on what response systems will be used in initial attacks on the problem. Marks has shown that vocalization of the elements of a problem is associated with effective concept attainment. It may be that this procedure did no more than assure that S would survey the entire problem, but it may also be that an active process of identifying and labeling the elements has other advantages. Perhaps discrimination of elements is fostered by such a procedure; Dollard and Miller seem to regard the discrimination which verbal labels make possible as a major value in problem solving. Kurtz and Hovland have observed that both recognition and recall are improved following verbalization during the study of an array of familiar objects, and the recent literature on stimulus pre-differentiation has suggested that the naming and association of stimuli may transfer to later perceptual-motor learning tasks. I think it is not unlikely that the results of these studies are relevant to this stage of problem solving.

In summary, and with very little to go on, it would seem that the verbal formulation of the problem forces constraints on the way the S attacks it. However, it may also force a survey of the situation, identification, discrimination and classification of elements, a statement of the nature of the problem, and start going the processes of the second stage.

Producing relevant material or elaborating alternative hypotheses

It is easy to see the rôle of verbal processes in this stage, and it is not unlikely that much or most of an S's activity in this stage is verbal. Mediating and associative linkages between verbal responses may well provide the basis for the generation of hypotheses.

Some time ago, Johnson and Reynolds postulated and demonstrated in a battery of verbal tests that there are a factor, "flow," which is "calling up various acts or responses," and a factor, "selection," which is "selecting those responses which meet the requirements of the problem." O. McNemar has compared good and poor reasoners, differentiated in terms of score on logical reasoning tests, and has found the good reasoners to perform significantly better on three verbal measures: (a) number of words beginning with the letter p written in three minutes; (b) number of words beginning with the letter s and ending with the letter l written in three minutes; (c) number of synonyms written in 13 minutes to eight stimulus words. But the two groups were not differentiated by productivity in a free or unrestricted association test. This suggests that the selection factor, as described by Johnson and Reynolds and as measured by verbal techniques, is the significant differentiator in McNemar's study. Vinacke cites evidence from studies with children which shows a substantial relationship between vocabulary and concept scores. Guilford's measures of originality also seem to emphasize certain aspects of verbal ability.

These studies suggest that effective problem solving is associated either with verbal fluency in general or with fluency under restricted conditions. This finding may indicate that the production or elaboration of hypotheses may often be a function of the controlled or relevant emission of verbal responses and probably reflects the mediating function of verbal response tendencies. The Judson-Gelfand adaptations of the Maier experiments may have achieved their results through operations leading to the production of relevant verbal associations at the proper time. May has reported data indicating that the more accurate were children's verbal formulations of the steps necessary to the assembly of puzzles the more quickly they learned to assemble the puzzles successfully.

An aspect of this stage deserving attention concerns the factors which enable the problem solver to produce relevant verbal material from memory. Does thinking about a topic for a while in some way strengthen relevant associations so that they may occur in the reasoning situation? Skinner has implied that this is the case, and Myers and Myers showed that such a phenomenon can occur. They asked Ss to attempt to recall poems or other material which they had learned as children and to continue in their attempts for a period of time with no outside aid. As these Ss worked at recalling, they increased the proportion of the material which they remembered accurately. In a preliminary study, I performed a somewhat similar investigation, obtaining results suggesting that attempts to recall will produce increments in what is recalled, at least under certain conditions. I do not know what these conditions are, the extent or the significance of the recall phenomenon, or its relevance to the phenomenon of reminiscence, but it would seem desirable to study it further, as it is likely that something of this kind occurs during the elaborate stage of problem solving. Perhaps this is involved in the process known as "incubation" or "unconscious cerebration."

Judging and verification

This involves the question which Miller puts as follows: "How is a correct solution recognized when it does occur?" Very little is known about this matter. In essence, I suppose the answer involves a comparison between the formulation of the problem and the formulation of the solution at hand. If they can be discriminated the search must continue; if not, the problem is solved. I will rest my discussion of this problem by quoting again from Miller: "The answer must come out in a sequence of words that seems possible against the background of our habitual intraverbal connections."

This brief review of the stages in problem solving has not yielded a great deal. We can point to verbal processes as aiding in the discrimination of stimuli and as factors leading associatively to other verbal responses perhaps more relevant to the problem. But there is another and broader problem with which we must contend, and I should like, in conclusion, to turn to it.

ON THE VERBAL CONTROL OF BEHAVIOR

The rôle of verbal processes in problem solving is but a part of the broader issue of the extent to which and the mechanisms by which human behavior in general occurs under the control of or through the mediation of verbal processes. We have not faced this issue squarely. The relatively limited consideration given to verbal behavior in our text books and systematic treatises attests to this point. Yet at the same time we would probably all agree that the high development in man of verbal-symbolic behavior has been an outstanding factor in his development of culture and in his solution of many complex problems. There is a hiatus here, of some magnitude.

Within the area of problem solving the material which I have surveyed demonstrates conclusively, I think, that thought is often closely associated with verbal processes. But one may assert that this is true because investigation has used chiefly verbal problems. However, I think the question is a legitimate one which asks whether any significant human problems will be or can be solved without the intermediation of verbal processes of some sort. I am not asserting here that no thought can occur unless there is verbal process, but I am asserting that such instances are perhaps infrequent and insignificant in terms of the over all problem. Perhaps my topic here could have been restated as follows: The rôle of verbal processes in verbal processes.

We often implicitly recognize that behavior is under verbal control, but we often try to ignore the fact. An experimental illustration may help to clarify this point. Under my guidance, Coonan studied the question whether punishment could be shown to lead to the response of stopping thinking or thinking of something else. He prepared a list of 48 words, half of which had been shown, independently, to produce a high proportion of synonyms as the first response in discrete free association and the other half to produce a high proportion of antonyms. We call these synonym producing words and antonym producing words, respectively. Coonan's plan was to present these words one at a time to individual Ss and to administer shock to half the Ss when they produced a synonym to a synonym producing word and to the other half when they produced an antonym to an antonym producing word. The effects of this procedure were to be observed on the latency and categories of response produced in the latter part of the list.

Coonan ran several Ss and found that when they were shocked every time they made the relevant response they quickly formulated the principle and stopped giving shockable responses. Then, with my concurrence, he modified the procedure to give only a few shocks so that the principle would not be readily grasped. Under the modified conditions the results were inconclusive.

Coonan's first few Ss clearly showed response suppression under the guidance of the principle which they formulated verbally. But we threw these data away, thinking them to be somehow contaminated. And this is characteristic of much research with human Ss; experiments are designed to make verbal control very difficult, and data are discarded if S "catches on" to what the experimenter is doing.

Perhaps the reason that we acted as we did in the case of Coonan's study is that we "know" that the behavior of Ss can be controlled by a verbally formulated principle, and hence the further demonstration of it resolves no uncertainty concerning the capabilities of human individuals. Yet I submit that this knowledge is illusory and that we know very little about the extent, the limitations, the varieties, the conditions, or the mechanisms of such verbal control. Study of this problem should clarify not only the rôle of verbal processes in problem solving but their rôle in behavior in general.

There is abundant evidence showing that behavior may be brought under verbal control, but this evidence is usually treated as an isolated fact. Perhaps our greatest need is for a theory of verbal behavior which would grapple with the problem of the verbal control of behavior. I think it is quite possible that the study of verbal behavior may be much more productive to our understanding of problem solving than further study of problem solving itself.

selection 37 / the influence of mental set on problem solving / Ian M. L. Hunter, University of Edinburgh

In his laboratory manual, Foster includes an experiment which aims to demonstrate the influence of mental set on speed of problem-solving. He uses six different lists of five-letter anagrams. Two series, containing miscellaneous words, are presented with an indefinite set, the subject being told nothing about the general nature of the words involved. Two series comprise words which "have something to do with eating" and another two series contain words "representing things about the house". Before attempting these, the subject is informed of the classification. Foster reports only that 'typical results show that the median time with indefinite set is about 2·5 times as long as for definite set' and that 'a typical median time for transposing anagrams with indefinite set is 25 sec.; for transposing anagrams referring to eating, 10 sec.; for anagrams referring to house, 10 sec.'

It seems likely that these results demonstrate the facilitating effect of definite as opposed to indefinite set. Nevertheless, an unambiguous interpretation is difficult to make. There is no adequate control of practice and fatigue effects. Also the specified and unspecified series employ different anagrams and there is no guarantee that the difference between the times taken to solve these is not attributable to a mere difference in their intrinsic difficulty. This note reports a class experiment in which Foster's materials and design were modified. The result demonstrates, of course, only one of the ways in which set can be established, and only one of the ways in which its effects can be observed (other investigations of set have been reviewed recently by Johnson). However, the experiment confirms, under better-controlled conditions, Foster's original findings. Moreover, it provides an interesting and instructive experiment for use in the teaching of experimental psychology.

From Ian M. L. Hunter, "The Influence of Mental Set on Problem Solving," *British Journal of Psychology*, 47:63–64, 1956. Reprinted by permission of the author and publisher.

The experiment was carried out with four laboratory sections of a first-year class in experimental psychology. A total of seventy-two students (thirty-five men, thirty-seven women) took part. The students were divided into groups of three, each member of the group acting, in turn, as subject, experimenter, and recorder. The material consisted of fifty-four five-letter anagrams, each of which permitted of only one solution. The solutions were nouns which fell into nine different categories as follows:

1. Animals: sheep, horse, tiger, skunk, camel, zebra.
2. Trees: birch, rowan, aspen, beech, hazel, holly.
3. Musical instruments: piano, flute, cello, organ, banjo, viola.
4. Birds: stork, eagle, goose, robin, heron, raven.
5. Fruit: peach, grape, olive, lemon (melon), prune, apple.
6. Parts of the body: wrist, mouth, waist, ankle, thigh, chest.
7. Countries: India, Spain, Wales, Italy, Japan, Tibet.
8. Wearing apparel: glove, skirt, apron, scarf, dress, shirt.
9. Flowers: pansy, lilac, daisy, tulip, lupin, poppy.

Each subject attempted two lists of six anagrams, one specified and the other unspecified. The specified lists used, for example, by the first group were lists 1, 2, and 3 above, while each unspecified list contained six nouns, one selected from each of the remaining categories. Using twelve groups of three subjects, lists were prepared so that: over the thirty-six subjects, each noun occurred the same number of times, i.e. twice, as specified and as unspecified; practice and fatigue effects were counterbalanced, half of the subjects attempting a specified list followed by an unspecified, and half attempting first an unspecified and then a specified list; in no group did an experimenter or recorder experience a noun which he would encounter while acting as subject.

Each group was given a six-page booklet, on each page of which the appropriate list was typed in capital letters on heavy white paper. Each list was headed either "Unspecified" or given a specific title, e.g., "Animals." Over the first list, the experimenter placed a long strip of hard-board in the centre of which was an aperture just large enough to expose a single anagram. The experimenter then moved the aperture down to expose the heading and told the subject whether the list was unspecified or specified in a particular way. He then exposed the first anagram for 30 sec. If the solution was given in this time, the experimenter waited until the recorder had noted the time taken for solution and then exposed the second anagram. If the anagram was not successfully transposed in 30 sec., a failure was recorded and the next anagram exposed. This procedure was continued until the end of the list. The same subject then attempted the second list. Members of the group then exchanged functions and the next two lists were presented to a new subject. This done, the third subject attempted the last two lists. Throughout, the recorder was responsible for timing the experiment by stop-watch and for entering the results in a specially prepared table. An hour gave the students time to perform the experiment, calculate the results for their own group of three, and discuss both their findings and the design of the experiment.

The results from the seventy-two subjects were as follows:

Median time to solve anagrams in specified lists   = 3 sec.
Median time to solve anagrams in unspecified lists = 12·5 sec.
Total number anagrams failed in specified lists   = 35 (8·10%)
Total number anagrams failed in unspecified lists = 129 (29·86%)

These results show clearly that the more specific the set the easier is the problem to solve. It is to be noted that the set involved here may not derive entirely from the instructions given but may, in part, have been established in the course of transposing a series of homogeneous anagrams. Even without specific instructions, a subject might, after solving four or five "animal" anagrams, be set for an animal name in the sixth anagram. Such a task-induced set can easily be demonstrated in the classroom by means of the water-jar problems of Luchins. However, the design of the present experiment does not permit any conclusion regarding the extent to which set established in this way contributes, if at all, to the results obtained.

selection 38 / does group participation when using brainstorming facilitate or inhibit creative thinking? / Donald W. Taylor, Paul C. Berry, and Clifford H. Block, Yale University

Brainstorming was originated and first used by Alex F. Osborn in 1939 in the advertising agency Batten, Barton, Durstine & Osborn, which he then headed. Within recent years its use has grown rapidly. A large number of major companies, units of the Army, Navy, and Air Force, and various federal, state, and local civilian agencies have employed the technique, and instruction has been given in a number of colleges and universities in its use. Although an occasional critical

Abridged from Donald W. Taylor, Paul C. Berry, and Clifford H. Block, "Does Group Participation When Using Brainstorming Facilitate or Inhibit Creative Thinking?" *Administrative Science Quarterly*, 3:23–47, 1958. Reprinted by permission of the author and the publisher.

voice has been raised, brainstorming may be said to have achieved wide acceptance as a means of facilitating creative thinking.

The purpose of brainstorming is to free individuals from inhibition, self-criticism, and criticism by others in order that in response to a specific problem they may produce as many different ideas as possible. The assumption is that the larger the number of ideas produced, the greater the probability of achieving an effective solution. Brainstorming is characterized by four basic rules:

1. *Criticism is ruled out.* Adverse judgment of ideas must be withheld until later.
2. *"Free-wheeling" is welcomed.* The wilder the idea, the better; it is easier to tame down than to think up.
3. *Quantity is wanted.* The greater the number of ideas, the more the likelihood of winners.
4. *Combination and improvement are sought.* In addition to contributing ideas of their own, participants should suggest how ideas of others can be turned into *better* ideas; or how two or more ideas can be joined into still another idea.

Brainstorming ordinarily involves not only following the four basic rules but also group collaboration in attacking the problem. Osborn emphasizes the value of group interaction in facilitating the flow of ideas. It was this characteristic of brainstorming which was of primary interest in the present study.

The present experiment employed a design previously developed by Taylor for use in studies of group problem solving where the problems involved have logically correct solutions. Earlier studies of such group problem solving were concerned with a comparison of the achievement of groups of various sizes with that of individuals. However, the performance of a group should be superior to that of an individual, simply because in the group more individuals are working on the problem. On the assumption of the appropriate null hypothesis, namely, that working in a group has no effect either positive or negative upon individual performance, Taylor and Lorge & Solomon independently have presented a simple mathematical model for predicting the performance of a group of a given size from a knowledge of individual performance. By comparing actual group achievement with that predicted from the model, one can determine whether group participation facilitates or inhibits problem solving.

Taylor has also developed an experimental design which provides an alternative method of testing the same null hypothesis as that represented by the model. Individuals are randomly assigned to work either alone or in groups of a given size on a series of problems. The number of individuals working alone should be about equal to that working in groups. After the experiment is completed, those who actually worked alone are divided at random into nominal groups of the same size as the real groups. The performance of the nominal groups is then scored as though the members of the group had worked together. The achievement of the nominal groups thus provides a measure of the performance to be expected under the null hypothesis. If the performance of the real groups is superior to that of the nominal groups, group participation facilitates performance; if it is inferior, group participation inhibits it.

This design, with appropriate modification in the scoring of responses for nominal groups, was employed in the present experiment to provide an answer to the question: Does group participation when using brainstorming facilitate or inhibit creative thinking?

The experiment

Subjects The ninety-six Yale juniors and seniors who served as subjects in this experiment were all at the time enrolled in a course in Psychology of Personnel Administration taught by the first author. Each week, in addition to two lectures to the entire class, the course included an analysis of a case carried out in small discussion groups; each group had its own student leader, this task being rotated among the members of the group. As a result of such case discussion and of the way in which subjects were assigned, each real group in the present experiment was not, as often must be the case in studies of group problem solving, an *ad hoc* group of individuals meeting for the first time; instead, each real group included men who not only knew each other but who also had worked together effectively in small-group discussion over a considerable period of time. At the same time, the procedure used in assigning subjects was such that those assigned to work in groups and those assigned to work alone could legitimately be regarded as random samples from the same population.

From each of the ten discussion groups in the class, four men were picked at random to form an experimental group, thus providing ten experimental groups; and from two of the ten discussion groups, an additional four men were picked at random to provide two more groups, for a total of twelve experimental groups. The remaining men in the ten discussion groups, forty-eight in all, served as individual subjects.

Problems On the basis of pretesting, three problems were selected which seemed to be of interest to Yale students, productive of many and varied responses, and appropriate for use with brainstorming. The three problems were as follows:

1. Each year a great many American tourists go to visit Europe. But now suppose that our country wished to get many more European

tourists to come to visit America during their vacations. What steps can you suggest that would get more European tourists to come to this country?

2. We don't think this is very likely to happen, but imagine for a moment what would happen if everyone born after 1960 had an extra thumb on each hand. This extra thumb will be built just as the present one is, but located on the other side of the hand. It faces inward, so that it can press against the fingers, just as the regular thumb does now. Here is a picture to help you see how it will be. (A line drawing of a hand with two thumbs was shown by the experimenter at this point in the reading of the problem and then left in full view on the table during the entire period of work on the problem.) Now the question is: What practical benefits or difficulties will arise when people start having this extra thumb?

3. Because of the rapidly increasing birth rate beginning in the 1940s, it is now clear that by 1970 public school enrollment will be very much greater than it is today. In fact, it has been estimated that if the student-teacher ratio were to be maintained at what it is today, 50 per cent of all individuals graduating from college would have to be induced to enter teaching. What different steps might be taken to insure that schools will continue to provide instruction at least equal in effectiveness to that now provided?

For brevity's sake, the three problems were referred to as the "Tourists Problem," the "Thumbs Problem," and the "Teachers Problem."

Procedure In a single experimental session lasting about one hour, the three problems were presented in the order in which they are listed above to each of the twelve groups and to each of the forty-eight individuals. The second and third authors of the present report conducted the sessions, each one conducting six group and twenty-four individual sessions. The assignment of groups and individuals to experimenters was largely a matter of chance. Group and individual sessions were alternated in such a way that on any given date about the same proportion of group and individual sessions had been completed.

Both experimenters were advanced graduate students in psychology. Both were familiar with Osborn's writing concerning brainstorming. Both had participated in the pretesting described above and thereby gained experience with the procedures of brainstorming. Both personally believed that group brainstorming was an effective procedure for facilitating the production of ideas.

Very shortly before the present experiment began, one lecture to the class as a whole was devoted to creative thinking, with particular attention to brainstorming. The origin, nature, and widespread use of brainstorming was described, the purpose being to create interest in the procedure and as favorable as possible an attitude toward it. The shortage of controlled experimental studies of this and similar procedures was described. Finally, the students were asked to participate as subjects in the experiment and were promised a report of the results when it was available.

During the pretesting, both with individuals and with small groups, attention was devoted to the question of what length of time should be allowed for work on each of the problems selected for use. What was wanted was a span of time long enough so that members of groups of four would have adequate opportunity to express all the ideas which occurred to them within the working period and at the same time short enough so that individuals would not become bored by being forced to continue work on a problem long after they had essentially exhausted their ideas. Pretesting showed that the rate at which ideas were produced on the problems decreased with time. A time limit of twelve minutes was finally selected as one which would permit group members to express all ideas occurring to them within the work period (though not to exhaust all possible ideas) and yet which would not result in excessive periods of silence for individual subjects. Actually, for both individuals and groups, appreciable periods of silence appeared between responses near the end of the twelve minutes.

Results

The first step following the completion of the experimental sessions was the division of the forty-eight individual subjects into twelve nominal groups of four each. This was done in order to permit comparison of real group performance not only with that of individuals but also with that to be expected on the basis of the hypothesis that working in the group has no effect either positive or negative upon the performance of its members. A table of random numbers was employed to divide the twenty-four individual subjects who had worked with the first experimenter into six nominal groups of four; the same procedure was used to divide the twenty-four who had worked with the second experimenter into an additional six nominal groups. This particular procedure was necessary if a test were to be made of any possible difference between the two sets of six nominal groups resulting from differences between the experimenters. Inspection of the data later obtained, however, revealed no possible significant difference between experimenters in the results.

Table 1 presents the mean number of responses by individuals and real groups to each of the three problems. On each of the three problems, the mean number of ideas presented by real groups is much larger than that presented by individuals. The appropriate analysis of variance briefly summarized in Table 1 shows that this difference

TABLE 1 MEAN TOTAL NUMBER OF RESPONSES TO EACH PROBLEM BY INDIVIDUALS AND REAL GROUPS

	Tourists	Thumbs	Teachers	Mean of means
Individuals	20.7	19.9	18.2	19.6
Real groups	38.4	41.3	32.6	37.5
Mean of means	29.6	30.6	25.4	
Analysis of variance	d. f.	F	p	
Individuals *vs.* real groups	1, 58	71.2	.0001	
Among problems	2, 116	8.5	.001	
Interaction	2, 116	4.96	.01	

between real groups and individuals with an *F* of 71.2 is significant at well beyond the .0001 level. The analysis also shows that the differences among the three problems in mean number of responses is significant at the .001 level and that the interaction between the two primary variables is also significant.

Table 2 shows that the mean number of responses produced by nominal groups was considerably larger than that produced by real groups on each of the three problems. The analysis of variance indicates that this superiority of nominal to real groups is significant at far beyond the .0001 level. The difference among the three problems in number of responses is again significant, but in this case the interaction does not even approach significance.

It seemed important to compare the performance of real and nominal groups not only in terms of the number of ideas produced

TABLE 2 MEAN TOTAL NUMBER OF RESPONSES TO EACH PROBLEM BY REAL GROUPS AND NOMINAL GROUPS

	Tourists	Thumbs	Teachers	Mean of means
Real groups	38.4	41.3	32.6	37.5
Nominal groups	68.3	72.6	63.5	68.1
Mean of means	53.4	57.0	48.0	
Analysis of variance	d. f.	F	p	
Real *vs.* nominal groups	1, 22	96.3	.0001	
Among problems	2, 44	7.8	.005	
Interaction	2, 44	.09	—	

TABLE 3   MEAN NUMBERS OF UNIQUE RESPONSES TO EACH PROBLEM

	Tourists	Thumbs	Teachers	Mean of means
Real groups	7.5	17.7	7.3	10.8
Nominal groups	13.7	28.1	17.5	19.8
Mean of means	10.6	22.9	12.4	
Analysis of variance		d. f.	F	p
Real vs. nominal groups		1, 22	11.4	.005
Among problems		2, 44	42.1	.0001
Interaction		2, 44	1.29	—

but also in terms of the originality and quality of these ideas. For this purpose, additional analyses were undertaken.

A large proportion of the responses to any one of the problems was, of course, produced by more than one of the nominal or real groups, a small number of the ideas on each of the problems being suggested by nearly all of the twenty-four groups. On each problem, however, an appreciable number of suggestions was made by only one of the twenty-four groups; these may be described as unique responses. The number of such unique ideas provides one satisfactory measure of the originality of the performance of a particular group.

In Table 3 are given the mean number of unique responses produced by real and nominal groups on each of the three problems. The superiority of the nominal to the real groups on this measure is significant at the .005 level. The difference among the three problems in mean number of unique responses is also significant, but the interaction is not.

Detailed examination of the 483 different suggestions for solution of the Tourists Problem and of the 513 different suggestions for solution of the Teachers Problem indicated that these suggestions differed in quality with respect to at least three dimensions: feasibility, effectiveness, and generality. Accordingly, five-step rating scales were constructed for use in measuring these three. The 791 different responses made to the Thumbs Problem differed from those made to the other two problems in that they represented anticipated consequences instead of suggested steps for solution. For this reason only one of the three rating scales constructed for rating responses to the other two problems, namely, generality, appeared equally applicable in the case of the Thumbs Problem. For this problem, however, analogous to feasibility and effectiveness on the other problems were the dimensions of probability and significance, respectively. Accordingly, two additional rating scales were constructed by the same method to measure these latter variables.

The responses to each problem were rated on three different scales by three different raters, presumably increasing the independence of the ratings of the three characteristics. Each rater employed a different scale for each of the three problems, thus presumably minimizing the possibility that a single idiosyncratic interpretation of any of the scales would occur for all three problems.

One additional point concerning the procedure used in rating deserves emphasis. All ratings were made of the responses as they appeared on the master list for the given problem and without any knowledge of whether the response had been made by real or nominal groups. This was done, of course, to eliminate any possible tendency of any rater to bias his ratings to favor either real or nominal groups. The score for each group for a given problem and a given dimension was simply the sum of the ratings on that dimension of the responses given by the group to that problem.

A comparison of the mean scores of real and nominal groups [shows that]: On each of the three dimensions for each of the three problems, the mean for the nominal groups is much larger than that for the real groups. The analyses of variance show that this superiority of the nominal to the real groups is significant well beyond the .0001 level for each of the three problems (see Tables 5, 6, and 7 of the original article).

Discussion

The first important finding was that on each of the three problems the mean total number of ideas produced by the twelve groups was considerably larger than the mean number produced by the forty-eight individuals, the difference being highly significant (Table 1). It is true that the interaction is significant, indicating that the difference between real group and individual performance does vary among the three problems. But on all three problems group performance is clearly superior to individual performance. Such group superiority may very well account for the widespread impression that group participation does facilitate production of ideas. The individual who compares his own performance working alone with that of a group in which he participates at another time may understandably conclude that group interaction stimulates creative thinking, whether or not this is in fact the case. Many of those participating in the groups in the present experiment made comments indicating that they believed such participation had been stimulating.

The comparison of group performance with individual performance does not, however, provide an adequate answer to the question: Does group participation when using brainstorming facilitate or inhibit creative thinking? To answer this question, the performance of the twelve real groups was compared with that of the twelve nominal groups on each of the three problems with respect to (*a*) mean total number of ideas produced, (*b*) mean number of unique ideas produced, and (*c*) the three measures which involved the weighting of the ideas with respect to quality. The results of these several analyses were both clear-cut and consistent.

The performance of the twelve real groups is markedly inferior to that of the twelve nominal groups both in terms of number of ideas produced (Table 2) and in terms of number of unique ideas produced (Table 3). Since in neither case was the interaction significant, these findings apply equally to all three problems. The mean scores of the real groups on the three weighted measures were also markedly inferior to those of the nominal groups for the Tourists, Thumbs, and Teachers Problem. In brief, the performance of the real groups is inferior to that of the nominal groups on all three problems with respect to each and all of the measures of performance employed.

To the extent that the results of the present experiment can be generalized, it must be concluded that group participation when using brainstorming *inhibits* creative thinking. What accounts for such inhibition? Although data are not available to provide an adequate answer, two suggestions may be made. In brainstorming strong emphasis is placed upon avoiding criticism both of one's own ideas and of the ideas of others. Nevertheless, it appears probable that the individual working in a group feels less free of possible criticism by others even when such criticism is not expressed at the time than does the individual working alone. To the extent that this is true, group participation is inhibiting. A second reason is that group participation may reduce the number of different ideas produced. A given number of individuals working in a group appear more likely to pursue the same train of thought—to have the same set or the same approach to the problem—than do the same number of individuals working alone. The greater the variety of set, train of thought, or approach, the greater would be the expected number of different ideas produced. To the extent that group participation reduces such variety, it inhibits production of ideas.

CHAPTER 9 ❂ INTELLIGENCE ❂

After studying the chapter on intelligence in textbooks in Introductory Psychology, students often ask, "But what do you mean by the term 'intelligence?'" The professor may define the term in a way which is satisfactory to the student, but in all likelihood the definition is not entirely satisfactory to the professor himself. Definitions of "intelligence" have ranged from the ultra-operational definition that "intelligence is what is measured by intelligence tests," to rather vague statements to the effect that "intelligence refers to the ability of the individual to maintain a flexible adjustment to his environment." Like all other attempts to pin down the meaning of the term, these definitions are inadequate in that they refer to only part of what we mean by intelligence. In lieu of accepting any particular explicit definition of intelligence, perhaps it is more important to emphasize that "intelligence" is not some "thing" that a person has, but is rather something that he does. It is an abstraction from his characteristic ways of behaving. We thus see that intelligence tests are important in understanding intelligence in that, to the extent that they are valid, they help us to predict how satisfactorily the individual will interact with his environment in everyday life. That is, we are never concerned about a person's intelligence test score per se; we are concerned about the typical level with which he can bring previous learning to bear on solutions of problems in his everyday living. In our society the most culturally important forms of learning are those which involve manipulation of abstract symbols (thinking). It is thus reasonable that most intelligence tests place great emphasis on verbal abilities. Although we may readily admit that there are different kinds of intellectual ability, we may still wonder if there is not some overall or more general intelligence which would encompass all these specific components. The statistical technique of factor analysis has permitted us to answer this question positively; that is, intelligence as measured by intelligence tests includes many specific abilities as well as an overall general intelligence factor.

The question is often raised by layman and scientist alike, "What is the relationship of intellectual functioning to the structures and functioning of the brain?" In attempting to answer this question the pseudo-science of phrenology assumed that (1) specific mental functions are localized in the brain; (2) the amount of brain tissue reflects the amount of mental ability; and (3) the shape of the skull indicates the amount of tissue and therefore the amount of ability. We now know that the latter two assumptions are most certainly wrong, and although there are specific areas of the brain which are related to specific functions, speech, for example, intelligence in general, or its subcomponents, does not seem to be so localized. In Selection 39 D. O. Hebb presents a hypothesis concerning the nature of adult intelligence which is based on examination of clinical and experimental data regarding the effects of brain injury on intelligence. He cites data to support the following empirical generalizations: (1) The degree of intellectual loss resulting from brain injury depends on the age at which the injury occurs and the specific intellectual factor being tested. (2) Destruction of brain tissue early in life has a less selective and more general effect than similar injury as an adult. (3) In the adult, extensive portions of the brain may be removed or destroyed without great loss of verbal abilities. *On the basis of these empirical generalizations Hebb offers the hypothesis that intellectual functioning may depend on two factors: present intellectual power or ability to develop new patterns of response; and the functioning of those patterns of response which are already developed. Thus, the test performance of an adult who suffered brain injury as a child is lowered by inadequate previous development of response patterns as well as by reduction of present intellectual power. On the other hand, brain injury as an adult influences only present intellectual power, whereas previously learned response patterns may continue to function relatively unimpaired.*

One of the inadequacies inherent in defining intelligence as the ability of the individual to adjust to his environment is indicated by the fact that even though two persons may have equivalent IQs, one may be highly neurotic and be making a poor adjustment, whereas the other may be making the most of his intellectual ability. It is thus clear that the level of intellectual functioning is greatly influenced by emotional factors. We make a grave error in our attempts to understand human behavior when we separate man's cognitive-self from his emotional-self. Behavior in the "microcosm" of the intelligence test situation is influenced by emotional factors, just as is behavior in "real life." Dr. Edith Weisskopf (Selection 40) presents a lucid discussion of the many facets of personality dynamics which may influence tested intelligence and intelligent behavior in general.

A question which is often heatedly argued by the layman is whether or not there are innate intellectual differences between the races of men. On the basis of our previous discussion of the interaction of hereditary and environmental factors in the determination of behavior, the discerning student will recognize that this problem is likely to be quite difficult to investigate scientifically. Further, since motivations, emotions, attitudes, and other facets of personality dynamics greatly influence intellectual functioning, it is evident that any adequate investigation of the problem must attempt to hold constant or to evaluate sociocultural influences. McCord and Demerath (Selection 41) show how a widely publicized statement regarding Negro-white intellectual differences is an inadequate scientific report. In addition, they present a further empirical study which in no way supports innate racial differences when environmental differences are eliminated. A joint statement made by eighteen outstanding social scientists further supports this view (cf. Selection 42).

selection 39 / the effect of early and late brain injury upon test scores, and the nature of normal adult intelligence / D. O. Hebb, McGill University

The effect of late injury outside the speech areas

Since the characteristics of aphasia are so unlike those of non-aphasic deterioration, the test scores made by aphasic patients will be considered in a separate section. For the effect of brain injury without aphasia, there are several sources of information. One is the fairly large number of cases of brain operation in which the Stanford-Binet has been used, sometimes both before and after operation. Although there are serious drawbacks to its use for the purpose, the high validity of much of its content with normal subjects gives a special interest to the scores of brain-operated patients.

Stanford-Binet scores in cases of brain operation

I have been able to find reports of Stanford-Binet IQ's after adult brain operation in 15 cases. The mean IQ for this group of 15 patients is 108, with scores ranging from 82 to 139 (not much weight can be given to the exact figures since in some cases the old Stanford-Binet was used, in others the new). In addition, I have records of 23 patients

Abridged from D. O. Hebb, "The Effect of Early and Late Brain Injury upon Test Scores, and the Nature of Normal Adult Intelligence," *Proceedings of the American Philosophical Society*, 85:275–292, 1942. Reprinted by permission of the author and publisher.

examined at the Montreal Neurological Institute with the new Stan-ford-Binet; the average here is 107, with scores ranging from 54 to 152. For the total group of 38 cases the mean score is 108. Since the true norm for adults is probably below 100, there is evidently some selection operating to give us an above-average group—how much above average, in original level, there is no way to tell.

Again, five of the writers cited above gave pre- and post-operative scores. In none was there post-operative loss. For 14 cases from the Montreal Neurological Institute with pre- and post-operative examination there was a mean loss of 1.3 points in IQ following operation. For the total group of 19 cases the mean drop in IQ is 1 point, the individual results ranging from a loss of 14 points to a gain of 11 points. Of the 19 cases, 7 show a loss, 6 a gain, and 6 no change following operation. Is this apparent lack of effect due to the compensating removal of dysfunction, with the effect of surgical destruction balanced by recovery from the pre-operative disturbance? To some extent, presumably; but in the cases from the Montreal Neurological Institute the pre-operative status was good (in each case the operation was for the purpose of removing scar tissue), and the case reports of other writers suggest the same thing. The data do not give an exact knowledge of the effect of cerebral destruction, *per se*, but they do suggest strongly that destruction outside the speech areas has no great effect on Binet score. We shall see later that this is not confined to cases of smaller excision.

Individual cases of large lesion or marked deterioration

The evidence discussed so far has been from cases of diffuse pathological destruction or relatively small surgical removals, and cases in which deterioration is not outstanding but evaluated by taking averages for large groups. Another approach to the question of the effect of brain damage is found in cases of unusually large surgical destruction or cases in which there has been marked deterioration.

The outstanding case is that of Rowe. Dr. Rowe, in a personal communication, has furnished further details of the Stanford-Binet examination of his patient after removal of the entire right hemisphere above the basal ganglia. These details are very valuable. Dandy, Gardner and O'Brien have reported cases which are similar surgically, but without psychometric examination. In such cases the bare statement that the patient showed "no obvious mental defect" must be particularly unconvincing to a psychologist, and a common-sense appraisal of intellectual ability may be especially fallible after brain injury. Yet for certain aspects of intelligence it is impressive to find independent observers reporting that there was little or no mental change after operation. The repeated statements of relatives or acquaintances that they found no defects cannot be wholly dismissed: they indicate that some of the components of adult intellectual ability are at most slightly affected. The psychometric data given by Rowe support this strongly. His patient had unfortunately become sensitive about her intellectual powers (after loss of half the cerebral cortex!) and was also found to tire very easily; the examination was not completed, but the results, while they do not make it possible to calculate an *IQ*, are of great significance.

This was the third time the test had been given the patient (others before the complete hemi-decortication), but more than a year had elapsed since the second examination, and it seems impossible to explain such a performance by practice effect, in the presence of any serious, generalized intellectual loss. The repetition of digits, forward and backward, should alone be enough to show that for some things the patient's abilities were above the average for the general population. It is clear, of course, that these data do not mean that other abilities were unaffected. We have already seen that the retention of one ability does not mean that others are also equally retained, and the psychometrist's report, that the patient "fatigued fairly rapidly, both physically and mentally" is positive evidence that in certain other tests the patient would have made lower scores. The significant fact here is the objective evidence supporting the clinical opinion that the patient's abilities were in some respects well retained; and the fact that even if other test abilities were impaired the patient still had average or above-average ability in the kind of task which is the core of the Binet test. Such things as comprehension of words, differentiation of abstract terms, memory for complex verbal material and solution of reasoning problems, are the kind of task which is most successful in differentiating various levels of intellectual development in normal subjects.

Summary of test data in non-aphasic cases of deterioration

The evidence from the larger groups of cases, and from the individual cases cited here, agrees on one point. Ability to do certain tasks which form an important part of Binet-type tests may not be greatly affected even by large injuries to the mature brain: these tasks include word definition, comprehension of and memory for complex verbal material, and the solution of unspeeded verbal problems which are hard to classify apart from the fact that they appear to be of a familiar kind, dealing with matters of general significance (though even this may not be true in all instances). The evidence shows also that there is likely to be deterioration in other abilities, although the extent and kind of loss in any individual case is unpredictable. The particular tests which have been found to show the effect of late brain injury, in the various cases cited, include: maze tracing, sentence completion, differentiation of abstract words, giving of opposites, analogies, speeded block-manipulation tasks, and picture absurdities.

Vocabulary is most noteworthy as an ability which is at most slightly affected; in all probability there are other things which are as well retained, but which are not measured directly by existing tests. This is suggested by the repeated and emphatic clinical statement that "intelligence" has been unaffected by surgical removal of cerebral tissue. The statement cannot be taken at face value but it is presumptive evidence that important components of normal adult ability are well retained.

Test scores after injury to the infant brain

The discussion here is confined to cases of "birth injury" in which test-score levels are not primarily determined by sensory or motor defects. The patient with hemiparesis cannot carry out certain tasks properly because of his motor defect; his test score is not then representative of an intellectual level. As far as can be determined, the scores to be discussed were not directly affected by such handicaps.

This makes for a selected sample. Athetosis or hemiparesis is detectable, but a case of cortical destruction without gross symptoms may pass for normal. The known birth-injury population therefore may deviate systematically from the total birth-injury population, so that one cannot compare the average test score of the birth-injured with the average score in cases of adult injury. The unknown degree of selection in the clinical birth-injury population is the principal difficulty of this study, and I shall return to it again.

A less direct comparison may be made, however, through the pattern of test scores. We do not know that the birth-injury sample is representative; but we can ask whether the defects, *when they do occur,* are similar in cases of early and late injury. In adult injury there are two psychometric patterns: the non-aphasic syndrome, with vocabulary in particular high and other abilities low, and the aphasic syndrome, with non-verbal abilities markedly higher than verbal abilities. For all cases of adult deterioration there would be, therefore, a bi-modal distribution of vocabulary scores and of differences between verbal (Binet) and performance scores, one mode due to the inclusion of cases of aphasia, the other to cases of deterioration without aphasia. Are the defects due to early injury at all similar? The available data, in cases of birth injury, are for children or young adolescents, which is another difficulty in making a direct comparison; but it is possible to compare brain-injured children with normal children, and brain-injured adults with normal adults, to see if deviations from the normal in each case are of the same kind, and of the same extent.

By the kindness of Dr. Heinz Werner, I have obtained details of test data in a series of 32 cases of "exogenous" mental defect, from the Wayne County Training School. These are not even representative of the known birth-injury cases without gross motor handicap, since those with Binet *IQ's* below 50 were excluded. As it happens, however, the selection here is on the safe side since it operates against the conclusions of this paper—namely, that certain test levels are lower with early than with late injury.

Werner's data include Stanford-Binet scores (in some of the cases the old, in some the new form was used); year level of vocabulary score; Stanford-Binet scatter; and Arthur Performance Test score. With these data I have included four comparable records from the Montreal Neurological Institute. Strauss has described the Wayne County Training School group as including only higher grade defectives, without gross motor handicap. The lack of motor disability makes an important difference between this group and that of Doll, Phelps and Melcher, the object of whose study was of course different.

The chronological age range, in the combined groups, is from 10 to 19 years, and the range of Binet *IQ* from 43 to 99. Vocabulary scores are available for 32 of the 36 cases. Taking the maximal chronological age as 15, Table I gives the differences between chronological age and vocabulary age level. In one case only the vocabulary age is (6 months) higher than the chronological age; the median vocabulary retardation is between 5 and 6 years, the greatest 9 years. This is evidence that vocabulary is generally depressed by birth injury. Vocabulary, also, does not tend, as it does with mature injury, to be one of the high Stanford-Binet subtest scores. Two of 30 cases have vocabulary at the highest year-level of successes; 10, on the contrary, have vocabulary scores at the basal age, and the rest are nearer the basal age than the highest year-level of successes. Scatter seems to be some-

TABLE 1   DISTRIBUTION OF VOCABULARY RETARDATION IN MONTHS, OBTAINED BY SUBTRACTING VOCABULARY AGE LEVEL FROM CHRONOLOGICAL AGE[1] IN 32 CASES OF BIRTH INJURY (DATA IN 28 CASES PROVIDED BY WERNER)

CA–VA[2] (months)	No. of cases	CA–VA (months)	No. of cases
−12 to −1	1	60 to 71	9
0 to 11	1	72 to 83	3
12 to 23	1	84 to 95	5
24 to 35	1	96 to 107	1
36 to 47	4	106 to 119	3
48 to 59	3		

[1] Range of chronological age was actually 10 to 19, but 15 is taken as a maximum; vocabulary age ranged from less than 6 to 14.

[2] VA = vocabulary age.

what greater than with normal children, but with vocabulary scores tending to be low it is not like the scatter that may be found in adult cases.

Obviously vocabulary is markedly depressed in these cases, and has not the relationship to other scores that is apt to be found in cases of adult deterioration. There is no evidence of a bi-modal vocabulary distribution, nor of a bi-modal distribution of the relationship between verbal and non-verbal ability. The low level of vocabulary score means that the "non-aphasic syndrome" of the adult is not to be found here.

Nor does the adult aphasic syndrome appear. "Speech-area" injury in the infant may affect later symbolic formulation and expression: indeed, it is possible that the more extreme defects of imbecility or idiocy (not represented in the group analyzed) may be the result of injury to what, in the adult, is the speech area. But it is characteristic of aphasics to have some non-verbal abilities well within the normal range, with the verbal abilities outside the normal range: in a large proportion, with a marked discrepancy between verbal and non-verbal abilities. No writer has discussed, as far as I am aware, the occurrence of aphasia as the result of birth injury (as distinct from lesions occurring or progressing after speech has developed), but it appears that when verbal defects are as serious as those of aphasia the level of other abilities is not far removed. In short, the only children whose verbal capacities are as poor as in the ordinary case of aphasia would be imbeciles at least. Doll refers to the effect of birth injury upon speech, pointing out that speech defects may be accompanied by normal ability elsewhere, but he appears to mean a kind of defect which is not at all like the aphasic disturbance of symbolic function. Such defects are to be thought of as disturbances of speech production, not of the cortical processes underlying speech organization (just as there are adult speech disturbances which have no relation to aphasia).

The development and retention of intelligence

The weight of evidence points to a more widespread and less selective effect of the large infant injury than of the large adult injury. Unless known cases of exogenous mental defect involve lesions in the speech areas (the possibility already discussed), to account for the uniformly low vocabulary and verbal test scores, it must be that *low verbal test scores are produced by early lesions outside the speech areas.* With vocabulary at least it appears that a cerebral lesion may be deleterious at infancy and not at maturity, for such lesions at maturity do not affect vocabulary to a detectable degree. If this is so, the development and the retention of an ability may depend on the brain in different ways. An intact cerebrum is necessary for the normal development of certain test abilities, but not for their retention at a nearly normal level. In other words, *more cerebral efficiency or more intellectual power is needed for intellectual development than for later functioning at the same level.*

Stating the problem in this way suggests a clue to a possible solution. The actual modifications of behavior which occur in intellectual development are mostly qualitative. Faced with a complex situation, the subject sees it in a new way and makes a new response—not more responses or harder responses. Now often in such modifications of behavior it is the first steps which demand intellectual capacity. Learning to solve a problem demands more intellectual effort than solving more problems of the same kind; this is obvious with formal problems, but it may also be true of the perception of relationships: in the figures used by the Gestalt psychologists, in puzzle pictures of the kind made to amuse children, in Street's Gestalt Completion test, there is ample evidence that the original perception of a relationship may make more intellectual demand than the same perception later. It is not far-fetched to suppose that this is also true of the perception of relationships in everyday events which the growing child does not set out consciously to master, as he must an arithmetic problem or a puzzle picture, but which make up the "problems" of everyday life. The intelligent child solves these problems without thinking of them as such, but nevertheless at a faster rate than the less intelligent: intellectual capacity must be important in the development and it is plausible to suppose that here, as in more formal intellectual undertakings, the first achievement is what requires the greater amount of intellect. The development of social appreciation, common sense and verbal comprehension, therefore, may demand an intact brain, while their retention does not.

Intellectual development then would involve stable, qualitative changes of behavior and perception, dependent for their first appearance upon more elaborate intellectual processes than for their later functioning. Physiologically, this implies that stable changes of neural organization may occur as the result of activity in other parts of the nervous system. Normal development of verbal comprehension demands an intact or almost intact cerebrum, but its persistence at a high level is possible after the removal of the right half of the cerebral cortex. This is accounted for on the supposition that the actual basis of the adult verbal response is in the middle regions of the left hemisphere (in right-handed individuals, of course), but that the physiological organization of this part of the brain is partly determined by earlier activities in the rest of the brain. The qualitatively good response is a modification due to an earlier and more elaborate kind of cerebral activity.

All this, however, emphasizes only one of the factors entering into test performance—the one accounting for high scores following mature brain injury. But verbal test indices, like non-verbal, vary in their susceptibility to the effect of injury outside the speech areas and no test is wholly unaffected. The stable qualitative changes of intellectual development are therefore not all that is rated by intelligence tests. To a varying degree, the tests must also measure something closer to the intellectual power that produced the qualitative changes in the first place.

An hypothesis can now be stated, to account for the high level of certain test scores following late brain injury, for the varying degree to which other test scores are affected, and for the differences of the effect of early and late injury:

In any test performance there are two factors involved, the relative importance of which varies with the test: one factor being present intellectual power, of the kind essential to normal intellectual development; the other being the lasting changes of perceptual organization and behavior induced by the first factor during the period of development. Roughly, the one concerns power of "reasoning," of synthesis and invention; the other skill (that is, a factor due to experience). The term "present intellectual power" is not altogether satisfactory; it is used in a special sense not equal to "present intellectual efficiency," since efficiency would be determined by both factors, not only one. The clinical data indicate that both are of essential importance in intelligence as it would be identified either by tests or by common sense. The contrast is not between intelligence and knowledge, but between capacity to develop new patterns of response and the functioning of those already developed.

Vocabulary, unspeeded verbal comprehension and so on may be regarded as primarily indices of a level of past development, while some other tests, more sensitive to the effect of injury to the mature brain, are better indices of "present intellectual power"; keeping in mind, however, the implication of the hypothesis presented—that adult intellectual efficiency in many matters is determined more by the highest past level of intellectual power than by the level of "present intellectual power." There are, in this view, two ways in which a test may function.

Weisenburg and McBride have made a somewhat similar distinction of test material, related to the familiarity or unfamiliarity of the task. Finding no evidence of loss, after right-sided cerebral destruction, in tests of sentence dictation, oral spelling, and vocabulary, they say:

It is noteworthy that these are language tests involving the reproduction of acquired knowledge in situations not unfamiliar to everyday experience. They [the patients] fall furthest below the normal on the Sentence Completion Test, which involves constructive synthetic mental activity in a situation which is not difficult for them to grasp, but still a less natural situation.

Emphasis here should be put on the kind and form of task rather than on "reproduction of acquired knowledge," if this phrase means the reproduction of material in the form in which it was learned. It must be insisted that in an oral vocabulary test the subject is not asked to repeat a form of words as he learned them, and a high score cannot be explained as due to rote memory. In spelling, this is often true; the child in school learns to repeat individual letters in the proper order; when he is tested as an adult he may make the same response from memory. Vocabulary tests are another matter. Common words are rarely learned by their definitions; still less are the definitions learned by heart. It is their use that is learned. The evidence in Rowe's case shows that comprehension and memory for complex verbal material heard *for the first time* are also insensitive to late injury. The kind of task is familiar; the specific content, and the actual response to be made, are not.

There is a still more cogent reason for not dismissing the vocabulary score of the adult brain-injured as a mere feat of memory. This is the correlation between vocabulary score and post-operative social competence, conversational ability (ability, that is, to understand and communicate ideas) and general level of functioning in ordinary life. I must revert here to the frequency with which relatives or friends, as well as the attending clinicians, report of the patient who has had successful removal of a large amount of cerebral tissue that his intelligence is unimpaired, and the inescapable conclusion that the patient has retained some essential and important part of his intellectual powers. Vocabulary score therefore would be a better index of level of functioning in such matters than test scores which are more sensitive to the effect of brain damage.

The implication of the hypothesis presented here is that the formation of the qualitative modifications of behavior may continue for some time after intellectual power has reached its peak, and that when tests of more genuinely adult interest are developed they may be found, unlike "power" tests but like vocabulary and some other tests, to continue to show a rise for some time after the onset of puberty. The functioning of intelligence in practice demands that these subjective products of earlier intellectual activity be available, that the understanding of common situations and the solution of routine problems occur without intellectual effort. The farther this process has gone, the more efficient intelligence will be. No amount of native mathematical aptitude, even to the extent of genius, will make original contributions to higher mathematics possible until the ideas of elementary algebra and geometry are second nature, so that real intellectual effort is saved for the advanced problem. Intellectual development, therefore, involves (A) the development of direct intellectual power, by neural maturation, and (B) the establishment of routine modes of response to common problems, or of perceptual and conceptual modifications leading to qualitative modifications of behavior.

The kind of test ability which is generally thought to reach its peak earliest, perhaps between the ages of 12 to 15 years, is the kind which is also more apt to be sensitive to the effect of brain injury after this period, and sensitive as well to the changes of senescence. Direct intellectual power, therefore, may be thought to be at a maximum before the age of 16 years. What we call intelligence, however, would involve both (A) and (B). It would therefore continue to rise to the point at which declining intellectual power offset the increase of intellectual products. For some problems, this peak of efficiency would be reached early; for others late, depending on the extent to which subsidiary problems are involved in the solution of the more difficult problems. Pure puzzle-solving might reach its peak early, for each puzzle would be more or less isolated; but insight into social relationships or skill at dealing with other people might reach a peak very much later and then be maintained. It is granted at once that this high level of problem solving by older subjects is likely to be within a strictly limited range, but this does not justify the psychological conclusion that intelligence begins to decline with adolescence, nor the idea that the older subject gives only an appearance of intelligence. He may not function as well in a wide range of tasks, and may not maintain as high a level of efficiency over long periods; but in all that kind of comprehension which is commonly thought of as demanding maturity of judgment it is likely that the older man has as high a level of functioning as the younger man, if not in many matters a higher one. We have as yet no good measures of "the integrative mental processes interpretative of [adult] experience," but when these processes can be measured one may expect to see a more adequate picture of psychological maturity.

selection 40 / intellectual malfunctioning and personality / Edith A. Weisskopf, Purdue University

It is one of the traditional tasks of the psychologist to evaluate the intellectual potentialities of individuals. The traditional tool for such evaluation is the intelligence test. At the same time, experience with the use of intelligence tests has shown that this instrument has serious

Abridged from Edith A. Weisskopf, "Intellectual Malfunctioning and Personality," *Journal of Abnormal and Social Psychology*, 46:410–423, 1951. Reprinted by permission of the author and the American Psychological Association.

limitations. If, for instance, of two individuals with the same IQ, one behaves considerably more "intelligently" outside the test situation than the other one, it becomes evident that intelligent behavior is affected by factors which may not be measured by traditional intelligence tests. More specifically, these factors are thought to be personality traits, such as persistence, emotional stability, curiosity, etc. However, it would be erroneous to say that these personality factors affect the degree to which an individual behaves intelligently outside the test situation without ever influencing the scores on intelligence tests. That psychometric performance also may be influenced by personality factors is a tacit assumption made by clinical psychologists and corroborated by various studies which submit the components of intelligence to factorial analysis.

Thus, a child with a comparatively high IQ, who functions on a low academic level, may be handicapped by personality factors unfavorable for high academic achievement. In this case, these unfavorable personality factors depress the individual's academic achievement more than they depress his psychometric performance. Stoddard indicates that the nature of the psychometric situation prevents certain personality factors from having an effect on test scores, while the same factors may be of potent influence on intellectual achievement outside the test situation. The ability to concentrate one's effort and interest over a long period of time on a problem, for example, is a factor which may have little effect on psychometric performances, since each problem in such performances requires only a very short amount of time. On the other hand, the ability to make a persistent effort may be an important factor affecting intellectual achievement outside the test situation. In other cases, nonintellective factors may depress test scores as much as they depress performance outside the test situation. For example, this is the case with certain individuals who are described as being pseudofeebleminded. The test scores of such individuals fall within the feebleminded range. Their behavior outside the test situation is in agreement with the test scores, i.e., on a defective level. Yet, there may be indicators in these individuals' performance on tests and projective techniques as well as in their present and past behavior outside test situations which make the clinician suspect that nonintellective personality factors rather than low intellectual ability are responsible for the defective behavior. Such suspicion is, of course, of great practical importance to the clinician, since unfavorable personality traits may yield to therapeutic effort. Thus, in studying nonintellective factors inhibiting intellectual functioning, the psychologist should not limit himself to cases where he finds a discrepancy between psychometric score and performance outside the test situation.

It will be noted that no attempt has been made, thus far, to draw, by definition, a line of demarcation between intellective and non-intellective factors. Wechsler says "personality traits *enter into* the effectiveness of intelligent behavior and, hence, into any global concept of intelligence itself." If this is the case, the question may arise how these personality traits can be distinguished from "intellective" factors. Probably the only way to distinguish the two kinds of factors is by enumeration, not by definition. We speak traditionally of the ability to do arithmetical computation or to grasp spatial relationships as intellective factors, while we do not include curiosity under the same heading. The recognition that intelligent behavior is influenced by every aspect of the personality may induce the psychologist to do away completely with any line of demarcation between intellective and nonintellective factors.

ETIOLOGICAL FACTORS

Lack of parental reward

It is well known that the emotional relationship of parents with their children may influence the children's intellectual efficiency. Thus, parental rejection may be a factor which blocks the child in the progress of his intellectual development. There are various possible connections between parental rejection and learning disabilities. The author has pointed out one connection in a previous treatment, the main points of which are as follows:

Learning processes of any kind and at any age are connected with frustration of more or less serious degree. The child feels frustrated when he has to learn to drink from a cup instead of a nipple. It is frustrating, too, for him to adjust the functioning of his bowels to the demands and taboos of the society in which he lives. Also, the acquisition of knowledge and skills at school is frustrating to a certain degree. What is it, then, that makes children put up with all the thwarting "do's and don'ts" which are impressed on them? It is obvious that children could never be induced to put on the tight corset of cultural demands unless they are given some reward which makes it worth while for them. Maybe the most powerful reward is love and approval, especially when given by the parents or parent substitutes. Thus, if the child develops intellectually, if he learns to master the three R's and to acquire the skill which enables him to perform the little tricks required by psychometric scales, he does it partly in exchange for approval, love, and security.[1] If he does not get this reward

---

[1] This statement does not negate heredity as a factor in the determination of intellectual differences. However, this article is concerned with the effect of environmental rather than hereditary factors.

because he has no parents or parent substitutes, or because the responsible adults fail to give love and security, he may fail to learn what is expected from him by society and to develop intellectually in the desired direction. This is usually an unconscious psychological mechanism rather than conscious malingering. Such a child appears dull to the superficial observer. However, he may actually be like a good businessman, who does not deliver the merchandise unless the price has been paid; sometimes it is smart to be dull.

Thus, if we encounter parents who seem to reject their children because they are dull and do not get along at school, we find frequently that the cart has been put before the horse. The children may not be rejected because they are dull, but they may be dull because they are rejected.

Desire to punish the parents

In our culture the most potent satisfiers of children's needs, namely the parents, are, at the same time, the most potent frustrators. Such a culture can be expected to create a frequent desire in children to punish their parents. This desire may be present even though the relationship between the parents and children is a "normal" one. It may become strongly enhanced by such maladaptive factors as domination, neglect, etc. Because of societal taboos and the child's dependence on his seemingly powerful, omnipotent parents, the hostile impulses of children against their parents remain frequently unconscious. For the same reason, punishing actions against the parents have often to be undertaken in an indirect, camouflaged manner whereby the connection between the action and its punishing significance may remain entirely unconscious. The refusal to eat, or to defecate regularly, is often an unconscious way of punishing parents, characteristic for the preschool child, but often carried on far beyond the first years of life, and even into adulthood. The refusal to develop intellectually —for example, to progress at school—may have the same unconscious significance. The following example illustrates the above.

Shirley, an 18-year-old girl, was referred to the author for psychotherapy because of her inability to meet the academic requirements of a junior college. Her Wechsler-Bellevue IQ was 120. She showed considerable blocking in her social relationships. She was overcome with feelings of despair and anxiety whenever she was in social contact with contemporaries, but she felt perfectly at ease with her parents and their friends. Her academic difficulties at school, however, were probably not a mere outcome of her inability to associate with people of her own age, since she exhibited the same blocking towards academic achievement when taking individual instructions from a tutor. Shirley's mother underwent psychotherapy simultaneously with Shirley. She was a woman who had great difficulties in accepting a feminine role. Her marriage and pregnancy forced her to give up her aim of getting graduate academic training and becoming a lawyer. She unconsciously resented Shirley for this reason. When Shirley reached school age and proved to have good intellectual endowment, her mother transferred her professional ambitions from herself to her daughter, hoping that Shirley would get a higher education and reach the goal which she herself had to give up. Shirley's father was a pediatrician and very fond of children. He wanted to have another child, a desire which met with strong resistance on the part of the mother. Shirley remained the only child. The father's arguments in favor of having a second child centered especially around the idea that Shirley's development might suffer by her being the only child. The mother tried to pacify her feelings of guilt about the matter by making herself believe that Shirley would associate with many other children and never be lonely on account of her onliness. Thus, the mother had two main ambitions for her daughter. She wanted her to get a higher education, and she wanted her to be a sociable person who is surrounded by and enjoys the company of a large number of contemporaries.

It is remarkable that Shirley blocked in exactly the activities which were most important to her mother, namely, in her association with contemporaries and in her intellectual growth. In the course of Shirley's therapy it became apparent that behind a façade of extreme submission she harboured a tremendous amount of resentment against her mother. The material brought out in the course of her treatment suggested that the two main symptoms of her neurosis were partially determined by her unconscious desire to hit her mother's two most sensitive spots.

Desire for self-punishment

Like many other neurotic symptoms, intellectual blocking may be brought about by an unconscious desire for self-punishment and, thus, for atonement of guilt feelings. These guilt feelings may stem from some of the sources discussed in this paper, or from other sources. The fact that a very high prestige premium is put on intellectual achievement in certain strata of society facilitates the use of learning disabilities as a self-punishing device.

Individuals whose intellect serves in the function of self-punishment frequently torture themselves through many other devices besides failure; for example, by compulsive pedantry in their intellectual work, through exaggeratedly long studying hours, etc.

Desire to maintain an infantile level of gratification

Intellectual malfunctioning may be a manifestation of a conscious resistance against growing up. Every step which the child undertakes in his development toward maturity brings about the necessity to forego more infantile gratifications. Thus, developmental progress is often accompanied by considerable nostalgia. Growing up means losing the privilege of entertaining sweet, dependent, protected relationships which are based on self-centered receiving rather than on a give-and-take basis. For example, the satisfaction of passive, irresponsible suck-ing at the mother's breast has to be given up, first for the sake of more active, less convenient cup-and-spoon feeding, which lacks the intimate physical contact with the mother and burdens the child with heavy responsibility, and much later for the strenuous and inconven-ient activity of making a living. Intellectual growth, too, means re-nouncement of the satisfaction of dependent needs. Learning to read may mean to a child not being read to; learning to think may mean not being thought for; learning to orient himself in his environment may mean not being guided and protected. The child who is exces-sively afraid of losing infantile gratifications may block in his intel-lectual development.

Mahler-Schoenberger reports on an 18-year-old boy suffering from pseudoim-becility. His behavior was seriously retarded. He walked with a shuffling gait like an automaton and sat with his arms listlessly hanging at his side. His mother and his siblings felt toward him as towards a small child and treated him accordingly. They exchanged kisses and caresses with him, a form of be-havior in which they could not have indulged if the patient were a normal 18-year-old boy. Mahler-Schoenberger considers the desire of obtaining such infantile gratification one of the etiological factors of the boy's neurosis.

In this connection it may be interesting to note that clinical workers are frequently concerned as to whether the mentally retarded child will encounter rejection by his parents and whether the parents will show favoritism towards the normal siblings. The opposite danger is discussed less frequently, namely, that the parents, especially the mother, may develop an unduly strong attachment toward the defec-tive child, so that the normal sibling may be at a disadvantage. In many ways mentally retarded children may offer certain libidinal satisfactions to parents which the normal child cannot supply, namely, complete, helpless dependence without the threat of a second child-birth, i.e., of a painful separation from the child at the time of adoles-cence. Such helplessness may satisfy the parents' need to protect, or to dominate. In a more indirect manner it may also satisfy the parents' dependency needs, since it offers them the possibility of identifying with a completely dependent individual. The parents may, thus, enjoy the care of a feebleminded child directly and vicariously. In this man-ner, *true* mental retardation may offer certain libidinal satisfactions to the child and to his parents. *Pseudo*retardation, on the other hand, may be caused by the unconscious desire of the child to gain such satisfaction, and unconsciously encouraged through the same desire in the parents.

A graduate student of the author who worked in an institution for the feebleminded remarked jokingly that if he would ever adopt a child, it would have to be a Mongolian imbecile. The remark was, of course, not serious, but humorous in a grim way. However, a genuine emotion may have given rise to his statement, namely, the sweet feeling of attachment which many adults experience towards creatures who are and will forever remain helpless. It is known that Mongolians with their characteristic clinging behavior often become the favorites of institutional staff members.

The previous discussion also throws some light on the problems of children who show intellectual regression, such as deterioration of speech, reading, or other mental skills, at the time of the birth of a younger sibling. At that time the advantages of the infant's way of life and the futility of trying to capture the parents' attention by "academic sophistication" seems especially apparent to the older child. If the child could express his feelings, he would say something like, "Why did I have to go through all the troubles of growing up, when this helpless and stupid baby receives so much affection?"

In this connection it may be enlightening to compare the attitude of adults toward children of very superior intelligence and toward less intelligent children. We often find that superior children are to a lesser degree recipients of adults' protective warmth. Many adults are inclined to handle superior children with objective detachment. Thus, the unconscious desire to avoid such curtailment in warmth and affection may result in intellectual blocking with children of superior ability. Gumpert says about the American woman that "she would rather be loved than respected." The same may be true for some children of superior intellect.

Displacement[2] of inhibitions from specific, threatening aspects of cognition to intellectual activity in general

Inhibitions caused by guilt feelings: (a) sexual curiosity   In certain strata of society the attitude of adults toward children's sexual knowledge is, in many ways, diametrically the opposite of their attitude toward other kinds of knowledge. This rather obvious fact becomes especially apparent if we examine the literature on sex education written for parents and teachers of young children. Many authors, for example, make statements to this effect:

A frank way of discussing the facts of life will, they say, stop the child's curiosity and interest in these matters and will put an end to his preoccupation and his questions. Now let us compare this alleged aim of sex education with the aim of any other branch of education. Is there any other field in which the teacher aims at squelching the

---

[2] In many instances where the term "displacement" is used in this paper, it would be more correct to use the term "displacement or stimulus generalization" since the exact nature of the mechanism cannot be determined.

children's intellectual thirst, at suffocating interest and curiosity, and at stopping further questions? On the contrary, educators measure the success of their teaching not so much according to the amount of knowledge or information they transmit, but according to the interest they create. Questions, stimulated curiosity, attempts to make further investigations are considered criteria of success in teaching. Thus, the aims of sex education appear to be the exact opposite of the aims of education in any other field.

It is no wonder that many children develop guilt feelings about their knowledge and curiosity concerning sexual matters. According to psychoanalytic theory, such guilt feelings do not always remain limited to knowledge about sex. Again, displacement upon similar stimuli may take place, i.e., the guilt feelings may spread to intellectual activity in general. Since the guilt is irrational, it usually remains unconscious, but may result in serious blocking of intellectual functioning.

The author treated an 11-year-old boy who was making poor progress at school. His school achievement improved considerably after treatment for several months. The main topic of conversation during the counseling sessions was "the facts of life." The boy had very drastic misconceptions about reproduction. His foster parents had never given him any sex information. He had acquired most of his knowledge from an older boy, whom he met secretly, against the wish of his foster parents. He considered the conversations about sex which he carried on with this boy as "bad." The treatment sessions taught him that it was not necessarily bad to talk, to know, or to be curious about sex. This relief of his guilt feelings about a specific type of knowledge may be one of the factors which decreased his blocking against school work.

Sylvester and Kunst report about an interesting fantasy of a boy with a reading disability.

He daydreamed that his father had invented a big machine and had cautioned the boy to stay away from it. It was a dangerous machine which made terrific noises. However, the boy disregarded his father's warning and looked at the machine. As an effect of this disobedience, he was forced to run with closed eyes for many years so that the machine could not catch him. He then pretended in his daydream that *he* was the inventor of the machine, and that he was not permitted to make any further inventions. The fantasy suggests that the boy feels guilty about curiosity, knowledge, and intellectual creativity, and that he believes it is safest to "keep his eyes closed." Since the boy is suffering from a reading disability, guilt may be one of the etiological factors of his difficulty.

Thus, the conventional parental reasoning—that if curiosity about sexual matters is suppressed, children will turn their thinking "to more wholesome and constructive matters"—may be a fallacy. In many cases the results may be the opposite from what the parents expect.

(*b*) *Aggression and sadism* The above discussion indicates that intellectual blocking may result from guilt feelings about a specific *kind* of knowledge and subsequent displacement upon intellectual work in general. Similarly, guilt feelings about a specific *aspect* of knowledge may develop and be displaced upon intellectual functioning in general. For example, the aggressive and sadistic aspect of thinking may, thus, become an instigator of learning difficulties.

There are various connections between the acquisition of knowledge, and aggression and sadism. One possible connection becomes apparent during preschool age, when the toddler tears apart toys, such as dolls, or living creatures, such as beetles, in order to investigate what is inside. Also the desire to know what is inside the human body may become associated with the aggressive desire to tear apart and to destroy.

Sylvester and Kunst report about an eight-year-old boy who was placed in a subnormal room at school even though he was of superior intelligence. His behavior during play therapy suggested strong aggression against the mother. He stated that the mother doll did not want to carry her baby since the baby might kick her. Finally the boy tied the baby doll to the mother doll's arm in order to prevent him from kicking. It also became apparent that the boy was filled with strong curiosity as to what was in his mother's body. During his play with dolls, he expressed the desire to tear the mother doll apart in order to see what was inside. Thus, intellectual curiosity and aggression were closely associated in the boy's personality structure. Furthermore, the situation was aggravated by the fact that the mother was seriously sick. The boy's magical thinking made his own aggressive desires responsible for her disease. In this manner, his guilt feelings were greatly increased. Finally, displacement of guilt from the aggressive aspect of "wanting to know" to intellectual functioning in general took place, and the boy developed a serious learning disability.

Aggression and intellectuality may become associated in various other ways. Intellective learning, for example, has a strong competitive aspect in certain strata of society. With some individuals competition may become the main motive for learning. Competition, however, implies aggression. Again, guilt feelings about competitive aggression may be displaced upon learning in general. Guilt feelings about competition are especially likely to arise in a culture where cooperative and competitive ideals are taught simultaneously. While tribes such as the Mundugumor stress competition and tribes such as the Arapesh preach mainly cooperative ideals, Western civilization finds itself in between the two contradictory ideals of competition and cooperation. Both attitudes are taught simultaneously. Thus, Western man is quasi forced to go out in the rain without getting wet. Indoctrinated with the ideal of competition, he finds it difficult to cooperate, and his training in cooperation makes him feel guilty about competitive activities.

In addition, some of the words used synonymously with "intelligent" and "stupid" suggest an association between intelligence and aggression in people's thinking, for example, the terms "sharp" and "dull." Similarly, Landauer points out that the German word "albern," meaning stupid, is derived from the obsolete word "alvari," meaning good or friendly.

Since intellectual work is related to a higher degree to the masculine role in our culture than to feminine activity, women often use their intellect as a device to compete aggressively with men. If such competition becomes the major motivating factor of intellectual endeavor, the ensuing guilt may become a serious block to progress.

Inhibitions caused by failure   Serious failure in specific intellectual endeavors may result in inhibition of intellectual functioning in general.

A child may be unsuccessful in his first attempts to master academic subject matter, not due to lack of intellectual endowment, but due to more extraneous factors such as a bad teacher, or a visual or auditory defect. The discouraging experience may condition the child in such a manner that he remains intellectually blocked even after all obstacles have been removed, e.g., after he has been placed with a better teacher or after his physical defects have been corrected.

According to psychoanalytic theory, such blocking is especially frequently instigated by children's failures in their investigations about sexual matters. These investigations are especially liable to meet with failure, since most adults tend to increase the obstacles of such endeavors or, at least, not to offer much constructive help. Moreover, his own psycho-sexual immaturity often prevents the young thinker from finding the truth. Instead, he may lose himself in a maze of contradictory hunches and fantastic sexual theories. Such "first failure" may have "a crippling effect forever after."

Desire to avoid self-evaluation

Some individuals fail intellectually because they do not make any effort to succeed. Such "lazy" individuals are often extremely ambitious. Their ambition may be so strong that they could not bear to become aware of their limitations. Since they do not make any effort to succeed, they can avoid getting a realistic and possibly disappointing conception of their capacity. Thus their laziness enables them to excuse their failure and to cling to the magical belief that they would be champions if they would care to participate in the contest.

Desire to be the recipient of love rather than of envy and aggression

The desire to succeed and the desire to be liked by one's fellow men are frequently incompatible. Success in climbing the ladder of achievement is often accompanied by loss of love. The successful individual may endanger himself by becoming the target of envy and aggression. Such envy and aggression against a successful person may be attitudes which are actually existing, or they may be projections on the part of the successful individual. In other cases actually existing aggression may be exaggerated in the recipient's perception through the mechanism of projection.

A very bright student of the author excelled in class by her stimulating contributions to the discussion, and by the quality of her written work. However, after a few weeks of class work her contributions dropped noticeably in quality and quantity. In conversation with the author she stated that several remarks made by her colleagues were reported to her, indicating that her intellectual superiority made her unpopular with her classmates. Thus, she decided to control her behavior at school in such a way that she would appear less outstanding. We would hesitate to designate this girl as a case of intellectual blocking, because her plan not to excel was conscious, intentional, and reversible through deliberate decision. However, the study of individuals' attitudes toward success in intellectual activities or in any other field indicates that the tendency to "hold back" in order to avoid hostility can lie anywhere on a continuum from complete conscious intention to entirely unconscious blocking. For example, "holding back" may start as a consciously planned maneuver and later develop into an automatic, uncontrollable habit.

Brilliant, well-educated, and sophisticated young women occasionally engage in diplomatic malingerings when associating with men in social situations such as dates. They try to hide their knowledge and sophistication in order not to be threatening to their companion and, thus, to enjoy the pleasures of unambivalent male affection rather than to be frustrated by the ambivalent emotional relationship of competitors and the pseudo-triumph of Pyrrhic victory. In other cases, the expectation of loss of gratification may automatically inhibit their intellectual development, without conscious planning or even against conscious planning. Every step which a man undertakes toward vocational success makes him more desirable as a love object, but every step undertaken by a woman in the same direction may make her less desirable as a partner for love and marriage. This conflict between two goals may become an etiological factor for the automatic inhibition of activity directed toward either goal.

The role played by the innocent, unsophisticated fool in myth, fairy tale, and fiction may serve as an illustration of the statement that intellectual blocking may be caused by fear of hostility. The fool in folk literature and other fiction is often an appealing figure, loved by everybody, envied by nobody. Since he is at the bottom of the ladder already, nobody can push him down.

CONCLUSION

The above is a discussion of some connecting bonds between intelligence and total personality. The discussion claims neither completeness nor originality. The emotional factors affecting thought processes covered in this paper have been described by others. However, the treatment of these topics is scattered through the psychiatric and psychological literature and interwoven with various other material. The author considered it a worth-while undertaking to extract pertinent material from various sources in order to present a more systematic discussion of intellect and total personality. Moreover, much of the subject matter surveyed in this paper is, in its original source, expressed in the often highly esoteric language of psychoanalysis, and interwoven with other psychoanalytic material which may be less acceptable to psychologically trained clinicians. In the author's opinion the above presentation discusses important aspects of intelligence, with emphasis on dynamic connections rather than quantitative comparisons. This approach has been relatively neglected by psychological investigators. Yet the objective research training of the academic psychologist is badly needed for the study of these aspects. Most emotional factors affecting intelligence have been ascertained "intuitively" rather than by objective methods. It will require all the ingenuity of psychologists to plan research designs which corroborate or disprove some of the "hunches" discussed in this paper.

selection 41 / negro vs. white intelligence: a continuing controversy / William M. McCord, Stanford University, and Nicholas J. Demerath III, Harvard University

On September 21, 1956, U.S. News and World Report fired the first round in a battle over Negro intelligence, a controversy with important implications for school integration. Under the awe-inspiring title, "A Scientist's Report on Race Differences," Frank C. J. McGurk, associate professor of psychology at Villanova University, set out to prove the innate intellectual inferiority of Negroes. After reviewing what he falsely claimed to be "the only existing studies that relate to the problem (of ethnic differences in intelligence)," McGurk asserted that improvements in the socio-economic status of Negroes do not

Abridged from William M. McCord and Nicholas J. Demerath III, "Negro vs. White Intelligence: A Continuing Controversy," *Harvard Educational Review*, 28:120–135, 1958. Reprinted by permission of the publisher.

result in an increase in their scores on intelligence tests. In addition, he categorically concluded, ". . . as far as psychological test performance is a measure of capacity for education, Negroes as a group do not possess as much of it as whites as a group. This has been demonstrated over and over."

The purpose of this article is: first, to demonstrate the specific inadequacies of McGurk's "proof" and second, to present a new study which investigates more closely several important factors influencing intelligence scores. These include father's social class, education, nationality and generation of entry into the United States, as well as the family's emotional atmosphere. Since the sample was drawn from the Cambridge-Somerville area near Boston and is both Northern and urban, the effects of two additional factors—the Southern milieu and segregated, unequal schooling—were eliminated.

THE INADEQUACIES OF "A SCIENTIST'S REPORT"

McGurk opened his attack by citing the famous studies of draftees' intelligence during World War I. A comparison of the Negro and white scores showed that only 27 per cent of the Negroes equaled or exceeded the average scores of the whites on the Alpha test and that only 29 per cent of the Negroes equaled the whites' average on the supposedly less "culture bound" Beta test. Using these results as a baseline, McGurk argued that the improvement in Negroes' socioeconomic status since 1918 should be revealed in higher scores on later tests of Negro and white intelligence; "If social and economic factors are *the* important thing in determining the test-score differences between these two racial groups, it would have to follow, as a matter of logic, that a decrease in the difference between the social and economic factors between Negroes and whites should be accompanied by a decrease in the difference between their average test scores." [Italics added.]

To test his point, McGurk examined the results of six later studies of Negro and white intelligence and concluded, ". . . when the Negro is given a better social and economic opportunity, the differences between Negroes and whites (in intelligence scores) actually *increase.*" Thus, in his opinion, the social and economic environment bears no causal relation to scores on intelligence tests. Before examining McGurk's six "authoritative" studies, one curious oversight in the article should be mentioned. At no point did McGurk state that Southern white scored consistently below Northern whites in the Army tests. Perhaps the oversight was intentional; for McGurk would find it uncomfortable to argue that inherent racial differences accounted for the poor performance of Southern whites.

Each of the six basic studies quoted by McGurk has serious inadequacies—when used as support for his opinion. A general criticism can be made of McGurk's description of this body of research. He consistently omits figures indicating the proportion of *whites* who equaled or exceeded the average score. One must remember that the average is not the median; if one or two testees scored extremely high, the average score for the entire group would be raised by several points.

The earliest study which was cited is H. A. Tanser's investigation of Canadian Negroes and whites. Tanser administered three standard tests to all Negro and white school children enrolled in the primary schools of Kent County, Ontario. On every test the Negroes scored lower than the whites; in no test did more than 20 per cent of the Negroes equal or exceed the average scores of the white children. The first question which a social scientist would ask about this study is: "Was the social and economic status of the two groups equal?" Innumerable studies have demonstrated that a close relationship exists between socio-economic status and intelligence scores; if the Negroes, as a group, were in a depressed status, their scores would inevitably have a lower average. McGurk recognized this criticism but cavalierly dismissed it by arguing that "social and economic opportunities had always been equal for all Negroes and whites in this area, *except for a few minor outbursts of oppression directed toward the Negroes.* [Italics added.] McGurk, in addition, *totally omitted* references to Tanser's own confession that the socio-economic status of Negroes in Kent County *was then and had always been inferior to whites.* We charge that such a critical omission could be only due to conscious biasing of the evidence.

As his second source of evidence, McGurk quoted research done in 1940 on Negro and white children living in rural areas of the South. The Negro children, not surprisingly, scored lower than the whites; from 15 to 20 per cent of the Negro children, depending on the test, equaled the average score of the whites. McGurk commented only in passing that the subjects attended rural segregated schools in Virginia. Knowing the economic deprivation of Southern Negro schools and the general psychological climate, it is difficult to believe that any social scientist could accept this study as a valid comparative measure of inherent capacity for education. Otto Klineberg's work, cited later in this paper, indicates the debilitating influence of the Southern milieu upon Negro children.

Third, McGurk drew upon a study of New York University freshmen published in 1942 by A. M. Shuey. Shuey matched forty-three pairs of Negro and white students on the basis of the birthplace of their father, their father's occupation and the students' earlier school education. Testing of the students revealed that only 18 per cent of the Negro subjects equaled the average score of the whites. In his summary, McGurk characteristically failed to note the author's caution concerning the work. Shuey conceded that many other factors influence performance on an intelligence test; not all influences could be "controlled." Indeed, Shuey was unable to hold constant one of the most important of these variables: the cultural background of the students' parents. The introduction of just this additional factor might have fundamentally changed the results; as is shown later in this article, test performance of children is closely related to the education of their fathers.

Throughout his entire paper, McGurk ignored all those subtle influences which affect an intelligence score: the motivation of the subjects; the emotional characteristics of the child, his parents, his culture; and the values and cultural stimulations to which he has been exposed. Until these variables are "controlled," every study of "racial" intelligence, including Shuey's and our own, must be taken with a grain of salt.

As a basic pillar of his argument, McGurk called upon his own work. In 1951, McGurk abandoned validated, standardized tests of intelligence and invented his own measure—half of it "drew heavily on the cultural background" of subjects, the other half was supposedly not "culture-bound." He administered this test to high school students in Pennsylvania and New Jersey and equated the students' socio-economic status—omitting any direct measure of the cultural or educational motivation of the students. As one would expect, the Negro students failed to equal the whites. In a later study, he paired the 25 per cent of the Negro and white subjects who were highest in socio-economic status and the 25 per cent who were lowest. Analysis showed that the Negroes in the *lowest* category equaled the whites' average score, but that only 18 per cent of those with the highest social status "overlapped" the white average (again, one wonders how many of the whites exceeded their own group's average score). The faults of McGurk's research—his failure to use a standardized test and his failure to match the cultural or emotional motivation of the subject—lead to the conclusion that his own studies only added to the confusions already abounding in this area.

Thus, what McGurk claimed as conclusive evidence appears to be far less than that. Many of the studies failed to control socio-economic influences and few considered the cultural background of the subjects. One study did not eliminate the influence of the Southern milieu and schooling; another investigation (McGurk's own) used a test which had not been sufficiently validated. None of the analyses explicitly considered the motivational or cognitive structure of the subjects or their environment.

From this insufficient evidence, McGurk drew untenable conclusions. The unreliability of his article becomes particularly apparent when one considers the information which he omitted. Although he claimed that the six articles were the only ones relating to the problem, McGurk—*consciously or unconsciously—eliminated all those studies which contradicted his bias*. Only three of these crucial omissions will be mentioned.

In 1923, W. W. Clark analyzed the intelligence of a large sample of children enrolled in Los Angeles schools. He administered the National Intelligence Test to 510 Negro children and 4326 white children. While there was no attempt to control the background of the children, no one could maintain that the Negroes were of *higher* socio-economic status than the whites. Clark's subjects lived in a non-Southern atmosphere and attended integrated schools. Clark found no statistically significant difference between the two "races." The white children had a median score of 106 and the Negro children achieved a median score of 104.7.

The famous work of Otto Klineberg is, of course, in direct contradiction to McGurk's position. McGurk mentioned Klineberg but ignored his research. Klineberg and his associates, over a number of years, analyzed the effect of the Northern environment on Southern-bred Negro children. Consistently, they found that intelligence scores increased the longer the children had resided in New York. Thus, scores were positively correlated with "Northernization" and "urbanization," two processes which commonly yield better social, cultural, educational, and occupational opportunities for the in-migrant Negro. In a variety of studies, the average scores increased by five to fifty points on the National Intelligence Test—a difficult result for McGurk to dismiss, if he is correct that an improved socio-economic environment does not affect Negro responses to intelligence tests.

Similar research has been conducted by H. H. Long. Long examined Negro children living in the urban atmosphere of Washington, D. C. He found that scores on the Kuhlman-Anderson intelligence test jumped by twelve to fourteen points when residence in Washington increased from under one year to more than eight years.

Admittedly, the work of Clark, Klineberg, and Long is inconclusive: Clark failed to hold constant a variety of influential factors; Klineberg and Long did not actually trace the *same* children's performance on intelligence tests. Yet, these inadequacies are no greater than those found in McGurk's studies. Why, then, did he omit them from his "authoritative" review of the evidence?

A NEW STUDY OF NEGRO AND WHITE INTELLIGENCE

No research which attempts to measure inherent biological differences between the intelligence of whites and Negroes can be conclusive. Too many unmeasurable factors—the pressures of inequality, motivational and cultural differences, the faults of the tests, and most importantly, the lack of consensus on the *nature* of intelligence itself —hamper research on this issue. Nevertheless, since our nation is passing through a great domestic crisis, studies of intelligence will inevitably be used as weapons in the social conflict. It is wise, therefore, to devote some scientific effort to the clarification, if not resolution, of the problem.

As part of another research project, Kuhlman-Anderson intelligence tests on a number of ten year old boys (562 whites and fifty Negroes) had been collected. The ratio of Negroes and whites in this group closely approximated the actual distribution in the general population of their cities, Cambridge and Somerville, Massachusetts. Stanford-Binet intelligence scores were also available for 238 children. The total sample had unique advantages for comparative research in that all of the children lived in a Northern, urban area and all attended integrated schools. We had additional information on the social class, national origin, and education of all the boys' families, and, for a smaller portion of the sample, information regarding the emotional climate of their families was available. Therefore, it was possible to control cultural, social and emotional factors which might influence intelligence.

This information was gathered between 1938 and 1945 as part of the "Cambridge-Somerville Youth Study"—a prolonged experiment in the prevention of juvenile delinquency. Founded by Dr. Richard Clarke Cabot, the project selected 650 boys, half of whom were considered as pre-delinquent and the other half as "normal." Half of the 650 boys were intensely observed and counseled for an average period of five years; the other half were left alone as a "control" group. Each group was composed of approximately equal proportions of "pre-delinquent" and of "normal" boys. In 1956, under a grant from the Ella Lyman Cabot Foundation and the Harvard Laboratory of Social Relations, an extended investigation of the adult criminality and alcoholism of these boys was begun. The results of these studies will be published elsewhere.[1] It should be noted, however, that no significant relation between criminal behavior and intelligence was found. We bring up this point, for it could be argued that the high proportion of "maladjusted" boys in this sample might render it an unrepresentative group. Since intelligence was not linked to crime, this possibility does not seem critical. The sample is unrepresentative in one other respect: most of the families belonged to the lower class

[1] See William McCord, Joan McCord, and Irving Zola, *The Genesis of Crime*, Columbia University Press, and William McCord and Joan McCord, *The Genesis of Alcoholism* (in preparation).

TABLE 1   KUHLMAN-ANDERSON INTELLIGENCE, NEGROES VERSUS WHITES (IN PERCENTAGE)

Intelligence	Negroes (N = 50)	Whites (N = 562)
Superior (105–above)	14.0	18.7
Average (104–95)	50.0	39.7
Low average (94–85)	34.0	35.0
Sub-normal (84–below)	2.0	6.6

Chi square: not significant

or the lower-middle class. This fact limits the generalizations which can be made; yet the other advantages of the sample make it an interesting "experiment" in the comparative study of intelligence.

As a first step, without holding constant those factors which previous research indicated were related to intelligence, the Kuhlman-Anderson scores of the white and Negro boys were compared. Even without specific controls, *no significant difference appeared. Both the Negro and the white groups achieved a median score ranging between 95 and 99* (see Table 1).

As a means of confirming this first finding, the scores of whites and Negroes on the Stanford-Binet test which had been given to 238 of the same boys were examined. In a variety of ways, the Stanford-Binet test differs from the Kuhlman-Anderson; perhaps most importantly, the Stanford-Binet was administered individually while the Kuhlman-Anderson was given to class-room groups. Once again, *no significant differences appeared.* The median score of the whites and the Negroes fell in the 90 to 95 range (see Table 2).

As compared to their scores on the other test, the boys scored generally lower on the Stanford-Binet; the "sub-normal" category increased considerably. Although the sample is relatively small, it is important that *different* tests agreed in indicating no significant racial

TABLE 2   STANFORD-BINET INTELLIGENCE, NEGROES VERSUS WHITES (IN PERCENTAGE)

Intelligence	Negroes (N = 21)	Whites (N = 217)
Superior (105–above)	28.6	18.4
Average (104–95)	19.0	23.1
Low average (94–85)	28.6	30.4
Sub-normal (84–below)	23.8	28.1

Chi square: not significant

differences. Only one interesting, albeit non-significant, trend appeared in both tests: more whites than Negroes exhibited sub-normal intelligence; a discomforting finding for the followers of McGurk.

Actually, *three important controls were built into the study:* the influence of segregated, inferior schooling on Negro performance was eliminated, for all the boys attended the same schools; the debilitating effects of the Southern atmosphere of virulent prejudice were held in check, since all the boys lived in Massachusetts; rural-urban differences were done away with since all the boys lived in an essentially similar urban environment.

Any study of inherent racial differences in intelligence must take account of those other environmental factors which are related to intelligence. Consequently, we examined the relationship between intelligence and social class, parental education, parental nationality, home atmosphere, and the personality of the boys' fathers. When a statistical relationship appears between these environmental factors and intelligence, it is impossible to disentangle the complicated causal web. High intelligence, for example, may *cause* high educational achievement, but it may also be a *result* of the cultural advantages inherent in extended education. Since we cannot know the causal link directly, it is necessary to control these environmental relationships, *if* one wishes to achieve a relatively "pure" comparative measure of innate racial intelligence.

The well-substantiated link between social class and intelligence appeared once again in this research. We rated social class on the generally accepted criterion of father's occupation. Professional people and business owners or managers composed the "middle" class; clerical, service, and white-collar employees made up the "lower-middle" class; while in the "lower" class, we separated four categories: skilled tradesmen, semi-skilled (mostly factory) laborers, unskilled workers, and workers on relief.

When the children's scores on the Kuhlman-Anderson test were compared to their fathers' occupations, a clear relationship emerged. At one end of the scale, 78.8 per cent of the middle class boys received an average or superior score. At the other end of the scale, less than half, 48.1 per cent of the relief children made the same scores.

We know that a statistical relationship exists; we do not know why it exists. Perhaps inferior intelligence leads to inferior status; perhaps the lower class environment—with its own values and stimulations—leads to certain cognitive and motivational disadvantages reflected in low scores on intelligence tests.

Two other factors which may influence performance on an intelligence test should be noted: the emotional atmosphere of the home and the personality of the child's parents. From the extensive records gathered by the Cambridge-Somerville social workers, it was possible to make a reliable judgment on the home atmosphere and the father's personality of a small number of the boys. These judgments were based on records, kept over a five year period, containing the observations of several social workers, teachers, a psychologist, a physician, and sometimes a psychiatrist or minister on each of the boys and their families.

Clinicians have long taken note of the force of emotional factors on a subject's performance. We wished to examine the influence of the emotional *milieu* on the child's measured intelligence. It was possible to categorize the general background of 243 boys into four divisions:

1. A *cohesive home*: an environment generally characterized by affection and pride in the family.
2. A *quarrelsome home*: one in which conflict dominated the atmosphere but where, nevertheless, affection still existed.
3. A *quarrelsome-neglecting home*: an environment torn by familial conflict and rejection of the child.
4. A *broken home*: a family separated by death, divorce, desertion, etc.

The cohesive homes, as one would expect, produced the largest percent of superior children and the smallest proportion of sub-normal children. Quarrelsome-neglecting homes made a poor showing, yet not as bad as the quarrelsome—but still affectionate—families. Perhaps the severe rejection characteristic of quarrelsome-neglecting families, creates, in a certain number of children, a drive toward independence and achievement which might be reflected in test performance. Although the level of statistical significance is low, it appears that home atmosphere may be related to intelligence.

It was also possible to categorize the fathers of 240 boys into five broad divisions of "personality":

1. *Loving fathers*: men who demonstrated active affection for their sons.
2. *Passive fathers*: men who played a minor role in family life and were generally phlegmatic individuals.
3. *Cruel fathers*: overtly rejecting, brutal men.
4. *Neglecting fathers*: overtly rejecting men, emotionally and materially indifferent toward their sons.
5. *Absent fathers*: men who had left the home because of divorce, desertion, or death.

Three independent judges agreed in 80 per cent of the cases in rating both home atmosphere and the father's personality.

TABLE 3   KUHLMAN-ANDERSON INTELLIGENCE, MATCHED PAIRS OF
NEGROES AND WHITES (IN PERCENTAGE)

Intelligence	Negroes (N = 30)	Whites (N = 30)
Superior (105–above)	16.7	20.0
Average (104–95)	50.0	36.7
Low-average (94–85)	30.0	33.3
Sub-normal (84–below)	3.3	10.0

Chi square: not significant

As might be predicted, the loving fathers turned out the highest proportion of superior children and the lowest number of sub-normal boys. Nevertheless, a consistent statistically significant pattern did not appear.

Although the results are far from conclusive, they do indicate that further research on the relation between intelligence and emotional background might well be productive.

Equipped with the knowledge that all of these environmental forces *might* bear a causal relation to intelligence, we were in a better position to analyze biological differences in intelligence. As a last comparative measure, therefore, we matched thirty pairs of Negroes and whites on a number of environmental factors—twenty of the original group of Negroes had to be eliminated since a perfect match could not be made with a white child in the sample. Each pair of boys was equated on the following standards: their father's social class, education, personality, generation of entry into America and the general atmosphere of their family. Thus, a number of influences—but by no means all possible factors—were held constant and a more precise approach could be made to the problem of innate racial differences. *There was no significant difference between the matched pairs in intelligence;* median scores for both groups fell in the 95 to 99 range.

CONCLUSIONS

In our sample of 612 Northern, urban boys, *we found no significant differences in intelligence between Negroes and whites.* Not surprisingly, however, we found that intelligence is significantly related to socio-economic status, parental education, and general home atmosphere. Our evidence, drawn from a straight racial comparison and from the analysis of matched pairs, contradicts McGurk's assertion of the innate inferiority of Negroes. In addition, our evidence suggests an explanation of why certain other studies tend to support his assertion.

From this research, we cannot conclude that Negroes as a group and whites as a group are equal in inherent intellectual ability; so many forces affect intelligence that a "pure" measure of innate differences is impossible. Those of McGurk's persuasion might argue, for example, that our group of children is unrepresentative. A comparison of primarily lower class whites with lower class Negroes, they could point out, may give an unfair advantage to Negroes. Since whites are offered relatively "equal opportunity" in competition with each other, those who remain in the lower class may be intellectually inferior. We grant this argument as a plausible explanation of our findings.

Yet if it is unjustified to claim that this study proves the equality of whites and Negroes, it is equally unjustified to claim, as McGurk has done, that one group has less "capacity for education" than the other. The evidence is inconclusive. We believe, however, that the present study lends weight to the argument that equalization of educational and social opportunities (as has partially occurred in Massachusetts) will result in the equalization of test performance of Negroes and whites.

selection 42 / on race and intelligence: a joint statement / Otto Klineberg, Columbia University

In connection with the process of school desegregation and the difficulties with which it has been accompanied in certain areas, the question has again arisen as to the existence of innate differences in intelligence between Negroes and Whites. The present statement is directed to that question. Those who have signed[1] it are not on this

[1] The signers include Prof. Otto Klineberg, Columbia University; Prof. Theodore Newcomb and Prof. Daniel Katz, University of Michigan; Dr. Gardner Murphy, Menninger Foundation; Prof. Nevitt Sanford, Vassar College; Prof. Robin Williams, Jr., Cornell University; Prof. David Krech, University of California; Prof. Jerome Bruner, Harvard University; Prof. Allison Davis, University of Chicago; Prof. Anne Anastasi, Fordham University; Prof. Stuart Cook, Prof. Isidor Chein and Prof. Marie Jahoda, New York University; Prof. Kenneth Clark, College of the City of New York; Prof. Bingham Dai, Duke University School of Medicine; Prof. Irving Lorge, Teachers College, Columbia University; Prof. Solomon Asch, Swarthmore College; and Dr. David Rapaport, Austen Riggs Center.

From Otto Klineberg, "Race and Intelligence: A Joint Statement," prepared with the Society for the Psychological Study of Social Issues, 1957. Reprinted by permission of the author and the Society for the Psychological Study of Social Issues.

occasion taking sides with regard to the problem of desegregation as a whole, nor with the manner or the rapidity with which it should be accomplished. They are for the moment concerned only with the facts and conclusions accepted by scientists with regard to racial comparisons in inborn intellectual capacity.

A number of years ago, at a time when Nazi race theories were receiving much publicity, several scientific organizations placed themselves on record as opposed to the conclusion that race was a determiner of innate psychological characteristics; their position was that no such relationship had ever been scientifically demonstrated. These organizations included, among others, the American Anthropological Association (in 1939) and the Society for the Psychological Study of Social Issues, a division of the American Psychological Association (in 1938). More recently (in 1950), a group of distinguished social scientists meeting in Unesco House in Paris issued a Statement on Race which reads in part as follows:

Whatever classification the anthropologist makes of man, he never includes mental characteristics as part of those classifications. It is now generally recognized that intelligence tests do not in themselves enable us to differentiate safely between what is due to innate capacity and what is the result of environmental influences, training and education. Wherever it has been possible to make allowances for differences in environmental opportunities, the tests have shown essential similarity in mental characters among all human groups. In short, given similar degrees of cultural opportunity to realize their potentialities, the average achievement of the members of each ethnic group is about the same.

Two years later an equally distinguished assembly of geneticists and physical anthropologists, also meeting in Paris, pointed out that:

The scientific material available to us at present does not justify the conclusion that inherited genetic differences are a major factor in producing the differences between the cultures and cultural achievements of different peoples or groups. It does indicate, on the contrary, that a major factor in explaining such differences is the cultural experience which each group has undergone.

In 1953, a Statement submitted to the United States Supreme Court by more than thirty American social scientists, included the following:

The available scientific evidence indicates that much, perhaps all, of the observable differences among various racial and national groups may be adequately explained in terms of environmental differences. . . . It seems clear, therefore, that fears based on the assumption of innate racial differences in intelligence are not well founded.

These statements still stand, and in our judgment represent the consensus among experts who have studied this question as objectively and as scientifically as is at present possible. We know of no new research which would reverse these conclusions.

Those few specialists who take a different position usually do so on two major grounds. The first is that Negro-White differences in intelligence test scores persist even when the two groups are "equated" for social and educational opportunities. To this we would point out that such "equation" is exceedingly difficult to achieve, since the opportunities related to test performance are by no means easy to assess in quantitative terms. We do know that the intelligence quotients of Southern Negro children improve markedly after a period of years in the schools available to them in New York or Philadelphia.

In the second place, it has been argued that the differences in IQ persist even when "noncultural questions" are used. We would deny the possibility of devising a "noncultural" test in the light of our present understanding of the problem.

In the early days of testing, many psychologists believed that the elimination of the handicap due to language was equivalent to eliminating the influence of culture in general. One psychologist, for example, Professor Florence L. Goodenough of the University of Minnesota, devised a performance test consisting in "Drawing a Man." She regarded this test as "culture-free." Many investigators have made use of this test, and they have been able to demonstrate that, contrary to the earlier view, the results are indeed affected by many aspects of previous experience. Professor Goodenough herself has now recognized this fact, and very honestly and courageously points out her former error. Writing with Dale B. Harris on "Studies in the Psychology of Children's drawings" in the *Psychological Bulletin* for September 1950, she expresses the opinion that "the search for a culture-free test, whether of intelligence, artistic ability, personal-social characteristics, or any other measurable trait is illusory." She goes on to state that her own earlier study "is certainly no exception to the rule" and adds, "The writer hereby apologizes for it."

No one can deny that at the present time the intellectual achievement of American Negro children, particularly those who come from segregated schools, is lower *on the average* than that of White children, nor that a reasonable amount of time must elapse before the gap can be closed. We would interpret the difference in terms of the *whole* pattern of educational opportunities associated with the social environment, and which may affect both the physical and mental development of the child. Even those few scholars, however, who prefer an explanation in terms of race, indicate that there is *overlapping* between the two racial groups. Overlapping is usually defined technically as the percentage in one group which is superior in test scores to the median or average score obtained by the other. *In every comparison with which we are familiar in this field there is some degree of overlapping.* This means more than that *some* Negro children do better than *some* White children. It means that some Negro children do better than the *average* White child, in spite of all the handicaps to which the former have in the past been subjected.

The conclusion is inescapable that any decision to use differences in the average achievement of the two racial groups as a basis for classifying in advance *any individual child,* Negro or White, is scientifically unjustified.

CHAPTER 10 ❂ SOCIAL PROCESSES: ATTITUDES AND ROLES ❂

The term "role" refers to the behavior which is typical of and thus expected of a person who occupies a particular status position in a society. In order to infer a particular status position from behavior, we must show that behavior changes or varies depending on the social-psychological category by which a person may be described. For example, since behavior changes with the age of the individual, we may infer an age status. Other readily observable behavioral differences may be related to sex status, marital status, occupational status, social status, and the like. In each of his statuses or positions a person learns to expect certain reactions from others. He also learns that other people have certain expectations of him as a person occupying a particular status. Informally speaking, a status position may be thought of as a system of rights and duties. More technically "a position is a cognitive organization of role expectations."[1]

The above conception implies that a role is learned in interaction with others and is continually defined or "acted out" in interaction with others. The learning of a role involves the acquiring of role expectations; the behavior resulting from the role expectations may be called role enactment. It should be clear, however, that role expectations and role enactment are influenced not only by the expectations of society but also by the individual's conception of himself. Thus, self, expectations of others, and role expectations interact with each other as strong influences in the determination of overt social behavior.

It is apparent that certain physical characteristics of the individual can have a great influence on position, role, and self concept. A person who is in some way biologically different from others, especially the dominant social group, the Negro, for instance, will be subjected

[1] Sarbin, T. R., "Role Theory," *Handbook of Social Psychology*, G. Lindzey, ed., Addison-Wesley Publishing Company, Reading, Mass., 1954, p. 225.

to expectations from others which will extensively mold his personality. However, it may not be so readily apparent that role enactment can vary greatly in the degree of biological involvement as reflected by the amount of physical effort and the degree to which normal physiological functions may be activated or inhibited. At the extreme of organismic involvement in role behavior the distinction between self and role becomes blurred. In Selection 43 Dr. T. R. Sarbin shows how such behavior as is involved in hypnosis, hysteria, mystical experiences, and Voodoo deaths illustrates increasing biological involvement in role enactment.

An attitude may be defined as a tendency to become motivated with respect to a certain object or person. Typically, it is implied that this motivation is consistently either adient (positive-approach) or abient (negative-avoidance). Of course, since this consistent motivational readiness to respond is a latent or unobservable characteristic, it must be inferred from consistency of behavior toward an object or person. This view is nicely encompassed by the following operational definition of attitude: "An individual's social attitude is an (enduring) syndrome of response consistency with regard to (a set of) social objects."[2]

Like roles, the learning of attitudes is greatly influenced by sociocultural factors, such as status position, and by psychological factors, such as the self concept. Expression of these learned attitudes may thus be made more understandable by taking into account certain principles of personality dynamics. One such principle postulates a relationship between frustration and aggression such that when a person is frustrated he is more likely to respond aggressively. *Cowen, Landes, and Schaet (Selection 44) report an experiment in which they demonstrate that even mild frustration, which is unrelated to the object of the attitude, may result in an increased expression of negative attitudes.*

Throughout this discussion we have emphasized the importance of sociocultural factors in the formation and expression of attitudes and role expectations. It should be apparent, however, that societies are not static but are constantly changing. How does cultural change influence role acquisition and expression? In Selection 45 Dr. Daniel G. Brown examines the effect of cultural changes on the development of sex roles. He provides data to support the generalization that in our culture males tend to prefer the male role more than females prefer the female role. *He also suggests that there is a cultural trend toward less sex role differentiation in our society. Although this trend results in greater personal flexibility and individual freedom, it may also make*

---

[2] Campbell, D. T., "The Indirect Assessment of Social Attitudes," *Psychological Bulletin*, 47:15–38, 1950.

the development of appropriate sexual identification more difficult. There is a good deal of clinical and experimental evidence to indicate that strong identification with the opposite sex and weak same-sex identification may greatly interfere with satisfactory sexual adjustment as an adult.

selection 43 / role enactment / Theodore R. Sarbin, University of California, Berkeley

Role enactment includes, among other segments of behavior, gross skeletal movements, the performance of verbal and motoric gestures, posture and gait, styles of speech and accent, the wearing of certain forms of dress and costume, the use of material objects, the wearing of emblems or ornamentation, including tattoos, etc. In short, role enactment embraces what may be called the mechanics of the role-taking process. These mechanics can be summarized by means of the following concepts: number of roles, organismic involvement, and accessibility or reportability.

Organismic dimension

Any role may be enacted with different degrees of organismic involvement. This is essentially an intensity dimension, the intensity of the enactment being manifest in the number of organic systems involved. At the low end of the dimension would be the kind of interaction which occurs with little affect and with little effort. The role of the customer in today's supermarket involves only minimal participation—the saying of a few words, plus a few movements involved in the exchange of money. Contrast this role with the intensity involved in enacting the role of the mother of a sick child.

In daily life, of course, most roles are enacted with minimal organismic involvement. Behavior would be inefficient indeed if all roles were enacted with maximal intensity. Not only are cultures organized so that the number of maximally intense roles is few, but there are autonomic safeguards which limit the time span of roles that call for great mobilization of energy. The organismic dimension can be understood as applying to all organized actions. The illustrations we have chosen are reference behaviors against which more conventional roles may be compared for intensity (Table 1).

Level I The low end of the scale is labeled "role and self differentiated." The self, a cognitive structure, and the role, also a cog-

From Gardner Lindzey, *Handbook of Social Psychology*, Addison-Wesley Publishing Company, Reading, Mass., 1954, pp. 232–235.

TABLE 1

Role and self differentiated Minimal involvement Few organic systems Little effort	Role and self undifferentiated Maximal involvement Entire organism Much effort

1. casual roles

II. dramatic role, mechanical acting

III. dramatic role, heated acting

IV. role of hypnotic subject

V. hysterical fugue, role of the amnestic

VI. roles involving ecstatic states; mystical experiences, possession, religious conversions, sexual climax

VII. role of the moribund person; object of sorcery and witchcraft (sometimes irreversible)

nitive structure, are minimally in contact. An example of a casual role is the customer in a supermarket. In fact, it is possible to perform this role at the motoric level while at the same time vicariously enacting other roles unrelated to the public role.

Level II   At the next level of organismic involvement, the reference is that of the dramatic actor who performs the motions necessary for the portrayal of the role assigned to him. In mechanical acting, the actor does not become involved; the self is relatively autonomous from the role. He must maintain a certain degree of consistency in the various response systems, which calls for more effort and precludes the degree of autonomy of the casual role. This degree of involvement is seen in many everyday interactions. For example, the employee who "puts on a good front" to impress the boss.

Level III   At the third level, "heated" acting is used as the illustrative reference behavior. Archer, in his classical study of the psychology of acting, was able to discern this kind of acting from the more automatic and mechanical mentioned before. Commonly called "living the role," the actor behaves as if he *is* the character in the drama. Of course, the successful actor maintains some contact with his role as actor in order to change his tempo, amplitude, intensity, etc., as conditions warrant. His involvement includes some affective as well as motoric components. In order to portray anger, for example, the actor may work up a rage by violently shaking a ladder in the wings before appearing on the stage.

Level IV The role of the hypnotic subject serves as a reference role for a moderate degree of organismic involvement. The classical behaviors of the hypnotic subject, the catalepsies, the compulsive posthypnotic actions, sensory and motoric changes, and so on, illustrate more cogently the operation of the *as if* mechanism. In enacting the role of the hypnotized subject as perceived against a background of generalized and specific expectations, a person demonstrates that more of the organism is responding than in play acting. He behaves *as if* he is blind, or deaf, or fearful, or analgesic, or whatever the specific instructions call for.

The hypnotic situation provides a suitable laboratory model for the demonstration of organismic involvement. An experiment conducted by Lewis and Sarbin demonstrates this involvement. These investigators addressed themselves to the question: Can *as if* behavior, as observed in the role taking of hypnosis, influence a basic physiological process, namely, the hunger cycle? Ten volunteer subjects, demonstrating different degrees of hypnotizability, participated in the experiment. The apparatus was essentially the same as used by Carlson in his studies of gastric hunger contractions. Each subject appeared for the experimental period each morning without his breakfast. He was hooked up to the recording apparatus. He was hypnotized and given no further instructions. One full gastric hunger cycle was recorded. During the middle of the second cycle, he was given a fictitious meal. The results indicated that for subjects rated high on the role-taking aptitude (see below), i.e., the ability to participate in *as if* behavior, the gastric hunger contractions stopped. That is, taking the role of the eater was effective in reducing or eliminating the gastric contractions even though no food was ingested. For subjects who were not hypnotizable, who were limited in their ability to participate in this form of *as if* behavior, no effect was produced on the gastric cycle. Thus, a range of the dimension of organismic involvement was demonstrated.

Level V The behaviors subsumed under the rubric hysteria may be used as a reference band on the organismic continuum. Responding *as if* one is afflicted with some organic dysfunction is the main characteristic of the hysteric. The range covered by hysteria overlaps considerably the range covered by hypnotic role taking. The organismic components in hysteria, however, are less self-limiting and more prolonged than in hypnosis. Descriptive cases may be found in any textbook of abnormal psychology. Common examples are hysterical seizures, hysterical anorexia, hysterical paralysis, and hysterical anesthesia. Both major varieties of hysteria, inactivation and autonomy, show how the role of the invalid may involve the entire organism. In the same range of intensity of involvement is the couvade. In this custom the husband lies-in; the essence of the custom is the husband's taking the role of the wife.

Level VI Ecstasy, a condition usually involving suspension of voluntary action, illustrates organismic involvement to a degree which is not ordinarily observed in day-to-day social interaction. Obviously, such states cannot be prolonged over time without damage to the functioning of the body. Ethnologists' accounts of ecstatic trance experiences, possession, religious revivals, conversion experiences, and mystical unions show many of the characteristics of hysteria. But in addition to the greater involvement of the skeletal musculature, there is a greater involvement of the organs that are served by the autonomic nervous system.

In our own wider culture, such roles are taken by participants in revival meetings, by adolescent bobby-soxers who swoon upon hearing "the voice," by participants in sexual congress, by marathon dancers, etc. What is common to these events is the intensity of involvement, the apparent relationship of this intensity to the activities of the sympathetico-adrenal system, and the automatic equilibratory controls. All these activities are terminated through institutionalized rituals, fatigue and exhaustion, and/or autonomic regulation.

In *rites de passage* the role of the celebrant is characterized by high organismic involvement. The manifest purpose of the intense role behaviors of the ritual is to signify the change from one position to another in the society; the effect of the intensity of role enactment is to modify the participant's self-concept so that the new role, e.g., adult, may not be incongruent with the self. If, for example, strength is an expected property of the adult person, and the rites of passage from adolescent to adult include passing a test of strength, then the successful completion of the test allows the person to add the adjective "strong" to his self-description. Thus he is better equipped to occupy the position of adult, not only because others know he has strength, but because he conceptualizes the self as strong.

Level VII The ultimate limit of the intensity dimension is an extension of the previous range. The effects of the sympathetico-adrenal system which is excessively activated in such role-taking sequences as described above may become irreversible under certain stimulus conditions. The end result of such a performance is death.

Well-authenticated cases of *Voodoo* death allow the employment of the descriptive phrase, taking-the-role-of-a-moribund person. Devereux has reported of the Mohave Indians that a person who learns that he has violated the incest taboo takes the role of the person who is about to die. Rivers reports of the Papuans and Melanesians: "Men who have offended one whom they believe to have magical powers sicken and die, as the direct result of their belief; and if the process has not gone too far they will recover if they can be convinced that the spell has been removed."

The case of a man dominated by a death wish is described by Alexander. Autopsy findings revealed no organic pathology. Apparently he took the role of the dying person so intensely that the equilibratory processes failed to work.

The eminent physiologist, Cannon, has provided a description of the physiological and social events associated with taking the role of the doomed person. He uses the description of bone pointing among the Australian aborigines provided by Basedow. This is a form of black magic in which the sorcerer points a sharpened bone at the intended victim.

Cannon explains the physiological events arising from the adoption of the victim's role. The fear response acts upon the soma in many ways. The sympathetico-adrenal system comes into action, exercising control over the viscera and blood vessels. The various internal changes render the organism ready for physical action (struggle or flight). If this state of extreme perturbation continues *without motoric discharge*, death may follow. But why do the equilibratory or internal constancy mechanisms fail to re-establish homeostasis, as in ecstatic experiences? One answer to this question is that the perturbation in the organism is maintained by the enactment of supporting roles by other members of the community.

These levels of organismic involvement are equivalent to, if not identical with, the concept of self-involvement. At one end of the continuum, we see relatively automatic responses, stereotyped habits, autonomous functioning of self and role. At the other end, we see the unitary functioning of self and role.

selection 44 / the effects of mild frustration on the expression of prejudiced attitudes / Emory L. Cowen, University of Rochester, Judah Landes, Stanford University, and Donald E. Schaet, U. S. Marine Corps

The concept that unacceptable aggressive or hostile impulses may be "displaced" to targets more suitable than the original one has been

From Emory L. Cowen, Judah Landes, and Donald E. Schaet, "The Effects of Mild Frustration on the Expression of Prejudiced Attitudes," *Journal of Abnormal and Social Psychology*, 58:33–38, 1959. Reprinted by permission of the authors and the American Psychological Association.

with us in psychology at least since the writings of Sigmund Freud. However, it is primarily as a result of the explicit formulation of frustration-aggression theory that concerted experimental test of this proposition has been attempted in diverse areas. One specific formulation derived from these conceptualizations is that increasing personal frustration may have, as one consequence, an increase in expression of prejudice. Such a theoretical notion has been referred to as a "scapegoat" theory of prejudice. A more detailed consideration of possible relations between frustration of personal needs and prejudice has been presented by Krech and Crutchfield under the heading of "a motivational analysis of prejudice."

Criticism has been directed to a scapegoat theory of prejudice both on theoretical and empirical grounds. In the former instance, the argument has been advanced that a scapegoat theory is an insufficient basis for explaining a sizeable number of instances of prejudice. As stated, there can be little question as to the justifiability of this argument. On the other hand, a scapegoat theory of prejudice may quite appropriately be viewed as no more than one of a series of explanatory principles required for complete understanding of the phenomena of prejudice. Gordon Allport, in his scholarly treatment of this problem, takes exactly such a position. Allport reviews six major classes of theoretical explanations of prejudice and points out that each seems to constitute a constructive vehicle for augmentation of our understanding of the phenomenon. Allport states ". . . as a rule most 'theories' are advanced by their authors to call attention to some one important causal factor, without implying that no other causal factors are operating." It may therefore be important to re-emphasize that when we are dealing with complex social processes such as, for example, prejudice, delinquency, industrial conflict, and international tensions, multiple determinants are likely to be involved. The identification of a single determinant does not in any way positively demonstrate that this is a sole determinant; nor does it necessarily preclude the operation of differing determinants toward the same end result.

An examination of some empirical data bearing on a scapegoat type theory indicates fairly conclusively that such an explanation should indeed be considered partial. For example, Morse and Allport, in a comprehensive investigation of seven hypotheses about the causes of anti-Semitism, found that only the factor of "national involvement" co-varied uniquely with anti-Semitism. "Circumstance frustration," the factor most directly derivable from a scapegoat theory, related only modestly to discriminatory treatment of Jews, leading the authors to conclude that scapegoat theories may not be taken as "general explanations of anti-Semitism."

Lindzey, in partial support of a scapegoat explanation, reported that both high and low prejudice Ss increased significantly in displaced aggression following frustration. On the other hand, since the high prejudice Ss (contrary to deductions) failed to displace more aggression than the lows, the author rejects scapegoating as a comprehensive explanatory principle.

Studies offering less qualified support for the existence of the scapegoating phenomenon are also reported in the literature. Thus Allport and Kramer, in their classic investigation of the "roots of prejudice," observe that among their Ss (Harvard, Dartmouth, and Radcliffe undergraduates) Catholic and Jewish Ss who saw themselves as more victimized also tended to be more prejudiced toward other minority groups. These findings, interpreted within a frustration aggression framework, were subsequently replicated by Rosenblith with South Dakota undergraduates. Gough found that high anti-Semite Ss are "less able to overlook and ignore minor irritations and frustrations." Mussen reports that high prejudice children had stronger aggressive and dominant needs than did low prejudice Ss, and that they also showed an increase in prejudiced feelings toward Negroes, in contrast to lows who showed a decrease, following four weeks in an interracial summer camp. Finally, Bettleheim and Janowitz have demonstrated significant contingencies between downward social mobility of veterans and intensity of anti-Semitic and anti-Negro attitudes.

With regard to the empirical data thus far reviewed, we may tentatively conclude that a scapegoat concept provides a basis for understanding some instances of prejudice, but is insufficient as a general explanatory principle. Two additional investigations, each of which constitutes a direct test of the scapegoat proposition, remain to be considered. Miller and Bugelski, working in the context of a CCC camp, were able to show a significant drop in positive attitudes and some trend toward increasing negative attitudes toward Mexicans and Japanese following a rather realistic experimental induction of frustration. On the basis of these findings the authors concluded that frustration increased aggression, which was in turn displaced in the form of deterioration of attitude to minority group members.

Recently, however, on the basis of some experimental work by Congdon, as reported by Stagner and Congdon, some question has been raised with respect to the generality, if not substance, of the Miller and Bugelski findings. Congdon assessed attitudes toward various in-groups and out-groups using a series of modified Osgood semantic-differential-type scales. Following this, experimental Ss in two groups were either mildly or strongly frustrated by failure on two of four or four of four subtests of the Grace-Arthur, respectively. A control group received no frustration. Subsequent readministration of the attitude scales indicated no differences in attitude change scores among the three groups. On the basis of these data, Congdon challenges the defensibility of a scapegoat theory of prejudice. He goes on to speculate that the failure to support the Miller and Bugelski findings may reflect some combination of: (*a*) having used a less arbitrary type of frustration, (*b*) having provided outlets for self-punitive behavior which were presumed not to have been present in the Miller and Bugelski experiment, and (*c*) the higher intellectual level of his subjects.

If on theoretical grounds one espouses, as we have, the view that a scapegoat theory of prejudice may be most useful as one of a series of complementary explanatory principles underlying the complex social phenomenon of prejudice, the Congdon findings raise the question as to whether such a view is useful *even* as a single particularist explanation for understanding some manifestations of prejudice. It is to this latter specific issue that the present research is addressed. In essence, we have attempted to re-examine the proposition that frustration will lead to an increased verbal expression of prejudice, preserving in our design the features of nonarbitrariness, opportunity for expressive and self punitive behavior, and high intelligence level of Ss, to which Congdon has attributed his negative findings.

Method

Instruments Two comparable subscales, each presumably measuring authoritarian attitudes and minority group prejudice, were drawn from a larger pool of items utilized in the California studies. These included the 30-item F scale (combined Forms 40 and 45), the 12-item Anti-Negro (AN) scale, and eight items each from the Anti-Minority (AM) and Patriotism (P) scales of the larger Ethnocentrism (E) scale. Items were assigned so that the subtests would be equated with respect to item discrimination quotients as reported in *The Authoritarian Personality*. The final forms (X and Q) each contained 29 items as follows. (*a*) F scale—15 items, (*b*) AN scale—6 items, (*c*) AM scale—4 items, (*d*) P scale—4 items.

Subjects and procedure Subjects (Ss) were 32 male and 32 female introductory psychology volunteers, all of whom were tested individually. The actual experiment consisted of three phases: the attitude pretest, frustration, and the attitude posttest. In the pretest phase, Ss were given either Form X or Form Q of the attitude scale, with order of presentation counterbalanced for both sexes. Immediately following completion of this first attitude scale, Ss were informed that we wished to collect some additional and separate data bearing on the problem-solving habits of college students. It was in this context that frustration was introduced.

In order to induce frustration, all Ss were given two puzzles which, though appearing soluble, were functionally nonsoluble in the time allotted. The actual puzzles used were the nine-dot problem reported by Cowen, and one of the Katona match stick problems. Fictitious time norms were given, so as to increase the likelihood that frustration would occur. The actual time allotted by E fell far short of what would be needed by most people to solve the problems. The attitude of the E during administration of the frustrating puzzles might best be described as aloof, nonsupporting, and disbelieving of Ss inability to achieve a correct solution. Upon the Ss failure to solve the second puzzle E stated simply, "I'm afraid our time is up for this problem too. We will have to complete the second part of the attitude scale now." The S then completed the alternate form of the combined attitude scale.

Results

Table 1 summarizes mean "pre" and "post" frustration test scores for each of the attitude test subscales. The data are presented separately by sex and for the two orders of administration.

For each of the constituent subscales, a three-way analysis of variance was carried out, involving the main effects of test form (A), sex (B), and pre-post frustration (C). Since both test form and pre-post frustration (the effect in which our major interest centered) are "within subjects" effects, a Lindquist Type IV design was employed as the basic model for the analysis. In general, the only subscale that presented consistently positive findings was the AN scale.

AN scale Table 2 presents the results of a three-way analysis of variance for the Anti-Negro scale. The most salient findings in this table are the significant F ratios involving pre-post frustration (C). Although the main effect here is highly significant, suggesting, in support of our hypothesis, the presence of stronger anti-Negro feelings following frustration, this finding may be pinpointed somewhat more specifically by noting other significant main effects and interactions, together with the means presented in Table 1. Thus it appears that there may be differences in the two supposedly equated subtests, with higher AN scores being given on Form Q. Perhaps more germane is the significant B × C interaction, indicating that male Ss express significantly stronger anti-Negro attitudes after frustration than do female Ss.

TABLE 1   MEAN "PRE" AND "POST" SCORES FOR ALL SUBSCALES

		Order			
Scale	Sex	X pre	Q post	Q pre	X post
AN	M	11.2	15.6	10.4	10.6
	F	9.9	11.3	11.3	10.8
F	M	49.7	44.9	44.0	55.2
	F	47.4	42.6	40.9	46.3
AM	M	8.6	9.4	10.3	9.4
	F	7.8	8.8	7.9	8.1
P	M	13.6	11.7	13.4	13.5
	F	12.4	11.4	12.1	12.9

TABLE 2 ANALYSIS OF VARIANCE FOR ANTI-NEGRO SCALE

Source	df	Sum of squares	Mean square	F	P
Between Ss	63	1942.5			
B	1	39.1	39.1	1.33	n.s.
A × C	1	48.5	48.5	1.64	n.s.
A × B × C	1	86.4	86.4	2.93	n.s.
Error (b)	60	1768.5	29.5		
Within Ss	64	345.5			
A	1	73.3	73.3	25.28	.001
C	1	58.0	58.0	20.00	.001
A × B	1	9.8	9.8	3.38	n.s.
B × C	1	30.2	30.2	10.41	.01
Error (w)	60	174.2	2.9		
Total	127	2228.0			

Note: A = Test form; B = Sex; and C = Pre-post frustration.

Incidental findings For the P scale, no significant main effects or interactions are observed. The pattern of findings for the AM and F scales is highly similar. In each case there are significant differences in the two test forms, a finding entirely tangential to our present focus, and on both scales there is either a significant (AM) or near significant (F) main effect of sex. Male Ss tend to score consistently higher (more negative attitudes) on both of these scales. This difference, however, is a general one, which does not vary systematically for "pre" vs. "post" frustration.

In order to test the generality of responses to the various subtests, a series of 12 Pearson product-moment correlations, in which AN scores were related to each of the other three scale scores (by sex, for both the "pre" and "post" tests), were computed. The correlations ranged in magnitude from .27 to .58 and averaged .40. These correlations are substantially lower than the ones reported by the California group.

Discussion

The most notable finding in the present experiment is the significant increase in anti-Negro feelings following experimental induction of frustration. Such a datum offers additional support for the existence of the scapegoat phenomenon and is quite consistent with earlier findings of Miller and Bugelski. Of incidental interest is the consistent trend observed on three of the subscales for male Ss to show greater prejudice (as well as greater increase in prejudice following frustration on the AN scale) than do females. This finding too is in line with empirical evidence and theoretical expectations discussed elsewhere.

There remains a sharp contrast between our basic findings in support of a scapegoat theory and those of Congdon which fail to support this view. The latter has proposed that his failure to obtain significant postfrustration effects may reflect some combination of less severe and less arbitrary frustration, provision of opportunities for self-punitive behavior, and the higher intellectual level of his Ss. In the present study, frustration was neither severe nor arbitrary or, at least insofar as can be judged, no more so than Congdon's. Opportunities for self-punitive behaviors should have been roughly comparable, as was the intellectual level of the Ss. These factors notwithstanding, it was possible to demonstrate the operation of the scapegoat effect in the present study.

The source of the discrepant findings in these two ostensibly comparable studies cannot be identified with any confidence, but several procedural variations may be noted that might have obscured the scapegoat effect in the Congdon experiment. The attitude dimensions used for the ratings tended to have quite highly crystallized social desirability values (e.g., *kind—cruel, strong—weak*, etc.). Both pre- and postscores may thus have been pushed toward the socially desirable response, obscuring differences. Then, too, the use of identical items in both pre- and posttest (in contrast to the alternate forms of the present study) may have operated to help sophisticated Ss sense the purpose of the experiment. Finally, Congdon used speed instructions, which may possibly have impaired the reliability of the attitude scales.

Possibly the most interesting issue raised by our findings is the fact that significantly higher anti-Negro attitudes are present following frustration, in the absence of a parallel increase in F, AM, and P scale scores. In the basic development of these scales, substantially high intercorrelations have been reported. Whether such correlations reflect a true clustering of these classes of attitudes, or a pervasiveness of response tendency behavior, the fact remains that there was reason to anticipate that they would have "behaved" similarly in our study. However, they did not. Our own pre- and postscale intercorrelations run substantially lower than those originally reported, suggesting that our Ss responded with a degree of independence to the subscales. The positive results on the AN scale can be seen most defensibly as an illustration of "targeting" a specific minority group. That the Negro is the targeted group in the present study may be a manifestation of a tendency noted earlier by Horowitz for this group to constitute a preferred target in this geographic locale. In another vein, Bettleheim and Janowitz observe that thresholds for anti-Negro prejudice may be lower than those for other minority groups to the point where negative attitudes may break through despite the presence of "relatively adequate controls." In agreement with such an interpretation is our observation that anti-Negro feelings seem to constitute a preferred prejudice in informal conversations of undergraduates at this institution.

In general overview, the present findings are viewed as confirming the hypothesis that frustration augments the expression of prejudice. The major limitation placed upon this conclusion is that the consequent increase in prejudice may be specific rather than generalized. Our findings in no way limit the role or importance of other types of antecedents of prejudice. Undoubtedly the relationships between many such antecedents and the same final product will have to be identified if we are ultimately to have an adequate, comprehensive theory of prejudice. For the present, however, the usefulness of a scapegoat theory, at least as one of a series of complementary explanatory principles, appears defensible.

Summary

The present study was designed to test the proposition that frustration may increase the expression of prejudice. Sixty-four Ss were given a series of attitude scales, following which all were exposed to a relatively mild, experimentally induced frustration. Immediately thereafter, alternate forms of the attitude scale were administered.

Significant increases were found in the expression of anti-Negro prejudice following frustration, this effect being more pronounced in male Ss. Since comparable postfrustration effects were not observed on other subscales, the results were interpreted as an instance of "targeting" of a minority group within the general framework of the scapegoat phenomenon.

selection 45 / sex-role development in a changing culture / Daniel G. Brown, United States Air Force Academy

One of the more significant psychosocial developments of contemporary American society would appear to be the relatively fluid state of the sex roles of individuals. Within a single generation, significant changes have taken place in the traditional conceptions of what is masculine and what is feminine. Whether such changes have been abrupt enough to be considered a cultural revolution or sufficiently

Abridged from Daniel G. Brown, "Sex-role Development in a Changing Culture," *Psychological Bulletin*, 55:232–242, 1958. Reprinted by permission of the author and the American Psychological Association.

gradual to be simply degrees of cultural variation is difficult to judge. In either case, however, this changed and changing cultural pattern has a number of implications and possible effects that bear directly on individual, group, and institutional behavior. In this connection such questions as the following might be asked: What are some of these changes that have taken place in the sex roles? Have such changes been more pronounced in the feminine role than in the masculine role? How have these changes affected the life adjustment of individuals? And the relationships of the sexes with each other? What about the effect on boys and girls at the present time and in the years ahead? These are just a few of the problems in the area of masculinity-femininity development and adjustment that need to be studied and investigated.

The present paper is primarily directed toward a consideration of the nature and theoretical implications of sex-role development in children.

DIFFERENTIATION OF SEX AND SEX ROLE

As a starting point, consideration might be given to the age at which the child becomes aware of biological sex differentiation per se as well as when the child becomes aware of the essential meaning of "masculine" and "feminine," i.e., sex-role behavior.[1] At what age for example is the average child able to distinguish between the sexes and to distinguish himself or herself as a boy or girl? Evidence suggests that between two thirds and three fourths of children by the age of three are able to make this basic distinction.

Evidence also suggests that sex-role differentiation is a gradual process, probably beginning in the second year of life and becoming definitely established by the age of three. By or during the fifth year most children make a clear differentiation between the more obvious biological cues of maleness and femaleness and psychological cues of masculinity and femininity. As in the other aspects of psychological development, there are undoubtedly wide individual differences in the clarity with which differences between the sexes are perceived by children.

In any event, whatever the exact age in a particular case, it seems safe to conclude that preschool children as a group become fully aware of the fact that the world is divided into two groups of people and that, depending on whether one belongs to one group or the other, different behavior patterns are expected accordingly. At an early age, then, children are being conditioned to and are actively acquiring their

[1] The concept, *sex role*, refers to those psychological characteristics and behavioral patterns that are typical of one sex in contrast to the other sex. The sex role of a person consists of the behavior that is socially defined and expected of that person because of his or her status as a male or female.

sex roles. One of the most important considerations here has to do with the *meaning* and *significance* to the child of the earliest perceptions of structural and sex-role differences between boys and girls. What does it mean to a child to become aware of his sex for the first time, and gradually, his sex role? For the child to feel safe, secure, and satisfied in his emerging sexual identity would appear to be one of the most important conditions in his entire development.

SEX-ROLE PREFERENCE IN CHILDREN

Related to the factor of age in sex and sex-role differentiation in children is the phenomenon of sex-role preference. Does preference for one sex role over the other parallel the developing awareness of the difference between the masculine and feminine roles? Or does preference come later, only after the child has been exposed sufficiently to the differential treatments accorded boys in contrast to girls? The origin and earliest occurrence of sex-role preference is a problem that awaits research investigation. That definite preferences exist in young children for one or the other sex role, however, has been reasonably well demonstrated by several studies. This problem has been investigated by the present writer by means of a technique known as the *It Scale for Children*, a scale composed of 36 picture cards, three by four, of objects and figures typically associated with the masculine or feminine roles in our culture (e.g., preferring to play with a tractor rather than a doll; wearing a dress rather than trousers; preferring to be a boy rather than a girl, etc.). A child-figure called "It," relatively ambiguous as to sexual identity, is used in administering the scale by having each child make choices for It, rather than the child himself or herself making the choices directly. Results based on the use of the It Scale with children between the ages of about 3½ and 11½, most of whom were from middle class homes, show that beginning with the youngest preschool group (Ages 3½ to 5½) and extending through the fourth grade (Ages 9½ to 10½) boys express a stronger preference for the masculine role than girls do for the feminine role. For example, at the kindergarten and third-grade levels, about 85% and 95% of the boys respectively indicate that It would rather be an "Indian Chief" than an "Indian Princess." And when asked which shoes It would rather "dress up and play house in," about 75% and 95% of the kindergarten and third-grade boys respectively chose men's rather than women's shoes.

Girls between the ages of 3½ and 6½ are quite heterogeneous as a group: some are predominantly feminine, choosing practically all of the feminine alternatives; others are predominantly masculine, and still others are "in-betweens," choosing both masculine and feminine alternatives. Taken as a group, for example, 50% express a preference for It "playing grownups" with cosmetic articles and 50% with shaving articles.

After about the sixth year and extending through the ninth year, most girls show a very strong preference for masculine in contrast to feminine things. For example, between 60% and 70% of the girls in the first, second, third, and fourth grades indicate that It would rather work with "building" tools than with "cooking and baking" utensils.

It is not known whether girls in the fifth grade and beyond (age group from about 10 to 11 and older) become less masculine in preference. Brown's study of fifth-grade subjects indicated a definite feminine changeover in girls, but Hogan failed to find any such change in the preference patterns of either fifth- or sixth-grade subjects. The whole problem of change in sex-role preference in relation to age needs further and more intensive study.

In contrast to girls, boys *at all ages* show a strong preference for the masculine role. This preference is evident in the youngest group (ages 3½ to 5½) and becomes even stronger until it reaches a near maximum at about the age of eight and thereafter. Thus, between 90% and 95% of boys in the second, third, fourth, and fifth grades indicate that, given a choice, It would rather wear a shirt and trousers than a dress.

SEX-ROLE PREFERENCE IN CHILDREN COMPARED TO ADULTS

To what extent are the sex-role preference patterns of children similar to those of adults? For comparative purposes the Parental Role section of the It Scale may be used. This section involves asking the child whether It would rather be a mother or a father. Results from this section may be summarized as follows: From about 80% to 95% of boys at all ages from kindergarten through the fifth grade express a preference for It becoming a father, only 5% to 20% for It becoming a mother. On the other hand, in the case of girls from kindergarten through the fourth grade, only about 25% to 45% express a preference for It becoming a mother, while between 55% and 75% for It becoming a father.

These results in the case of children are quite consistent with studies of adults in our culture which asked men and women: "Have you sometimes wished you were of the opposite sex?" or "If you could be born over again, would you rather be a man or a woman?" or "Have you ever wished that you belonged to the opposite sex?" Results may be summarized as follows: only between 2½% and 4% of adult men compared to between 20% and 31% of adult women recall *consciously* having been aware of the desire to be of the opposite sex. And in Puerto Rico only 33% of a group of adult female students compared to about 93% of male students indicated they would prefer to be female and male respectively if they "could come to life again after death." This lopsided preference for being male in preference to being female is also reflected in a recent survey of several hundred university students at Ohio State University who were asked whether they would rather have a male or female child in their family if they could have only one child. The results showed that 91% of the men and 66% of the women students expressed a preference for a male child. When both groups are combined, boys were preferred by approximately 75% and girls by only 25% of these students.

A significant problem connected with these findings concerns the psychological effect on large numbers of women who openly admit having preferred to be male. How does such awareness affect the self-concept of a girl or woman? The result, according to White is to undermine a woman's respect for herself as a woman and to derogate the feminine role in general.

An important anthropological analysis in connection with sex differences in acceptance of appropriate sex roles would be a *cross-cultural* comparison of the percentage of men compared to women who had preferred to be of the opposite sex. Compared to those cultures, for example, where male domination reaches exaggerated proportions, very different results might be expected among the Burmese, Ojibwa Indians and Tchambuli where females have relatively high status and a favorable position in their society.

FACTORS RELATED TO MASCULINE ROLE PREFERENCE

What factors are functionally related to the much greater preference that boys show for the masculine role than girls show for the feminine role and for the definite preference that many girls show for the masculine role? Although this is a problem in relation to which much research is needed, several conditions or factors may be suggested as contributory.

First, there is the emphasis by Freud on the *anatomical difference* between males and females, the effect of which is supposed to make the boy proud of his status and the girl dissatisfied with hers. Having versus not having a penis allegedly "explains" why girls as well as boys prefer to be boys.

Another attempt to account for sex differences in role preference is the emphasis by Adler on *sociocultural advantages* that go with being male in contrast to being female. The little girl may early perceive the greater prestige and numerous privileges connected with the masculine role. This would tend to arouse envy and drive her in the direction of wanting that which she does not have, namely, masculine status. Adler introduced the concept of "masculine protest" to refer to this phenomenon. That our culture has been and still is masculine-centered and masculine-oriented is obvious. The superior position and privileged status of the male permeates nearly every aspect, minor and major, of our social life. The gadgets and prizes in boxes of breakfast cereal, for example, commonly have a strong masculine rather than feminine appeal.[2] And the most basic social institutions perpetuate this pattern of masculine aggrandizement. Thus, the Judeo-Christian faiths involve worshipping God, a "Father," rather than a "Mother," and Christ, a "Son," rather than a "Daughter."

A third factor relative to the difference between the sexes in role preference is the *greater latitude* of the girls compared to the boys in sex-role development. It appears somewhat paradoxical that, although restricted much more in practically all other respects, girls are allowed *more* freedom than boys in sex-role learning. This is, however, simply consistent with the idea that masculine status is so superior to feminine status that many girls are not even discouraged from striving to attain the former. For a girl to be a tomboy does not involve the censure that results when a boy is a sissy. With little, if any, embarrassment or threat, girls may show strong preference for the masculine role; this is not true in the case of boys.

Further evidence of the fact that girls in contrast to boys not only have much more opportunity to pattern their behavior after the model of the opposite sex but in many cases actually do so is cited by Cunningham. She reports on a group of fourth- and fifth-grade students who, when asked to describe what they consider to be some of the "pressing problems in human relations" included the following: "How can I stop my sister from being a tomboy?" Other examples that may be cited include:

Clothing Girls may wear shirts and trousers with little or no social disapproval, but boys do not wear skirts or dresses; in fact, men who wear feminine clothing, i.e., transvestites, do so at the risk of severe social censure and even legal punishment.

Names Many girls are given masculinized names such as Jackie, Stephanie, Billie, Pauline, Jo, Roberta, Frankie, etc., but few boys are given feminized names.

Toys and play activities Girls may play with any or all of the toys typically associated with boys (e.g., cars, trucks, erector sets, guns, etc.) but boys are discouraged from playing with toys that are considered feminine (e.g., dolls, dishes, sewing materials, etc.).

Goodenough has commented on the greater freedom of girls in sex-typed play as follows: "A boy is not likely to be a Dale Evans, but a girl often becomes Roy Rogers, or any of his masculine col-

[2] Typical examples include: military equipment, cowboy paraphernalia, police badges, airplanes, boats, trains, spaceships, marbles, yo-yoes, miniature auto license plates, etc.

leagues. Boys are rarely glamour girls, but many little girls fall eagerly into the roles of space men, or masculine rough riders."

Based on research findings that show boys consistently making more appropriate sex-typed choices than girls, Rabban and Hurlock conclude that "boys are more aware of sex-appropriate behavior than girls." Rather than being "more aware" than girls, however, it is the relative lack of flexibility of boys in sex-role choices that probably accounts for some of the difference between boys and girls in this regard. Boys simply do not have the same freedom of choice as girls when it comes to sex-typed objects and activities. In this connection, Hartley raises the question as to whether or not results of studies of sex-role preference in children, rather than measuring role preference as such, might not simply reflect the fact that girls are given much and boys little opportunity for variation in expressing preferences for sex-typed objects and activities. This is a good point and should be explored further.

As to the basis of the narrow, rigid sex-typing pattern in males, Goodenough presents evidence that suggests fathers show *greater concern* than mothers for sex-appropriate behavior in their children. In other words, father is more likely than mother to insist that "junior" look and talk and act like a *man*. This pattern, which would tend to have greater impact on the boy than the girl, is consistent with findings presented in the present paper, showing boys are much more likely than girls to make sex-appropriate choices.

Related to these differences in sex roles in childhood appears to be a parallel difference in adult occupational roles. Even though women traditionally have been subject to various kinds of vocational and economic discrimination, it is still true that a woman may and does enter a "masculine" vocation or profession, e.g., bus driver, engineer, lawyer, etc., with less social disapproval or concern as to one's sex-role "normality" than a man who enters a "feminine" field, e.g., hair stylist, dress designer, nurse, etc. The census in 1950, for example, revealed that women are now in all of the 446 occupations reported by the census. Among the 16,000,000 American women employed, there are "lady" carpenters, sailors, tractor drivers, pilots, telephone linesmen, locomotive engineers, lumbermen, firemen, and even stevedores and longshoremen!

SEX-ROLE IDENTIFICATION AND SEX-ROLE PREFERENCE

In dealing with the complex problem of sex-role behavior it seems particularly important to distinguish between sex-role identification and sex-role preference. *Identification* is the basic process in which a child, at first involuntarily, and later consciously, learns to think, feel, and act like members of one sex in contrast to the other sex. *Prefer-*

ence refers to the tendency to adopt the sex role of one sex in contrast to that of the other sex, the former being perceived as more desirable and attractive. With this distinction in mind it is possible to delineate three major sex-role patterns: (*a*) Identification with and preference for the sex role of one's own sex, e.g., a girl may identify with and prefer the feminine role; (*b*) Identification with the sex role of one's own sex but preference for the sex role of the opposite sex, e.g., a girl may identify with the feminine role but prefer the masculine role; (*c*) Identification with the sex role of the opposite sex but preference for the sex role of one's own sex, e.g., a girl may identify with the masculine role but prefer the feminine role. Of the two processes, identification appears to be primary, while preference is more or less secondary relative to sex-role behavior. In normal development the two form a single, integrative process.

In view of the finding that masculine role preference appears to be widespread among girls, it might be hypothesized that conflict or confusion will be conspicuous in their sex-role development. Thus, the fact that girls are destined for feminine functions in adulthood, yet envy and attempt to emulate the masculine role in childhood, would tend to produce ambivalence and a lack of clarity in the feminine role. On the basis of a study of sex-role learning in five-year-olds, for example, Fauls and Smith refer to the "lack of clear definition" of a sex role in the case of female children. Related to this is the contradiction between the sex-role identification of many girls with the feminine model and the tendency for them to prefer the masculine role.

On the other hand, boys do not necessarily escape difficulties in sex-role development. Even though the culture greatly favors the male, the fact that boys must shift *from* an original identification-attachment with the mother *to* an identification with the father may create difficulties for boys that girls do not experience. Thus, Sears reports that six-year-old boys have not identified with their fathers as well as girls have with their mothers. On the basis of extensive observations of children in preschools, Hartley arrives at a conclusion similar to that of Sears and, in addition, raises the question as to whether many boys really experience their fathers in their paternal role. She also questions whether many boys even picture themselves as "future fathers."

It is also true that a considerable number of boys get overly exposed to the feminine model in early life when the mother is much more prominent in the life of the child than the father. This is especially likely to occur if for any reason the father is psychologically distant or a predominantly negative figure for the son and there is no adequate substitute.

According to Parsons and Gorer a major effect of the situation in which the father is typically away most of the time while the mother is around continually exemplifying the feminine model is to facilitate the role development of the girl and to complicate the role development of the boy. These writers seem to emphasize the *quantity* of the parent-child relationship rather than the *quality* of such a relationship. In other words, the degree that the child respects, admires and loves the parent may be much more significant than the sheer amount of contact, per se.

SEX-ROLE DEVELOPMENT AND ADULT SEXUAL ADJUSTMENT

A boy who incorporates the basic features of the feminine model via predominant identification with the mother intrinsically will feel most comfortable in the feminine role, which to him is "normal" and "natural." Such a boy will show a "feminine protest," i.e., he will protest any restriction of his desire and effort to become thoroughly feminine. He will often plead and even demand the freedom to adopt the feminine role. This is the developmental pattern in childhood that seems to provide the basis for sex-role inversion in adulthood. In fact, inversion refers precisely to the adoption of the basic behavior patterns that are characteristic of the opposite sex.

In cases of males that do not involve a relatively complete inversion of sex role but do show considerable feminine identification, the result may be boys who become rebellious and develop strong defensive reactions in the form of extreme aggressiveness as a means of attempting to counteract their underlying inverted tendencies. MacDonald has presented a number of cases of "effeminate" boys who developed pathological aggressive reactions.

Although direct evidence is limited it appears that the child's eventual sexual orientation and adjustment in adolescence and adulthood bears a direct relationship with the nature of his sex-role development in childhood. Adult sexual behavior, at least in part, appears to be an outgrowth of the individual's underlying sex role. Thus, a normal male is one who has identified with, incorporated, and prefers the masculine role; his sexual desire for the female is one aspect of this role. A boy who has identified with, incorporated, and prefers the feminine role will most likely desire a male as a sexual partner in adulthood in keeping with the inverted role pattern. The problem of normal and inverted sex-role development has been discussed in another paper.

SEX-ROLE CONVERGENCE: A NEW CULTURAL PATTERN EMERGING?

Despite the fact that boys, much more than girls, show a concern for behaving along sex-appropriate lines, there has been considerable change in the direction of both masculine and feminine roles becoming broader, less rigidly defined, less sex-typed, and more overlapping with each other. As Seward observes, "Today in the post-World War II United States, there is a good deal less self-consciousness about sex roles and probably more freedom of choice for the individual than ever before." In line with this observation is a new course in domestic arts for eighth-graders in a public school in Jersey City, New Jersey, in which boys learn how to cook, sew, and become "efficient housewives," and in which girls learn how to handle "man-sized tools," do woodwork, plumbing repairs, and become the "man-of-the-house." This course is described as so successful that the sexes may be switched in all eighth-grade homemaking and shop courses in the Jersey City system. The same type of course has been established recently in a junior high school in St. Petersburg, Florida. And in the public senior high schools in Denver, Colorado, courses in cooking for boys, metal crafts and lathe work for girls, and child care and training for both boys and girls are offered.

Other indications of the trend toward increasing similarity of sex roles include: (a) similarity of educational experiences of girls and boys from kindergarten through the secondary school system; (b) husbands doing the dishes, cleaning the house and carrying out other domestic tasks historically considered exclusively "feminine"; (c) wives holding down jobs outside the home, many of which have been traditionally "masculine"; and (d) the apparel of boys and men that emphasize color, softness, and more delicate features along with the adoption by girls and women of all kinds of "masculine" clothing, hair styles, etc.

Mead and Seward have pointed out that this greater flexibility in sex-role learning makes for increased interfamily variability and, hence, increasing cultural diversity in this regard. Is it still possible, in our culture for example, to speak of *the* feminine role or *the* masculine role? Or is it necessary to refer to various *roles?* Thus, within a single neighborhood, the role of the husband-father in one home involves almost absolute control, while the role of the wife-mother is strictly subservient and dependent. Next door, the dominating control of the family may be maintained by the wife-mother, while the husband-father is little more than a financially convenient "boarder." Across the street there may be hostile competitiveness and a continual "power struggle" between the husband-father and the wife-mother, each at times emerging "victorious," the other "defeated." And, in still another home, the respective roles of husband-father and wife-mother are largely complementary and equalitarian rather than hierarchical. What must be the effect of these very different parental role patterns on the sex-role identifications and preferences of children who are developing in these respective familial environments? For example, how is the process by which a boy becomes like his father (i.e., "a man") influenced by the various role structures in such families? It is plausible that degree of ease and normality or difficulty and abnormality is directly related to the particular parental role relationships. Intensive study in this area is very much needed.

Finally, on a culture-wide level, the rapid changes in the sex roles of the Japanese during the past decade might be cited. Among other contributing factors, the cultural diffusion stemming from American occupation of Japan has brought about far-reaching changes, particularly in the feminine role. In a country that gave rise to the expression "as unimportant as a Japanese woman," the traditional and relatively complete subordination of the female to the male appears to be on the way out and is being replaced by a status of women that is beginning to approach that of men. This trend is reflected not only in the fact that women can now vote, an unheard of practice ten years ago, but also in the hopes and aspirations of Japanese children as revealed in their drawings. When asked to draw pictures depicting what they wanted to be when they were grown, many girls drew pictures of teachers, secretaries, industrial workers, beauticians, scientists, etc.

A somewhat parallel development to that in Japan has been taking place in Germany during the past decade or so. Here, too, feminine status has undergone marked change in the direction of greater freedom and opportunity for women in the educational and economic spheres. A continuing sociopsychological analysis of such significant and rapid changes in the feminine sex role of the Japanese and Germans should be very informative and valuable, especially in terms of the impact on the present and future generation of children.

SUMMARY

The young child, as early as the second year of life, begins to distinguish between male and female and between masculine and feminine. Preference for one sex role or the other also begins to emerge early in the life of the child, probably by the third year.

Beginning at the kindergarten level and extending through the fourth grade, boys show a much stronger preference for aspects of the masculine role than girls show for aspects of the feminine role. In fact, a majority of girls in Grades 1 through 4 express greater preference for masculine things than for feminine things. These results are based on the It Scale for Children, a masculinity-femininity projective technique for use with young children.

The finding that girls more than boys show a preference for the role of the opposite sex is paralleled by studies of adults in our culture which reveal that between five and twelve times as many women as men recall having wished they were of the opposite sex.

As to the basis of masculine role preference in both sexes, three factors are mentioned: (*a*) the Freudian emphasis on the anatomical differences between males and females; (*b*) the Adlerian emphasis on sociocultural favoritism of the male compared to the female; and (*c*) the fact that the girl has more latitude than the boy in expressing a preference for sex-typed objects and activities.

A child may identify with and prefer the sex role appropriate to his own sex; or he may identify with and prefer the sex role of the opposite sex; or he may identify with one sex role and prefer the other. A distinction between sex-role identification and sex-role preference is emphasized.

In some ways girls would appear to have a more difficult time than boys in sex-role development; in other ways the development of boys would seem to be more complicated. The general problem of sex differences in ease of masculinity-femininity development is discussed.

Adult sexual adjustment or maladjustment is related to the nature and outcome of sex-role development in childhood.

There are definite signs that a convergence of the two sex roles gradually is taking place in our society. This cultural trend is evident in the increasing overlap between things and activities formerly considered "exclusively masculine" or "exclusively feminine." A major effect of this emerging cultural pattern is widespread interfamily variability in the sex roles of family members.

Finally, attention is called to the rapid changes in the feminine sex role in Japan and Germany during the past ten years. Emphasis is placed on the need for a continuing sociopsychological analysis of sex-role development in such changing cultures as those of the Japanese and Germans as well as that of our own.

CHAPTER 11 ⚙ THE SELF
AND BEHAVIOR ⚙

Perhaps no other word is used more frequently in conversation than the personal pronoun "I." Each of us lives in a universe which seems to have himself as its center. Although psychologists disagree as to the kinds of behavior from which this concept of self may be validly inferred, there is increasing agreement that understanding of human behavior is greatly facilitated by the use of this concept. Definitions of the term are diverse but seem to agree that "self" refers to the organized structure of conceptions that each person has about his feelings, motivations, attitudes, roles, etc. Simply put, self may be thought of as a person's conception of who he is. Some aspects of the individual's self concept may be quite conscious and easily verbalized, for example, "I am a college student." Other facets may be quite difficult to think about without great anxiety, for example, "I feel an intense hatred for my mother." In this latter case the person may automatically avoid perceiving these negative aspects of himself. In psychoanalytic terms, these motivations become repressed.

The development of this cognitive-emotive self-structure begins with the child's discrimination that his body is somehow different from other objects or persons. Further, one's self-concept continues throughout life to be closely associated with his conception of his body (bodyimage). Children take great pride in the development and growth of their bodies. However, there is perhaps no other period of life during which the individual is so body-conscious as during adolescence and early adulthood; witness the hours which teen-agers (both boys and girls) spend before the mirror. It is also during this period that there is most rapid change in the self-concept. Much of teen-age anxiety, hostility, and changeability reflects the person's attempts to define himself more independently of the views of himself which he has learned from other people. As was noted in our discussion of roles, expectations of others and of self may be greatly influenced by any biological factors which tend to make the person different from his reference group. Drs. Mary Cover Jones and Paul Henry Mussen have performed a series of investigations which help us to understand better the importance of early and late sexual development on the self-concepts, motives, and attitudes of adolescents. Their research, reported in Selection 46, indicates that early maturing girls have significantly more favorable conceptions of themselves and greater need for recognition by others than do late maturing girls. You may wonder, *"Since early maturation would certainly make these girls 'different,' why would this not be detrimental to their conception of self?" The answer seems to lie in the fact that this difference is in the positively valued direction. It is interpreted as a sign of superior growth and maturity rather than a deficit.*

Several previous selections in this book have emphasized the tendency toward growth which seems to be characteristic of organisms from birth onwards (Gesell, Selection 11, and Maslow, Selections 15 and 16). Even though in neurotics this growth tendency may be hidden by self-defeating and self-depreciating behavior, the experiences of clinical psychologists with patients in psychotherapy suggest that the tendency toward growth can make itself manifest. The individual can become more adequate in his everyday relationships with others and come to evaluate himself more realistically. The assumption that each person has a capacity to grow beyond his present state of functioning is central to the personality theory and the nondirective psychotherapy which has been presented by Dr. Carl R. Rogers. In Selection 47 Dr. Rogers shares with us some of his hypotheses about changes in a person's self-concept, feelings, and behavior which occur as a result of psychotherapy. He indicates that the person becomes more accurately sensitive to his real feelings and trusts these experiences to redefine continually his conception of self. As a result, he becomes more independent of the evaluations of others in defining who he is. Rogers expresses this new discovery of self most beautifully in these words: ". . . to an increasing degree he becomes himself— not a facade of conformity to others, nor a cynical denial of all feeling, nor a front of intellectual rationality, but a living, breathing, feeling, fluctuating process—in short, he becomes a person."

In the previous chapter on role behavior it was emphasized that self and role conceptions interact as important determiners of behavior in social situations. A concrete example of the usefulness of the self and role concepts in understanding behavior is presented by Sarbin in Selection 48. Inferences about self-concept and role perceptions obtained from the Rorschach and Draw-A-Person tests provided a meaningful framework for describing behavior in the complex social interactions involved in hypnotic age regression. Sarbin generalizes that the validity of role taking behavior depends on the validity of perception of the interact situation, the person's ability to assume an "as if" relationship, and his self-concept.

selection 46 / self-conceptions, motivations, and interpersonal attitudes of early- and late-maturing girls / Mary Cover Jones and Paul Henry Mussen, University of California, Berkeley

"The changing body and the changing self" is a phrase associated with adolescent development. It suggests that the shaping into mature form of the childhood body pattern is accompanied by new self-concepts. These altered attitudes toward the self reflect at least in part the youth's response to his physical metamorphosis.

What "growing-up" connotes for the individual adolescent depends upon a complex of psychobiological factors. One of the most important of these is rate of physical maturation. Adolescent growth may be relatively regular and even, or it may be uneven or abrupt. The timing of puberty, in relation to social norms of the peer group, may present problems of special importance for some adolescents.

Previous reports of systematic comparisons between the behavior and personality characteristics of early- and late-maturing adolescents have indicated that acceleration in growth tends to carry social advantages for boys but disadvantages for girls. At their peak of growth, early maturing girls are not only taller than their girl classmates but are actually taller than most of the boys in their class. They are conspicuously large at a time when physical size is not an asset for girls in our culture. Many girls consider tallness to be a physical stigma. At the end of adolescence the early-maturing are no longer taller than their age-mates, but in body proportion they tend to have a broad and stocky build, less attractive (in terms of current feminine standards) than the more slender physique of the late-maturing.

Among boys, ascendance in size and musculature is an asset because of our cultural values and the functional advantages of such a build for athletic prowess. This more favorable status is indicated in observational records for early-maturing boys. Staff members rated them as physically more attractive and better-groomed than the late-maturing,

From Mary Cover Jones and Paul Henry Mussen, "Self-conceptions, Motivations and Inter-personal Attitudes of Early- and Late-Maturing Girls," *Child Development*, 29:491–501, 1958. Reprinted by permission of the authors and the Society for Research in Child Development Inc., Purdue University.

and in social situations they were more poised and matter-of-fact, and less attention-seeking.

In contrast, both classmates and adult observers saw the early-maturing girls as relatively submissive, listless or indifferent in social situations, and lacking in poise. Such girls have little influence upon the group and seldom attain a high degree of popularity, prestige or leadership.

The girls in the slower-maturing classification were seen as relatively more outgoing and more assured. They were eager, animated, peppy, and talkative. This behavior seems to be acceptable among girls since those who exhibit it are also described as confident and having leadership abilities.

While the same characteristics of expressiveness are attributed to slow-growing boys, it is associated in their case more specifically (and especially in later adolescence) with show-off behavior, affectation, and tenseness.

In accounting for these sex differences in the response to early or late puberty, we may note that although early-maturing boys have physical advantages over other boys and are socially in step with girls, the girl who develops earlier than her classmates may be temporarily isolated. H. E. Jones has expressed this as follows:

The early-maturing girl quite naturally has interests in boys and in social usages and activities more mature than those of her chronological age group. But the males of her own age are unreceptive, for while she is physiologically a year or two out of step with the girls in her class, she is three or four years out of step with the boys—a vast and terrifying degree of developmental distance.

A study of responses to the Thematic Apperception Test, given to members of the Adolescent Growth Study when they were seniors in high school, yielded a somewhat unfavorable psychological picture for the late-maturing boys. Compared with their early-maturing peers, they showed greater evidence of negative self-concepts, prolonged dependency needs, feelings of rejection by others, rebellious attitudes toward parents, and strong affiliative needs. These findings were in agreement with evidence from other sources.

A similar TAT comparison of early- and late-maturing girls should be expected to show results different from those obtained for boys. Thus, it might be expected that early-maturing girls would reveal negative self-feeling and less satisfactory interpersonal attitudes.

Procedure

The present study, paralleling that for boys, was designed to investigate the relationship between maturational status and self-conceptions, motivations, and interpersonal attitudes in a normal public school sample of girls. Personality assessment was made on the basis of their responses to the Thematic Apperception Test (TAT).

The 34 17-year-old girls of this investigation constitute approximately the 20 per cent at each extreme of the total sample of the Adolescent Growth Study, selected on the basis of their physical maturity status as determined by X-rays of the wrists and hands. Sixteen had been among the most consistently accelerated over a four-year period during adolescence; the other 18 were among the most consistently retarded. All of the subjects took the TAT at around age 17 when they were seniors in high school.

The TAT consisted of 18 pictures: nine from the Murray set which is now standard (cards 1, 5, 6, 7BM, 10, 11, 14, 15, 17); five pictures from the set generally used in 1938 when these data were collected (a man and woman seated on a park bench; a bearded old man writing in an open book; a thin, sullen, young man standing behind a well-dressed older man; a tea table and two chairs; an abstract drawing of two bearded men); and four cards not in the Murray series (a madonna and child, the nave of a large church, a dramatic view of mountains, a boy gazing at a cross which is wreathed in clouds.

The tests were administered individually. Each card was projected on a screen while the subject told a story which was recorded verbatim. Standard instructions were given for the Murray cards, and subjects were asked to describe the feelings elicited by the other four pictures. Most of the stories were brief.

The scoring scheme involved counting the relevant needs, press, and descriptions of the heroes of the stories, the assumption being that the storyteller has identified with the hero; the hero's needs are the same as the girl's; the press that impinge upon the hero are the ones that affect the girl telling the story. A total of 20 needs, press, and descriptive categories, each defined as specifically as possible, was developed in the analysis of the protocols. A score for each subject for each TAT category was derived by counting the number of stories in which it appeared.

To test the reliability of this analysis, one of the authors (PM) and another psychologist independently scored 15 complete protocols (300 stories). The percentage of interrater agreement was 90, computed by the usual formula (number of agreements divided by number of agreements plus number of disagreements).

In order to eliminate bias, the scoring used in the present study was done "blind," that is, independently of knowledge of the subject's maturational status.

Results

Frequency distributions of the scores of all subjects were made for all the TAT variables. Each distribution was then dichotomized at the point which most nearly enabled the placing of half of the 34 subjects above, and half of them below, the dividing point. Subjects having scores above this point were considered high in this particular variable; those with scores below this point were considered low in this variable.

Early- and late-maturing boys differed from each other on many more characteristics than the two groups of girls did. The boys' groups were significantly different from each other, at the 5 per cent level or better, in six of the 20 variables scored, while the early- and late-maturing girls differ significantly in only two of the variables (*negative characteristics* and *n Recognition*). It should be noted, however, that the *direction* of the differences tended to be the same, rather than reversed, in the two sets of data. For example, the following similarities may be noted:

1. In this list of characteristics a significantly greater proportion of late-maturing girls than of early-maturing girls have high scores on *negative characteristics*. This finding is similar to that found in the comparison of early- and late-maturing boys. For girls, it is contrary to expectation.

2. The differences between early- and late-maturing girls in respect to *p Dominance* and *p Rejection* are similar to those for early- and late-maturing boys in these variables. These may be interpreted to indicate slightly poorer parent-child relationships among the late-maturing.

3. The early- and late-maturing boys differ significantly on *n Autonomy 1*, suggesting a greater tendency for the late-maturing to avoid or defy authority. The differences are in the same direction for girls, but are not significant.

4. Similar results for boys and girls in *n Succorance* may be interpreted as showing some tendency for stronger dependency needs in the late-maturing.

5. Similar results for boys and girls in *p Nurturance* (significant in one variable for boys) may also be interpreted as indirect indications of stronger dependency needs in the late-maturing.

The chief differences between the sexes are as follows:

1. With respect to *n Aggression* more early- than late-maturing girls show "argumentative aggression," but the two groups of girls do not differ in physical aggression. On the other hand, more early-maturing than late-maturing boys show high degrees of both kinds of aggression.

2. On one category of *n Affiliation* (involving romantic love) higher proportions of high scores are shown for early-maturing girls as contrasted with their late-maturing peers. The differences between the early-maturing and the late-maturing boys are in the opposite direction for this category.

3. The variables *n Achievement* and *n Recognition* do not differen-

tiate the two groups of boys. Among girls scores are higher for the late-maturing, very significantly so in the case of *n Recognition*.

4. *Denial of feeling* does not differentiate early- and late-maturing girls but tends to yield higher scores for early-maturing boys.

Discussion

The failure of the TAT data to support observational findings, especially with reference to the variable, negative characteristics, might be accounted for in a number of ways. Some writers report that in many cases thematic fantasies and manifest behavior operate independently and are even negatively related. If we assume this to be the case for our subjects, no further explanation would be needed. But there is also evidence from the literature that, for some groups, TAT findings and overt behavior may be congruent. Our data on boys are in line with this assumption, since, according to observational ratings, late-maturing boys tend to be socially disadvantaged, and, according to the TAT, personally more maladjusted.

The findings for girls are quite different, however. The early-maturing received more unfavorable ratings from both peers and adult observers on many characteristics. But in the TAT they appear to be somewhat better adjusted than their late-maturing peers. This discrepancy between observers' ratings and the picture derived from the personality tests may stem partly from the fact that the reported observational records represented an average of repeated ratings taken over a period of time (from 11 to 17 years) while the TAT stories were collected at the end of this period.

Girls who enter puberty early would be expected to have more difficulties in personal-social relations when they are out of phase with their group. However, after the peer group "catches up," these difficulties would be reduced. By the end of senior high school maturational discrepancies, and social distance due to this factor, would be less marked. It is also possible that even a slight improvement in status would bolster morale and be reflected in a projective technique designed to register attitudes and self-concepts.

There is some slight evidence of a trend toward improved social status for the early-maturing in observational ratings over the seven-year period. Twenty-five items concerned with appearance, emotional tone, social participation, responsiveness, and assurance, were used in the comparison. Three of these reflected an improved status at the twelfth grade level for early-maturing girls. In two of these, "laughing" vs. "sober" and "sociable" vs. "unsociable," the accelerated girls, while still rated lower than the late-maturing, had improved sufficiently so that the differences between the two groups were no longer significant. But for one important characteristic, "popular" vs. "unpopular," the average ratings for the accelerated girls were now actually slightly higher than for the late-maturing, though the differences were not significant. This last year at high school was the only period when the early-maturing girls were rated by observers as above average in popularity.

It is conceivable that other improvements in social relationships were undetected because of the "halo effect" which, in spite of precautions, may have influenced observers who had rated these same adolescents in earlier years. It is not unlikely that if these girls of more mature status had been observed in social groups of their own choosing (presumably outside of school) the behavior picture might have been more favorable.

It may be noted that over the seven-year period the observational records received little corroboration from a self-report inventory. Although differences were not consistent in all categories, the early-maturing girls tended to score more favorably than the slow-maturing on "total adjustment," and also on family adjustment and feelings of personal adequacy. These data from the self-report inventory seem to be generally consistent with the findings from the TAT.

However, we may note that in both the inventory and the TAT the early-maturing girls appear in a somewhat better light than in their reputation scores or in ratings by adult observers. In some individual cases a favorable self-report score should not be taken at face value, in view of the tendency for some individuals to cover up or deny their deficiencies.

The only other variable which yields a significant difference between the maturity groups is the category *n Recognition*, late-maturing girls manifesting a greater desire for personal recognition. The results for *n Achievement*, though not showing significant differences, tend to support these findings. Other data for this group of girls would lead us to expect this relationship between maturity status and desire for recognition. Late-maturing girls were rated by adult observers as attaining higher prestige, showing more leadership, and having greater stimulus value than their early-maturing peers. They were also mentioned more frequently in the high school daily paper over a three-year period and were elected to more offices in extra-curricular activities. The late-maturing girls' leadership abilities, their greater social participation, and their apparent social success may have been more closely related to desires for recognition and achievement in the social sphere than to a need for affiliation.

It should be noted that, among boys, *n Achievement* and *n Recognition* were not significantly associated with rate of physical maturation. Perhaps this is due to the fact that for boys in our culture the pressures to strive for achievement and personal recognition are powerful and pervasive; hence, the boy's physical status may have little influence on his acquisition of strong achievement and recognition needs. Since these cultural pressures are undoubtedly less severe for girls, the strength of these personal needs may be more influenced by such factors as rate of physical maturation.

As we have pointed out in an earlier article, the relationship between physical status and psychological characteristics in boys is by no means simple. The evidence of the present study indicates that this relationship is even more complex in the case of girls. While the TAT analysis reported in this study suggests that early-maturing girls have fewer negative self-concepts and fewer needs for personal recognition, the results must be interpreted very cautiously. Since only two variables were found to be significantly related to physical status, it is obvious that many psychological and social factors are more important than rate of maturing in determining girls' self-concepts and personality characteristics. Furthermore, these data, considered together with the data from earlier studies on girls, suggest that the rate of maturation may affect overt behavior and covert characteristics in different— sometimes seemingly contradictory—ways.

It is also possible that, at least for girls, early- or late-maturing means different things at different stages of adolescent development. It has been proposed that since girls who enter puberty early are out of step physically with both the boys and girls in their classrooms, they tend to be socially handicapped during early adolescence. We have assumed that this would carry emotional hazards, and evidence is available from observational data and reputation measures to indicate that this is the case.

However, the accelerated girl may gain assurance from knowing that she is on the way toward a goal which is a common task for all adolescents, that of being an adult. By the end of high school, many girls in this group were beginning to feel that they had made satisfactory progress toward this goal. If, in addition to this, she can cope with the problems of this period without too much stress, her self-esteem and feelings of adequacy may be enhanced. A resulting improvement in self-concepts may be reflected in the relative infrequency of negative characteristics in TAT stories.

In conclusion, it is evident that each individual's unique personality structure is determined by a complex of interacting variables, including rate of maturation. Comments made by these subjects as young adults indicate that they were aware of a variety of surface phenomena which affected their adolescent adjustment:

"High school is not a pleasant memory. I felt remote from my mother. If I could have talked to her, it would have helped" (a slow-maturer).

"I wasn't very happy in adolescence. My father was out of work. I felt inferior outside my own circle of friends—I always aimed to please" (a very popular late-maturing girl).

"I was slightly rattle-brained" (a popular late-maturing girl).

"I didn't have much fun in high school. I look forward to more happiness now than I did when I was in high school. I was an ugly duckling" (a slow-maturer who ascribed many negative characteristics to the hero).

"I seemed to be separated from friends in high school. I'm more outgoing now, less cautious and fearful" (accelerated girl).

"I was overweight and sensitive about it—now I take things more for granted" (accelerated girl).

"I had a feeling of being different when growing up" (accelerated).

"I felt stupid in school" (accelerated girl).

"I was very lacking in self-confidence in high school" (accelerated girl).

"I'm more optimistic now. I didn't know many people in high school. I would make an effort to get on with people if I had it to do over again" (accelerated).

Feelings of inadequacy and isolation are expressed by these girls and they are attributed to lack of mental ability, financial difficulties, separation from parents, poor social status, overweight, and unattractiveness. They are about equally common among those whose maturational status was at one extreme or the other.

It is obvious that the findings for this specific group of girls need to be particularized for each individual. These results might be modified also for girls in another geographical area or social level or in another generation. It is possible that school and community programs may be able to de-emphasize maturational status by providing an easier access to mixed social groups through classroom, extra-curricular, and recreational activities which cut across age classifications.

Summary

The present study was designed to investigate the relationship between maturational status and TAT scores for a group of physically-accelerated as contrasted with a group of slow-developing girls from a normal classroom sample. The TAT protocols of 34 17-year-old girls —16 who had been consistently accelerated and 18 who had been consistently retarded—were analyzed according to a scoring scheme involving 20 needs, press, and descriptive categories.

The scores of early- and late-maturing in each of the categories were compared. Earlier reports had indicated that girls who reach puberty early are likely to be socially disadvantaged, at least until the rest of their age group "catch up" with them. It was assumed that this social disadvantage would be reflected in the TAT protocols and that differences between the two maturity groups in self-concepts, attitudes, and motivations would be found. Analysis of the data of the present study found few striking differences between the two groups of girls. However, early-maturing girls had significantly lower scores on the category *negative characteristics*, indicating more favorable self-concepts. This finding is contrary to what might have been expected on the basis of observational ratings by adults and reputational ratings by classmates. On the other hand, the TAT results are in line with scores (total adjustment, self-adequacy, family adjustment) on a self-report inventory.

Late-maturing girls have significantly higher scores on *n Recoginition*, which is corroborated by data from other sources.

When the differences between early- and late-maturing girls are compared with the differences between early- and late-maturing boys, they are found to be in the same direction more often than in the opposite. These findings are interpreted to indicate that late-maturing adolescents of both sexes are characterized by less adequate self-concepts, slightly poorer parent-child relationships, and some tendency for stronger dependency needs.

It has been emphasized that complex psychological and cultural factors as well as maturational status contribute to personality development and that the pattern of these influences varies for each individual.

selection 47 / becoming a person / Carl R. Rogers, University of Wisconsin

SOME HYPOTHESES REGARDING THE FACILITATION OF PERSONAL GROWTH

To be faced by a troubled, conflicted person who is seeking and expecting help, has always constituted a great challenge to me. Do I have the knowledge, the resources, the psychological strength, the skill—do I have whatever it takes to be of help to such an individual?

For more than twenty-five years I have been trying to meet this kind of challenge. It has caused me to draw upon every element of my professional background: the rigorous methods of personality measurement which I first learned at Teachers College, Columbia; the Freudian psychoanalytic insights and methods of the Institute for Child Guidance where I worked as intern; the continuing developments in the field of clinical psychology, with which I have been closely associated; the briefer exposure to the work of Otto Rank, the methods of psychiatric social work, and other contacts too numerous to mention. But most of all it has meant a continual learning from my own experience and that of my colleagues at the Counseling Center as we have

Abridged from Carl R. Rogers, "Becoming a Person," The Hogg Foundation for Mental Hygiene, The University of Texas, 1956, pp. 9–23. Lectures delivered on the Nellie Heldt Lecture Fund at Oberlin College. Reprinted here by permission of The Board of Trustees of Oberlin College.

endeavored to discover for ourselves effective means of working with people in distress. Gradually I have developed a way of working which grows out of that experience, and which can be tested, refined, and reshaped by further experience and by research.

One brief way of describing the change which has taken place in me is to say that in my early professional years I was asking the question: How can I treat, or cure, or change this person? Now I would phrase the question this way: How can I provide a relationship which this person may use for his own personal growth?

It is as I have come to put the question in this second way that I realize that whatever I have learned is applicable to all of my human relationships, not just to working with clients with problems. It is for this reason that I feel it is possible that the learnings which have had meaning for me in my experience may have some meaning for you in your experience, since all of us are involved in human relationships.

Perhaps I should start with a negative learning. It has gradually been driven home to me that I cannot be of help to this troubled person by means of any intellectual or training procedure. No approach which relies upon knowledge, upon training, upon the acceptance of something that is *taught*, is of any use. These approaches seem so tempting and direct that I have, in the past, tried a great many of them. It is possible to explain a person to himself, to prescribe steps which should lead him forward, to train him in knowledge about a more satisfying mode of life. But such methods are, in my experience, futile and inconsequential. The most they can accomplish is some temporary change, which soon disappears, leaving the individual more than ever convinced of his inadequacy.

The failure of any such approach through the intellect has forced me to recognize that change appears to come about through *experience* in a *relationship*. So I am going to try to state very briefly and informally some of the essential hypotheses regarding a helping relationship which have seemed to gain increasing confirmation both from experience and research.

I can state the over-all hypothesis in one sentence, as follows. If I can provide a certain type of relationship, the other person will discover within himself the capacity to use that relationship for growth, and change and personal development will occur.

WHAT IT MEANS TO BECOME A PERSON

A frequently-raised question is: "What problems do people bring to you and other counselors at the Counseling Center?" I always feel baffled by this question. One reply is that they bring every kind of problem one can imagine, and quite a number that I believe no one would imagine. There is the student concerned about failing in college; the housewife disturbed about her marriage; the individual who feels he is teetering on the edge of a complete breakdown or psychosis; the responsible professional man who spends much of his time in sexual fantasies and functions inefficiently in his work; the brilliant student, at the top of his class, who is paralyzed by the conviction that he is hopelessly and helplessly inadequate; the parent who is distressed by his child's behavior; the popular girl who finds herself unaccountably overtaken by sharp spells of black depression; the woman who fears that life and love are passing her by, and that her good graduate record is a poor recompense; the man who has become convinced that powerful and sinister forces are plotting against him;— I could go on and on with the many different and unique problems which people bring to us. They run the gamut of life's experiences. Yet there is no satisfaction in giving this type of catalog, for, as counselor, I know that the problem as stated in the first interview will not be the problem as seen in the second or third hour, and by the tenth interview it will be a still different problem or series of problems. You can see why I feel baffled as to how to answer this simple question.

I have however come to believe that in spite of this bewildering horizontal multiplicity, and the layer upon layer of vertical complexity, there is a simple answer. As I follow the experience of many clients in the therapeutic relationship which we endeavor to create for them, it seems to me that each one has the same problem. Below the level of the problem situation about which the individual is complaining— behind the trouble with studies, or wife, or employer, or with his own uncontrollable or bizarre behavior, or with his frightening feelings, lies one central search. It seems to me that at bottom each person is asking: "Who am I, *really?* How can I get in touch with this real self, underlying all my surface behavior? How can I become myself?"

The process of becoming

Getting behind the mask   Let me try to explain what I mean when I say that it appears that the goal the individual most wishes to achieve, the end which he knowingly and unknowingly pursues, is to become himself.

When a person comes to me, troubled by his unique combination of difficulties, I have found it most worth while to try to create a relationship with him in which he is safe and free. It is my purpose to understand the way he feels in his own inner world, to accept him as he is, to create an atmosphere of freedom in which he can move in his thinking and feeling and being, in any direction he desires. How does he use this freedom?

It is my experience that he uses it to become more and more himself. He begins to drop the false fronts, or the masks, or the roles, with which he has faced life. He appears to be trying to discover something more basic, something more truly himself. At first he lays aside masks which he is to some degree aware of using. One young woman describes in a counseling interview one of the masks she has been using, and how uncertain she is whether underneath this appeasing, ingratiating front there is any real self with convictions.

I was thinking about this business of standards. I somehow developed a sort of knack, I guess, of—well—a habit—of trying to make people feel at ease around me, or to make things go along smoothly. There always had to be some appeaser around, being sorta the oil that soothed the waters. At a small meeting, or a little party, or something—I could help things go along nicely and appear to be having a good time. And sometimes I'd surprise myself by arguing against what I really thought when I saw that the person in charge would be quite unhappy about it if I didn't. In other words I just wasn't ever —I mean, I didn't find myself ever being set and definite about things. Now the reason why I did it probably was I'd been doing it around home so much. I just didn't stand up for my own convictions, until I don't know whether I have any convictions to stand up for. I haven't been really honestly being myself, or actually knowing what my real self is, and I've been just playing a sort of false role.

You can, in this excerpt, see her examining the mask she has been using, recognizing her dissatisfaction with it, and wondering how to get to the real self underneath, if such a self exists.

In this attempt to discover his own self, the client typically uses the therapeutic relationship to explore, to examine the various aspects of his own experience, to recognize and face up to the deep contradictions which he often discovers. He learns how much of his behavior, even how much of the feeling he experiences, is not real, is not something which flows from the genuine reactions of his organism, but is a facade, a front, behind which he has been hiding. He discovers how much of his life is guided by what he thinks he *should* be, not by what he is. Often he discovers that he exists only in response to the demands of others, that he seems to have no self of his own, that he is only trying to think, and feel, and behave in the way that others believe he *ought* to think, and feel, and behave.

In this connection I have been astonished to find how accurately the Danish philosopher, Soren Kierkegaard, pictured the dilemma of the individual more than a century ago, with keen psychological insight. He points out that the most common despair is to be in despair at not choosing, or willing, to be one's self; but that the deepest form of despair is to choose "to be another than himself." On the other hand "to will to be that self which one truly is, is indeed the opposite of despair," and this choice is the deepest responsibility of man. As I read some of his writings I almost feel that he must have listened in on the statements made by our clients as they search and explore for the reality of self—often a painful and troubling search.

This exploration becomes even more disturbing when they find themselves involved in removing the false faces which they had not known were false faces. They begin to engage in the frightening task of exploring the turbulent and sometimes violent feelings within themselves. To remove a mask which you had thought was part of your real self can be a deeply disturbing experience, yet when there is freedom to think and feel and be, the individual moves toward such a goal. A few statements from a person who had completed a series of psychotherapeutic interviews will illustrate this. She uses many metaphors as she tells how she struggled to get to the core of herself.

As I look at it now, I was peeling off layer after layer of defenses, I'd build them up, try them, and then discard them when you remained the same. I didn't know what was at the bottom and I was very much afraid to find out, but I *had* to keep on trying. At first I felt there was *nothing* within me—just a great emptiness where I needed and wanted a solid core. Then I began to feel that I was facing a solid brick wall, too high to get over and too thick to go through. One day the wall became translucent, rather than solid. After this, the wall seemed to disappear, but beyond it I discovered a dam holding back violent, churning waters. I felt as if I were holding back the force of these waters and if I opened even a tiny hole I and all about me would be destroyed in the ensuing torrent of feelings represented by the water. Finally I could stand the strain no longer and I let go. All I did, actually, was to succumb to complete and utter self-pity, then hate, then love. After this experience, I felt as if I had leaped a brink and was safely on the other side, though still tottering a bit on the edge. I don't know what I was searching for or where I was going, but I felt then, as I have always felt whenever I really lived, that I was moving forward.

I believe this represents rather well the feelings of many an individual that if the false front, the wall, the dam, is not maintained, that everything will be swept away in the violence of the feelings that he discovers pent-up in his private world. Yet it also illustrates the compelling necessity which the individual feels to search for and become himself. It also begins to indicate the way in which the individual determines the reality in himself—that when he fully experiences the feelings which at an organic level he *is*, as this client experienced her self-pity, hatred, and love, then he feels an assurance that he is being a part of his real self.

The experiencing of feeling I would like to say something more about this experiencing of feeling. It is really the discovery of unknown elements of self. The phenomenon I am trying to describe is something which I think is quite difficult to get across in any meaningful way. In our daily lives there are a thousand and one reasons for not letting ourselves experience our attitudes fully, reasons from our past and from the present, reasons that reside within the social situation. It seems too dangerous, too potentially damaging, to experience them freely and fully. But in the safety and freedom of the therapeutic relationship, they can be experienced fully, clear to the limit of what they are. They can be and are experienced in a fashion that I like to think of as a "pure culture," so that for the moment the person *is* his fear, or he *is* his anger, or he *is* his tenderness, or whatever.

Perhaps again I can indicate that somewhat better by giving an example from a client that will indicate and convey something of what I mean. This comes from the recording of the thirty-first interview with this woman. She has talked several times of a recurrent feeling which troubles her and which she can't quite pin down and define. Is it a feeling that developed because she practically had no relationship with her parents? Is it a guilty feeling? She is not quite sure, and she ends this kind of talk with this statement:

Client: And I have the feeling that it isn't guilt. (Pause: she weeps) So . . . I mean, I can't verbalize it yet. It's just being *terribly hurt!*

Therapist: M-hm. It isn't guilt except in the sense of being very much wounded somehow.

C: (Weeping) It's . . . you know, often I've been guilty of it myself, but in later years, when I've heard parents . . . say to their children, "stop crying," I've had a feeling, as though, well, why should they tell them to stop crying? They feel sorry for themselves, and who can feel more adequately sorry for himself than a child. Well, that is sort of what . . . I mean, as-as though I thought that they should let him cry. And . . . feel sorry for him too, maybe. In a . . . rather objective kind of way. Well, that's . . . that's something of the kind of thing I've been experiencing. I mean, now . . . just right now.

T: That catches a little more of the flavor of the feeling, that it's almost as if you're really weeping for yourself. . . .

C: And then of course, I've come to . . . to see and to feel that over this . . . see, I've covered it up. (Weeps) I've covered it up with so much *bitterness*, which in turn I've had to cover up. (Weeps) *That's* what I want to get rid of! I almost don't *care* if I hurt.

T: (Gently) You feel that here at the basis of it as you experienced it, is a feeling of real tears for yourself. But that you *can't* show, mustn't show, so that's been covered by bitterness that you don't like, that you'd like to be rid of. You almost feel you'd rather absorb the hurt than to . . . than to feel the bitterness. (Pause) And what you seem to be saying quite strongly is, I do *hurt*, and I've tried to cover it up.

C: I didn't *know* it.

T: M-hm. Like a new discovery really.

C: (Speaking at the same time) I never really did know. It's almost a physical thing. It's . . . it's sort of as though I were looking within myself at all kinds of . . . nerve endings and-and bits of-of . . . things that have been sort of mashed. (Weeping)

T: As though some of the most delicate aspects of you—physically almost —have been crushed or hurt.

C: Yes. And you know, I do get the feeling, oh, you poor thing. (Pause)

T: Just can't help but feel very deeply sorry for the person that is you.

I hope that perhaps this excerpt conveys a little bit of the thing I have been talking about, the experiencing of a feeling all the way to the limit. She was feeling herself as though she were nothing but hurt at that moment, nothing but sorrow for her crushed self. It is not only hurt and sorrow that are experienced in this all-out kind of fashion. It may be jealousy, or destructive anger, or deep desire, or confidence and pride, or sensitive tenderness, or shuddering fear, or outgoing love. It may be any of the emotions of which man is capable.

What I have gradually learned from experiences such as this is that the individual in such a moment is coming to *be* what he *is*. When a person has, throughout therapy, experienced in this fashion all the emotions which organismically arise in him, and has experienced them in this knowing and open manner, then he has experienced *himself*, in all the richness that exists within himself. He has become what he is.

The discovery of self in experience   Let us pursue a bit further this question of what it means to become one's self. It is a most perplexing question and again I will try to take from a statement by a client, written between interviews, a suggestion of an answer. She tells how the various facades by which she has been living have somehow crumpled and collapsed, bringing a feeling of confusion, but also a feeling of relief. She continues:

You know, it seems as if all the energy that went into holding the arbitrary pattern together was quite unnecessary—a waste. You think you have to make the pattern yourself; but there are so many pieces, and it's so hard to see where they fit. Sometimes you put them in the wrong place, and the more pieces not fitted, the more effort it takes to hold them in place, until at last you are so tired that even that awful confusion is better than holding on any longer. Then you discover that left to themselves the jumbled pieces fall quite naturally into their own places, and a living pattern emerges without any effort at all on your part. Your job is just to discover it, and in the course of that, you will find yourself. You must even let your own experience tell you its own meaning; the minute *you* tell it what it means, you are at war with yourself.

Let me see if I can take her poetic expression and translate it into the meaning it has for me. I believe she is saying that to be herself means to find the pattern, the underlying order, which exists in the ceaselessly changing flow of her experience. Rather than to try to hold her experience into the form of a mask, or to make it be a form or structure that it is not, being herself means to discover the unity and harmony which exists in her own actual feelings and reactions. It means that the real self is something which is comfortably discovered *in* one's experience, not something imposed *upon* it.

Through giving excerpts from the statements of these clients, I have been trying to suggest what happens in the warmth and understanding of a facilitating relationship with a therapist. It seems that gradually, painfully, the individual explores what is behind the masks he presents to the world, and even behind the masks with which he has been deceiving himself. Deeply and often vividly he experiences the various elements of himself which have been hidden within. Thus to an increasing degree he becomes himself—not a facade of conformity to others, nor a cynical denial of all feeling, nor a front of intellectual rationality, but a living, breathing, feeling, fluctuating process—in short, he becomes a person.

The person who emerges

I imagine that some of you are asking: "But what *kind* of a person does he become? It isn't enough to say that he drops the facades. What kind of person lies underneath?" Since one of the most obvious facts is that each individual tends to become a separate and distinct and unique person, the answer is not easy. However I would like to point out some of the characteristic trends which I see. No one person would fully exemplify these characteristics, no one person fully achieves the description I will give, but I do see certain generalizations which can be drawn, based upon living a therapeutic relationship with many clients.

Openness to experience First of all I would say that in this process the individual becomes more open to his experience. This is a phrase which has come to have a great deal of meaning to me. It is the opposite of defensiveness. Psychological research has shown the way in which sensory evidence, if it runs contrary to the pattern of organization of the self, tends to be distorted in awareness. In other words we cannot see all that our senses report, but only the things which fit the picture we have.

Now in a safe relationship of the sort I have described, this defensiveness, or rigidity, tends to be replaced by an increasing openness to experience. The individual becomes more openly aware of his own feelings and attitudes as they exist in him at an organic level. He also becomes more aware of reality as it exists outside of himself, instead of perceiving it in preconceived categories. He sees that not all trees are green, not all men are stern fathers, not all women are rejecting, not all failure experiences prove that he is no good, and the like. He is able to take in the evidence in a new situation, *as it is*, rather than distorting it to fit a pattern which he already holds. As you might expect, this increasing ability to be open to experience makes him far more realistic in dealing with new people, new situations, new problems. It means that his beliefs are not rigid, that he can tolerate ambiguity. He can receive much conflicting evidence without forcing closure upon the situation. This openness of awareness to what exists at *this moment* in *this situation* is, I believe, an important element in the description of the person who emerges from therapy.

Perhaps I can give this concept a more vivid meaning if I illustrate it from a recorded interview. A young professional man reports in the forty-eighth interview the way in which he has become more open to some of his bodily sensations, as well as other feelings.

Client: It doesn't seem to me that it would be possible for anybody to relate all the changes that I feel. But I certainly have felt recently that I have more respect for, more objectivity toward, my physical makeup. I mean I don't expect too much of myself. This is how it works out. It feels to me that in the past I used to fight a certain tiredness that I felt after supper. Well, now I feel pretty sure that I really *am tired*—that I am not making myself tired—that I am just physiologically lower. It seemed that I was just constantly criticizing my tiredness.

Therapist: So you can let yourself *be* tired, instead of feeling along with it a kind of criticism of it.

C: Yes, that I shouldn't be tired or something. And it seems in a way to be pretty profound that I can just not fight this tiredness, and along with it goes a real feeling that being tired isn't such an awful thing. I think I can also kind of pick up a thread here of why I should be that way in the way my father is and the way he looks at some of these things. For instance, say that I was sick, and I would report this, and it would seem that overtly he would want to do something about it but he would also communicate, "Oh, my gosh, more trouble." You know, something like that.

T: As though there were something quite annoying really about being physically ill.

C: Yeah, I am sure that my father has the same disrespect for his own physiology that I have had. Now last summer I twisted my back, I wrenched it, I heard it snap and everything. There was real pain there all the time at first, real sharp. And I had the doctor look at it and he said it wasn't serious, it should heal by itself as long as I didn't bend too much. Well this was months ago—and I have been noticing recently that—hell, this is real pain and it's still there—and it's not my fault.

T: It doesn't prove something bad about you—

C: No—and one of the reasons I seem to get more tired than I should maybe is because of this constant strain and so—I have already made an appointment with one of the doctors at the hospital that he would look at it and take an X-ray or something. In a way I guess you could say that I am just more accurately sensitive—or objectively sensitive to this kind of thing. I can say with certainty that this has also spread to what I eat and how much I eat. And this is really a profound change, and of course my relationship with my wife and the two children is—well, you just wouldn't recognize it if you could see me inside—as you have—I mean—there just doesn't seem to be anything more wonderful than really and *genuinely*— really *feeling* love for your own children and at the same time receiving it. I don't know how to put this. We have such an increased respect—both of us—for Judy and we've noticed just—as we participate in this—we have noticed such a tremendous change in her—it seems to be a pretty deep kind of thing.

T: It seems to me you are saying that you can listen more accurately to yourself. If your body says its tired, you listen to it and believe it, instead of criticizing it; if it's in pain, you can listen to that; if the feeling is really loving your wife or children, you can *feel* that, and it seems to show up in the differences in them too.

Here, in a relatively minor but symbolically important excerpt, can be seen much of what I have been trying to say about openness to experience. Formerly he could not freely feel pain or illness, because being ill meant being unacceptable. Neither could he feel tenderness and love for his child, because such feelings meant being weak, and he had to maintain his facade of being strong and masculine. But now he can be genuinely open to the experiences of his organism— he can be tired when he is tired, he can feel pain when his organism is in pain, he can freely experience the love he feels for his daughter, and he can also feel and express annoyance toward her, as he goes on to say in the next portion of the interview. He can fully live the experiences of his total organism, rather than shutting them out of awareness.

Trust in one's organism A second characteristic of the persons who emerge from therapy is that the person increasingly discovers that his own organism is trustworthy, that it is a suitable instrument for discovering the most satisfying behavior in each immediate situation.

If this seems strange, let me try to state it more fully. Perhaps it will help to understand my description if you think of the individual as faced with some existential choice: "Shall I go home to my family during vacation, or strike out on my own?" "Shall I drink this third cocktail which is being offered?" "Is this the person whom I would like to have as my partner in love and in life?" Thinking of such situations, what seems to be true of the person who emerges from the therapeutic process? To the extent that this person is open to all of his experience, he has access to all of the available data in the situation on which to base his behavior. He has knowledge of his own feelings and impulses, which are often complex and contradictory. He is freely able to sense the social demands, from the relatively rigid social "laws" to the desires of friends and family. He has access to his memories of similar situations, and the consequences of different behaviors in those situations. He has a relatively accurate perception of this existential situation in all of its complexity. He is better able to permit his total organism, his conscious thought participating, to consider, weigh, and balance each stimulus, need, and demand, and its relative weight and intensity. Out of this complex weighing and balancing he is able to discover that course of action which seems to come closest to satisfying all his needs in the situation, long-range as well as immediate needs.

In such a weighing and balancing of all of the components of a given life choice, his organism would not by any means be infallible. Mistaken choices might be made. But because he tends to be open to his experience, there is a greater and more immediate awareness of unsatisfying consequences, a quicker correction of choices which are in error.

It may help to realize that in most of us the defects which interfere with this weighing and balancing are that we include things which are not a part of our experience, and exclude elements which are. Thus an individual may persist in the concept that "I can handle liquor," when openness to his past experience would indicate that this is scarcely correct. Or a young woman may see only the good qualities of her prospective mate, where an openness to experience would indicate that he possesses faults as well.

In general, then, it appears to be true that when a client is open to his experience, he comes to find his organism more trustworthy. He feels less fear of the emotional reactions which he has. There is a gradual growth of trust in, and even affection for, the complex, rich, varied assortment of feelings and tendencies which exist in him at the organic level. Consciousness, instead of being the watchman over a dangerous and unpredictable lot of impulses, of which few can be permitted to see the light of day, becomes the comfortable inhabitant of a society of impulses and feelings and thoughts, which are discovered to be very satisfactorily self-governing when not fearfully guarded.

An internal locus of evaluation Another trend which is evident in this process of becoming a person relates to the source or locus of choices and decisions, of evaluative judgments. The individual increasingly comes to feel that this locus of evaluation lies within himself. Less and less does he look to others for approval or disapproval; for standards to live by; for decisions and choices. He recognizes that it rests within himself to choose; that the only question which matters is: "Am I living in a way which is deeply satisfying to me, and which truly expresses me?" This I think is perhaps *the* most important question for the creative individual.

Perhaps it will help if I give an illustration. I would like to give a brief portion of a recorded interview with a young woman, a graduate student, who had come for counseling help. She was initially very much disturbed about many problems, and had been contemplating suicide. During the interviews one of the feelings she discovered was her great desire to be dependent, just to let someone else take over the direction of her life. She was very critical of those who had not given her enough guidance. She talked about one after another of her professors, feeling bitterly that none of them had taught her anything with deep meaning. Gradually she began to realize that part of the difficulty was the fact that she had taken no initiative in *participating* in these classes. Then comes the portion I wish to quote.

I think you will find that this excerpt gives you some indication of what it means in experience to accept the locus of evaluation as being within oneself. Here then is the quotation from one of the later interviews with this young woman as she has begun to realize that perhaps she is partly responsible for the deficiencies in her own education.

Client: Well now, I wonder if I've been going around doing that, getting smatterings of things, and not getting hold, not really getting down to things.

Therapist: Maybe you've been getting just spoonfuls here and there rather than really digging in somewhere rather deeply.

C: M-hm. That's why I say—(slowly and very thoughtfully) well, with that sort of a foundation, well, it's really up to *me*. I mean, it seems to be really apparent to me that I *can't depend on someone else* to give me an education. (very softly) I'll really have to get it myself.

T: It really begins to come home—there's only one person that can educate you—a realization that perhaps nobody else *can give* you an education.

C: M-hm. (long pause—while she sits thinking) I have all the symptoms of fright. (laughs softly).

T: Fright? That this is a scary thing, is that what you mean?

C: M-hm. (very long pause—obviously struggling with feelings in herself).

T: Do you want to say any more about what you mean by that? That it really does give you the symptoms of fright?

C: (laughs) I, uh—I don't know whether I quite know. I mean—well, it really seems like I'm cut loose (pause), and it seems that I'm very—I don't know—in a vulnerable position, but I, uh, I brought this up and it, uh, somehow it almost came out without my saying it. It seems to be—it's something I let out.

T: Hardly a part of you.

C: Well, I felt surprised.

T: As though: "Well for goodness sake, did I say that?" (both chuckle).

C: Really, I don't think I've had that feeling before. I've—uh, well, this really feels like I'm saying something that, uh, *is* a part of me really. (pause) Or, uh, (quite perplexed) it feels like I sort of have, uh, I don't know. I have a feeling of *strength*, and yet, I have a feeling of—realizing it's so sort of fearful, of fright.

T: That is, do you mean that saying something of that sort gives you at the same time a feeling of, of strength in saying it, and yet at the same time a frightened feeling of *what* you have said, is that it?

C: M-hm. I am feeling that. For instance, I'm feeling it internally now— a sort of surging up, or force. As if that's something really big and strong. And yet, uh, well at first it was almost a physical feeling of just being out alone, and sort of cut off from a—support I had been carrying around.

T: You feel that it's something deep and strong, and surging forth, and at the same time, you just feel as though you'd cut yourself loose from any support when you say it.

C: M-hm. Maybe that's—I don't know—it's a disturbance of a kind of pattern I've been carrying around, I think.

T: It sort of shakes a rather significant pattern, jars it loose.

C: M-hm. (pause, then cautiously, but with conviction) I, I think—I don't know, but I have the feeling that then I am going to begin to *do* more things that I know I should do. . . . There are so many things that I need to do. It seems in so many avenues of my living I have to work out new ways of behaving, but—maybe—I can see myself doing a little better in some things.

I hope that this illustration gives some sense of the strength which is experienced in being a unique person, responsible for oneself, and also the uneasiness that accompanies this assumption of responsibility.

Willingness to be a process I should like to point out one final characteristic of these individuals as they strive to discover and become themselves. It is that the individual seems to become more content to be a process than a product. When he enters the therapeutic relationship, the client is likely to wish to achieve some fixed state; he wants to reach the point where his problems are solved, or where he is effective in his work, or where his marriage is satisfactory. He tends, in the freedom of the therapeutic relationship, to drop such fixed goals, and to accept a more satisfying realization that he is not a fixed entity, but a process of becoming.

One client, at the conclusion of therapy, says in rather puzzled fashion: "I haven't finished the job of integrating and reorganizing myself, but that's only confusing, not discouraging, now that I realize this is a continuing process. . . . It is exciting, sometimes upsetting, but deeply encouraging to feel yourself in action, apparently knowing where you are going even though you don't always consciously know what that is." One can see here both the expression of trust in the organism, which I have mentioned, and also the realization of self as a process.

Here is another statement of this same element of fluidity of existential living. "This whole train of experiencing, and the meanings that I have thus far discovered in it, seem to have launched me on a process which is both fascinating and at times a little frightening. It seems to mean letting my experience carry me on, in a direction which appears to be forward, toward goals that I can but dimly define, as I try to understand at least the current meaning of that experience. The sensation is that of floating with a complex stream of experience, with the fascinating possibility of trying to comprehend its ever-changing complexity." Here again is a personal description of what it seems like to accept oneself as a stream of becoming, not a finished product. It means that a person is a fluid process, not a fixed and static entity; a flowing river of change, not a block of solid material; a continually changing constellation of potentialities, not a fixed quantity of traits.

Conclusion

I have tried to tell you what has seemed to occur in the lives of people with whom I have had the privilege of being in a relationship as they struggled toward becoming themselves. I have endeavored to describe, as accurately as I can, the meanings which seem to be involved in this process of becoming a person. I am sure that I do not see it clearly or completely, since I keep changing in my comprehension and understanding of it. I hope you will accept it as a current and tentative picture, not as something final.

One reason for stressing the tentative nature of what I have said is that I wish to make it clear that I am *not* saying: "This is what you should become; here is the goal for you." Rather, I am saying that these are some of the meanings I see in the experiences that my clients and I have shared. Perhaps this picture of the experience of others may illuminate or give more meaning to some of your own experiences.

I have pointed out that the individual appears to have a strong desire to become himself; that given a favorable psychological climate he drops the defensive masks with which he has faced life, and begins to discover and to experience the stranger who lives behind these masks —the hidden parts of himself. I have pictured some of the attributes of the person who emerges—the tendency to be more open to all elements of his organic experience; the growth of trust in one's organism as an instrument of sensitive living; the acceptance of the fearsome responsibility of being a unique person; and finally the sense of living in one's life as a participant in a fluid, ongoing process, continually discovering new aspects of one's self in the flow of experience. These are some of the things which seem to me to be involved in becoming a person.

selection 48 / contributions to role-taking theory: a clinical study of self and role / Theodore R. Sarbin, University of California, Berkeley, and Norman L. Farberow, Veterans Administration, Los Angeles

The purpose of this paper is twofold: first, to throw some light on the phenomenon of age-regression; and second, to illustrate the heuristic value of the concepts of self and role. In the succeeding pages, we shall try to review some of the pertinent features of age-regression as a social psychological phenomenon. This will lead us into a brief examination of hypnosis—the procedure which apparently facilitates age-regression. With this discussion as a background, we present the findings of our experiment. Our results, together with those of other investigators, are then interpreted with the aid of the aforementioned social psychological concepts—self and role. This interpretation leads us into the final section of our paper—a brief formulation of a general theoretical position that complex social psychological phenomena (such as age-regression) can be more readily understood at the present stage of our knowledge with the aid of self and role concepts.

AGE-REGRESSION

A survey of the literature reveals only a limited number of articles that deal with the hypothesis that through hypnotic age-regression earlier life roles can be relived with a precise degree of authenticity. The experimental procedure in these studies is somewhat as follows. The adult S is hypnotized and given instructions to return to an earlier age-role. An example of such instructions would be: "You are now a little boy. Instead of being 25 years old, you are 8 years old. You will think, act, feel, and talk like an 8-year-old boy. Today is your birthday and you are 8 years old, . . . etc." The S is then given some task to perform which is age-graded. The conclusions drawn from such experiments have been equivocal.

The study reported by Platonow has been used as a point of

Abridged from Theodore R. Sarbin and Norman L. Farberow, "Contributions to Role-Taking Theory: A Clinical Study of Self and Role," *Journal of Abnormal and Social Psychology*, 47:117–125, 1952. Reprinted by permission of the authors and the American Psychological Association.

departure for subsequent discussions. He hypnotically regressed three Ss to ages 4, 6, and 10 and claimed he obtained mental ages which were suitable, using a brief intelligence test. He makes a specific note of the fact that the accompanying behavior was also comparable. He adds his impression that there was a definite "unity" or "stability" to the complex of knowledge for each age. P. C. Young used the Stanford Binet test to obtain the mental ages of nine hypnotizable Ss who were regressed to age 3, and of seven non-hypnotizable Ss who were asked to simulate age 3. The former averaged 5 years, 11 months, and the latter averaged 5 years, 5 months mental age. He raised the question: Do trance Ss play their roles unwittingly and thus become less skillful than the controls because of the surrender of their critical attitudes? He implied that hypnotic age-regression was an artifact and that dissimulation might explain the phenomenon. A study by Sarbin attempted a more controlled test of Young's conclusion that regression in hypnosis is an artifact. Twelve young adults, average age 19, were asked to simulate the behavior of 8-year-olds. At another time, they were given the same instruction in hypnosis. Binet tests were administered in both instances and compared with the actual Binets which had been given to each of these Ss ten years before. The Ss, when enacting the 8-year role in hypnosis, overestimated on the average of 3.5 years; in simulating the role, the same Ss overestimated on the average of 5.3 years. In no case was regression to an earlier role as precise as the reflexologists would have us believe. This study demonstrated, however, that certain changes in role-behavior can and do occur under the special interpersonal conditions prevailing in hypnosis. Levine, Grassi, and Gerson report that one S in whom they induced various affective moods and then tested by means of the Rorschach produced pronounced variations. The similarity in the tests was always great enough to show the same underlying personality structure. Sarbin also reported important differences in content when one S was given different role-instructions or "sets" and then tested with the Rorschach.

In all the studies reported above, including Young's, the hypnotic Ss were described as behaving very realistically, that is, their speech, gestures, gait, etc., were "childish." Young's nonhypnotized Ss did not behave childishly at all, and yet were able to perform as well as the hypnotized Ss. He cites this as evidence for dissimulation on the part of the hypnotic Ss.

The disagreement among these writers would appear to stem from a dependence on outworn concepts and from a failure to regard hypnosis as a form of social psychological behavior. For example, Young's explanation of his results as dissimulation is a reflection of the failure to note that the enactment of a role (this is essentially the task he set for his Ss) can occur in *any* interact situation, that is, in any situation where the occupant of a specified position perceives his own role and the role of the other. Enactment of a role follows upon role-perception, variations in role-perception being dependent in part on the S's self-perceptions. Thus, from this approach we would conclude that Young's hypnotic Ss had different role-perceptions from the nonhypnotic Ss. The observed differential role-enactment of the two groups, then, could be related to differential self-perception rather than to dissimulation on the part of the hypnotic Ss.

The implication of the preceding paragraph is that hypnotic age-regression—a complex kind of social psychological behavior—can be viewed from a more comprehensive and nonmyopic theoretical structure than before. As a preface to the findings of our experiment and to the discussion that follows, a brief outline of this theoretical structure follows.

Theoretical background

First, hypnosis is looked upon as a form of a more general kind of social psychological activity known as role-taking. This activity has been described by various writers, among them Cameron, G. H. Mead, Newcomb, and Sarbin. Role-taking can best be described as an organismic process, dependent on prior experience, either overt or symbolic, which experience contributes both to the validity of role-perception and to the skill in role-enactment. Variations in the perception and enactment of roles are in part a function of the contribution of the self (*vide infra*).

Second, a role is a set of behaviors prescribed for the occupant of a specified position or status in an interact situation. Put in another way, the role is what the person does to validate his occupancy of a given position or status. For cultural or social roles, the behaviors are prescribed or expected by the social group that supports the differentiation of the particular position or status. For idiosyncratic or personal roles, the behaviors may be prescribed by small groups or even by single individuals. The role of the hypnotic S, for example, is made up of behaviors prescribed or expected by the larger culture. Dorcus *et al.* have shown that in a large group of college undergraduates the role behaviors expected of the S are well known. Sarbin, working with a similar population in unpublished studies, learned that the role-expectations of the hypnotist are also quite uniform. Thus, when the positions of hypnotist and S are perceived, each acts according to the social role-perception. However, since persons who correctly perceive the role of the hypnotic S do not enact the role in the same way, we must invoke a third concept to which we now turn.

Third, variations in role-taking behavior are dependent on the participation or involvement of the self. This is a restatement of general motivation theory. In our terms, motivation is defined as the degree to which a role is congruent with the S's self-perceptions. Where there is a high degree of congruency, motivation is said to be favorable. Where there is a low degree or absence of congruency, the motivation is not favorable.

The concept of the self is assumed to be a cognitively derived, inferred structure which usually develops in ordered steps through the early years of infancy and childhood. The development of this structure is more fully elaborated by the senior author in his epistemogenic theory of the self. Emphasizing cognitive factors, this theory postulates that the human organism can regard itself as an object and make inferences concerning this object. Cognitive substructures, called empirical selves, or reference-schemata, are developed as a result of interaction with the total interbehavioral field. Which empirical self may occupy the focus of the field at any given time depends upon the organization of the various object- and self-perceptions. The social self first appears around two years of age, on the average, and is the reference-schema by which the individual begins to perceive a number of roles which, in addition to other factors, determine his behavior. The elaboration of the social self from this stage onward depends on the amount and kind of practice in performing the role-behaviors appropriate to the various age, sex, class, and other positions which are occupied from time to time. Roles are thus seen as further differentiations of the social self at constantly increasing levels of complexity.

In hypnosis, S enacts the role of an hypnotic subject. The effectiveness of his role-taking depends upon: (a) the accuracy of role-perception, which may be inferred from what he communicates via verbal reports, motor behavior, posture, etc., (b) role-taking aptitude, which depends on imaginative processes, or the ability of S to engage in *as-if* activities, and (c) favorable motivation, which depends on the congruence of the demands of the role with the self-concept. The closer the congruence, the more favorable the motivation, and the better the role-enactment, providing, of course, that the role-perception has veridical properties and that an appropriate degree of the role-taking aptitude is present. The fact that a person can be hypnotized is taken as evidence that he possesses at least a minimal degree of role-taking aptitude.

Hypnotic age-regression can be described with the same terms. The effectiveness of the enactment of an age-role depends upon the same set of factors. The S's perception of the child's role must have some veridical properties; there must be present evidence of the role-taking aptitude, and the assigned role must not be incongruent with the S's current self-perceptions. In the preceding paper of this series, these three notions were elaborated in detail. We might add here that in an earlier study, a high correlation was reported between a measure of role-taking aptitude (hynotizability) and the ability to enact the role of an eight-year-old child.

Method

In our study it has been assumed that the changes occurring in the various hypnotically regressed ages will manifest themselves in fairly specific ways on our test instruments. A child of six when given the Rorschach test will produce imaginative behavior representative of his current self-perceptions and object-perceptions. However, an S who is 20 years old and whose self-reactions are appropriate to his age level, when asked to enact the role of a 6-year-old, will give a Rorschach which is consistent with his perceptions of the role of a 6-year-old as integrated into his perceptions of self as a 20-year-old. The more congruent the perceptions of self and role, the closer the test results would approach the average for 6-year-old children. Individuals will vary in the congruency exhibited, depending upon the state of development of the self-structure. It would follow, then, that an adult whose self-development is retarded in regard to age-grade characteristics would be able better to integrate a 6-year-old role with his self-perceptions.

The Rorschach test lends itself to the task of assessing self-perception and role-perception. Self-perceptions are inferred by the experimenters from the structural features of the protocols, such as M, FM, FC, etc. The more stable features of the personality, the self, are adduced from this aspect of the test. The variation in quantity and time of appearance of these components reflects the level of selfhood. These components we shall call "validating" factors.

Role-perceptions, on the other hand, may be inferred from the content, from verbal and vocal characteristics, as well as from mannerisms and gestural responses which may be noted by E. These aspects of behavior will be consistent with other expressions of the voluntary musculature. The Draw-A-Person test also serves to reflect the operation of peripheral factors because its performance draws so much upon the activity of the voluntary muscular system. These expressive features of behavior are the vehicles of communication; it is by the use of such expressive behaviors that the person makes known to others his current role. We shall call these aspects of behavior expressive or peripheral factors.

Data have so far been collected on six Ss, a number too small to treat statistically with any satisfaction, but from which it is possible to infer some trends and to view some of the more salient characteristics. The Ss were all students, ranging in age from 19 to 26, with an average age of 21. The hypnotizability of the one male and five females had previously been determined by means of the Friedlander-Sarbin scale. The Rorschach, Draw-A-Person, graphological material, and interview material were obtained, where possible, at suggested age levels 3, 6, 13, and 18, chosen because they represent, in general, those years which are considered especially significant in development. Each was regressed to his birthday so that the age level would be comparable for the group. The order of ages to which regression was effected was varied among the Ss to equate the practice effects. A total of 21 Rorschachs was obtained, 4 from age 3, 4 from age 6, 4 from age 13, 2 from age 18, and 6 from the waking state. In addition one record was obtained from one S who was asked to simulate age 6.

Parenthetically, we noted what has been reported elsewhere, that the depth of hypnosis was associated with the effectiveness of role-enactment. In two previous studies, depth of hypnosis was found to be correlated with two varieties of role-enactment. In the first, reported by Lewis and Sarbin, hungry Ss were given the task (under hypnosis) of taking the role of a person eating a hearty breakfast. The role-enactment brought about cessation of gastric hunger contractions. The relative frequency with which this could be accomplished was associated with degree of hypnotizability. The second study showed a positive correlation between hypnotizability and ability to enact the role of an 8-year-old.

Results

Prior to analysis, our results appeared equivocal. Some of the Ss seemed to enact with remarkable fidelity the assigned role as evidenced by their speech, posture, mannerisms, etc., at the same time giving test performances which were incompatible with the assigned role. An example of the consistency and realism of the Ss' role-enactment is given in the postural analysis of one of the Ss. "S began to adduct her feet as E counted back the years until she was sitting pigeon-toed, and finally brought one foot under to sit on it in a way which is characteristic of young children." Another protocol illustrates the realism of the role-enactment: "S would only print block letters when asked to write her name. She had been late in starting school."

Other Ss did not show the same proficiency in role-enactment, yet their test performances were in the range of the assigned age-role.

The apparent lack of consistency in our findings could be explained most readily in terms of the interrelation of the two variables already described: the matrix of self-perceptions and the particular set of role-perceptions.

In order to clarify these conceptions, we shall illustrate with two of our cases, identified as Olga and Jeanne. To introduce these Ss we present the main features of their adult waking state Rorschach psychographs.

From the psychograms and from other clinical data, Jeanne may be considered the more mature, better adjusted, and more adequate person of the two, although she revealed the presence of a situational conflict which she was controlling by suppression.

In order to compare the responses of our Ss with those of average

TABLE 1   RORSCHACH FEATURES, WAKING STATE

	R	W	D,d	DdS	M	FM	m	K	F	Fc	c	C'	FC	CF	C
Olga	55	8	33	14	7	5	0	1	29	11	1	1	2	2	0
Jeanne	73	10	36	27	12	3	9	0	41	6	0	2	4	1	0

TABLE 2   **RORSCHACH FEATURES, REGRESSED AGE THREE**

	R	W	D,d	DdS	M	FM	F	FC	CF	C
Average	10	7	3	0.3	0.4	1.2	5.4	0.9	0.4	1
Olga	10	9	1	0	1	1	5	0	1	1
Jeanne	44	4	29	17	2	5	31	1	1	0

children of stated ages, we have made use of the extensive norms for 3- and 6-year-olds given by Klopfer and Margulies and Kay and Vorhaus. Table 2 presents selected features of the Rorschach psychograph for average 3-year-old children and for Olga and Jeanne regressed hypnotically to age 3. How much each S approaches the norm for that age is readily apparent. Olga approximates it, while Jeanne shows some changes from the adult test record but does not nearly approach Olga's performance.

Table 3 shows the comparison for age 6. Again, there is a marked difference in the performance of the two Ss. This is most apparent in the movement column where Jeanne gives 20 responses. Olga gives none, which is common for that age. The last line indicates the results for Jeanne's *simulated* age 6. As can be seen, she reacted in almost the same way, except that the number of form responses increased and the number of responses to color decreased. Apparently (following the customary interpretations of this kind of data) she became much more constricted when she was asked to enact a role on a conscious awareness basis, without the interpersonal elements that accompany the hypnotic situation.

The adolescent records may be compared with the norms established by McFate and Orr. Their results are given in terms of medians for girls. Table 4 shows the comparison for age 13. It is apparent that Olga begins to deviate much more from the norms for this age than she did before. It would be assumed under our hypothesis that her regressed self was more congruent with her perceived self at ages 3 and 6, and that it would not be expected that a close approximation

TABLE 3   **RORSCHACH FEATURES, REGRESSED AGE SIX**

	R	W	D,d	DdS	M	FM	F	FC	CF	C
Average	20	8	11	2	1	3	9	2	1	1
Olga	15	8	6	1	0	1	6	3	2	0
Jeanne	48	11	28	9	20	6	10	3	1	0
Jeanne (Simulated age six)	54	8	35	11	9	5	36	2	0	0

TABLE 4   RORSCHACH FEATURES, REGRESSED AGE THIRTEEN

	R	W	D,d	DdS	M	FM	F	FC	CF	C
Average	14	8	6	0	3	2	6	1	0	0
Olga	29	5	20	4	3	1	21	0	0	0
Jeanne	58	7	35	16	9	8	33	3	0	0

would be found for any of the other ages to which she might be regressed. The validating elements from Jeanne's record are still not similar to the norms.

Each of the categories in the tables is viewed as a "validating" factor, affected both by role-perceptions and by self-perceptions, but to a greater extent by the latter. It is safe to assume that our naive Ss could not have acquired a role-perception which includes such specialized cognitive elements as "wholes are more common than large parts in the location choices of average 3-year-olds" or "form responses are generally around 50 per cent of the total." Some of these validating factors, of course, are directly influenced by the role-perception. Thus, one finds that animal movement is more common than human movement in young children, and that this ratio reverses itself with increase in chronological age. It is conceivable that an adult may perceive the child as concerned with Bunnies and Mickey Mouses, thus yielding a higher animal-movement score (FM). If, however, the adult perceives the child as preoccupied with fairy tales of giants and princesses, the chances are that a higher human-movement score (M) would occur in the Rorschach test administered with age regression instructions. Likewise, the number of responses would be another factor which would be somewhat influenced by the role-perception. It is within everyday knowledge that the child has a more limited vocabulary than the adult. This role-perceived limitation would tend to lower the number of responses in the lower ages, merely because the adult in his enactment of the role has denied himself the usage of certain words. It does not seem possible, however, that the role-perception of Rorschach-naive adults could include such a cognitive element as: "The number of responses (R) decreases in the Rorschach as one goes farther down the age scale."

The drawing productions may be similarly interpreted. We present Draw-A-Person pictures for the same two Ss at regressed ages 3, 6, and 13. A typical Goodenough drawing for a child of the stipulated age is introduced for comparison (Figure 1).

The most apparent result is that the productions are superior to the norms for the same ages. This coincides with the findings of other experiments in age-regression.

Fig. 1 *Selected D-A-P protocols of two subjects. Top row illustrates deviation from Goodenough standard for age 6 of drawings at regressed age three. Left-hand column illustrates Olga's lack of role-differentiation. Compare with right-hand column which shows Jeanne's more adequate role-differentiation. The lower-center drawing and the lower right-hand drawings illustrate marked differences in Jeanne's role-perception under conditions of simulated regression and hypnotic regression. [See text.]*

The differences between these two Ss is noteworthy. Olga's productions for age 3 and age 6 show stereotypy and only minor changes in moving from one role to another. This might be interpreted in the same way as the Rorschach data. Her role-perceptions were relatively invariant. Compare these drawings with those of the second S, Jeanne. Here the S showed different role-perceptions in her drawing. Although both are superior drawings for the stated ages, they show marked differences in conceptualization. Also compare with the quality and choice of subject-matter when the S was taking the role in the absence of the facilitating effects of hypnosis. In the drawings of Olga, we see some primitivation, but not to the same extent as in Jeanne's drawings. Her drawings do not extend over as much of the scale and do not differentiate the assigned age-roles as well as Jeanne's. Thus, the Draw-A-Person pictures lend support to some of the inferences drawn from the Rorschach data. A fuller exposition in terms of our theoretical conceptions follows.

Discussion

The interaction of role and self in behavior may now be more fully expounded using the performances of these two subjects as illustrations. The self-organization of each S is inferred (by the experimenters) from the validating features of the Rorschach test. Thus, Olga is seen as having self-perceptions which are relatively unstable—the validating features of the Rorschach show that she is able to perceive the age-roles assigned to her, particularly the younger age-roles. Her enactment of these roles, however, is deficient as evidenced by her expressive behavior: the content features of the Rorschach, the Draw-A-Person, and other behavior such as posture, inflections, etc. The clinical history of Olga revealed a relatively immature person who had not yet solved the adolescent problem of independence from mother. Her self-perceptions are those appropriate to a person occupying the position of a young child in our society. Although in daily life she tried to enact the role of an adult, she was unhappy and anxious because of the lack of congruence between the role-demands and the self-concept. When instructed to take the role of the 3-year-old or the 6-year-old she could perceive herself in this role quite accurately —probably because her self-concept included relatively sharp perceptions of self in these earlier age-grades. She was deficient in enacting the role, however, because her role-taking skills were not so well developed—probably as a result of the fixation of the self at an immature level, thus allowing for fewer opportunities for moving through the usual sequence of social positions with the accompanying role-behavior. We can infer, then, that Olga's self-concept is relatively unstable and her role-perceptions are relatively invariant.

The test results and clinical data on Jeanne reveal a different organization of self- and role-perceptions. The validating features of the Rorschach show a relatively stable self-concept in the various role-assignments. Unlike Olga, she had solved the problem of autonomy. She has been married and leads an active social life. Under the various role-assignments, the validating features changed but little. The expressive features, however, showed gross changes as she moved from one age-role to another. The drawing test results, the content analysis, the child-like postures, etc., revealed flexibility in role-enactment.

The results lead to the further inference that Jeanne has many more roles in her repertory than has Olga—roles which make for a better adjusted, well-rounded social person. This would be consistent with her ability to communicate, via expressive behavior, the multiple roles demanded in the experiment. Olga, on the other hand, with the self-concept at a less mature level, has fewer roles in her repertory. The perceptions of the assigned roles were screened through this less developed self-organization. It is as if Olga had verbalized: "I feel I really am a 6-year-old child, but I *have* to act like an adult. I can't let myself *act* as if I am a 6-year-old, because then others would know I really am one, and then, too, I'm not sure I could regain my adult role." Jeanne, however, might have said: "I've acted all kinds of roles and feel secure enough to act like a 6-year-old even though I am grown up." Having perceived and enacted (differentiated) more roles in her lifetime, Jeanne can readily communicate them to others via expressive channels.

The Rorschach protocols, the Draw-A-Person test, and the observations during the experimental sessions are all consistent in revealing the self-role derivation of human conduct. The data seem to fit into the hypothesis that conduct can be predicted from a knowledge of the self-perceptions and the role-perceptions of the individual. The self-perceptions may be thought of as lying on a continuum with stability at one end and instability at the other end. The role-perceptions may be regarded as lying on a continuum with variability or flexibility at one end and inflexibility at the other. In our two illustrative cases, Olga's behavior is seen as the result of interaction of a relatively inflexible set of role-perceptions with a relatively unstable set of self-perceptions. Jeanne's behavior is seen as the result of interaction of a relatively varied set of role-perceptions with a relatively stable set of self-perceptions. The reader should not draw the inference that these two sets of perceptions are reciprocal. Another of our Ss showed a different organization of self- and role-perceptions. Both unstable self-perceptions and varied role-perceptions were present— each to a marked degree. (Parenthetically, this S was subsequently found to be a psychopathic delinquent.)

Summary

In this paper, we have illustrated the use of the concepts of role and self in interaction in explaining apparently equivocal results in age-regression experiments. By means of the method of hypnotic age-regression, various age roles were assigned to six Ss. The Rorschach and Draw-A-Person tests were administered and clinical observations were noted. The formal scoring categories of the Rorschach test were taken as indicative of the organization of self-perceptions. The content of the responses, together with other linguistic and motor behavior (including the drawings) were taken as representative of the perception of the roles. Using two of our Ss as illustrative examples, we have shown how the use of the concepts self and role contributes to an understanding of behavior.

We have essayed to demonstrate how these conceptions are useful in describing one kind of complex social psychological behavior— hypnotic age-regression. The suggestion is apposite that all social-psychological behavior can be more readily understood with these concepts. A brief generalized statement of this position would be something like this:

1. Persons, through assignment, selection, achievement, birth, etc., occupy positions or statuses in interact situations.
2. The organized systems of behavior prescribed for or expected from the occupants of these positions or statuses make up the role.
3. The occupant of a given position enacts the role in order to validate his occupancy of the position.
4. The variations in the social validity of his role-taking are a function of at least three variables:
    a. the validity of the perception of the interact situation (i.e., the perception of the position of self and the position of other);
    b. role-taking aptitude (apparently related to practice in the use of *as-if* formulations); and
    c. the current organization of the self—a cognitive structure that exercises a selective effect in role-perception and role-enactment.

CHAPTER 12 ❁ PERSONALITY ❁

As a psychological concept comes to encompass an increasingly wide
variety of behavior, it becomes more difficult to provide an explicit
definition which approaches completeness. The term "personality" is
a case in point. In a very real sense each personality theory provides
us with new meaning for the term. Nevertheless, there are certain
core characteristics ·to which all psychologists would probably agree.
We may thus provide a partial definition of the study of personality
as being that part of the total subject matter of psychology which
attempts to understand the complex behavior of the human organism
as a whole. In contrast to those psychologists who concentrate their
efforts on components of behavior, such as learning or perception, the
"personologist" attempts to understand how these part processes
interact to yield behavior. We may thus somewhat more completely
define personality as the study of the dynamic organization of those
part processes within the individual which motivate and guide his
adjustment to his environment. More than any other topic of psychology, the study of personality requires the view which has been
maintained throughout this book: namely, that the ongoing behavior
of human beings depends upon complex interactions of biological,
psychological, and sociocultural determinants.

A biological approach to personality is presented in Selection 49
by Dr. Roger J. Williams, a biochemist. He emphasizes the often
overlooked fact that there are not only individual differences in behavior but also considerable variations among people in internal anatomy,
physiology, and biochemistry. Although he admits that differences in
brain and endocrine structure have not yet been demonstrated to
"have much to do with personality differences," he suggests that
neither have such psychological variables as toilet training experiences.
Although Dr. Williams strongly defends the position that biochemical

differences are quite likely to be related to personality differences, he feels that "it is not a substitute for all other valid approaches," that is, we must be concerned with the whole organism.

Our definition of personality suggests that the adequacy of an individual's organization of part processes might be judged by the adequacy of his adjustment. The concept of adjustment is closely related to the biological notion of adaptation. Both terms refer to the degree to which an organism uses its abilities in coping with its environment. Although specific adjustive reactions vary in complexity and form, we may describe general types of reactions as involving attack, withdrawal, or compromise behavior. Dr. James C. Coleman presents, in Selection 50, a brief but lucid introduction to these general adjustment patterns and indicates their interactions with motivational patterns and self-concepts under conditions of stress. If the stress represents a threat to the person's self-concept, then the adjustive reactions become complicated by the use of ego defense mechanisms such as rationalization, projection, and identification.

The process of identification may be thought of either as a defensive reaction to threat or as a process in which the child learns to imitate the actions and simulate the attitudes and feelings for those persons with whom he has affectionate relationships. A third possibility proposed by role theorists is that both factors are operating; the child identifies to the extent that the other person possesses power for both reward and punishment. In Selection 51 Mussen and Distler report an investigation which attempted to differentiate between these three theories. Their results are interpreted as supporting role theory, since they found that boys identify most with a father who is perceived as a powerful source of both reward and punishment.

In order to understand personality development in our culture, Dr. Robert R. Sears suggests, in Selection 52, that increased knowledge of the part processes of motivation and social learning is imperative. Our learned wants and the ways in which we satisfy them are extensively determined by the culture in which we live. In growing up we internalize the cultural attitudes and to a greater or lesser degree tend to conform to societal norms. Thus, in the adult culturally appropriate behavior depends on our having learned certain kinds of motives in childhood. The crucial role of parents in shaping personality is emphasized since it is through parent-child interactions which are mutually need-satisfying or need-frustrating that new motives are learned. Sears also analyzes the influence of sex differences, ordinal position in the family, aggression, and dependency within the framework of an instrumental interaction sequence leading to satisfaction or frustration.

selection 49 / the biological approach to the study of personality / Roger J. Williams, University of Texas

The study of personality logically involves trying to answer three questions: First, of what is personality composed; e.g., if two people have differing personalities in what specific ways do they or may they differ? Secondly, how do distinctive personalities arise? Thirdly, how can improvement or modification of personality be brought about?

The first question: Of what is personality composed? is a difficult and complicated one, and the answers to the second and third questions hinge upon the answer to it. Our discussion this evening will be a contribution toward the answering of all these questions. Our approach is in a sense not new but it is largely unexplored, and we believe, rich in potentialities. It has the advantage that it can be used to supplement all other approaches; it does not require the rejection of older insights regardless of their origin or how time-honored they may be.

Certainly one of the earliest attempts to account for personality differences was made by the astrologers who recognized that people differed one from another and sought to explain these differences on the basis of the influence of the heavenly bodies. The hypothesis of the astrologers has not stood up well in scientific circles, but there are numerous citizens who still believe in horoscopes and many magazines and newspapers that publish them. This tenacious belief rests, I believe, on a fundamental failure of real scientists to come up with other reasons and explanations which satisfy.

In the beginning of the nineteenth century Gall and Spurzheim developed phrenology which was destined to be in public vogue for a number of decades. This purported to be a science essentially concerned with the relation between personality traits and the contours of people's heads. Partly because it lacked scientific validity and partly because its implications were fatalistic and deterministic, the fundamental idea has largely been discarded.

In the middle portion of the nineteenth century the possible importance of heredity as a factor in the production of personality dif-

Abridged from Roger J. Williams, "The Biological Approach to the Study of Personality." This paper was presented to The Berkeley Conference on Personality Development in Childhood, University of California, May 5, 1960. Reprinted by permission of the author and the Elizabeth McCormick Memorial Fund.

ferences was brought to the fore by the investigations and writings of Darwin and his nephew, Galton. Galton, the founder of Eugenics, had none of our modern information as to how complicated heredity is; his emphasis on "good" and "bad" heredity (his own, of course, was "good") was misleading and his ideas of improving the race not only flew in the face of religious teachings but were so over-simplified that they came to be regarded as unsound scientifically. The eugenic view also had the disadvantage from the standpoint of public acceptance of being impregnated with determinism.

Before the end of the nineteenth century Freudianism came into being and has subsequently received such wide acceptance that it has dominated the field of psychiatry for several decades. Fundamentally, Freudianism is a system of surmises of such a nature that they have not and cannot be tested by controlled experiments. These surmises appear to some minds to be plausible to such a high degree that they demand acceptance. On the other hand, to some minds, some of the surmises appear so implausible as to demand rejection. Controlled experiments are quite outside the routine thoughts and discussions of adherents of the Freudian school.

The surmises which form the basis of the Freudian doctrine include the essential idea that personalities are built during the lifetime of the individual and that the prime factors which enter are the environmental happenings beginning on the day of birth—possibly even before—and the thoughts that are developed as a result of these happenings. Therapeutic psychoanalysis is based upon the idea that if an individual can come to understand how the events of his earlier life have developed his present unfortunate attitudes, his personality difficulties tend to evaporate. Inherent in this approach is the idea that minds are much more complex than they superficially appear to be; they are like icebergs in that there is much more "out of sight" than there is in open view.

That the Freudian approach to personality has elements of strength is so obvious as not to require argument. It leaves room for the unknown and unexpected in human behavior (which is needed); it emphasizes the dynamic aspects of personality, and strongly encourages the belief that human beings are not powerless to change and modify their personalities, and that parents have tremendous potentialities in developing the lives of their children. The wide acceptance of Freudian ideas bears out the thought that the public, including the physicians, are people first and secondly, if at all, scientists. Certainly a cold-blooded scientific approach would never have developed and fostered the Freudian concepts.

Behavioristic psychology which at its inception was *completely* environmentalistic has bolstered the environmental approach of Freudianism. This school of psychology has as a fundamental basis the facts discovered by Pavlov using dogs, and commonly designated as conditioned reflexes. The development of personality thus becomes a pyramiding conditioning process whereby the developing infant is continuously modified in his responses by the stimuli he or she received.

What was not quoted by the behavioristic school were correlative findings by Pavlov which are highly pertinent. Pavlov found as a result of extensive study of many dogs that they often exhibited innate tendencies to react very differently to the same stimulus. He recognized in his dogs four basic types (1) excitable, (2) inhibitory, (3) equilibrated, and (4) active, as well as intermediate types. He recognized enormous differences in dogs with respect to their conditionability, and was by no means inclined to focus his attention solely upon the behavior of "*the* dog." Scott and others have in more recent times found ample justification for Pavlov's concern over the fundamental differences between dogs of different breeds and between individual dogs within each breed. These differences, which can be studied under controlled conditions in dogs vastly easier than in human beings, are *not* the result of training.

Before we proceed to the principal part of our discussion it should be pointed out that the pronouncements of men whose memories we may revere must be taken in their historical context. Freud, for example, developed most of his fundamental ideas before there was any knowledge of hormones, indeed before the term "hormone" was coined. He had at this time no knowledge of present day biochemistry; the chemical factors involved in nutrition were almost wholly unknown, and he certainly had no knowledge of the close ties which exist between biochemistry and genetics. It can safely be assumed that if the youthful Sigmund Freud were reincarnated today, he would include these vast developments in endocrinology, biochemistry, and genetics in his purview, and that his thinking would follow quite different paths from those which it followed about the turn of the century.

A biological approach to personality should seek to bring from biology *everything* that can help to explain what personality is, how it originates and how it can be modified and improved. Biology has much to contribute, particularly in an area of biology which has received relatively little attention; namely that involving anatomical, physiological, biochemical (and psychological) individuality.

It seems indefensible to assume that people are built in separate compartments, one anatomical, one physiological, one biochemical, one psychological, and that these compartments are unrelated or only distantly related to each other. Each human being possesses and exhibits unity. Certainly anatomy is basic to physiology and biochemistry, and it may logically be presumed that it is also basic to psychology.

Let us look therefore in the field of anatomy for facts which are pertinent to our problem.

Anatomists, partly for reasons of simplicity, have been prone in centuries past to concentrate on a single picture of the human body. Obvious concessions are made, when necessary, in considering the male and the female of the species, and always anatomists have been aware that within these two groups there are variations and anomalies. Only within the past decade, however, has comprehensive information been published which indicates how great these inter-individual variations are and how widespread they are in the general population.

It makes no difference where we look, whether at the skeletal system, the digestive tract, the muscular system, the circulatory system, the respiratory system, the endocrine system, the nervous system, or even at the microscopic anatomy of the blood, we find tremendous morphological variations within the so-called normal range.

For example, normal stomachs vary greatly in shape, and about six-fold in size. Transverse colons vary widely in the positions at which they cross over in the abdomen, pelvic colon patterns vary widely. Arising from the aortic arch are two, three, four, and sometimes five and six branch arteries; the aorta itself varies greatly in size and hearts differ morphologically and physiologically so that their pumping capacities in healthy young men vary widely. The size of arteries and the branching patterns are such that in each individual the various tissues and organs are supplied with blood unequally well, resulting in a distinctive pattern of blood supply for each.

Each endocrine gland is subject to wide variation among "normal" individuals. Thyroid glands vary in weight about six-fold, and the protein-bound iodine of the blood which measures the hormonal output varies to about the same degree. Parathyroid glands also vary about six-fold in total weight in so-called "normal" individuals, and the number of lobes vary from 2–12. The most prevalent number of lobes is 4, but some anatomists estimate that not over fifty per cent of the population have this number. The number of islets of Langerhans, which are responsible for insulin production, vary over a ten-fold range in diabetes-free individuals. The thickness of the adrenal cortex where the critical adrenal hormones arise is said to vary from 0.5 mm to 5 mm (ten-fold).

The morphology of the pituitary glands which produce about eight different hormones is so variable, when different healthy individuals are compared, as to allow for several fold differences in the production of the individual hormones. The male sex glands vary in weight from 10 to 45 grams in so-called "normal" males and much more than this if those with "sub-normal" sex development are included. The female sex glands vary in weight over a five-fold range and the number of primordial ova present at the birth of "normal" female infants varies over a thirteen-fold range. It is evident that all individuals possess distinctive endocrine systems and that the individual hormonal activities may vary over a several fold range in individuals who have no recognized hormonal difficulty.

The nervous system is, of course, particularly interesting in connection with the personality problem, and the question arises whether substantial variations exist. The classification of the various kinds of sensory nerve endings, for example, is by no means complete nor satisfactory, and the precise functioning of many of the recognized types is unknown. Investigations involving "cold spots," "warm spots," and "pain spots" on the skin indicate that each individual exhibits a distinctive pattern of each. In a relatively recent study of pain spots in twenty-one healthy young adults, a high degree of variation was observed. When subjected to carefully controlled test conditions the right hand of one young man "A" showed seven per cent of the area tested to be "highly sensitive," while in another, "B," the right hand showed one hundred per cent "highly sensitive" areas. On A's hand, forty-nine per cent of the area registered "no pain" under standard pain producing test conditions. On B's hand, however, there was no area which registered "no pain."

It is evident that there is room for wide variations with respect to the numbers and distributions of sensory nerve endings in different individuals. That such differences exist is indicated by the extreme diversity in the reactions of individuals to many stimuli such as those involving seeing, hearing, and tasting. An entire lecture could easily be devoted to this subject alone.

Variations in brain anatomy have received little attention. Thirteen years ago, however, Lashly in a review wrote: "The brain is extremely variable in every character that has been subjected to measurement. Its diversities of structure within the species are of the same general character as are the differences between related species or even between orders of animals." . . . "Even the limited evidence at hand, however, shows that individuals start life with brains differing enormously in structure; unlike in number, size, and arrangement of neurons as well as in grosser features."

Unfortunately, partly due to the complexity of the problem, there is no information whatever available as to how these enormous anatomical differences are related to the equally striking personality differences which are commonplace. Recently there has been published, primarily for the use of surgeons, an extensive study of differences in brain anatomy.

Up to the present in our discussion we have paid attention only to certain facts of biology—those in the field of anatomy. Before we consider other areas—physiology, biochemistry, and psychology —it seems appropriate to note whether we have made any progress in uncovering facts that have important implications for personality development.

Consider the fact (I do regard it a fact and not a theory) that every individual person is endowed with a distinctive gastro-intestinal tract, a distinctive circulatory system, a distinctive respiratory system, a distinctive endocrine system, a distinctive nervous system, and a morphologically distinctive brain; furthermore that the differences involved in this distinctiveness are never trifling and often are enormous. Can it be that this fact is inconsequential, in relation to the problem of personality differences?

I am willing to take the position that this fact is of the *utmost* importance. The material in the area of anatomy alone is sufficient to convince anyone who comes upon the problem with an open mind that here is an obvious frontier which should yield many insights. Those who have accepted the Freudian idea that personality disorders arise from infantile conditioning will surely be led to see that *in addition*, the distinctive bodily equipment of each individual infant is potentially important.

The failure of psychologists—and of biologists too—to deal seriously with innate individual differences in connection with many problems probably has deep roots.

McGill has said "Experimental psychologists . . . ignore individual differences almost as an item of faith." The same statement holds, in the main, for physiological psychologists, physiologists, and biochemists. Anatomists have adopted in the past (and some do even at present) the same attitude. Generally speaking, individual differences are flies in the ointment which need to be removed and disregarded. Every subject becomes vastly simpler and more "scientific" when this is done.

If one is pursuing knowledge about personality, however, neglect of innate individual differences is fatal. All of biology and all of psychology have suffered, in my opinion, from at least a mild case of "universalitis," an overruling desire to generalize immediately—oftentimes long before sufficient facts are gathered to give the generalization validity. This desire to generalize is of itself laudable, but the willingness to do so without an adequate background of information is unscientific and has devastating effects in the area of personality study.

With these ideas as additional background for our thinking let us consider some of the other aspects of biology. Physiologically and biochemically distinctiveness in gastro-intestinal tracts is just as marked as is the distinctiveness in anatomy. The gastric juices of 5,000 individuals free from gastric disease were found to contain from 0–4300 units of pepsin. The range of hydrochloric acid in a smaller study of normal individuals was from 0.0 to 66.0 millequivalents per liter. No one can deny the probability that large variations also exist in the digestive juices which cannot be so readily investigated. Some "normal" hearts beat more than twice as fast as others, some have pumping capacities at least three times as large as others, and the blood of each individual is distinctive. The discovery of the existence of "blood groups" was just the beginning of our knowledge of the individuality of the blood. Enzyme levels in the blood, which are a reflection of fundamental biochemical differences, vary from one well individual to another over substantial ranges, sometimes ten-fold or even thirty-fold or more.

Our neuromuscular systems are far from assembly line products as can easily be demonstrated by a study of motor skills and by a large number of physiological tests. Our senses are by no means identical as has been made clear by taste tests for PTC and many other substances, by tests involving sense of smell (verbenas, hydrocyanic acid), sense of sight (peripheral vision, foveal size, flicker fusion, and related phenomena, eighteen types of color "blindness"), sense of balance, pitch discriminations and hearing acuities at different frequencies, etc., etc. From the tremendous variation in the action of specific drugs and chemicals on different individuals, we gain further evidence of fundamental differences in physiology and biochemistry.

Thurston's pioneering work on primary mental abilities called attention to the fact that human minds have different facets, and that some individuals may be relatively well endowed with respect to arithmetical facility, for example, while being relatively deficient in word familiarity or spatial imagery. Others may be strong in the area of word familiarity but weak in rote memory or arithmetic. Guilford has more recently suggested that there are at least forty facets to human minds, involving a group of memory factors, four groups of thinking factors, the latter involving abilities relating to discovering, evaluating and generating ideas. All of this leaves room for a multitude of mental patterns (patterns of conditionability) which it seems reasonable to suppose must be related to the enormous variation in the anatomy of human brains. People, even when confronted with the same facts, do not think alike, and this appears to have a sound anatomical as well as psychological basis.

Those social anthropologists and other social scientists who regard culture as the one factor which determines what an individual will be like often say or imply that adult members of a society bear a very great resemblance to each other because of the similarities of their upbringing. In view of this common implication it may be well to ask whether inborn differentness and distinctiveness fade out as a result of the adjustment of the individuals to the culture to which they are exposed.

At the risk of being naive, it appears that the whole story we have been unfolding hangs together. Individual infants are endowed with far-reaching anatomical distinctiveness; each has a distinctive endocrine system, a highly distinctive nervous system, a highly distinctive brain. The same distinctiveness carries over into the sensory and biochemical realms, and into their individual psychologies. It is not surprising therefore that each individual, upon reaching adulthood, exhibits a distinctive pattern of likes and dislikes not only with respect to trivialities but also with respect to what may be regarded the most important things in life.

That culture has a profound influence on our lives no one should deny. The serious question arises, however, as to the relative position that different factors occupy in producing distinctive personalities. To me it seems probable that one's distinctive endocrine system and one's distinctive brain morphology are more important factors than the toilet training one receives as an infant.

We cannot state as a demonstrated fact that differences in brain morphology or in endocrine systems have much to do with personality differences. On the other hand we have no rigorous scientific proof that toilet training has any substantial effect on personality development. We can only surmise. In one sense, personality study is in its very early infancy.

Another pertinent question—simple but important—awaits a clear answer: Are patterns of brain morphology inherited? On the basis of what is known about the inheritance of other morphological features including fingerprints and the branching of blood vessels on the chest, etc., it may be *inferred* that specific morphological features in brain are handed down by inheritance, but we do not have definitive proof.

A fact which makes the study of the inheritance of such morphological features difficult is that expressed by geneticists David and Snyder ". . . it has become more and more widely recognized that single-gene differences which produce readily distinguishable discontinuities in phenotype variation are completely non-representative of the bulk of genetic variability in any species." Multiple gene effects are extremely common and in many cases, because of the complexity of the inheritance process, it is impossible to trace them in families or to know when and where such effects may be expected to arise. This complication is not the only one which exists; there is also the possibility (and certainty in some species) of maternal influence (cytoplasmic) which does not follow the rules of gene-centered genetics, and can thus throw one's calculations off.

Consideration of the available facts leads me to suppose, in the absence of completely definitive information, that differences in brain morphology, in endocrine patterns, in digestive, circulatory, muscular and nervous systems, etc., have important roots in heredity. It is difficult to see how such differences as exist could arise independent of heredity. The exact mechanisms whereby all these differences are inherited will probably be obscure many decades hence.

The recognition of hereditary factors does not by any means exclude from consideration the dynamic aspects of personality development. Potentialities and conditionabilities are inherited; not fixed characteristics. The widespread idea that personalities are developed from early childhood is fully in accord with an appreciation of the hereditary factors. Conditioning still takes place but the recognition of innate biological differences calls attention to distinct make-up that each newborn baby possesses. Conditioning does not take place starting with assembly-line babies, each one, according to Watson, possessing exactly the same potentialities to develop into a "doctor, lawyer, artist, merchant, chief, and yes, even beggar-man and thief."

To tackle in one giant undertaking the problem of understanding, characterizing and cataloguing all personalities from the biological or any other point of view seems hopeless. A strategy which seems far from hopeless, however, involves studying *one at a time* various personality characteristics to ascertain what biological roots they may have. The personality characteristics to be chosen for investigation should, obviously, be as definite as possible. They might include not only matters of temperament or emotion but also the ability to perform specified types of mental processes, or they might include personality problems of numerous types.

Studying even one particular personality characteristic to ascertain its biological roots is a large undertaking and might involve making scores, possibly hundreds, of measurements on every individual subjected to study. If one has some rational basis for selecting wisely the measurements to be made, the number of desirable measurements might be reduced. This fact would constitute an argument for selecting, as the "personality problem" to be investigated, one for which the type of biological roots *might be* successfully guessed in advance. Such might include hyper- or hyposexuality, homosexuality, obesity, depressions, alcoholism, insomnia, accident proneness, etc. When one after another of personality disorders have been studied from this standpoint, it seems very likely that the whole picture will begin to clear and that the study of specific personality characteristics and problems will become successively easier the farther it progresses. What I am considering is obviously a relatively long range proposal.

Such a type of study as I am suggesting is not in line with the vast amount of experimentation which is currently fashionable. It is very common, for example, to develop a measurement and then apply it to large numbers of people. It is almost or totally unheard of to apply a large series of measurements to a relatively few individuals to determine their individual distinctive patterns. This must be done if we are to find the biological roots of personality characteristics, and psychologists should be warned that the major part of the work must be done in the area of biology, and the biological scientists concerned cannot be looked upon as minor contributors.

Digressing for a moment it has been with this thought in mind that I have objected strenuously to the current widespread implication that "behavioral sciences" constitute a distinct group including psychology, sociology, and social anthropology and excluding the biological sciences. Hidden in this classification is the *assumption* that biological factors are of no importance in behavior and that conditioning is the whole story. It actually may well be, however, that anatomy, physiology, and biochemistry are, from the standpoint of their practical potentialities, the most important behavioral sciences at our disposal.

Time will not permit a discussion of the numerous ways in which my own discipline, biochemistry, impinges on personality problems. The effects of various chemicals on personality behavior, the correlations between brain metabolism and behavior, the effects of various hormones on personality characteristics are all well recognized. What is not so well recognized is that each individual's body chemistry is distinctive and different, and that complex biochemical roots of personality characteristics are likely to be found when we look for them with due care and thoroughness.

Before I close this discussion, I want to stress a most important environmental factor which is capable of contributing enormously to healthy personality development.

The monumental work of Beadle and Tatum demonstrated for the first time the vital connection between genes and enzymes, and in effect, between heredity and biochemistry. Their work made clear the inevitable basis for individual body chemistry. As a direct consequence of this finding, it becomes inevitable that the nutritional needs of genetically distinctive individuals are quantitatively not the same. Carrying the idea still further it becomes inescapable that the brain cells of individual people do not have quantitatively identical nutritional needs.

It has been amply demonstrated that malnutrition of various kinds can induce personality disorders. This was observed in the starvation studies of Keys and associates, in thiamin deficiency studies, in amino acid deficiency studies and perhaps most notably in pellagra where unequivocal insanity may result from niacin deficiency and can be abolished promptly by administration of the missing vitamin. It has also been shown repeatedly that inadequacy of prenatal nutrition can cause all sorts of developmental difficulties and abnormalities in the growing fetus.

One of the most obvious environmental measures that can be taken to insure favorable personality development is to see, for example, that the nervous system of each distinctive individual with his distinctive needs receives prenatally and postnatally the best possible nourishment. Nourishment of brain cells like the nourishment of other cells throughout the body can be maintained at many levels of excellence, and of course achieving the best is no small order.

Serious attention to nutrition which must involve the utilization of substantial manpower and a great deal of human ingenuity and persistence can, I believe, make tremendous contributions to our knowledge of personality states and personality disorders, and to the alleviation and prevention of personality difficulties.

In conclusion I would emphasize that the biological approach to personality, outstandingly important as I believe it to be, is not a substitute for all other valid approaches. Whatever we may know or may be able to accomplish by other approaches, if valid, is not lost. Consideration of the biological approach expands our horizon and gives us a much broader view. In my opinion the insight we may gain from this approach will be mostly valuable and productive. I should reiterate also what I have said before, that personality study is in its early infancy.

selection 50 / types of adjustive reactions / James C. Coleman, University of California, Los Angeles

Adjustive reactions can best be understood in terms of the total personality organization of the individual and his specific life situation. The particular adjustive reaction that occurs will vary widely depending upon these two sets of factors. However, even the most divergent attempts at adjustment follow certain basic dynamic principles and can be understood as attempts to cope with actual or perceived stress in such a way as to maintain psychobiological integrity by satisfying basic needs.

From James C. Coleman, *Abnormal Psychology and Modern Life*, Scott, Foresman and Company, Chicago, 1950, pp. 78–80. Copyright 1950 by Scott, Foresman and Company.

General patterns

In general the individual deals with his adjustive problems by either attack, withdrawal, or compromise, complicated by various ego defense mechanisms and by varying degrees of emotional involvement.

Attack, aggression, hostility In attack behavior we attempt to remove or surmount the obstacles through increased effort or a variation in mode of approach. We have seen that biological frustration leads to various compensatory or corrective activities such as the release of stored energy to allow increased activity by the organism in an attempt to meet the need and restore equilibrium. This increased tension and variant activity is apparently the primary origin of aggressive or attack-type behavior. In primitive form it is seen in the restless behavior of the infant deprived of food; such behavior is at first relatively uncoordinated and generalized, but as motor and intellectual abilities increase, the individual learns to evaluate and deal directly with an ever-increasing variety of specific obstacles.

Despite these improvements in efficiency, only a small number of stress situations can be adequately dealt with by means of direct aggression. This means that in infancy, as well as later in life, direct attack may be unsuccessful, the frustration continues, and the irritation, pain, and unpleasantness connected with it become attached to the objects or persons viewed as obstacles and sources of frustration. Such conditions, of course, lead to the arousal of emergency emotional reactions, particularly hostility. Thus aggressive reactions, which at first involve only a tendency toward increased activity and variation in mode of attack, may eventually be reinforced by hate or hostility.

Attack behavior may be primarily constructive or destructive in nature. With hostility there is a tendency to destroy as well as attack; hence we find that where hostility is extremely intense, attack behavior may be primarily destructive. For example, an individual who feels unwanted, unjustly treated, and deprived of opportunities afforded to others may build up intense resentment and hostility which may be manifested in hostile, aggressive activities, perhaps of a delinquent or criminal nature. Stealing, destroying property, setting fires, sexual misbehavior, and assault frequently represent attack patterns involving defiant hostile reactions of this sort.

The way in which hostility is discharged is very important in personality dynamics. For example, it may be expressed directly in overt behavior (physical or verbal), in fantasies (in which the individual may machine-gun or otherwise attack and destroy his enemies), or in competitive sports and other activities; or it may be discharged internally through the visceral organs. Although hostility is ordinarily directed toward external objects and persons viewed as sources of frustration, it may be evoked by personal limitations and mistakes and directed toward the self in terms of self-recrimination, self-punishment, and even self-mutilation and suicide.

Where the hostility is felt toward more powerful persons—authority figures—the individual may inhibit any actual outward manifestations. However, such hostile tensions may build up to high levels of intensity and become extremely difficult to manage; for we may not only view hostility as morally wrong, particularly if it is directed toward parents or siblings, but we know from unpleasant experience that overt hostile acts toward others lead to retaliation in the form of punishment and frustration. So, as we shall see, such hostility may come to be expressed in various deviant but "safe" ways.

Flight, withdrawal, fear Simple withdrawal is the second fundamental type of reaction to stress. Many animals seem capable of fairly well-coordinated withdrawal or flight reactions shortly after birth, but the human infant is relatively helpless for a long period and is unable to execute any well-coordinated withdrawal reaction. However, he is able to withdraw a bodily part from a painful stimulus such as a hot object and as Watson has demonstrated, he may on the occasion of sudden, unexpected stimuli tend to curl up into a ball, which appears to be sort of a primitive fear reaction.

As the growing infant learns to associate certain objects and situations with frustration and hurt, he may avoid instead of attacking them. His action tendency to withdraw in the face of such dangerous situations is typically reinforced by emotional processes involving fear. With time, his fears involve a wide range of real and imagined dangers as well as being usually induced by any strong, sudden, unexpected stimulation. And in a related way his withdrawal behavior becomes more complicated; in addition to mere physical withdrawal, he may withdraw in various psychological ways: he may inhibit dangerous internal desires, or consciously suppress them, or abandon goals, or restrict the situations to which he reacts, or even become emotionally passive.

So just as simple aggression becomes complicated by hostility we find simple withdrawal or flight reactions becoming complicated by fear. In both cases the individual's action tendencies are reinforced by mobilization of reserve resources, with a high degree of psychobiological tension demanding discharge. But here again social living provides few situations in which such mobilized energy can be utilized in direct physical action. Taking final examinations, being interviewed for jobs, excessive competition, cannot ordinarily be met by direct physical withdrawal. Rather the individual is forced to face the dangerous situation despite fears and anticipated frustration. It is of interest here to note that Shaffer found, in a study of fear in aerial combat, that situations permitting no adjustive response, such as "being fired upon when you have no chance to shoot back," were the most frequently reported causes of increased fear. On the other hand, he found that engaging in some effective activity was frequently conducive to reducing fear, even though such activities did not make possible the avoidance of the real danger.

Anxiety is very similar to fear, involving the same general pattern of emergency physiological changes and arising in connection with anticipated frustration or hurt. However, it differs from fear in certain essential respects. Fear is usually related to some immediate concrete situation, whereas the stress giving rise to anxiety is usually vague and ill-defined. Often the individual is unaware of what is causing his anxiety. Likewise, fear involves a definite action tendency of flight whereas anxiety is more in the nature of diffuse apprehension not leading to any action tendency. Thus anxiety seems to be a sort of preliminary or primitive fear reaction which mobilizes energy reserves to meet some threat, but in which neither the threat nor the appropriate direction of response is clearly discernible by the individual. Perhaps this feeling of vagueness and uncertainty adds to the unpleasantness of anxiety; in any event anxiety is one of the most painful and intolerable of all conscious experiences.

Compromise, substitution   Since most situations cannot be dealt with successfully by either direct attack or withdrawal, it usually becomes necessary to work out some sort of compromise. This represents our most common method of dealing with conflicts. Such compromises may mean accepting substitute goals or lowering one's aspirations or internal ethical or reality restraints. An individual faced with starvation may compromise with his conscience and steal "just this one time" because of the special nature of the conditions, or he may resort to eating worms, bugs, spiders, and even human flesh, or he may revise his ethical standards. Often, too, we resort to symbolic

Fig. 1 *Personality development determines motivational patterns. Motivational pattern and stress jointly determine reactions to stress, which will include ego defensive mechanisms if the stress is ego-involved.*

satisfactions under conditions of severe frustration. Thus a soldier may gain some substitutive satisfaction out of pin-up pictures or out of wish-fulfilling daydreams. In fact, Masserman has shown that under frustration, the individual becomes increasingly willing to accept substitutive goals—both symbolic and nonsymbolic ones. Hate, fear, and other emotional reactions may, of course, also reinforce or be involved in compromise reactions, as well as in attack or withdrawal reactions.

selection 51 / masculinity, identification, and father-son relationships / Paul Mussen and Luther Distler, University of California, Berkeley

By identifying with his parents—i.e., endeavoring "to mold (his) own ego after the fashion of one that has been taken as a model"—the child begins to acquire his parents' personality characteristics, behavior, values, motivations, and attitudes. Two of the major consequents of the processes of identification are the development of the superego, or conscience, and the acquisition of behavior and personality characteristics appropriate to his own sex (sex-typing).

It has been hypothesized that both boys and girls form their first identification with a female, the mother, because she is likely to be the most gratifying and affectionate person with whom the child has contact. Continued identification with the mother is appropriate for a girl, for she must acquire feminine personality characteristics and interests, but the boy "must shift to a masculine identification, sometime in his early years, if he is to develop normally masculine personality."

According to psychoanalytic theory, the boy's shift to identification with his father begins during the Oedipal phase of development and is motivated by fears and anxieties related to his hostility toward that parent. By identifying with his father, the boy's fears of counteraggression are reduced and, at the same time, he vicariously obtains his mother's attention and affection. This is the defense mechanism that has been called "identification with the aggressor" and "defensive identification."

In contrast to this, the developmental hypothesis states that identification with the father depends on a positive, affectionate relationship between father and son. If the father is an important source of nur-

From Paul Mussen and Luther Distler, "Masculinity, Identification, and Father-Son Relationships," *Journal of Abnormal and Social Psychology*, 59: 350–356, 1959. Reprinted by permission of the authors and the American Psychological Association.

turance, reward, and satisfaction, his responses and characteristics acquire secondary reward value and the boy imitates his father's behavior in order to "reproduce bits of the beloved and longed for parent."

Although the two hypothesized explanations of the dynamics underlying identification with the father seem to be vastly different from each other, there is some supportive evidence for each of them. The validity of the developmental identification hypothesis has been tested in a number of recent studies. Thus in one study, five-year-old boys with warm and affectionate fathers (as judged by home interviews) showed stronger father identifications than did boys with "cold" fathers. It has also been reported that adolescent boys who perceive their fathers as nurturant (according to projective tests) are more likely to identify strongly with this parent than are boys who do not perceive their fathers as rewarding. Moreover, certain characteristics of boys generally regarded as consequents of identification with the father—sex-typed behavior such as aggression, masculine interests and attitudes, and highly developed conscience—tend to be associated with favorable father-son relationships.

The hypothesis of defensive identification is a complex one that is difficult to investigate empirically. However, there are extensive clinical observations indicating that, as this hypothesis would predict, many children attempt to reduce their anxieties by adopting the aggressive characteristics of individuals whom they perceive as threatening to them.

It is quite possible, of course, that the two hypothesized identification processes are not mutually exclusive but may function together to facilitate the boy's shift from a feminine to a masculine identification. This view is consistent with that of the role theorists who equate identification with the father with "father role playing." These theorists maintain that identification, or role-playing, depends on the *power* of the identificand—a combination of his reward value *and* his threat or punishment potential. More specifically:

Given two . . . persons with whom one interacts and who differ in power over the actor (the identifier), i.e., differ in the degree to which they control rewards and punishments for the actor, one would predict that the actor would adopt many of the characteristics of the powerful as contrasted to the less powerful other person. This follows from the fact that it is more important to the actor to predict the behavior of the powerful figure, that he is motivated more strongly to take his role (i.e., to identify), that rewards and punishments are more impressive and the learning consequently better.

The present paper reports the results of an investigation that attempted to evaluate the validity of the three hypothesized explanations of identification—developmental, defensive, and role-playing. It was assumed that, for young boys, appropriate sex-typing of interests is an indication of identification with the father, and that amount of identification can be estimated from the degree of sex-typing. The rewarding-nurturant and threatening-punitive qualities of the father were evaluated in terms of the child's *perceptions* of the father, rather than in terms of the father's actual behavior, the criterion used in some previous studies.

There were several central questions. How do boys who are strongly identified with their fathers, i.e., highly masculine in their interests, perceive their fathers: as basically nurturant and rewarding, as would be predicted from the developmental identification hypothesis, or as punitive and threatening, in accordance with the defensive identification hypothesis? Or are they viewed as powerful agents of both reward and punishment, as the role-playing hypothesis of identification maintains?

Method

Subjects According to psychoanalytic theory and observational data, the late preschool period is a critical time in the boy's shift from feminine to masculine identification. For this reason, it seemed best to use kindergarten boys as Ss for this investigation.

Initially, 38 white five-year-old boys in two kindergarten classes of a predominantly middle-class public school were given the IT Scale for Children (ITSC), a projective test of sex-role preference. The test consists of 36 picture cards depicting various objects, figures, and activities commonly associated with masculine or feminine roles. The child is given a card with a figure drawing unstructured as to sex and referred to as IT. He is then presented with groups of pictures of toys and with paired choices of activities, and asked to choose what IT would like.

"In using IT the assumption is made that the child will project himself or herself into the IT-figure on the basis of his own or her own sex-role preference, and will attribute to IT the child's own role preference." The possible range of scores on the test is from zero, an exclusively feminine score, to 84, an exclusively masculine score.

The 10 boys with the highest scores (range 79-84, with a mean of 83) and the 10 boys with the lowest scores (range 30-63, with a mean of 53) were selected for further study. The two groups were matched in socioeconomic status, each of them having the same number of upper-lower, lower-middle, and upper-middle class boys. Ten of the Ss, 5 high scorers and 5 low scorers, came from one kindergarten class, and 10 from the other.

Measures of parent-child relations Between one and four weeks after he had taken the ITSC, each of the 20 boys was tested individually in a structured doll-play session. Early in the session, the child familiarized himself with three easily manipulated dolls, representing a mother, a father, and a boy doll, and some very simple toy furniture, which were on a low table in the testing room. S was told that these were to be used in a story telling game in which the examiner would make up the first part of the story and S would complete it.

The examiner then presented, with appropriate manipulations of the dolls, a series of nine incomplete, family situation stories, and the child was asked to complete each one in play. The stories were structured in such a way that the child could depict either or both parents as nurturant and/or punitive. Five of the incomplete stories follow:

1. The child wants a certain toy. He can't reach it. He goes into the living room to get help. Both Mommy and Daddy are busy reading. What happens?

3. The child lives on a very busy street. Mommy and Daddy told him never to cross the street alone. The child is playing in the front yard, and Mommy and Daddy are not there. A friend is on the other side of the street playing with his new bike. The child wants to cross the street very much. What happens?

4. The child is having fun playing with his toys. Mommy and Daddy say "It's time to go to bed now." The child says "I don't want to go to bed now." Then the child throws a toy on the floor and it breaks. What happens?

5. The child is getting ready to go to school. He has a knot in his shoelace. He can't fix it. What happens?

8. Let's pretend the little boy had a bad dream. Now the little boy wakes up from his bad dream, screaming. He calls for Mommy or Daddy. Which one does he call for, Mommy or Daddy? Then what happens?

If the child failed to respond to one of the stories or said "I don't know," the story was repeated or the question rephrased. If S did not mention the parents in his play, the examiner asked "What did Mommy or Daddy say or do?" When the child did not designate a specific parent in his response, the examiner inquired "Who did that, the Mommy or the Daddy?" Each doll-play session was completely recorded.

Scoring the doll-play responses The major hypotheses with which the study was concerned dealt with the relationship between boys' masculinity scores and their perceptions of their fathers. The structured doll-play situation, however, permitted evaluations of the child's perceptions not only of his father but also of his mother and his parents as a unit (when mentioned without specific designation of mother or father) as nurturant and/or punishing. The assumption underlying the use of this technique is that the boy's responses in doll play reveal his own feelings about his parents' treatment of him.

Each story was scored for the presence of nurturance or punishment by the father, mother, or "they" (parents undifferentiated). The stories were scored without the scorer's knowledge of the child's ITSC score.

The following scoring categories were used:

Father Nurturance (FN) score was the total number of stories in which the child character in the stories received help, comfort, attention, or reassurance from the father (e.g., "his Daddy gets it for him" in response to Story 1 described above).

A Mother Nurturance (MN) score was derived by counting the number of stories in which the mother was depicted as nurturant. (For example, in response to the story about the dream, "He calls his Mommy and she says it's just a dream and he can sleep with her.")

They Nurturance (TN) score was the number of stories in which the parents as a unit were nurturant. (For example, S, in response to Story 3: "They help him cross the street." E: "Who helps, Mommy or Daddy?" S: "His Mommy and Daddy.")

Total Nurturance (TotN) score was the sum of the MN (Mother Nurturance), FN (Father Nurturance), and TN (They Nurturance) scores.

The total number of stories in which the father, mother, or "they" disciplined, spanked, criticized, or admonished the child in the story constituted, respectively, the Father Punishment (FP), Mother Punishment (MP), and They Punishment (TP) scores.

Total Punishment (TotP) score was the sum of the FP (Father Punishment), MP (Mother Punishment), and TP (They Punishment) scores.

It should be noted that a given story could be scored for more than one variable. For example, if the mother in the story spanked the child and later comforted him, the story would be scored both Mother Punishment (MP) and Mother Nurturance (MN).

The total number of stories involving relationships with the father, either nurturant or punitive (i.e., FN plus FP), constituted the Father Power (FPow) score. Analogously, Mother Power (MPow) was the sum of the Mother Nurturance (MN) and Mother Punishment (MP) scores.

Results

The three theoretical formulations of the dynamics underlying the shift from feminine to masculine identification, outlined above, could be evaluated by determining the relationships between masculinity status and perceptions of parents, as measured by the child's responses in doll play. If the developmental hypothesis is valid, highly masculine boys would perceive their fathers as more rewarding and affectionate or, operationally, would have higher Father Nurturance (FN) scores than boys with low masculinity scores. On the basis of the defensive identification hypothesis, however, it would be predicted that boys who were most strongly identified with their fathers—as this is reflected in their highly masculine interests—would regard their fathers as more threatening and punitive, i.e., would have higher Father Punishment (FP) scores than boys whose father identifications are weak. The role-playing hypothesis of identification offers a third prediction. According to this theory, boys with strong tendencies to play the father role or to identify with the father would feel that their fathers were powerful figures and important sources of both rewards and punishments. In terms of the variables of this study, this would mean that highly masculine boys would have higher Father Power (FPow) scores than boys who have not achieved strong masculine identifications.

Since responses to the structured doll-play situation were scored for perceptions of the mother and "they" (parents as a unit) as nurturant-gratifying and/or punitive-threatening, it was also possible to assess

TABLE 1   MEAN SCORES OF BOYS HIGH AND LOW MASCULINITY
GROUPS ON FAMILY PERCEPTION VARIABLES

Variable	High masculinity group	Low masculinity group
Mother Nurturance (MN)	2.1	1.7
Father Nurturance (FN)	3.7	2.2
They Nurturance (TN)	.8	.7
Total Nurturance (TotN)	6.6	4.7
Mother Punishment (MP)	1.2	1.5
Father Punishment (FP)	2.8	2.1
They Punishment (TP)	.2	.7
Total Punishment (TotP)	4.2	4.3
Mother Power (MPow)	3.3	3.2
Father Power (FPow)	6.5	4.3

the relationships between these variables and strong or weak sex-typing
among five-year-old boys.

Table 1 presents the mean scores of the high and low masculinity
groups on all the doll-play scores.

In view of the facts that the number of Ss in each group was small
and that the distribution of scores on these variables was non-normal,
U tests were employed to compare rank transformation scores on all
doll-play scores of Ss scoring high and low on the ITSC. The results
of these tests and their significance levels are summarized in Table 2.

TABLE 2   DIFFERENCES BETWEEN HIGH AND LOW MASCULINITY
GROUPS ON FAMILY PERCEPTION VARIABLES

Variable	U	P	Group with higher scores
Mother Nurturance (MN)	45.5	NS	—
Father Nurturance (FN)	23.5	.02	Highs
They Nurturance (TN)	48.5	NS	—
Total Nurturance (TotN)	16.0	.004	Highs
Mother Punishment (MP)	44.0	NS	—
Father Punishment (FP)	30.5	.06	Highs
They Punishment (TP)	34.0	.07	Lows
Total Punishment (TotP)	47.0	NS	—
Mother Power (MPow)	49.5	NS	—
Father Power (FPow)	18.5	.007	Highs

It is obvious from this table that the two groups of Ss differ significantly in many of their perceptions of their families. Compared with boys low in masculine identification, as measured by the ITSC, those who were high in this characteristic perceived themselves as receiving more Total Nurturance (TotN) (i.e., more nurturance from all sources combined). Evidently, this difference is primarily attributable to differences in one major component of TotN, the perceptions of father's nurturance, for the two groups differ significantly in Father Nurturance (FN) scores but not in the Mother Nurturance (MN) or They Nurturance (TN) scores.

This finding seems clearly consistent with the developmental identification hypothesis. It supports the prediction, made on the basis of this hypothesis, that young boys are more likely to identify strongly with their fathers, and thus to acquire masculine interests, if they perceive their fathers as highly nurturant and rewarding.

The data also appear to lend support to the second, or defensive identification, hypothesis, which predicted that high masculine identification would be related to views of the father as threatening and punitive. Highly masculine boys tended to attribute more punishment to the fathers in their doll-play stories than boys low in masculine identification did, although the difference between the two groups in the father punishment score was not quite as marked as the difference in the father nurturance variable.

The third, or role-taking, hypothesis states that the degree of identification and, consequently, sex-role learning varies with the amount of the child's interaction with the identificand and the degree to which the latter has power over him, i.e., controls both his rewards and his punishments. The data of the present study seem to be fully in accord with this hypothesis, since the low and high masculinity groups differ markedly in Father Power (FPow) scores, the high identifiers giving a significantly greater number of these responses. This finding is exactly what would be anticipated, since this score is composed of the FN and FP scores, and the highly identified group scored significantly higher in each of these.

The high and low masculinity groups were not significantly different in any of the variables related to perceptions of the mother. However, compared with those scoring low on the ITSC, high scorers tended to perceive their parents as a unit as less punitive, i.e., tended to have lower They Punishment (TP) scores ($p = .07$). This would seem to be further confirmation of the findings of another study which concluded that adolescent "boys who feel comfortable in their relationships with their parents adopt more of their father's behavior and attitudes than boys who experience less favorable parent-child relationships."

It may be that the boy who scores high in They Punishment (TP) views his family milieu as hostile and unfriendly. While he may not feel that either parent is particularly threatening, he may feel generally rejected, unwanted, and unimportant. Insofar as this is true, the child may be expected to attempt to avoid intensive interactions with his parents. Under these circumstances, he should not identify strongly with his father and, consequently, should not acquire highly masculine interests.

Discussion

The data of the present study indicate that for boys, sex-typing of interests is more directly related to their perceptions of their fathers than to perceptions of their mothers. This finding is in accord with the findings of previous studies as well as with an assumption underlying all three of the identification hypotheses outlined above; namely, that the acquisition of masculine interests, attitudes, and patterns of behavior is primarily determined by the boy's interactions with his father.

Some of the findings of this study lend support to the defensive identification hypothesis; others seem to support the developmental hypothesis. Since the two hypotheses generate predictions that are in some respects diametrically opposed, there are also data that are inconsistent with both hypotheses. Thus, since the developmental hypothesis postulates that identification with the father is dependent upon nurturant rewarding interactions with that parent, the finding that boys also identify with punitive, threatening fathers must be inconsistent with this hypothesis. Conversely, the finding that boys are more likely to identify with a nurturant father is inconsistent with the view of defensive identification or identification with the aggressor.

A high level of masculine identification does not appear to depend on any one specific type of father-son relationship. From the child's point of view, the significant factor seems to be the father's *salience*—his importance in the child's life—rather than the particular techniques he uses in dealing with his child. Thus, as a group, boys who have made substantial father-identifications—reflected in their strongly sex-typed interests—perceived their fathers as both more nurturant *and* more punitive. Hence, masculine sex-role identification cannot be attributed exclusively to either the reward value or the threat potential of the father.

For these reasons, it seems to us that the role theory of identification is most fully consistent with—and most adequately integrates—the present data. The two groups were clearly differentiated on the Father Power (FPow) score, indicating that, compared with the other group, the highly masculine boys had—or at least perceived that they had—more intensive interactions with their fathers. This is exactly what is predicted by the role theory of sex-role identification, which maintains that more interaction with another individual, e.g., the father, leads to greater assimilation of his role.

Moreover, role theory states most explicitly that an individual is most likely to assimilate the role of, or identify with, individuals he sees as powerful. From the child's point of view, the most powerful individual is probably the one who most effectively controls his rewards and punishments. In this way, the theory implies that both reward and punishment strongly influence the course of role learning.

It follows from these postulates of role theory that the boy should be most strongly motivated to imitate or to practice his father's role frequently if he has a great deal of interaction with his father and sees him as a powerful source of rewards and punishments. Under these circumstances, the child gets extensive experience playing the father's role and adopts more of the father's characteristics, including those connected specifically with his sex-role. Our data are substantially in accordance with these theoretical predictions. The highly father-identified Ss—those who had adopted masculine interests and behavior—did in fact perceive their fathers as more interactive with them and as major providers of rewards *and* punishments.

There is also a psychoanalytic hypothesis which these data seem to confirm. In summarizing psychoanalytic writings on identification, Bronfenbrenner notes that one of the "syndromes of parent-child relationship . . . predisposing the child to incorporate or introject the parent" is "a relationship based on conditional love, in which the parent, willfully or unconsciously, withholds expression of affection as the price of conformity." This means that the boy is most likely to identify with his father if his feelings toward him are affectionate, while the father's love is given conditionally. According to this hypothesis, high nurturance from the father, together with the threat of withdrawal of his love (high FP), would lead to strong father identification. This prediction seems to be verified by the finding that highly masculine boys have relatively high Father Power scores, indicating a high degree of combined father nurturance and father punishment.

The findings may also be conceptualized in terms of general behavior theory. Among those with whom the preschool boy has intimate associations, the father is the one who has the most adequate knowledge of appropriate masculine behavior. If there is a high level of father-son interaction (high FPow scores), the father should frequently, and fairly regularly, reward the son's sex-appropriate responses and punish sex-inappropriate responses when they occur. Consequently, the boy's masculine responses should be relatively rapidly and effectively strengthened, while his sex-inappropriate responses become extinguished. In short, vigorous application of both rewards and punishments by the father facilitate the son's shift from feminine to masculine identification.

On the other hand, the condition of relatively little father-son interaction implies sporadic, and at best ineffective, rewards and punishments by the father. Under these circumstances, the shift in identification may be a difficult one, and the child's acquisition of sex-typed interests and behavior may be considerably retarded.

It seems that the father's use of *both* reward *and* punishment is his most effective method of "teaching" his son masculine behavior. It must be emphasized, however, that the high masculine and low masculine groups also differed significantly in the individual variables relating to perceptions of father reward and father punishment. From this it may be inferred that sex-appropriate behavior may be "taught" primarily by rewarding appropriate responses *or* punishing inappropriate responses. In short, from the child's point of view, the important factor is the salience of his relationship with his father, not the particular techniques that the father uses in handling him.

Of course, the present data refer *only* to masculinity of interests. Other possible long-range consequents of different processes of identification cannot be evaluated. For example, it is quite possible that boys who learn their sex roles primarily as a result of being punished or threatened by their fathers differ in many ways (e.g., in personality characteristics, self-conceptions, or basic motivations) from those who achieve their masculine identifications by means of developmental identification or through learning based on some combination of reward and punishment by the father. As the data stand, however, we can only state that five-year-old boys may shift from feminine to masculine identification, as measured by the acquisition of masculine interests, as a result of either developmental or defensive identification processes or, as role theory suggests, by some combination of the two.

Summary

The IT Scale for Children (ITSC), a test of sex-typing of interests, was administered to 38 white, middle-class, kindergarten boys. The 10 Ss scoring highest in the test were assumed to have developed the highest degree of male role identification, while the 10 scoring lowest were considered the least strongly identified with this role.

In order to determine the relationship between parental perceptions and degree of masculine identification, each of the 20 boys was tested in a structured doll-play situation. During the session, the child completed, in play, nine incomplete stories involving parent-child relations. Responses were scored in terms of the amount of nurturance, punishment, and power (nurturance plus punishment) attributed to the mother, father, and parents as a unit.

The study was designed to evaluate three hypothesized processes of identification—developmental, defensive, and role-taking. Analysis of the data provided evidence consistent with all three hypotheses. As predicted from the developmental identification hypothesis, young boys who were strongly identified with the male role perceived their fathers as more rewarding and nurturant ($p = .02$) than their weakly identified peers did. According to the defensive identification hypothesis, the strongly father-identified boys perceived their fathers as more punitive and threatening. This hypothesis was also supported ($p = .06$). Boys high and low in masculinity were also clearly differentiated on the Father Power score ($p = .007$). This finding indicates that those who have made substantial male identifications view their fathers as powerful sources of *both* reward and punishment, and is in accordance with role theory, which maintains that the child is most likely to assimilate the role of an individual with whom he has intensive interactions, especially if this individual is powerful. To the present authors, it seems that role theory, with its explicit emphasis on the importance of both reward and punishment in role-learning, best integrates all these data.

selection 52 / personality development in contemporary culture / Robert R. Sears, State University of Iowa

The problem of relating culture and personality is essentially one of defining the variables and measuring the constants of human motivation and social learning. Although the practical research tasks implied by this statement are both great and complex, the logical framework within which the work must be done is entirely unambiguous.

The individual is the molar unit of his society. During his lifetime, he develops motivational systems the action components of which enable him to interact with others. Certain aspects of his behavior are unique to him; the particular objects that call forth his love and hate, his language and gestural mannerisms, the strength of his affiliations and the style of his living differentiate him from his fellows. Other aspects, however, are stereotyped and virtually universal among the members of his society; these include such things as role-playing

From Robert R. Sears, "Personality Development in Contemporary Culture," *Proceedings of the American Philosophical Society*, 92:363–370, 1948. Reprinted by permission of the author and the publisher.

in institutional settings and the use of common language forms in naming family relationships. Whether the individual's behavior appears to be unique or common depends in some degree on the molecularity of description.

The complexity of these motivational systems is almost limitless. Some of them involve no more than appetites for certain foods or, in adults, routinized methods of maintaining cleanliness. Others involve elaborate interactions with other people. When these require the adoption of different roles by different people, and when the ensuing interactions solve such problems as the exchange of material goods or the rearing of children, the total pattern of societal behavior is described as an institution. The individual also learns to formulate rules and principles to guide his own behavior; that is, he verbalizes what he does and what goal he must reach. Each society possesses a set of more or less official formulations about the customary, and proper, way of solving some of its living problems. These formulations are the culture.

These various abstractions must not blind us to the fact that the ultimate operational referent of social science is the behavior of individual persons. Such terms as *class, family, institution,* and *status position* can be systematically commensurate with terms relating to an individual's behavior only if they are defined as forms of behavior and if the relevant motivational structures are fully described. Every criterion of class membership, for example, is a behavior item that exists in some person's repertory of actions. It may involve a linguistic form, a food preference, a method of rearing children, a way of dressing or the purchase of a kind of furniture. However nonbehavioral the immediate description of the criterion item may be (e.g., "owns a suburban home"), the fact is ultimately a behavior fact.

Socially relevant behavior is based on motives that are gradually built up through social experiences. These systems exist within the individual himself. They are constituted of drives to secure gratification through the making of consummatory or goal responses, and of action patterns that are primarily instrumental in the sense that they enable the person to get in such context with his environment as to permit him to secure the gratification.

These instrumental responses compose the great bulk of what is commonly called culture-conforming behavior. They are of significance because they not only provide the manipulative matrix within which other persons' behavior must occur, but by virtue of the learning process become secondary goal responses themselves. That is, they provide gratification when they occur and the individual will seek to manipulate his environment in order to permit them to occur.

When a man marries one wife at a time in the United States, for example, he is conforming to the marriage rules of a monogamous society. It is not only the verbal rules that make him conform, but a combination of antecedents that includes learned motivation as well. The rule gives him guidance as to what he must do, but the very word *must* suggests the sanctions that exist for the support or enforcement of the rule. These sanctions are by no means limited to immediate threats of punishment for bigamy; in the healthy man who is thoroughly assimilated in his culture, they also include secondary drives that can be gratified only by his behaving monogamously. Breaking the rules would lead to difficulties of adjustment with other persons who do conform, to be sure, but more importantly, it would frustrate motivational systems inherent in the man himself. He would fail to secure the gratifications he anticipated from the marital relationship and would suffer positive anxieties and frustrations as well.

The fact that adult culture-conforming behavior is dependent on the existence of appropriate supporting motives makes child development a key area for the construction of a systematic social science. As will be seen, the nature of these motives, the kind of behavior which provides him with gratification, depends on the kind of environment he has in childhood. This means that the personalities of his parents are a crucial element. What they do to reward or punish his efforts at social interaction determines the kinds of social interaction that will be desirable or undesirable, in his view, in his later life. In turn, what he does to and with other people in later life will determine not only his adjustment to his society but the extent to which he will stabilize or modify his society's culture patterns.

Origins of motives

A newborn infant has various biological needs that have associated with them primary drives. He needs food, warmth, and an opportunity to eliminate waste products. He is so constructed as to have internal stimulation that persists until these needs are satisfied. When he performs the appropriate acts, such as eating or shivering or defecating, to reduce these needs, there is a reduction also in the internal stimulation. Performance of such acts, or goal responses, also strengthens the connection between the stimulus conditions that existed at that moment and the various acts he performed just preceding the goal response. This is a statement of the principle of reinforcement.

The reinforced acts are in most instances instrumental to securing the necessary conditions for further reinforcement. Or if they are not instrumental at first, they become so in either one of two ways. First, the useless acts drop out because on the occasions on which they do not occur the goal response eventually occurs anyway. Second, the adults in the child's environment gradually learn to recognize the child's behavior as having a signal quality. For example, a child is likely to cry when it is hungry. It may also twist its left foot sideways by a species of physiological chance. There is small likelihood, however, that every time he gets fed he will have just twisted his foot. This movement therefore suffers extinction and does not enter into the eventual instrumental act sequence by which food is obtained.

The cry is another matter, however. The mother soon learns to recognize this as a signal that the child wants feeding. Later on in his life, the youngster will develop a whole host of signal acts to control the people around him. His primitive crying response may be reflex in character, and its ease of becoming a signal for feeding may be because it is painful to the mother. This will not be true of language habits; there is nothing intrinsically painful about the words "I'm hungry, mommy!" nor do they become a part of the child's repertory without great effort, but the words are none the less effective as controllers of behavior.

Another consequence of the reinforcement process is that the instrumental acts become secondary or learned goal responses. In Figure 1 the various parts of a behavior sequence are indicated. The drive stimuli that accompany the existence of a primary biological need are indicated by S_D. Other simultaneous stimulation that impinges on the child's sense organs is shown as S_1; this includes lights and sounds, odors and tastes, proprioceptive stimuli, and central symbolic processes. When the appropriate instrumental activity is carried out, exogenous agencies (in this discourse—people) do something and create new environmental conditions, or events, that permit the child to make a goal response (R_G). The instrumental acts gradually become goal responses in their own right after a large number of successful completions of the behavior sequence. Furthermore, the objects that create the favorable environmental event become secondary rewards.

This process has been clearly exemplified in a study by Wolfe (1936), who gave young chimpanzees an opportunity to get food from a vending machine by inserting poker chips in a slot. Although the animals showed no interest in the chips initially, the constant

Fig. 1 *Instigation-action sequence. This is the basic unit of individual behavior.*

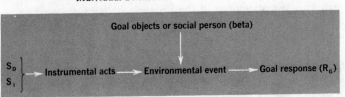

use of them instrumentally in the eating sequence made them desired objects. After the animals had become thoroughly accustomed to their use, they would work for the chips and would hoard them when the vending machine was not available. Later studies have shown that such secondary rewards may be used for motivating learning.

Since the instrumental activities are designed to manipulate the environment, the nature of the environment becomes an important determiner of the kinds of activities that will be learned. Likewise, the new motivational systems will be composed of secondary goal responses that require certain environmental events for their occurrence. Hence, the characteristics of the behavior of people who surround the child become the primary determiners of the kinds of motives he will develop.

The social person

This situation is schematized in Figure 1. Both the goal object and the social person who collaborates with the child in the interaction sequence are indicated as entering the sequence at the point where the new environmental event is created. The full implications of this social relationship are better exhibited by Figure 2. Alpha is the child in this instance and beta is the parental adult. At a given moment each has certain basic drives (S_D) and non-drive stimuli (S_1) operating. Let us suppose the child is hungry and the mother has a nurturant drive. The child cries; this stimulation is part of the S_1 impinging on beta, the mother. The cry is one of the child's instrumental acts. The mother then performs an instrumental act that will lead to satisfaction for her nurturant drive; she picks the child up, holds him against her breast, smiles at him and talks softly as she presents the breast to him. Both of them thereupon have the necessary environmental events for performing the goal response. The child eats $(R_G$, a goal response to a primary drive), and the mother nurtures her child $(Rg$, a goal response to a probably secondary drive). The instrumental activities of each have been required for the production of the environmental events needed by the other. This situation describes the fundamental unit of social interaction, with reference not only to ongoing social behavior but also to the formation of motivational systems involving interdependence between people.

Schematic diagrams like Figure 2 are so simplified as to rob the process of its human meaningfulness, however. Emphasis must be given to the kind of behavior performed by beta. Mothers do not merely feed their children; they talk to them and snuggle them, they pick them up frequently or rarely, they are tense or relaxed. When such major problems of socialization as weaning, toilet training, cleanliness and orderliness training, and the control of emotional

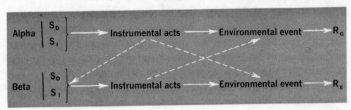

Fig. 2 *Instrumental interaction sequence. This is the basic unit of social behavior.*

dependency and aggression present themselves, there are innumerable ways in which parents can vary from one another, and at the same time be consistent in the treatment of their own children.

It is to these finer and yet very pervasive dimensions of behavior that we must look for the origin of individual differences in motivational systems. While the gross outlines of social action are determined by parental reflection of cultural standards, there are many aspects of their behavior toward their children that derive from non-culturally determined characteristics of their own motivational systems. For example, it is commonly said that middle-class American culture puts a high premium on orderliness and the care of material household goods. In comparison with lower class standards this may be so. But within the group of middle class people there are great variations in the style of orderly behavior and great differences in the relative importance of orderliness. To some women, a toy-strewn living room floor is but another chore; if the day is over and the children are in bed, the floor will be cleaned up, as an instrumental act, in order that adults will not stumble and that the next day may start fresh. To other women, the situation is distressing, offensive. It creates discomforting anxiety and represents a threat to the neatness status of the household, possibly a threat to social status. Orderliness has high value in its own right. These contrasting kinds of mothers inevitably treat their children differently. The first ignore messy play, permit children great latitude in manipulative activities within the house, reinforce within-the-house motility. The other group are restrictive and inhibitive with reference to children's play, more frequently commanding, demand low within-the-house motility and reduce manipulative play to a high extent. Because children enjoy exploration and manipulation, the orderly mothers will be more often frustrated by their children and will have a tenser and more hostile attitude toward them; they will set more rigid standards and be more punishing.

These differences between parents can be understood as influences in child training only if they are introduced into the learning situation presented by Figure 2. Each mannerism, each approach or withdrawal, each facial expression, laughter and frowning, each command or plea, is a quality of the social person, beta, in the interaction sequence. These qualities, to the extent that they occur with reasonable consistency in the parental interaction with the child, become essential properties of the goal object or social person around whose behavior the child's secondary motives are developed. He becomes a person who is accustomed to orderliness or its lack, hostility or friendliness, much or little help. More importantly, he is motivated to modify his environment to make it like that which he has known if its properties have been associated with reward. And he will be motivated to rebel if there has been too much associated hostility and punishment.

To put the matter briefly, what the parents do and how they do it determine the content of the motivational systems of the child.

The field for research

In spite of its empirical complexity, the field for research can be summed up simply. A society has verbal formulations of the way it solves many of its problems, both material and social. The people who compose the society behave with varying degrees of conformity to these formulations. Children reared in a particular culture learn not only the verbal formulations but the necessary motivational systems that will ensure their conforming to the culture. But the kinds of behavior required by the society's adults determine in some degree the kinds of training used for the children. And the kind of people the adults are, defined in terms of their behavior toward their children, determines the kind of motivational systems developed by the children.

This formulation of the relationship between culture and personality development rests on the process of social learning. It requires that systematic analysis be made of the conditions of learning and of the nature of the behavior learned. Such an approach is compounded of ethnography and a detailed psychological study of parent-child interaction. The former is essential for securing a description of the culture, and the latter for discovering how the methods used for socializing the child create the qualities of personality in him that generally characterize members of his culture and specifically characterize him.

The current research program at the Iowa Child Welfare Station is organized around one segment of this dual problem. It would be impractical to try to secure measures of large areas of contemporary American culture at one time, and equally confusing to try to take into consideration a large number of variables in the personalities of children. Therefore, we are limiting our investigation at the start to a few highly significant factors that gain their importance from their universality; they represent problems of social adjustment to all societies.

Two of these relate to biological differences among people that each society must find a way of coping with; these are the fact of there being two sexes and the fact that children have different ordinal positions in a given family. The roles of the two sexes are differentiated by all societies, but there are sharp differences among cultures as to the responsibilities allocated to each, and corresponding to these role differences are motivational differences. Personality characteristics such as aggression have been shown to differ sharply, also; in our own society these differences can be detected as early as age three.

The question as to what learning situations and parental training techniques are responsible for these differential personality developments is by no means a purely academic one, although the study of sex typing should prove an excellent place to discover the basic principles of certain types of motivational development. From a practical standpoint, the degree to which a given child fits his or her sex role is an important determiner of the success of later marital adjustment, a point of crucial importance for the child and a significant variable in its effect on the institutionalized culture pattern of the family.

The significance of ordinal position is greater in some societies than others, because of the formulations that surround primogeniture. Even in our own society, however, which has little formalized role provided for the various ordinal positions, rather startling and consistent differences have been observed between the personality characteristics of first and second children. The fact that different ordinal positions provide well-defined differences in the in-family social learning situation makes this dimension a useful one for studying the effects of variation in parental treatment.

Two other universal problems, inherent in the nature of man's societal living, derive from biological similarities rather than differences. It is evident from the analysis of social interaction schematized in Figure 2 that the social person, beta, can either help or hinder alpha, the individual whose behavior we observe. If he hinders, alpha is described as frustrated. In order to enforce his demands for assistance, or at least non-interference, alpha can make use of the fact that all people can suffer pain or injury and that they withdraw from the injuring stimulus. Since there are certain vocal and manneristic expressions associated with this withdrawal, expressions that are part of the reaction to pain, alpha has an opportunity to develop a secondary drive to produce injury that will be satisfied by perceiving such evidences of pain. This is the drive of aggression. Aggressive behavior in one form or another is found in all societies, and all societies develop procedures for controlling it. To some extent these different aggressions, counter aggressions, and controls are formulated by the society's members, but formulated or not most societies, and particularly our own, have difficulties in providing appropriate aggression training for their children.

The other problem posed by the interaction sequence of Figure 2 is that of dependency. The care of children during their early years involves repeated contact between parent and child, and many of these contacts are the environmental events required for the satisfaction of primary drives. Hence, the child has an opportunity to develop secondary drives for the satisfaction of which specific kinds of helping responses by others are the secondary rewards or environmental events. As the child grows older, some of these drives must be extinguished if he is to become an independent person able to play the adult role in his society. Recent psychiatric analyses, especially those by Levy, have focused attention on the more extreme forms of the failure to establish adequate independence motivation, but dependency is necessarily a universal consequence of the very nature of child-rearing in any culture. It is the root of affiliative and cooperative behavior, and the problems any society faces have not to do with its total elimination, but with its control and utilization in the maintenance of societal stability.

In our research design, sex groups and ordinal position groups are being handled as independent variables comparable to cultures, while aggression and dependency are considered as dependent variables. The *processes* of sex typing and ordinal position typing are similar to the processes of the development of aggression and dependency drives, and all four represent areas for investigation in which the relationship between culture and personality is intimate. The inculcation of children into the society is largely a problem of training or rearing for which, in most cultures, the parents are primarily responsible during the first few years of the child's life.

Ethnography

The first step appears to be an ethnographic one. In order to relate the specifics of personality formation to cultural antecedents, there must be an adequate account of what happens to the child. This account must contain several things. First, it must describe the ideals of personality or behavior toward which parents are training their children. Second, it must present the details of how parents formulate the methods by which these ideals are being achieved. And third, it must give a description of both the range and the modality of the actual practices of the parents in their child-rearing.

It would be impossible to cover all aspects of child development in such an ethnographic study; too many ideals would be unique to particular parents or to specific sub-cultures, and there are too many areas of interaction between parent and child to be able to sample them all. As a beginning, the ethnography will be useful if it emphasizes those aspects of the child's behavior that are related to the major primary drives (hunger, sex, sleep and fatigue, elimination), the major secondary drives dependent on social interaction (aggression, dependency, independence, status striving, affection), certain of the routines that play an important part in our own culture (cleanliness, orderliness, hygiene), and reactions to disciplinary control. Parental practices in these areas probably account for the chief influence the parents have on their children's developing motivational systems.

Such data are needed for several purposes. First, they will permit the detailed comparison of various sub-cultures within our own society. Observations by Davis and Havighurst have shown that lower and middle-class child-rearing practices differ radically in certain respects, and that Negro and white practices are different to some degree even when class position is taken into account. These differences, and many others based on ethnic and religious affiliations, provide the bases for differences in the motivational characteristics of the sub-groups involved. Comparison of ideals of personality will indicate the extent to which there are conflicts within contemporary society and the extent to which specific culture groups are operating out of context with the ideals of contiguous groups. The data will also provide a sample of contemporary American practices for comparison with data on primitive cultures. At present the Navaho, Alorese, Hopi, Kwoma and several Micronesian cultures have been studied with more thoroughness in respect to the basic facts of child training procedures than has the American culture.

Second, child-rearing practices can be matched with the personality characteristics of the children. Data concerning children's behavior are being sought through several procedures, and the ethnographic report of practices is necessary to provide tests of hypotheses relating practices to behavior. The two comparisons having immediate priority are those between the sexes and between ordinal positions within any one culture group. Before antecedent-consequent relations can be evaluated, however, it is first necessary to discover what the parental aims are for their children, and what, if any, differences these differential aims make in the parents' formulations of their child-rearing procedures.

Finally, analysis of the parental formulations of their child-rearing methods will throw light on the relationship between formulation and intra-cultural consistency.

Measurement of personality

Two main approaches are being made to the problem of personality measurement in the children. One is on the level of overt behavior and the other on the fantasy level. Various procedures for getting samples of overt behavior are necessary; no one appears to encompass a large enough sphere of the child's life to provide a full picture of his behavior characteristics. One study is in process that involves the repeated observation of aggressive and dependent behavior in a relatively free social situation in the preschool. This work is requiring the definition of these two motivational systems in terms of concrete behavior items that can be isolated and counted through a behavior unit sampling method. Another study is comparing interview data obtained from teachers with performance exhibited by the child in test situations created in the laboratory and designed to facilitate the occurrence of aggressive and dependent behavior. Both studies are oriented around the question of the interrelationships between different manifestations of the dependency drive and of the aggressive drive. A third study is exploring the use of public reputation in a community as a means of measuring child behavior. Comparisons are being made between ethnic sub-groups in communities containing two or more clearly differentiated groups. Judgments about the aggressive, dependent and self-reliant or independent behavior of school children are being obtained from church members, police, teachers, social workers, and others whose public positions require them to deal on an institutional basis with the children under consideration.

Exploratory studies have been completed on another method of measuring overt behavior. Merrill has introduced the child and his mother jointly into a laboratory setting and has worked out a method of time sampling for the measurement of methods of maternal control and of types of child response. This method was shown to have a potential source of serious error in it, however, and it is questionable how far one can go with it. Mothers in whom some anxiety about the "goodness" of their child's behavior had been evoked changed so markedly in their methods of dealing with the child that the obtained sample was unsatisfactory as a measure of everyday behavior. Whether it was satisfactory as a measure of the mother's behavior under conditions of strain remains to be determined.

Still another method, currently being investigated by Dr. Vincent Nowlis, is that of securing data about a child's behavior from an interview with the mother. The interview technique is in part adapted from the methods worked out by Kinsey, but factual emphasis is being laid on the child's reactions to specific instances of disciplinary control exerted in connection with the channeling and control of the primary and secondary drive systems. This procedure will provide not only information about the child's immediate responses to the training situation, but will give a measure of individual differences among the members of a homogeneous culture group with respect to the kinds of disciplinary practices of the parents. This will permit the correlation of the data with other data, both overt and fantasy, obtained from the same children.

Since, from a practical standpoint, the measurement of overt behavior in children is often tedious, expensive, and difficult to manage for many research projects, collateral research is being carried out with projective procedures. Techniques such as doll play permit a study of the child in camera, as it were, and require less equipment, time, and environmental control than do overt behavior measures. Parallel studies on doll play performances are being directed to the measurement of dependency and aggression. The same children who are being observed in the preschool, and whose parents are being interviewed, are being examined in a standardized projective doll play setting by Dr. Pauline S. Sears.

Conclusion

This research program is based on the assumptions that the formalized patterns of a society's behavior on the one hand are a product of motivational systems established in its people and on the other partly determine what the adults will do in rearing their children; and that the personalities, or motivational systems, of the children are in turn a function of the society's child-rearing practices. The methods of research being used have been chosen for their effectiveness in providing a measure of the conditions under which children's motivational systems are learned, the process by which the learning is reinforced by parents, and the products of the learning in the children.

CHAPTER 13 ✸ BEHAVIOR DISORDERS ✸

The two major classes of behavior disorders are neurosis and psychosis. Neurotic behavior often follows certain general patterns which may involve (1) loss of memory or function of a portion of the body (hysteria); (2) recurring thoughts or actions over which the person has little or no control (psychasthenia); (3) excessive fatigue and anxiety-related body complaints (neurasthenia); (4) chronic low-grade anxiety which occasionally flares into an acute anxiety attack (anxiety neurosis). Although such behavior syndromes are certainly maladaptive in the long run, they are attempts on the person's part to adjust to his environment as he perceives it. It is unfortunately the case that his perception of his social environment is distorted. It is not surprising that perceptual distortions first manifest themselves in relation to the social environment; since the behavior of others is more ambiguous, it requires more interpretation based on one's own feelings than is the case in perception of our physical environment. One recurring perceptual distortion of the neurotic person is that he is an inadequate and inferior person. In effect, he generalizes his real limitations and failures too far. He defines his "self" on the basis of his weaknesses rather than a realistic evaluation of both strengths and weaknesses. This chronic feeling of inadequacy generates emotions of anxiety and fear, and the anxiety and fear make the person less capable of using his rational thinking processes in order to solve his adjustment problems. Many aspects of his environment, especially other people, are perceived as frustrating and threatening. This generates more anxiety which perpetuates the vicious circle. He then begins to rely more and more on defense mechanisms to reduce this anxiety. Although the ego defenses may reduce his anxiety, without responsible constructive action they tend to be used to excess. Thus, in the short run they are adjustive, but in the long run they are maladaptive since in the neurotic their excessive use renders him less capable of more realistic nondefensive solutions to his adjustment problems.

Psychoses may be divided into two general classes:

The organic psychoses are those which are based on actual destruc-

tion of portions of the central nervous system, for example general paresis and alcoholic psychosis. The functional psychoses are those in which no central nervous system damage is present, for example, schizophrenia and manic depressive psychosis. Since the organic psychoses have been found to be related to biological factors, it has long been the hope that biological determinants of functional psychoses could be discovered. Considerable research effort is being expended by biochemists, physiologists, psychiatrists, and psychologists toward the resolution of this problem. One of the most exciting leads is being investigated by Dr. Robert G. Heath and his co-workers. They have found that the administration of taraxein, a protein substance extracted from the blood of schizophrenics, produces temporary schizophrenic-like behavior in normal persons (cf. Selection 53). Furthermore, it is their impression that schizophrenia may really be one disease entity in that the different types of schizophrenia may be related to the amount of taraxein in the blood. However, they admit that this latter conclusion is quite speculative and will require considerably more research. Let us suppose that eventually we are successful in determining a specific biochemical imbalance which causes schizophrenia. Will this invalidate the importance of psychological and sociological factors? On the contrary, we will then be ready for further research to explore the distinct possibility that the biochemical imbalance itself is related to psycho-social stress situations.

What are some of the psychological factors which are important in the development of psychoses? In Selection 54 Professor Coleman reviews some of the factors which are important in psychoses in general and then discusses in more detail these factors as they are related to the most frequently occurring functional psychosis, schizophrenia. It should be no surprise that frustration, conflict, and distortions of interpersonal relations are intimately connected with the psychotic adjustment. In all psychoses we find perceptual distortion present in a more intense degree than in neurosis. The neurotic may distort the intentions of his wife or boss, but the psychotic often distorts the intentions of all people. The schizophrenic, in particular, tends to perceive others as basically untrustworthy. He thus tends to withdraw from those very social contacts which might provide an opportunity for correction of his misconceptions. His faulty perceptions eventually become organized into a consistent but distorted system of beliefs about other people (delusions). His distorted perceptions may extend beyond his social environment to the physical environment in such a way that he perceives objects or voices which are not actually present in the external world (hallucinations).

The involved student may be thinking at this point, "I think I can understand some of the personality dynamics in neurosis and psychosis, but how does this distorted perception of self and others get started in the first place?" The foundations for schizophrenia seem to be laid in childhood by certain types of relationships within the family. The central role played by the parents, especially the mother, is emphasized in Selection 55 by Dr. Richard L. Jenkins. He also describes in detail the progression of the schizophrenic reaction from schizoid withdrawal, through personality disorganization, to reorganization of the personality into the "schizophrenic way of life." The full-blown psychosis is thus an attempt to organize perceptions and thought processes into an integrated, although distorted, conception of the person and his surroundings. It is adjustive, albeit maladaptive.

Further insight into the dynamics and development of neurosis is presented by Dr. Karen Horney in her paper "Culture and Neurosis." She emphasizes that the cultural tendency to encourage competition and rivalry among people results in a constant need for measuring up to others, a need for perfection, and a chronic reaction of hostility toward others (although, of course, the neurotic's hostility may be concealed from others and from himself). However, our culture is not consistent; it requires competition but also encourages the person to be self-sacrificing and modest. When this culturally induced conflict is imposed on a person who already is in a state of "Basic Anxiety" (cf. Selection 56), a vicious circle develops. The neurotic has a need for reassurance from other people, but he chronically expects a rejection from them; this in turn results in his interpreting their behavior as being rejecting in fact. More hostility is generated by the perceived rejection, and the person becomes more anxious and insecure. This vicious circle is an excellent example of some of the general characteristics of the neurotic which we noted at the beginning of this section. His attempts to adjust to his environment are self-defeating because his perception of others is distorted in such a way as to emphasize their competitive prowess and his own inadequacy.

selection 53 / effects on behavior in humans with the administration of taraxein / Robert G. Heath, Sten Martens, Byron E. Leach, Matthew Cohen, and Charles Angel, Tulane University School of Medicine

In this report of work in progress, we describe the effect of the administration of a protein substance, which we have named taraxein,

Abridged from Robert G. Heath, Sten Martens, Byron E. Leach, Matthew Cohen, and Charles Angel, "Effects on Behavior in Humans with the Administration of Taraxein," *American Journal of Psychiatry*, 114:14–24, 1957. Reproduced by permission of the American Psychiatric Association.

extracted from the serum of schizophrenic patients. Taraxein has been given on 17 occasions to nonpsychotic volunteers and on 1 occasion to a schizophrenic in remission. In all, 20 human subjects have been used in this study.

Factors leading up to the isolation of this blood fraction were briefly reviewed in the presentation at the APA meeting in Chicago, 1956. For several years we had obtained subcortical and cortical recordings from a group of schizophrenic patients which revealed a characteristic spike and slow wave pattern in the septal region and rostral hippocampus. Accumulated evidence indicated that the introduction of physiological variables to this region produced profound changes in blood chemistry. This led to the exploration of the comparative effects of schizophrenic and normal serum on the speed of adrenaline oxidation. Our findings suggested that adrenaline was more rapidly oxidized by the serum of schizophrenics who were free of systemic disease than in normal control subjects. Similarly, we found in confirmation of Altschule's work that levels of reduced glutathione were lower in a statistically significant number of schizophrenics without systemic disease than in normal control subjects. Both indicators, *i.e.* the speed of adrenaline oxidation and the low glutathione levels, were, however, nonspecific since nonpsychotic persons with various systemic diseases showed similar alterations. It was known from work of others that copper levels were increased in chronic disease processes and in schizophrenia, and that in diseases other than schizophrenia, the elevated copper levels were due to increased levels of the copper globulin oxidase, ceruloplasmin. In investigating the adrenaline oxidation phenomenon, we noted that the addition of copper speeded the process considerably. In one study we isolated ceruloplasmin from serum and found that this was the substance in serum responsible for the increased oxidation. Details of this study including the isolation of one inhibitor of the process (albumin) are given in a separate article. Recent evidence suggests the presence of additional inhibitors. Inasmuch as patients with schizophrenia showed the increased speed of oxidation of adrenaline and lowered levels of reduced glutathione in the absence of systemic diseases, we postulated that perhaps a copper protein accounting for these differences might be qualitatively different if this chemical phenomenon, namely increased levels of oxidizing enzymes, was an important factor in psychotic behavior. To test this hypothesis we isolated ceruloplasmin from the serum of normals and schizophrenics and administered it to monkeys with chronically implanted electrodes. With the intravenous administration of ceruloplasmin from schizophrenic patients, the monkeys occasionally showed mild behavioral changes characterized by reduction in level of awareness resembling incipient catatonic symptoms. This did not occur with the administration of the substance extracted from normals. It was noted during the extraction procedure, however, that at one point in the process a blue color was present in the precipitate from schizophrenic serum but not in the precipitate from normal serum. Since we had these mild behavioral changes with administration of schizophrenic ceruloplasmin, we postulated that perhaps this apparently different precipitate might be significant. Therefore, instead of discarding it, as is routinely done in the extraction of ceruloplasmin, we set up a procedure for processing this substance. When the end-product of this procedure was administered to the monkeys, most profound behavioral changes resulted; the behavior resembling very closely that seen in schizophrenic patients. The monkeys appeared dazed and out of contact. They were catatonic and the extremities could be readily molded into various positions. In association with this, there were clear-cut alterations in the electrical recordings, particularly from the septal region. Since we had accumulated considerable data on recordings from human schizophrenics which showed essentially the same characteristics, we reasoned that if our recordings in schizophrenics were significant, then administration of this substance should induce schizophrenic-like behavior in the humans (we could not reasonably call the monkeys' behavior schizophrenic since this diagnosis is dependent upon the reporting of the patient). In this regard, our previous data on electrical recordings from humans were of extreme importance since we would otherwise have had no logical reasons for assuming that the behavioral reactions we observed in monkeys were anything more than simple toxic effects which many compounds are capable of producing. Other compounds which altered behavior in monkeys have never produced this characteristic type of recording. Thus, by means of the electrical recording, we are apparently able to make meaningful cross-interpretations of behavior from animals to man.

The experimental design for each group and the questions to be answered by each were as follows:

Group I This experiment, which included 2 subjects, was designed to answer the major question as to whether or not administration of the blood substance from schizophrenics which produced characteristic behavioral and subcorticogram changes in monkeys would result in schizophrenic-like behavior in humans. In contrast to the monkeys, the humans could report their thoughts and feelings, thus providing the data necessary to compare these reactions with behavioral changes seen in schizophrenic patients. Each of the subjects received 1 injection of active taraxein from pooled schizophrenic serum and 1 of the subjects first received 2 injections of an inert substance as a control.

Group II This experiment included 5 subjects and was designed to provide a larger and more thorough study with more controls. Each subject was examined by 4 psychiatrists. Psychological testing was conducted before, during, and at conclusion of the reaction. Very active substance was given to 2 subjects; normal saline to the third; the protein fraction obtained by the same procedure from normal serum was administered to the fourth subject; the fifth volunteer received a weak taraxein injection. The subject receiving the fraction from normals was later given a weak solution of taraxein. The weaker solutions provided information regarding dosage levels. In this experiment, pooled serum subdivided according to the conventional subcategories of schizophrenia was employed.

Group III This was a heterogeneous group and included the 3 nonprisoner volunteers. Our motivation in administering taraxein to a schizophrenic in remission was to determine if there would be a difference in reaction from that seen in nonpsychotic subjects. Our reasoning was that we might obtain some leads as to possible underlying mechanisms in the phenomenon. Inclusion of the 2 additional subjects served to determine if residency in a state prison was prerequisite for the reaction.

Group IV This group included 6 subjects. Four were given taraxein. In addition, 6 injections of control substances were made, 3 of which consisted of the protein extracted by the taraxein isolation method from serum of normals and 3 were of the ceruloplasmin fraction from normal serum. As is apparent, some of the subjects received 2 injections, either 1 of taraxein and 1 of the substance similarly extracted from normal serum or 2 injections of different normal fractions (1 subject). In this experiment we selected as volunteers only first offenders who had minimal prison sentences in an attempt to obtain a prisoner group with the least degree of psychopathy. Also in this experiment, pooled serum subdivided according to the conventional diagnostic subcategories of schizophrenia was employed. Our purpose in doing this was to determine if the taraxein extracted from serum of patients with one particular subcategory of schizophrenia would, when injected, induce similar symptoms in the recipient.

Group V Two of the 4 subjects of this group received 2 injections at least 3½ hours apart; a third subject, 3 injections each separated by at least 3½ hours; a fourth subject received only 1 injection—a total of 8 injections: 5 of active taraxein; 1, the fraction extracted from normal serum; 1 of normal saline; 1, a weak solution of sodium amytal. All injections contained the same volume of fluid and were purposely made to be of exactly the same color. This experiment was designed to determine whether or not the same individual would react differently upon receiving taraxein of one subcategory of schizophrenia than he would when receiving taraxein of another subcategory.

On all experiments, moving picture films were taken before and at various periods following the administration of the compounds.

Results

All patients receiving taraxein developed symptoms which have been described for schizophrenia. This does not imply that each time we have processed taraxein, especially in the earlier stages, we obtained an active product. It has been our policy always to test at least 1 dose of each preparation on monkeys prior to setting up a study with human volunteers. The details of information we have gathered concerning the factors in processing which might inactivate this substance will be given in our paper on identification. With the exception of a few early occasions, we have always processed blood from normals along with that of the schizophrenics, usually isolating the ceruloplasmin as well as the fraction that comes out by the extraction method for taraxein. In monkeys we have given the fraction extracted from normal serum by the taraxein isolation method on 10 occasions to 7 monkeys without producing behavioral or EEG changes. In the 5 human subjects to whom this fraction obtained from normal serum was administered as a control, we induced no reaction. Likewise, in the 3 normal subjects who received ceruloplasmin extracted from normal serum, there was no reaction. There is, however, one questionable situation in regard to the administration of the protein fraction from normals which is detailed below under Complications. In none of the other control experiments which included 2 doses of known inactivated taraxein and, on 3 occasions the administration of saline, or Sodium Amytal, has there been any behavioral change.

Some rather consistent basic alterations in behavior have occurred in every subject receiving taraxein. This is in contrast to rather marked variability in secondary symptoms which have appeared. Basic alterations are similar to those described by Bleuler as "fundamental symptoms." Secondary symptoms resemble Bleuler's "accessory symptoms." The onset of symptoms is gradual beginning in every instance between 2 and 10 minutes following the injection. Symptoms increased slowly in intensity reaching a peak between 15 minutes and 40 minutes, after which they begin to subside. The longest duration of clinically detectable symptomatology in the nonpsychotic population has been 2 hours. No residual abnormalities have ever been observed beyond this period except in the case of the 1 schizophrenic patient.

General reactions

The characteristic general change is evidence of impairment of the central integrative process resulting in a variety of symptoms. There is marked blocking with disorganization and fragmentation of thought.

There is impairment of concentration. Each subject has described this in his own words—some saying merely "I can't think"; "my thoughts break off"; others, "I have a thought but I lose it before I can tell you anything about it," etc. "My mind is a blank" is another common expression. It becomes impossible to express a complete thought. Often they will state only a part of a sentence. They appear generally dazed and out of contact with a rather blank look in their eyes. They become autistic, displaying a lessening of animation in facial expression. Subjective complaints of depersonalization are frequent. Attention span is markedly shortened with increase in reaction time. The symptoms often produce apprehension in the patients. The commonest verbalization of their concern is "I never felt like this in my life before." Virtually all have made this statement. Memory was impaired only during states of profound stupor. Recall was excellent in all cases except for what transpired during periods of deep stupor. Sensorium has always been clear when subjects are capable of reporting.

Specific reactions

The test subjects have developed secondary symptoms of various types and degrees. In an effort to gain some knowledge as to whether or not the subcategories of schizophrenia represented different diseases, we have carried out a variety of studies with the various test groups.

In the first test group of 2 subjects, 1 batch of taraxein was extracted from pooled serum of schizophrenics of various subtypes. Each subject received one-half the material and the secondary symptoms in one were predominantly catatonic whereas in the other they were predominantly paranoid.

In 3 of the test groups, II, IV, and V, taraxein was extracted from schizophrenic serum which was pooled in accordance with the classical subcategories, *i.e.* paranoid, catatonic, hebephrenic, and undifferentiated. There has been no consistent correlation between the presenting symptoms of the donors and those of the recipients with regard to secondary symptoms. On one or more occasions, symptoms characteristic of all the schizophrenic subcategories have been induced. Thirteen subjects in these 3 test groups received taraxein extracted from serum pooled according to subcategories. On 4 occasions, the recipient presented predominantly the symptomatology of the donor group, whereas on 9 occasions, predominant symptoms of the recipient fitted into schizophrenic subcategories other than those presented by the donor group.

After our experience with the first 2 prisoner volunteers, we were interested in determining if, on the basis of mental status examination, we could accurately predict the type of secondary symptoms that would be induced by the administration of taraxein. As indicated in our preliminary presentation, our predictions were not accurate. In Groups II, IV, and V, all examiners independently listed their predictions prior to the administration of the substance. Although there was almost universal agreement among the examiners, the reactions in the subjects were not at all in accordance with the predictions—in fact, the predictions were wrong in the majority of cases. It must be pointed out, however, that the predictions of the examiners were based on only one interview. It is possible that longer observation may have resulted in more accurate predictions, but this does not seem likely since the character traits in the group were quite distinct.

On 2 occasions (Group V), a single subject was given 2 test doses of taraxein extracted from patients with different types of schizophrenia. In 1 instance a subject first received taraxein from paranoid patients and developed some paranoid symptoms; namely, referential ideas, suspicion and auditory hallucinations. Later, after all effects had cleared, he was given taraxein from patients with undifferentiated schizophrenia which induced predominantly catatonic symptoms. The other subject, receiving 2 injections, first received taraxein from undifferentiated schizophrenics and developed a mild undifferentiated schizophrenic reaction with predominantly primary symptoms. His second injection of taraxein, after all symptoms had cleared, was from catatonic patients. This induced full-blown catatonic symptoms. It may be an important observation that the symptoms were much more intense in both individuals following the second injection.

In test Group IV in which all subjects were first offenders and whose history of antisocial behavior was shorter, the reactions were the same. Two subjects in Group V were also first offenders. Reactions were in no way different from those induced in more chronic offenders. In the 2 nonschizophrenic volunteers of test Group III, the induced reactions were again essentially the same. These observations indicate that the effect of taraxein on inducing schizophrenic symptoms is not related to intensity of psychopathic behavior nor to residency in state prisons.

The response in the 1 schizophrenic patient in remission who received taraxein was quite different from that seen in the nonpsychotic volunteers. We know of no way to evaluate accurately intensity of reaction once full-blown secondary symptoms appear, but the symptoms induced were quite marked and were characterized by more profound depersonalization than those seen in the nonpsychotic volunteer group. The principal differing characteristic, however, was the duration of reaction. The full-blown open psychotic symptoms induced persisted to a gradually diminishing extent for 4 days, in contrast with the maximum duration of 2 hours in the nonpsychotic volunteers.

Psychological tests given some of our taraxein subjects by H. E. King have shown clearly a defect in performance roughly approximating the dosage administered and the observed clinical effects.

Complications

In these clinical studies we have had two noteworthy complications. On 3 of the 18 occasions when taraxein was administered to humans, the subjects developed nausea and 1 subject vomited. These effects persisted for less than 5 minutes following the injection and prior to the onset of the psychotic symptoms. All occurred in the earlier experiments. We believe that they were caused by insufficient destruction of nonspecific proteins at one stage of the processing. With a minor modification of the processing, they have been eliminated.

Another serious complication occurred when one subject, receiving a fraction labelled as coming from serum of normals, developed a full-blown psychotic reaction. Though it appears that this was a case of mislabelling, we believe it necessary to report it along with all evidence surrounding the incident. The tubes were labelled by the chemists at 6:00 a.m. after they had worked on the procedure throughout the previous night without sleep. This fraction was processed along with several batches of schizophrenic serum. One batch of schizophrenic serum consisted of 2 doses of undifferentiated schizophrenic serum. One dose of the fraction labelled undifferentiated was active and produced psychotic symptoms in a human subject. When we administered the second dose labelled "undifferentiated" (other half of the total amount) to the same subject who developed a full-blown reaction from the fraction labelled "normal," it produced absolutely no response. We thought that if one dose consisting of one-half of the match of undifferentiated taraxein was active, then this second dose consisting of the other half of the same batch should have been also. On the basis of these factors, we strongly suspect that one dose of normal and one dose of undifferentiated schizophrenic fraction were mislabelled. In addition to this, we have administered the fraction extracted from normals to 5 other human subjects and 10 monkeys with no effect whatsoever. Despite this evidence, however, we recognize that because of this complication we must test many more normal fractions before being absolutely certain that the effects cannot be induced by administration of the fraction from normals.

Discussion

It is obvious that although we have accumulated considerable data there are still many unanswered questions. At this stage we feel it would be unwise to attempt to draw any sweeping conclusions or to enter into lengthy theoretical speculation. Our data tentatively suggest that schizophrenia, despite the nature of presenting symptomatology, may be one common disease entity. Several other factors seem apparent. One is that different test subjects have different thresholds for the appearance of psychotic symptoms with the administration of this substance. This is based on the observation that similar amounts from the same batch produce varying intensity of symptoms in different subjects. Also, duration of effects following the reaction vary considerably suggesting a different speed of breakdown of the substance. Although cognizant of the danger of speculating on the basis of one case, the results in our one schizophrenic subject suggest that in schizophrenic persons, the ability to detoxify this substance or a product formed by the interaction of this substance with some constituent of the human organism is impaired.

We have gained the impression, although it is difficult to substantiate, that the nature of the presenting symptoms is a function of dosage rather than of the recipient's character traits or the disease symptoms presented by the donor. So-called primary or fundamental symptoms have appeared with lower dosages whereas hebephrenic and catatonic symptoms predominate with high dosages. Supporting evidence for this speculation is the observation that a more intense color is usually noted in the precipitated fraction from catatonic and hebephrenic donors. Of course this observation is highly speculative since we as yet do not have a method for accurately quantitating the amount of taraxein present. Several questions have been raised concerning the similarities between reactions in subjects receiving this substance and those in volunteers receiving the psychomimetic drugs, D-lysergic acid and mescaline. The principal difference is that subjects in this study have presented the characteristic picture of schizophrenia whereas those receiving the conventional psychomimetic drugs had only some schizophrenic symptoms and the most prevalent were typical of toxic psychosis (visual disturbances, disturbances of perception and sensorium, etc.). Our subjects have never shown symptoms of autonomic nervous system stimulation so characteristic of D-lysergic acid reactions.

We considered the possibility that an immune reaction might develop from taraxein which perhaps would render the subject insensitive to later injections. We therefore repeated the experiment after an interval of 11 weeks in one subject. Response to the second injection was virtually the same as to the first.

In our preliminary paper we reported that we had extracted taraxein from the blood of so-called pseudoneurotic or ambulatory schizophrenics. These were patients in our outpatient department who presented some fundamental or primary schizophrenic symptoms without secondary or accessory symptoms. We noted, however, that in order to produce a reaction in monkeys, taraxein from a larger amount of serum was required. As yet we have been unable to explore this area further, but hope to report on it in the near future.

Summary

Work in progress centered about the isolation of taraxein from the serum of schizophrenic patients and its administration to monkeys and human volunteers is presented. The taraxein was extracted from a variety of schizophrenic patients in 4 institutions and administered on 17 occasions to nonpsychotic human volunteers and on one occasion to a schizophrenic patient in remission. Several additional studies are planned or in progress and we expect that in the near future it will be possible to present considerably more information.

selection 54 / psychological factors in schizophrenia / James C. Coleman, University of California, Los Angeles

PSYCHOLOGICAL FACTORS

Among the psychological factors which seem to play a major role in the development of psychoses are faulty parent-child relations, trauma, frustration, and conflict.

Parent-child relations

The exact role of various parent-child and other social relationships in the development of psychotic reactions is not clearly understood. Apparently, however, rejection, excessive conscience development, overly severe discipline, overprotection, rigid sexual morals, chronic insecurity, and inconsistent discipline are some of the more important family conditions which predispose a child to the development of later psychopathology. In a study of the psychoses of children, Yerbury and Newell emphasize the total lack of security in human relationships, the disturbed home life, the beatings and brutal treatment the children had experienced, and the hatred many of them bore toward their parents. Many of these children were also found to be burdened with excessively high standards, leading to conflicts and feelings of inferiority, guilt, and inadequacy.

Apparently the effect of these undesirable parent-child relations is to prevent children from developing the ability to achieve satisfactory

Abridged from James C. Coleman, *Abnormal Psychology and Modern Life*, Scott, Foresman and Company, Chicago, 1950, pp. 254–255, 276–285. Copyright © 1956, 1950 by Scott, Foresman and Company.

psychological adjustments to stress. This handicapping may, of course, result partially from constitutional inadequacies and may in turn reinforce any constitutional weakness; in any event, the final result is a psychologically handicapped person. As Escalona points out in her report on psychotic children,

One may say that they present a large variety of behavior pictures which in all cases lead to a generalized and far-reaching inadequacy on the part of the child. This inadequacy, whatever form it took, made it impossible for these children to cope with whatever life situations are ordinarily appropriate at a given age and under given environmental circumstances.

However, the question still remains as to how one child is seemingly able to surmount undesirable early conditions while another under comparable conditions becomes a psychotic casualty. Again the possibility of constitutional inadequacies reinforced by undesirable psychological factors appears relevant.

Trauma, frustration, conflict

Many individuals, though psychologically handicapped by faulty parent-child relations, manage to make successful adjustments in childhood and later life, as, for example, in cases where there is no severe trauma from social and other environmental experiences and where the life situation does not involve severe and prolonged conflicts. But in instances where the child's early experiences are severely traumatizing and where severe conflicts centering around sex, hostility, dependence, independence, and self-acceptance are aroused, the outlook is not so favorable.

Added to other conflicts and frustrations may be the terrifying experience of ego decompensation—of realizing that one is losing control of his thoughts and impulses, that he is "losing his mind." Many patients state that this experience was one of the most traumatic of their entire lives. Since trauma, frustration, and conflict play such important roles in all mental disorders, we shall consider their specific significance in some detail in our discussion of the various psychoses.

Frustration and conflict Since the time of Bleuler there has been increasing agreement among psychiatrists and psychologists that schizophrenia is primarily the result of faulty responses to frustration and conflict. In the face of stress which the individual feels inadequate to cope with, he resorts to the extreme use of rationalization, projection, emotional insulation, fantasy, and other ego defensive measures. Below is a summary of Adolf Meyer's[1] conclusions concerning the development of this pattern.

[1] H. A. Christian, *Psychiatry for Practitioners*, Oxford University Press, New York, 1936.

In the process of personality development, the individual learns various methods of coping with his problems. Some of these methods involve dealing directly with life's problems and making the most effective adjustment to them that is possible. However, other adjustive reactions are in the nature of evasive substitutions—utilizing rationalization, projection, fantasy satisfactions, and emotional withdrawal and insulation. These evasive reactions inevitably lead to failure and self-devaluation which in turn makes their use even more necessary. Thus vicious habits of response become established which lead to a complete miscarriage of ego defenses—instead of helping the individual to adjust successfully, they actually make such an adjustment impossible.

The individual who later develops schizophrenia usually manifests an early withdrawal from a world he interprets as frustrating and hostile. This withdrawal is often concealed behind what seems to be an exemplary childhood, but which on closer examination reveals adherence to meekness and formally good behavior in order to avoid fights and struggles. Instead of participating in an active and healthy way in the activities of childhood, the individual withdraws behind a façade of goodness and meekness. This withdrawal, of course, inevitably leads to failures and disappointments which in turn serve to encourage further withdrawal from the world of reality and foster the use of fantasy satisfactions to compensate for real life failures.

As this "good" child enters the adolescent period, he tends to be overly serious, painfully self-conscious, inhibited, and prone to prefer his own company. Often he is unduly preoccupied with various religious and philosophical issues. Normal interest in the opposite sex is lacking, and vivid ideas of the evilness of sexual behavior are usually only too apparent. As the adolescent enters the period of adulthood, with its demands for independency, responsibility, and family relationships, the youth's lack of adequate socialization and preparation for meeting these problems proves fatal. Instead of increased effort and a vigorous attack on the problems associated with the assumption of adult status, the youth finds the world unbearably hurtful and turns progressively inward to fantasy satisfactions.

It is out of this type of background that schizophrenic reactions develop. These reactions may be precipitated by the increased stress placed on the individual during the period of puberty and young adulthood, or by stresses occurring later in life. However, it is particularly in coping with the ordinary adolescent and young adult conflicts centering around dependency-independency problems and the handling of hostility and sexual drives that the insecure, withdrawn personality seems to get into serious difficulty. It is usually difficult for such an individual to enter into vigorous social competition for jobs and adult status. Rather he tends to find the competitive aspects of adult life terrifying and disillusioning; it seems much safer to maintain his childhood position of dependency upon the family. His whole problem is often complicated too by unrealistic levels of aspiration and altruistic ethical ideals to which he expects others to conform. Such a psychologically vulnerable individual is of course easily hurt by the inevitable setbacks and frustrations of adult life.

In the sexual sphere, his problems are usually complicated by his highly moralistic attitude toward sex and his failure to develop to a normal heterosexual level of adjustment. In general, his sexual behavior is relatively immature and undifferentiated. Usually he has had few if any sexual contacts with the other sex (it is not unusual to find schizophrenics over 30 years of age who have never even had a date). Even if he has been married and so has had what appear to be more adequate sexual patterns, these are usually found on closer examination to have been hopelessly unsatisfactory and conducive to feelings of repugnance and guilt. As a result of his sexual immaturity, his sexual fantasies, like those of the early adolescent, may include a wide range of sexual objects, including members of the same sex. Since even heterosexual fantasies are considered immoral and unacceptable, it is not surprising that homosexual fantasies often lead to severe personality conflicts, to self-devaluation, and in some instances, as in paranoid schizophrenia, to the use of projection and other defense mechanisms for protecting the "self" against these immoral inner desires.

Homosexual fantasies, as well as overt homosexual behavior, involve far more males than is ordinarily realized, and need not lead to schizophrenia. They have a part in schizophrenia only in cases where the individual evaluates them as horribly immoral and repugnant. It is the resulting conflict and self-devaluation, rather than the homosexual fantasies or behavior, which lead to mental illness.

In a similar way, the handling of hostility is a particularly stressful problem for such an individual, because he usually considers it completely immoral and terribly dangerous. The hostility generated by his feelings of hurt and frustration is often more than he can bear, yet as a consequence of his withdrawal from normal social participation, he typically lacks any adequate comprehension of the role of hostility in normal everyday social relations. He does not know how to express it in socially acceptable ways and he is completely upset when he is the object of other people's hostility. Consequently he usually tries to repress his hostility and to deny even to himself that he is the kind of person who has such unacceptable impulses. The author is reminded here of a schizophrenic patient whose adjustment difficulties centered in part around his complete inability to express hostility. After several group therapy sessions, this patient proudly related to the group how for the first time in his life he had told a fellow who shoved in front of him in the cafeteria line to wait his turn.

As in the case of the neurotic, the schizophrenic's conflicts get him into a vicious circle. He withdraws from social participation because he is hurt and scared. But this withdrawal does not necessarily reduce his need or desire for social approval, status, and love. However, it does materially reduce his chances of gratifying these desires by removing him from the normal stream of social development and preventing him from acquiring the necessary attitudes and skills requisite to the attainment of his desires. Thus it can readily be seen that individuals who are severely sensitized to the hurts and frustrations of social relations, and who are handicapped by their subsequent withdrawal from the educative effects of normal social give and take, find the stresses of young adulthood too much to handle. Studying the backgrounds of 341 schizophrenic patients treated in a combat zone during World War II Ripley and Wolf emphasized the importance of a "prominent lack of productive and satisfying relationships with other individuals and groups of individuals."

Disturbed family relations and early psychic trauma This general developmental picture of schizophrenia as a failure in socialization with gradual accumulation of faulty attitudes and habits of reaction is supplemented by increasing evidence of early psychic wounds in schizophrenic patients. These wounds may be the result of specific episodes or of a long-term, unhealthy family pattern. Many take place in what seem to be exceptionally good homes, and often the parents are quite unaware of any trauma to the child. In a study of the parent-child relations of childhood schizophrenics, Kanner found that many of the parents were prominent, respected citizens of the community, but that toward their children they showed an almost complete lack of any real warmth.

Other studies have found the mothers of schizophrenic patients to be typically rejecting, overanxious, dominating, overpossessive, moralistic, and perfectionistic. Their children are infantilized and overprotected, while being made to feel that motherhood is martyrdom. Often combined with this are rigid, moralistic attitudes toward sexual behavior which make any evidence of such behavior on the part of their children especially horrifying to them and lead of course to serious sexual conflicts and accompanying self-devaluation for the children.

There are fewer studies on paternal attitudes. They have generally revealed a somewhat inadequate, indifferent, or passive father or the loss of the father at an early age although paternal overprotection has also been noted. Several studies have also revealed serious disturbances in emotional relationships between the parents and a lack of coordination in parental control and guidance of the child.

These parental attitudes and home situations are of course not exclusive to the background of schizophrenia. The important point here seems to be the contribution which they make to the patterning of events that produces a "good" child who tends to be sensitive, rigid, unrealistic in his expectations, moralistic, and lacking in warmth, spontaneity, and good socialization. The schizophrenic process thus becomes a method of adjusting to an unbearably hurtful world—of protecting oneself against overwhelming feelings of helplessness and worthlessness.

Lack of reality checks As we have seen, many schizophrenics are handicapped in their social development by oversolicitous, overprotective mothers. This, together with their early social withdrawal, has a variety of effects which are of developmental significance. Perhaps most important, these factors tend to cut him off from the normal activities of social reality testing—from social give and take—so that he tends to be passive and protected and fails to develop the necessary skills and emotional attitudes for healthy social participation. For example, in the matter of role playing, the schizophrenic is handicapped by a lack of social experience. We all model our behavior after that of others and attempt many roles which we test out in the group and either adopt as successful or discard. Since this eliminative process does not take place in the schizophrenic's social development, he may have very unrealistic ideas of the types of social roles that are open to him, and it may be easy to fantasy himself as a great religious savior or some other remarkable or unusual person.

Our self-evaluation is to a large extent determined by the way other people react to us. We gradually learn to see ourselves somewhat as others see us and to evaluate ourselves accordingly. However, the schizophrenic is handicapped by a lack of ability to see himself from the perspective of others; consequently his attitudes toward himself are apt to be fantasy ridden and distorted. The same point holds, of course, for his environmental attitudes, which suffer from the rigidity and lack of perspective of his own limited viewpoint, uncorrected by social experience.

Such a lack of constant reality checks in the development of a frame of reference would in itself make for an ever-widening breach between the schizophrenic and other people. As might be expected, his language and thought patterns become progressively more individualistic. He becomes "an emotional stranger in a strange land, with his own inner problems and conflicts dictating what he sees in the world around him. . . ."

Regression Considerable interest has been shown in the dynamics underlying the disorganization or disintegration of thought processes in schizophrenia. Kasanin, Goldstein, and others (Levy) have advanced the belief that in schizophrenia there is a reduction from conceptual thinking to a more primitive "concrete" thinking in which the individual is dominated by the external and internal stimuli acting upon him at the moment and reacts to parts of the perceptual field as if they were wholes. As a result of this "concrete" approach, the patient loses the normal demarcations between himself and the world, his words lose their usual representative character, and his perceptions no longer show the expected relation of parts to a whole. Kasanin attributes this concretization or fragmentation of thought processes to extreme regression to immature and childish levels of thinking.

Here Kasanin points out that the child lives in a world which is partly real and partly magic, and that he forms all sorts of fantastic notions and ideas about the things around him. He tends to personify and vitalize inanimate objects and to endow them with various powers. He may also tend to feel that he is the center of the universe and to develop ideas of his own omnipotence. Also commonly found, according to Kasanin, is the belief that adults can read his thoughts.

Kasanin then attempts to relate many of the odd and bizarre delusions of schizophrenics to the magical thinking and other characteristics of children's thinking. For example, he points out that most schizophrenics at one time or another express ideas of omnipotence. This may be expressed by the patient who sits quietly in his chair with his index finger flexed in a certain way, afraid to change its position because the world would suddenly be destroyed if he moved. Similarly, many schizophrenics are convinced that other people can read their minds and know their thoughts. Everyone knows what they are thinking about, and when questioned by the psychiatrist, they may look at him in amusement and consider the whole thing a farce since he obviously knows their thoughts already without being told.

Ego defensive values of symptoms As we have noted, the emotional blunting and distortion in schizophrenic reactions protect the individual from the hurt of disappointment and frustration. Regression enables him to lower his level of aspiration and to accept a position of dependency. Projection helps him to maintain some semblance of ego integrity by placing the blame for his difficulties on others and attributing his own unacceptable desires to them. Wish-fulfilling fantasy enables him to achieve some measure of compensation for his feelings of inferiority and self-devaluation. In various combinations and degrees, these mechanisms seem to constitute the basic defensive framework of schizophrenic reactions.

In the exaggerated use of fantasy and projection, we find the two mechanisms which are most apt to lead to the development of delusions and hallucinations with their many ego defensive values. Delusions of influence enable the patient to blame others for causing his own inadmissible thoughts and behavior. Fantasies of being the focus of widespread interest and attention help the patient to compensate for feelings of isolation and lack of social recognition and status. Delusions of persecution explain away the patient's failure to achieve a satisfactory adjustment in the real world by placing the blame on his enemies. Delusions of grandeur and omnipotence may grow out of simple wishful thinking and may help to counteract feelings of inferiority and inadequacy by a sense of great personal worth and power.

Hallucinations in functional psychoses are interrelated with delusions and have similar dynamic functions. They are closely related to wishful thinking, the projection of unacceptable desires and impulses, feelings of unbearable guilt, and so on. Schizophrenic patients may speak to God and hear him confer great powers upon them and assign them the mission of saving the world. Or the patient with guilt feelings over homosexual thoughts may hear voices which accuse him of being a homosexual or of being guilty of other sexual misdeeds. Occasionally patients hallucinate sexual relations.

Of course, it may be noted that acutely disturbed patients may be so upset by their emotional conflicts that almost a delirious ideation occurs; here the delusions and hallucinations are part of a picture of acute mental turmoil in which their ego defensive value is greatly reduced or comes to be nonexistent.

Finally, the stereotypies and other symbolic behavior of the schizophrenic can also be understood in terms of the patient's mental processes and general reactive pattern. Thus the patient who thinks he is Christ may prostrate himself on the floor with his arms spread at right angles to form a cross, or dangerous obsessive desires may be counteracted by various magical rituals. Often the symbolism is by no means easy to fathom, but the study of it may be of value in furthering an understanding of apparently meaningless behavioral symptoms.

selection 55 / the schizophrenic sequence: withdrawal, disorganization, psychotic reorganization / Richard L. Jenkins, Psychiatry and Neurology Division, Veterans Administration

Adolf Meyer first significantly stressed the understandability of schizophrenia as a progressive maladaptation with habit disorganization. He emphasized what he called the adaptive insufficiency of the schizophrenic.

Norman Maier furnished a basic link in the understanding of the

Abridged from Richard L. Jenkins, "The Schizophrenic Sequence: Withdrawal, Disorganization, Psychotic Reorganization," *American Journal of Orthopsychiatry*, 22:738–748, 1952. Reprinted by permission of the author and the publisher.

schizophrenic process by demonstrating experimentally that rats, subjected to continued frustration, show a replacement of adaptive behavior by a frozen stereotyped behavior which he calls frustration behavior.

These two elements together give the basis for a hypothesis concerning the nature of the schizophrenic process. We all know from personal experience the extremely depressing effect continued and profound frustration has on our effort to adapt to a situation. There is a breaking point in the capacity of the individual—rat or human—to sustain adaptive effort in the face of continued frustration. The breakdown of the adaptive process represents a disorganization or illness of the personality.

Since adaptive behavior is a more highly evolved behavior than stereotyped behavior, the latter also represents a regression, a step backward in the evolutionary process. Since such nonadaptive behavior typically leads to further frustration, and this in turn leads to further replacement of adaptive responses with stereotyped nonadaptive responses, we see the regressive process of schizophrenic disorganization. This process is potentially reversible.

The breakdown which we are discussing here must be distinguished from the quick panicky reaction which may occur in almost anyone and which is temporarily disruptive of adjustive behavior, but is brief in duration, easily dispelled, and is accompanied by few if any serious aftereffects. These two kinds of breakdowns must be distinguished, but the distinction may be made much more easily in terms of the course than in terms of the momentary clinical picture. It may be that the key to the difference is to be found much more in the resilience and recuperative power of the patient than in the nature of the breakdown itself.

The schizophrenic sequence typically begins with the process of schizoid withdrawal. Schizoid withdrawal is a relative withdrawal of attention and interest from the outer environment, particularly withdrawal from empathic contact with the human environment. Autistic fantasy tends to replace external reality as a focus of attention, and the capacity for reality testing is reduced.

While schizoid withdrawal is a typical precursor of schizophrenia, and is in this sense an initial phase of the schizophrenic sequence, we should not regard it as a phase of the schizophrenic process itself, for such withdrawal from empathic contact with the human environment is a stable long-term characteristic of many personalities who never show schizophrenic disorganization.

Schizoid withdrawal frequently begins in childhood, and appears typically to bear some relation to the character of the parent-child and child-parent relationship.

While examination of the literature for description of the typical parent-child relations in the background of schizophrenia reveals some range of description, the descriptions of various investigators seem to agree in giving a picture of a parent overpowering to a child, a parent with whom it would be more than usually difficult for the child to establish his individuality, his selfhood, without doing so through negativism or schizoid withdrawal.

A recent study by Joseph Mark records the agreement and disagreement of 100 mothers of male schizophrenic patients with 139 statements, and compares it with the agreement and disagreement of 100 mothers of nonschizophrenics. The mothers of schizophrenics show a tendency to agree with some of these statements more than the mothers of nonschizophrenics. In the case of 15 statements, the difference between the two groups is great enough to be significant at the .001 level—that is, a difference of this magnitude would not occur more than once in a thousand times on the basis of chance.

As you read these 15 statements, with which mothers of schizophrenic patients showed a significantly greater tendency to agree than the control mothers, I ask that you try to form a mental picture of the kind of mothers who would agree in these statements:

Children should be taken to and from school until the age of eight just to make sure there are no accidents.

A mother should make it her business to know everything her children are thinking.

If the children are quiet for a little while a mother should immediately find out what they are thinking about.

Children should not annoy parents with their unimportant problems.

A devoted mother has no time for social life.

A watchful mother can keep her child out of all accidents.

Playing too much with a child will spoil him.

A parent must never make mistakes in front of the child.

Parents should sacrifice everything for their children.

When the father punishes a child for no good reason the mother should take the child's side.

A mother has to suffer much and say little.

Most children are toilet-trained by 15 months of age.

Children who take part in sex play become sex criminals when they grow up.

A child should not plan to enter any occupation that his parents don't approve of.

Too much affection will make a child a "softie."

I believe you will agree with me that this composite picture of attitudes which tend to be characteristic of the mothers of schizophrenics is impressive. The focus is upon maternal responsibility, authority and control. Maternal understanding of the feelings and emotional needs of the child seems conspicuously lacking. These mothers are more disapproving of freely showing affection to a child or of freely playing with him than are mothers in general, and justify this disapproval in terms of the child's welfare.

Does not the composite picture suggest a mother who is relatively lacking in warmth, in affection for the child, and most of all in a readiness to respect the individuality and feelings of the child? She is willing to allow the child no privacy, even in his thoughts. She is overprotective and oversolicitous, expresses a need for perfection, feels that a mother has to suffer much and say little, and in return for this martyrdom of motherhood feels and conveys to the child that he is under a deep moral obligation to conform to maternal wishes. She is particularly horrified by and intolerant of any expression of sexual impulses by the child, for she is prone to regard them as a forerunner of sexual crime.

The above elements give a composite picture which is doubtless more extreme than that of the typical mother of a schizophrenic. However, these statements seem clearly to reveal, as characteristic, parental tendencies which would make it more than usually difficult for a child to establish or maintain a sense of his individuality, except in the autistic withdrawal of fantasy. The child is expected to surrender his individuality to his parent, but even when he does so, he gets little love. What refuge from the dominance of such a mother can a child find other than retreat into autism?

The question may fairly be asked, since these attitudes were expressed by the mothers of schizophrenic patients, Were these maternal attitudes a causal factor in, or solely a result of, the schizophrenic breakdown of the son? In my own judgment, I cannot regard them primarily as a result, although possibly some of them have been intensified by the care of a schizoid child.

Less fairly the question may be asked, What profit is there in inquiring about a mother's conscious attitudes, when it is her unconscious ones which are determining? This type of challenge has been developed to the point of a subtle sophistry which is highly destructive to the advance of our knowledge. It is true that the attitudes mothers express consciously do not always govern their behavior, and that expressing the "right" attitudes verbally does not necessarily mean that a mother will behave accordingly. When, however, a careful inquiry reveals clear evidence of morbid attitudes on the conscious level, it is sophistry to throw this evidence out of court.

We have, then, something of a characterization of the maternal attitudes which contribute to schizoid withdrawal and in turn, toward a schizophrenic illness. Another factor which appears to be significant and which may have a constitutional basis is a low energy endowment. This is understandable since we all know from personal experience that it is less difficult to sustain goal-directed behavior in the face of frustration when our energy level is high.

The second phase of the schizophrenic sequence, the actual schizophrenic process, as distinguished from mere schizoid withdrawal, is a process of progressive personality disorganization. It has a regressive course which tends to recapitulate in reverse order developments related to the evolutionary process.

The evolutionary process has represented, so far as behavior is concerned, progression along several pathways which all lead in the same general direction. Behavior tends to evolve from a very limited range of responses which are relatively invariable, automatic, stable and even rigid, toward responses which are much more highly variable, flexible, modifiable and differentiatingly adaptive. The former type of response we may call primitive, and the latter highly evolved. The determination of the latter type of response is likely to involve a conscious, reflective and even deliberative process.

Characteristically, the schizophrenic process first becomes noticeable in those mental processes which are of most recent development, and of the most evolved, most indeterminate and most conditional nature. As it progresses, it tends progressively to invade lower, more primitive, and more automatic levels of behavior.

This is all in accord with a recognition of schizophrenia as a regressive process resulting from the breakdown of the adaptive process, and substituted for it. It is an evolution of behavior in reverse, toward more stereotyped fixed invariable patterns. A personal world which offers little span for self-realization predisposes, and a frustration beyond the tolerance of the individual precipitates the process.

Usually, one of the first symptoms of reaction to a frustrating problem insoluble for the patient is anxiety. Anxiety is, of course, a common state and its resolution may proceed in various ways. Although the vast majority of patients with acute anxiety do not become schizophrenic, yet acute anxiety is a typical prodromal symptom of an acute schizophrenic psychosis. A schizophrenic break appears sometimes to afford an avenue for the relief of otherwise unresolved anxiety.

Anxiety tends to block the freedom of clear and effective decision. It may lead to preoccupation, to indecision, and to perplexity and puzzling in which the real nature of the issues becomes increasingly clouded and obscured. These tendencies in turn may give rise to the typical blocking of the schizophrenic patient.

With the progression of the schizophrenic process, the perplexity and puzzling lead to a weakening of the efficiency of the conceptual process. Anxiety relating to inner tensions tends to overshadow, color and obscure the patient's perception of external reality. For example, the patient may interpret the meaning of speech, not in terms of a real grasp of the situation being discussed, but rather in terms of his own anxious preoccupations. Meanings tend to become private, and the capacity to recognize their wider application is impaired. Recollection of the meaning of words learned in childhood is retained, and there is consequent regression to a lower level of comprehension, a naïvely literal interpretation of speech, with loss of capacity to modify this interpretation by an effective appraisal of the situation and the intent of the speaker. This is so likely to be conspicuous in the case of proverbs and fables, which are concrete in form and abstract in meaning, that the tendency to interpret proverbs literally is used as an indication or even a test of schizophrenic thinking. The important fact for us is that the emotional separation of the schizophrenic from the common pattern of human feeling, plus the impairment of effective conceptual thinking due to the schizophrenic process, leads to the fumbling approximations of meaning, the vagueness, the tendency to interpret the metaphor literally, which betoken the early schizophrenic disintegration of conceptual thinking. At a later stage, more severe disintegration is reflected in the growing incapacity of the schizophrenic to detect absurdity and ultimately in the "word salad" level of disintegration of symbolization which may be seen in the regressed hebephrenic.

Disorder involving the functions of perception as well as the functions of conceptualization betokens a more deeply extending disorganization than does a conceptual disorder by itself.

The perceptive functions themselves differ widely in the degree to which they lend themselves to finely discriminated alternatives of action. Some sensory perceptions (such as the pain of the burned extremity) arouse emotional values immediately; others are translated into emotional values only through, or as a result of, an evaluative process which is essentially and necessarily highly conditional.

Since the highest and most conditional perceptions are those relating to the language functions, it is not surprising that perceptual disorders involving the language functions—morbid misinterpretations of speech or the hearing of "voices"—are the most common type of perceptual disorders in schizophrenia, and their presence does not betoken as deep a degree of disorganization as do other types of perceptual disorders. The illusion, or misinterpretation is, of course, not so severe a sign of disorder as the outright hallucination. Typically, the hallucinatory "voice" seems in fact almost as close to a conceptual as to a perceptual disorder, as most patients, when queried, will describe it as something heard in the mind or in the head, rather than as something heard with the ears.

The third element of the schizophrenic sequence is the process of psychotic reorganization. This is the integration of morbid ideas and rational processes into the coherent whole of a well-organized psychosis. This is best exemplified in the slow evolution of the morbid suspicion of a paranoid trend into the delusions of paranoia. This process of integration tends to stabilize the psychosis so that its progression is less rapid and recovery is less likely.

This stabilizing tendency results in some special effects on the process of recovery. Since experience has shown that the schizophrenic process is potentially reversible, we might, in general, expect that in the course of improvement the schizophrenic disorganization will disappear first from the most primitive functions and remain longest in the higher functions. This is, in general, true, but there are some exceptions occasioned by this third major factor in schizophrenia, the process of psychotic reorganization.

A system of fixed false beliefs may be evolved which serves to reduce some of the intolerable inner tensions of the personality at the expense of reality distortion. This system of beliefs acquires a vitality of its own and acquires some capacity to maintain or even extend its influence even when it no longer serves a function. In such instances, the morbid process leads from pathology at the higher levels (e.g., paranoid suspicion) to a disorganization extending to paranoid hallucinosis. With treatment, the morbid suspicion may be cleared away, only to recur in active form as a result of a new hallucination. Thus hallucination represents a persistence of the psychotic reorganization at a more primitive and more fixed level. Probably it is particularly in regard to the disruption of such entrenchments of the morbid process that shock therapy is valuable. It does not cure, but it makes easier the reorganization of the personality along adaptive and healthy patterns. It serves the process of recovery by rendering the patient more accessible to our therapeutic efforts.

It seems possible, then, to distinguish the three major elements or factors underlying the schizophrenic sequence. There is, first of all, the protective isolation of schizoid withdrawal from a social world, contact with which has become painful. This protective withdrawal, if pronounced, reduces the capacity for social adaptation. It predisposes to the schizophrenic disorganization, which is the second factor. Yet, despite this predisposition, most schizoid personalities never become schizophrenic, and in many cases schizophrenic disorganization occurs without much evidence of prior schizoid withdrawal. The schizophrenic disorganization itself may be viewed as a result of frustration overwhelming to the individual, beyond his level of tolerance, and paralyzing to his adaptive capacity.

Finally, there is the stabilizing factor of psychotic reorganization. This is a process which may be regarded as an effort to maintain the integration of a disintegrating personality. It is a morbid adaptation of the individual's personality to his psychotic trends, an adaptation which retards progress of the psychosis and recovery from the disorder alike. It occurs most commonly in the stronger, older, better-integrated personalities among those who develop schizophrenic symptoms. Since schizophrenics in general lack adaptability, their strength tends to be rigid in character and paranoid in effect.

Dealing therapeutically with the third factor, psychotic reorganization, would seem to depend upon more disruptive procedures such as shock therapy. Electroshock and metrazol might be expected to have a merely disruptive effect, while insulin coma, which has been demonstrated to have a greater therapeutic value in schizophrenia, not only produces a temporary disruption of consciousness with slow recovery, but also activates the patient, through intensification of the basic biological drive of hunger, to the adjustive satisfaction of this hunger tension through the process of eating. Eating satisfies the hunger. The satisfaction of actively felt inner need by adaptive behavior, on however simple a level, is a therapeutic experience for the patient. The fact that the patients who improve psychiatrically under insulin therapy are in general those who gain in weight on insulin therapy would support this conception.

The operation of prefrontal lobotomy, which appears to be therapeutic in its net effect in selected cases of schizophrenia, may achieve its value partly by the disruption of psychotic reorganization, but probably its therapeutic effect occurs more through a reduction of the anxiety responsible for both schizoid withdrawal and the progressive schizophrenic disorganization. On this basis, it would seem that the logical time for a prefrontal lobotomy is in the early stages of the psychosis. However, at such a time, it would seem that less drastic methods of treatment should suffice if skillfully utilized.

In conclusion, there are three distinguishable factors in schizophrenia, and a consideration of these factors appears significant for the process of therapy.

selection 56 / culture and neurosis / Karen Horney, New York City

In the psychoanalytic concept of neuroses a shift of emphasis has taken place: whereas originally interest was focussed on the dramatic symptomatic picture, it is now being realized more and more that the real source of these psychic disorders lies in character disturbances, that the symptoms are a manifest result of conflicting character traits,

From Karen Horney, "Culture and Neurosis," *American Sociological Review*, 1:221–235, 1936. Reprinted by permission of the publisher.

and that without uncovering and straightening out the neurotic character structure we cannot cure a neurosis. When analyzing these character traits, in a great many cases one is struck by the observation that, in marked contrast to the divergency of the symptomatic pictures, character difficulties invariably center around the same basic conflicts.

These similarities in the content of conflicts present a problem. They suggest, to minds open to the importance of cultural implications, the question of whether and to what extent neuroses are moulded by cultural processes in essentially the same way as "normal" character formation is determined by these influences; and, if so, how far such a concept would necessitate certain modifications in Freud's views of the relation between culture and neurosis.

In the following remarks I shall try to outline roughly some characteristics typically recurring in all our neuroses. The limitations of time will allow us to present neither data—good case histories—nor method, but only results. I shall try to select from the extremely complex and diversified observational material the essential points.

There is another difficulty in the presentation. I wish to show how these neurotic persons are trapped in a vicious circle. Unable to present in detail the factors leading up to the vicious circle, I must start rather arbitrarily with one of the outstanding features, although this in itself is already a complex product of several interrelated, developed mental factors. I start, therefore, with the problem of competition.

The problem of competition, or rivalry, appears to be a never-failing center of neurotic conflicts. How to deal with competition presents a problem for everyone in our culture; for the neurotic, however, it assumes dimensions which generally surpass actual vicissitudes. It does so in three respects:

1. There is a constant measuring-up with others, even in situations which do not call for it. While striving to surpass others is essential for all competitive situations, the neurotic measures up even with persons who are in no way potential competitors and have no goal in common with him. The question as to who is the more intelligent, more attractive, more popular, is indiscriminately applied towards everyone.

2. The content of neurotic ambitions is not only to accomplish something worth while, or to be successful, but to be absolutely best of all. These ambitions, however, exist in fantasy mainly—fantasies which may or may not be conscious. The degree of awareness differs widely in different persons. The ambitions may appear in occasional flashes of fantasy only. There is never a clear realization of the powerful dramatic role these ambitions play in the neurotic's life, or of the great part they have in accounting for his behavior and mental reactions. The challenge of these ambitions is not met by adequate efforts which might lead to realization of the aims. They are in queer

contrast to existing inhibitions towards work, towards assuming leadership, towards all means which would effectually secure success. There are many ways in which these fantastic ambitions influence the emotional lives of the persons concerned: by hypersensitivity to criticism, by depressions or inhibitions following failures, etc. These failures need not necessarily be real. Everything which falls short of the realization of the grandiose ambitions is felt as failure. The success of another person is felt as one's own failure.

This competitive attitude not only exists in reference to the external world, but is also internalized, and appears as a constant measuring-up to an ego-ideal. The fantastic ambitions appear on this score as excessive and rigid demands towards the self, and failure in living up to these demands produces depressions and irritations similar to those produced in competition with others.

3. The third characteristic is the amount of hostility involved in neurotic ambition. While intense competition implicitly contains elements of hostility—the defeat of a competitor meaning victory for oneself—the reactions of neurotic persons are determined by an insatiable and irrational expectation that no one in the universe other than themselves should be intelligent, influential, attractive, or popular. They become infuriated, or feel their own endeavors condemned to futility, if someone else writes a good play or a scientific paper or plays a prominent role in society. If this attitude is strongly accentuated, one may observe in the analytical situation, for example, that these patients regard any progress made as a victory on the part of the analyst, completely disregarding the fact that progress is of vital concern to their own interests. In such situations they will disparage the analyst, betraying, by the intense hostility displayed, that they feel endangered in a position of paramount importance to themselves. They are as a rule completely unaware of the existence and intensity of this "no one but me" attitude, but one may safely assume and eventually always uncover this attitude from reactions observable in the analytical situation, as indicated above.

This attitude easily leads to a fear of retaliation. It results in a fear of success and also in a fear of failure: "If I want to crush everyone who is successful, then I will automatically assume identical reactions in others, so that the way to success implies exposing me to the hostility of others. Furthermore: if I make any move towards this goal and fail, then I shall be crushed." Success thus becomes a peril and any possible failure becomes a danger which must at all costs be avoided. From the point of view of all these dangers it appears much safer to stay in the corner, be modest and inconspicuous. In other and more positive terms, this fear leads to a definite recoiling from any aim which implies competition. This safety device is assured by a constant, accurately working process of automatic self-checking.

This self-checking process results in inhibitions, particularly inhibitions towards work, but also towards all steps necessary to the pursuit of one's aims, such as seizing opportunities, or revealing to others that one has certain goals or capacities. This eventually results in an incapacity to stand up for one's own wishes. The peculiar nature of these inhibitions is best demonstrated by the fact that these persons may be quite capable of fighting for the needs of others or for an impersonal cause. They will, for instance, act like this:

When playing an instrument with a poor partner, they will instinctively play worse than he, although otherwise they may be very competent. When discussing a subject with someone less intelligent than themselves, they will compulsively descend below his level. They will prefer to be in the rank and file, not to be identified with the superiors, not even to get an increase in salary, rationalizing this attitude in some way. Even their dreams will be dictated by this need for reassurance. Instead of utilizing the liberty of a dream to imagine themselves in glorious situations, they will actually see themselves, in their dreams, in humble or even humiliating situations.

This self-checking process does not restrict itself to activities in the pursuit of some aim, but going beyond that, tends to undermine the self-confidence, which is a prerequisite for any accomplishment, by means of self-belittling. The function of self-belittling in this context is to eliminate oneself from any competition. In most cases these persons are not aware of actually disparaging themselves, but are aware of the results only as they feel themselves inferior to others and take for granted their own inadequacy.

The presence of these feelings of inferiority is one of the most common psychic disorders of our time and culture. Let me say a few more words about them. The genesis of inferiority feelings is not always in neurotic competition. They present complex phenomena and may be determined by various conditions. But that they do result from, and stand in the service of, a recoiling from competition, is a basic and ever-present implication. They result from a recoiling inasmuch as they are the expression of a discrepancy between high-pitched ideals and real accomplishment. The fact, however, that these painful feelings at the same time fulfill the important function of making secure the recoiling attitude itself becomes evident through the vigor with which this position is defended when attacked. Not only will no evidence of competence or attractiveness ever convince these persons, but they may actually become scared or angered by any attempt to convince them of their positive qualities.

The surface pictures resulting from this situation may be widely divergent. Some persons appear thoroughly convinced of their unique importance and may be anxious to demonstrate their superiority on every occasion, but betray their insecurity in an excessive sensitivity to every criticism, to every dissenting opinion, or every lack of responsive admiration. Others are just as thoroughly convinced of their incompetence or unworthiness, or of being unwanted or unappreciated; yet they betray their actually great demands in that they react with open or concealed hostility to every frustration of their unacknowledged demands. Still others will waver constantly in their self-estimation between feeling themselves all-important and feeling, for instance, honestly amazed that anyone pays any attention to them.

If you have followed me thus far, I can now proceed to outline the particular vicious circle in which these persons are moving. It is important here, as in every complex neurotic picture, to recognize the vicious circle, because, if we overlook it and simplify the complexity of the processes going on by assuming a simple cause-effect relation, we either fail to get an understanding of the emotions involved, or attribute an undue importance to some one cause. As an example of this error, I might mention regarding a highly emotion-charged rivalry attitude as derived directly from rivalry with the father. Roughly, the vicious circle looks like this:

The failures, in conjunction with a feeling of weakness and defeat, lead to a feeling of envy towards all persons who are more successful, or merely more secure or better contented with life. This envy may be manifest or it may be repressed under the pressure of the same anxiety which led to a repression of, and a recoiling from, rivalry. It may be entirely wiped out of consciousness and represented by the substitution of a blind admiration; it may be kept from awareness by a disparaging attitude towards the person concerned. Its effect, however, is apparent in the incapacity to grant to others what one has been forced to deny oneself. At any rate, no matter to what degree the envy is repressed or expressed, it implies an increase in the existing hostility against people and consequently an increase in the anxiety, which now takes the particular form of an irrational fear of the envy of others.

The irrational nature of this fear is shown in two ways: (1) it exists regardless of the presence or absence of envy in the given situation; and (2) its intensity is out of proportion to the dangers menacing from the side of the envious competitors. This irrational side of the fear of envy always remains unconscious, at least in non-psychotic persons, therefore it is never corrected by a reality-testing process, and is all the more effective in the direction of reinforcing the existing tendencies to recoil.

Consequently the feeling of own insignificance grows, the hostility against people grows, and the anxiety grows. We thus return to the beginning, because now the fantasies come up, with about this content: "I wish I were more powerful, more attractive, more intelligent than all the others, then I should be safe, and besides, I could defeat them and step on them." Thus we see an ever-increasing deviation of the ambitions towards the stringent, fantastic, and hostile.

This pyramiding process may come to a standstill under various conditions, usually at an inordinate expense in loss of expansiveness and vitality. There is often some sort of resignation as to personal ambitions, in turn permitting the diminution of anxieties as to competition, with the inferiority feelings and inhibitions continuing.

It is now time, however, to make a reservation. It is in no way self-evident that ambition of the "no-one-but-me" type must necessarily evoke anxieties. There are persons quite capable of brushing aside or crushing everyone in the way of their ruthless pursuit of personal power. The question then is: Under what special condition is anxiety invoked in neurotically competitive people?

The answer is that they at the same time want to be loved. While most persons who pursue an asocial ambition in life care little for the affection or the opinion of others, the neurotics, although possessed by the same kind of competitiveness, simultaneously have a boundless craving for affection and appreciation. Therefore, as soon as they make any move towards self-assertion, competition, or success, they begin to dread losing the affection of others, and must automatically check their aggressive impulses. This conflict between ambition and affection is one of the gravest and most typical dilemmas of the neurotics of our time.

Why are these two incompatible strivings so frequently present in the same individual? They are related to each other in more than one way. The briefest formulation of this relationship would perhaps be that they both grow out of the same sources, namely, anxieties, and they both serve as a means of reassurance against the anxieties. Power and affection may both be safeguards. They generate each other, check each other, and reinforce each other. These interrelations can be observed most accurately within the analytic situation, but sometimes are obvious from only a casual knowledge of the life history.

In the life history may be found, for instance, an atmosphere in childhood lacking in warmth and reliability, but rife with frightening elements—battles between the parents, injustice, cruelty, oversolicitousness—generation of an increased need for affection—disappointments—development of an outspoken competitiveness—inhibition—attempts to get affection on the basis of weakness, helplessness, or suffering. We sometimes hear that a youngster has suddenly turned to ambition after an acute disappointment in his need for affection, and then given up the ambition on falling in love.

Particularly when the expansive and aggressive desires have been severely curbed in early life by a forbidding atmosphere, the excessive need for reassuring affection will play a major role. As a guiding principle for behavior this implies a yielding to the wishes or opinions of others rather than asserting one's own wishes or opinions; an overvaluation of the significance for one's own life of expressions of fondness from others, and a dependence on such expressions. And similarly, it implies an overvaluation of signs of rejection and a reacting to such signs with apprehension and defensive hostility. Here again a vicious circle begins easily and reinforces the single elements: In diagram it looks somewhat like this:

Anxiety plus repressed hostility
   ↘ Need for reassuring affection
     ↘ Anticipation of, sensitivity to, rejection
       ↘ Hostile reactions to feeling rejected

These reactions explain why emotional contact with others that is attained on the basis of anxiety can be at best only a very shaky and easily shattered bridge between individuals, and why it always fails to bring them out of their emotional isolation. It may, however, serve to cope with anxieties and even get one through life rather smoothly, but only at the expense of growth and personality development, and only if circumstances are quite favorable.

Let us ask now, which special features in our culture may be responsible for the frequent occurrence of the neurotic structures just described?

We live in a competitive, individualistic culture. Whether the enormous economic and technical achievements of our culture were and are possible only on the basis of the competitive principle is a question for the economist or sociologist to decide. The psychologist, however, can evaluate the personal price we have paid for it.

It must be kept in mind that competition not only is a driving force in economic activities, but that it also pervades our personal life in every respect. The character of all our human relationships is moulded by a more or less outspoken competition. It is effective in the family between siblings, at school, in social relations (keeping up with the Joneses), and in love life.

In love, it may show itself in two ways: the genuine erotic wish is often overshadowed or replaced by the merely competitive goal of being the most popular, having the most dates, love letters, lovers, being seen with the most desirable man or woman. Again, it may pervade the love relationship itself. Marriage partners, for example, may be living in an endless struggle for supremacy, with or without being aware of the nature or even of the existence of this combat.

The influence on human relations of this competitiveness lies in the fact that it creates easily aroused envy towards the stronger ones, contempt for the weaker, distrust towards everyone. In consequence of all these potentially hostile tensions, the satisfaction and reassurance which one can get out of human relations are limited and the individual becomes more or less emotionally isolated. It seems that here, too, mutually reinforcing interactions take place, so far as insecurity and dissatisfaction in human relations in turn compel people to seek gratification and security in ambitious strivings, and vice versa.

Another cultural factor relevant to the structure of our neurosis lies in our attitude toward failure and success. We are inclined to attribute success to good personal qualities and capacities, such as competence, courage, enterprise. In religious terms this attitude was expressed by saying that success was due to God's grace. While these qualities may be effective—and in certain periods, such as the pioneer days, may have represented the only conditions necessary—this ideology omits two essential facts: (1) that the possibility for success is strictly limited; even external conditions and personal qualities being equal, only a comparative few can possibly attain success; and (2) that other factors than those mentioned may play the decisive role, such as, for example, unscrupulousness or fortuitous circumstances. Inasmuch as these factors are overlooked in the general evaluation of success, failures, besides putting the person concerned in a factually disadvantageous position, are bound to reflect on his self-esteem.

The confusion involved in this situation is enhanced by a sort of double moral. Although, in fact, success meets with adoration almost without regard to the means employed in securing it, we are at the same time taught to regard modesty and an undemanding, unselfish attitude as social or religious virtues, and are rewarded for them by praise and affection. The particular difficulties which confront the individual in our culture may be summarized as follows: for the competitive struggle he needs a certain amount of available aggressiveness; at the same time, he is required to be modest, unselfish, even self-sacrificing. While the competitive life situation with the hostile tensions involved in it creates an enhanced need of security, the chances of attaining a feeling of safety in human relations—love, friendship, social contacts—are at the same time diminished. The estimation of one's personal value is all too dependent on the degree of success attained, while at the same time the possibilities for success are limited and the success itself is dependent, to a great extent, on fortuitous circumstances or on personal qualities of an asocial character.

Perhaps these sketchy comments have suggested to you the direction in which to explore the actual relationship of our culture to our personality and its neurotic deviations. Let us now consider the relation of this conception to the views of Freud on culture and neurosis.

The essence of Freud's views on this subject can be summarized, briefly, as follows: Culture is the result of a sublimation of biologically given sexual and aggressive drives—"sexual" in the extended connotation Freud has given the term. Sublimation presupposes unwitting suppression of these instinctual drives. The more complete the suppression of these drives, the higher the cultural development. As the capacity for sublimating is limited, and as the intensive suppression of primitive drives without sublimation may lead to neurosis, the growth of civilization must inevitably imply a growth of neurosis. Neuroses are the price humanity has to pay for cultural development.

The implicit theoretical presupposition underlying this train of thought is the belief in the existence of biologically determined human nature, or, more precisely, the belief that oral, anal, genital, and aggressive drives exist in all human beings in approximately equal quantities. Variations in character formation from individual to individual, as from culture to culture, are due, then, to the varying intensity of the suppression required, with the addition that this suppression can affect the different kinds of drives in varying degrees.

This viewpoint of Freud's seems actually to encounter difficulties with two groups of data. (1) Historical and anthropological findings do not support the assumption that the growth of civilization is in a direct ratio to the growth of instinct suppression. (2) Clinical experience of the kind indicated in this paper suggests that neurosis is due not simply to the quantity of suppression of one or the other instinctual drives, but rather to difficulties caused by the conflicting character of the demands which a culture imposes on its individuals. The differences in neuroses typical of different cultures may be understood to be conditioned by the amount and quality of conflicting demands within the particular culture.

In a given culture, those persons are likely to become neurotic who have met these culturally determined difficulties in accentuated form, mostly through the medium of childhood experiences; and who have not been able to solve their difficulties, or have solved them only at great expense to personality.